W9-CEB-490

Blue Pills

a positive love story

Frederik Peeters

Translated from the French by Anjali Singh

Houghton Mifflin Company • Boston • New York • 2008

Swiss edition copyright © 2001 by Atrabile

English translation copyright © 2008 by Anjali Singh

For information about permission to reproduce selections from this book, write to Permissions, Houghton Mifflin Company, 215 Park Avenue South, New York, New York 10003.

www.houghtonmifflinbooks.com

Library of Congress Cataloging-in-Publication Data
Peeters, Frederik.
 [Pilules bleues. English]
 Blue pills : a positive love story / Frederik Peeters.
    p.   cm.
 Originally published: Genève : Atrabile, 2001.
 ISBN-13: 978-0-618-82099-3
 ISBN-10: 0-618-82099-X
 1. Graphic novels—Switzerland—Translations into English.
 2. HIV positive persons—Comic books, strips, etc. I. Title.
 PN6790.S93P44 2008
 741.5'9494—dc22   2007008914

Printed in the United States of America

MP 10 9 8 7 6 5 4 3 2 1

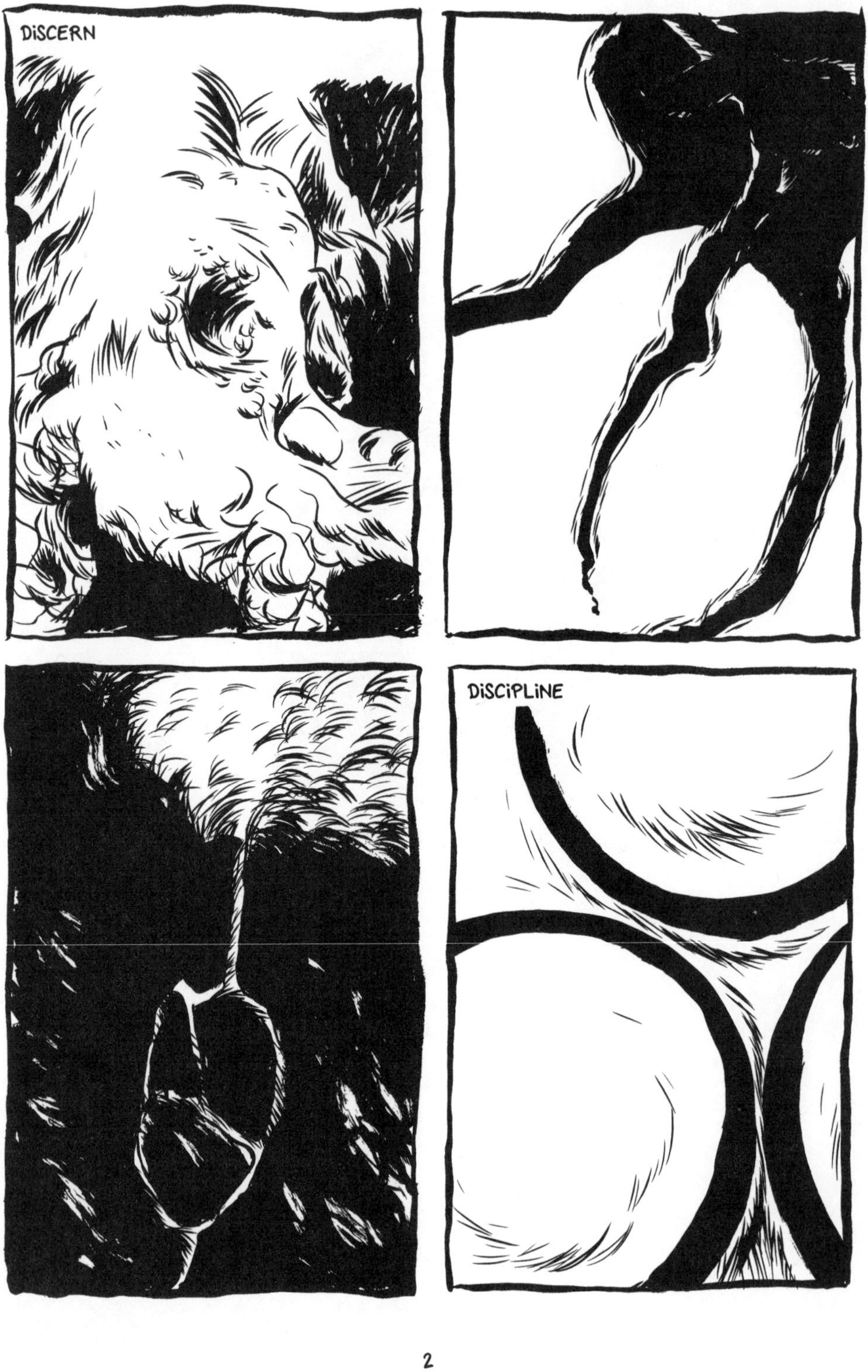
DiSCERN
DiSCiPLiNE

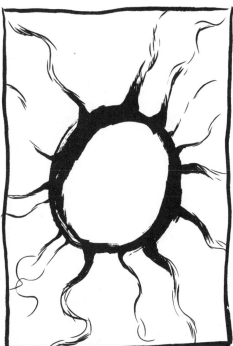

MMM . . . DISCOBULOS . . .

... DISCONTINUOUS

AH! HERE it iS! ... DISCORDANT! ...

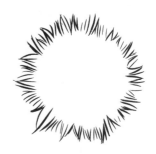

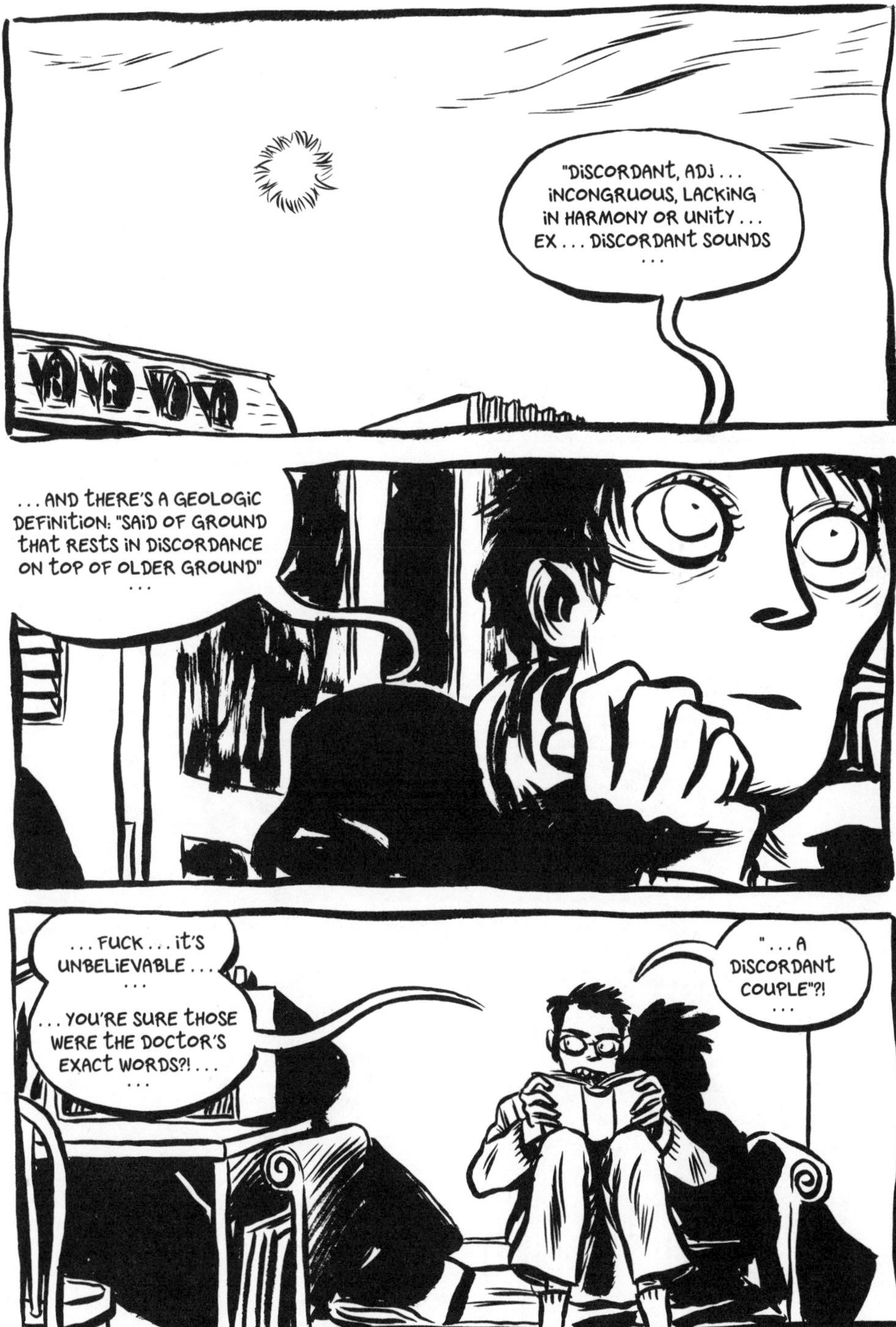
"DISCORDANT, ADJ . . . INCONGRUOUS, LACKING IN HARMONY OR UNITY . . . EX . . . DISCORDANT SOUNDS . . .
. . . AND THERE'S A GEOLOGIC DEFINITION: "SAID OF GROUND THAT RESTS IN DISCORDANCE ON TOP OF OLDER GROUND" . . .
. . . FUCK . . . IT'S UNBELIEVABLE . . . . . .
. . . YOU'RE SURE THOSE WERE THE DOCTOR'S EXACT WORDS?! . . . . . .
" . . . A DISCORDANT COUPLE"?! . . .

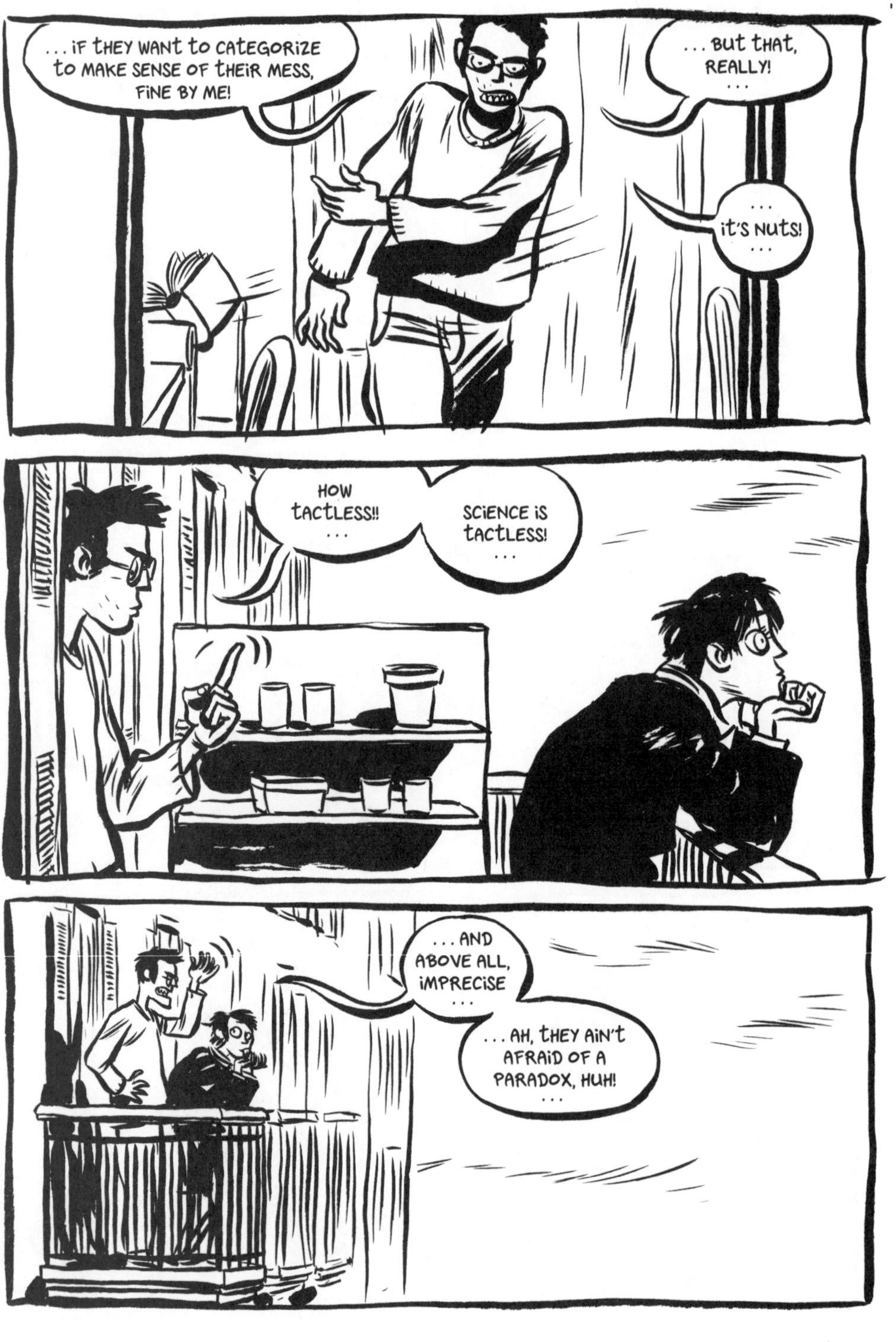
. . . iF THEY WANT TO CATEGORIZE TO MAKE SENSE OF THEIR MESS, FINE BY ME!
. . . BUT THAT, REALLY! . . .
. . . iT'S NUTS! . . .
HOW TACTLESS!! . . .
SCIENCE iS TACTLESS! . . .
. . . AND ABOVE ALL, iMPRECISE . . .
. . . AH, THEY AiN'T AFRAiD OF A PARADOX, HUH! . . .

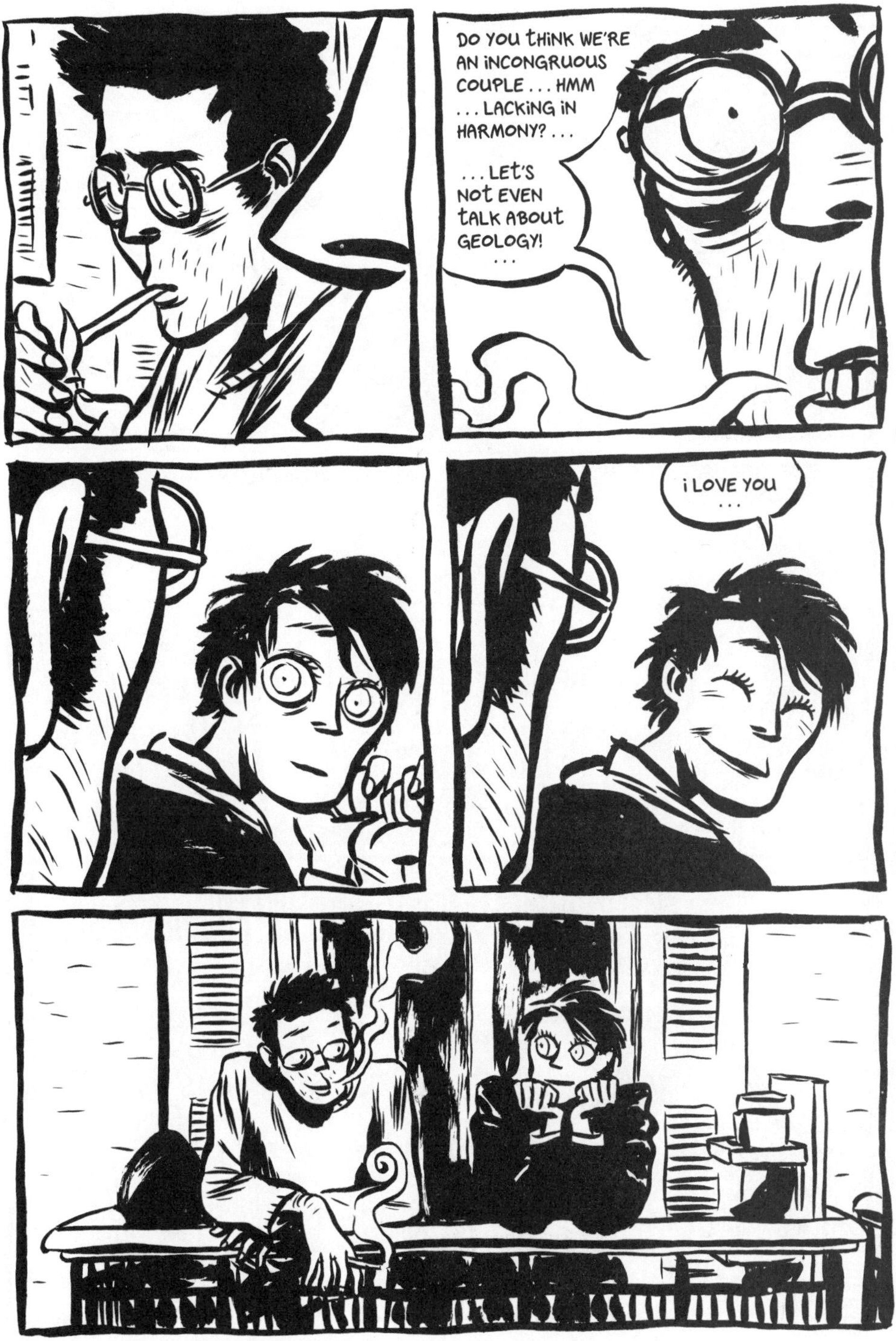
DO YOU THINK WE'RE AN INCONGRUOUS COUPLE... HMM ...LACKING IN HARMONY?...
...LET'S NOT EVEN TALK ABOUT GEOLOGY! ...
I LOVE YOU ...

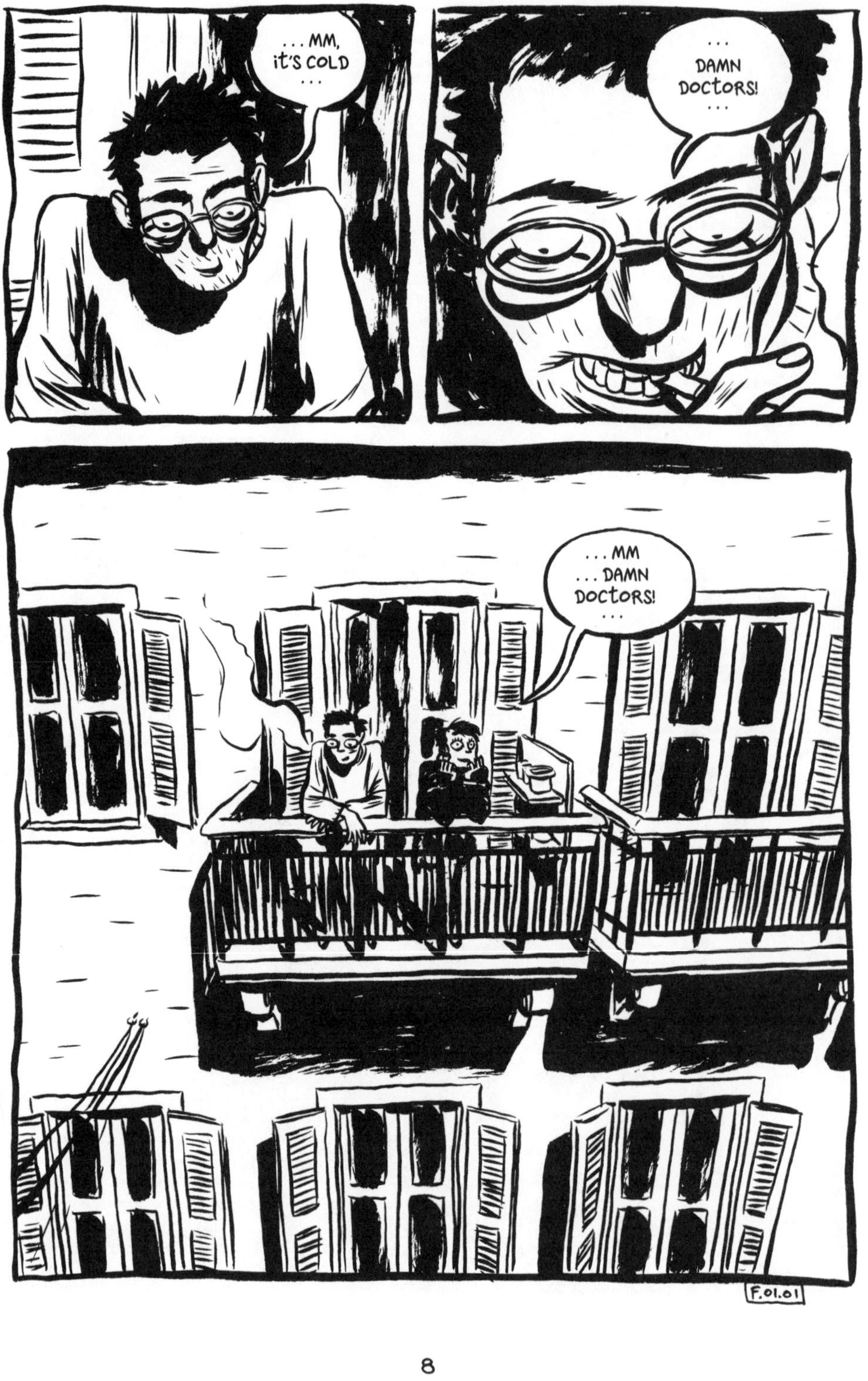
. . . MM,
it's COLD
. . .
. . .
DAMN
DOCTORS!
. . .
. . . MM
. . . DAMN
DOCTORS!
. . .
F.01.01

. . . i CAN JUSt iMAGiNE A PEDANtiC tHiRtY-SOMEtHiNG WitH tHREE GRAY HAiRS AND BLUE-GREEN tiNtED GLASSES, SCRAtCHiNG HiS tHREE-DAY-OLD BEARD WHiLE SAYiNG: "OH . . . YOU KNOW, ULtiMAtELY NEW YORK iS LiKE A ViLLAGE . . ."

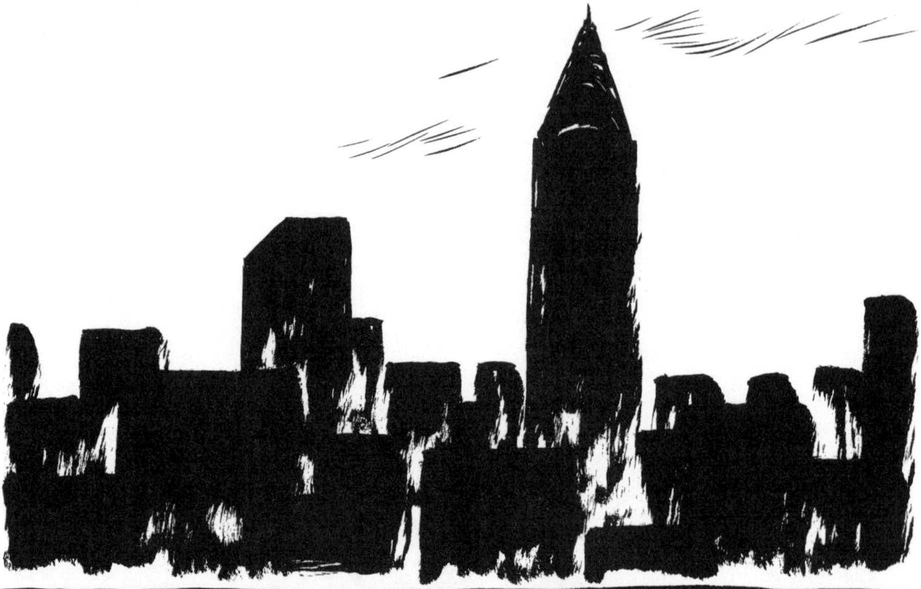

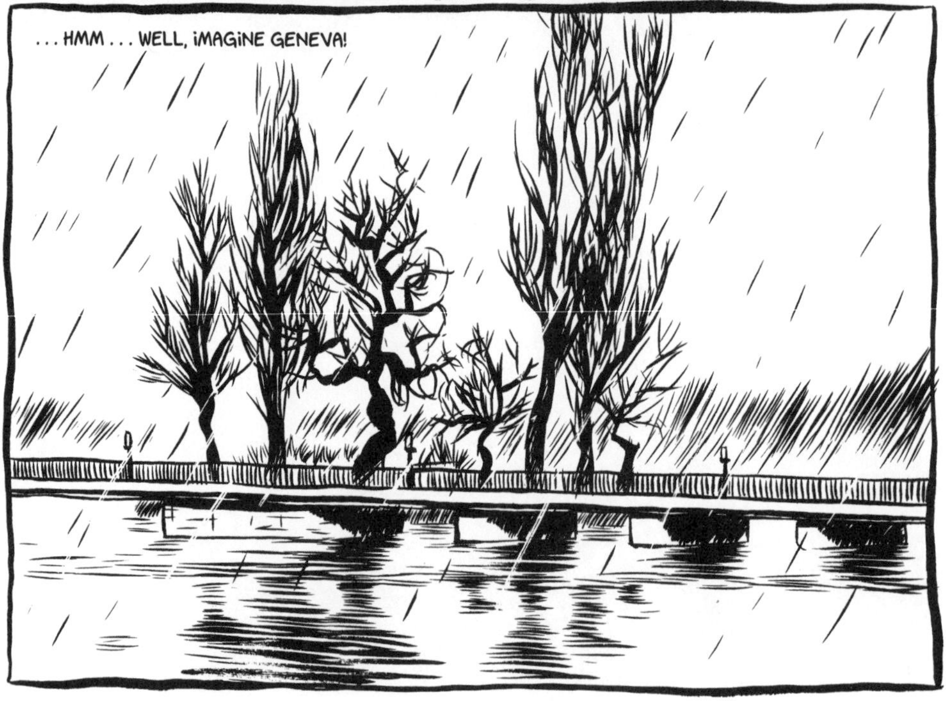
. . . HMM . . . WELL, iMAGiNE GENEVA!

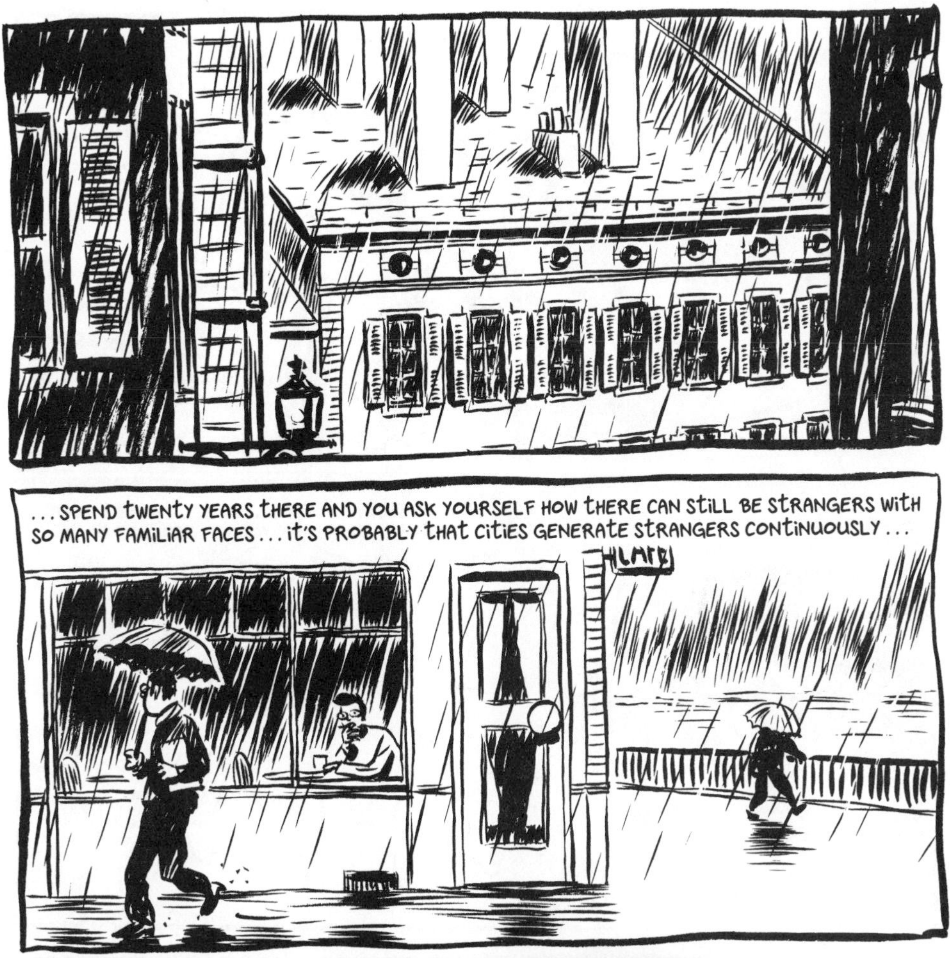
. . . SPEND TWENTY YEARS THERE AND YOU ASK YOURSELF HOW THERE CAN STILL BE STRANGERS WITH SO MANY FAMILIAR FACES . . . IT'S PROBABLY THAT CITIES GENERATE STRANGERS CONTINUOUSLY . . .
. . . WITH A SLOW AND VITAL BREATH . . .

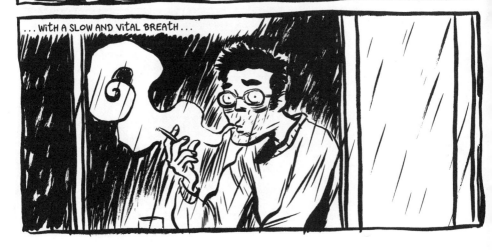

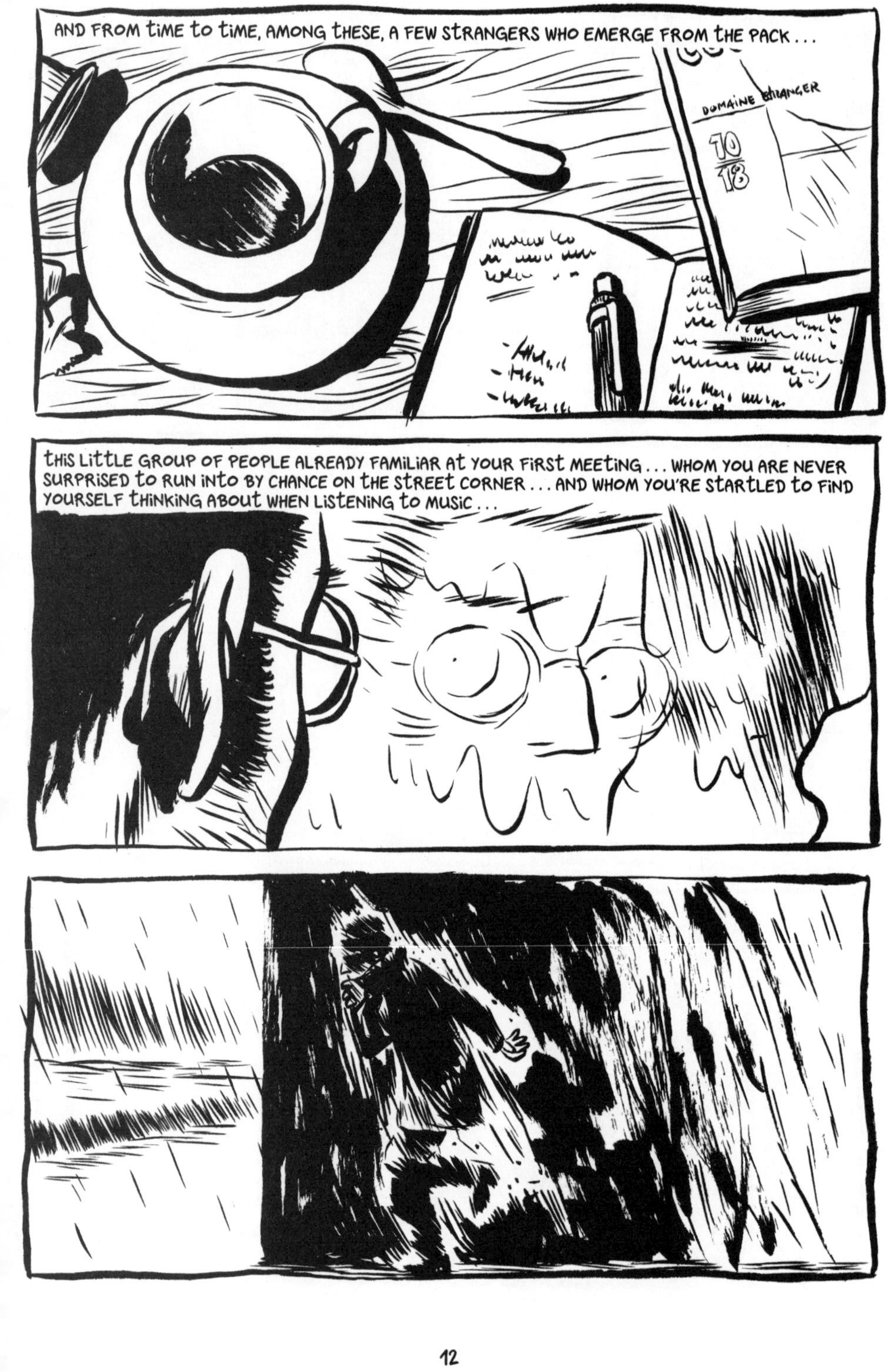
AND FROM TIME TO TIME, AMONG THESE, A FEW STRANGERS WHO EMERGE FROM THE PACK . . .
DOMAINE ÉTRANGER
10
18
THIS LITTLE GROUP OF PEOPLE ALREADY FAMILIAR AT YOUR FIRST MEETING . . . WHOM YOU ARE NEVER SURPRISED TO RUN INTO BY CHANCE ON THE STREET CORNER . . . AND WHOM YOU'RE STARTLED TO FIND YOURSELF THINKING ABOUT WHEN LISTENING TO MUSIC . . .

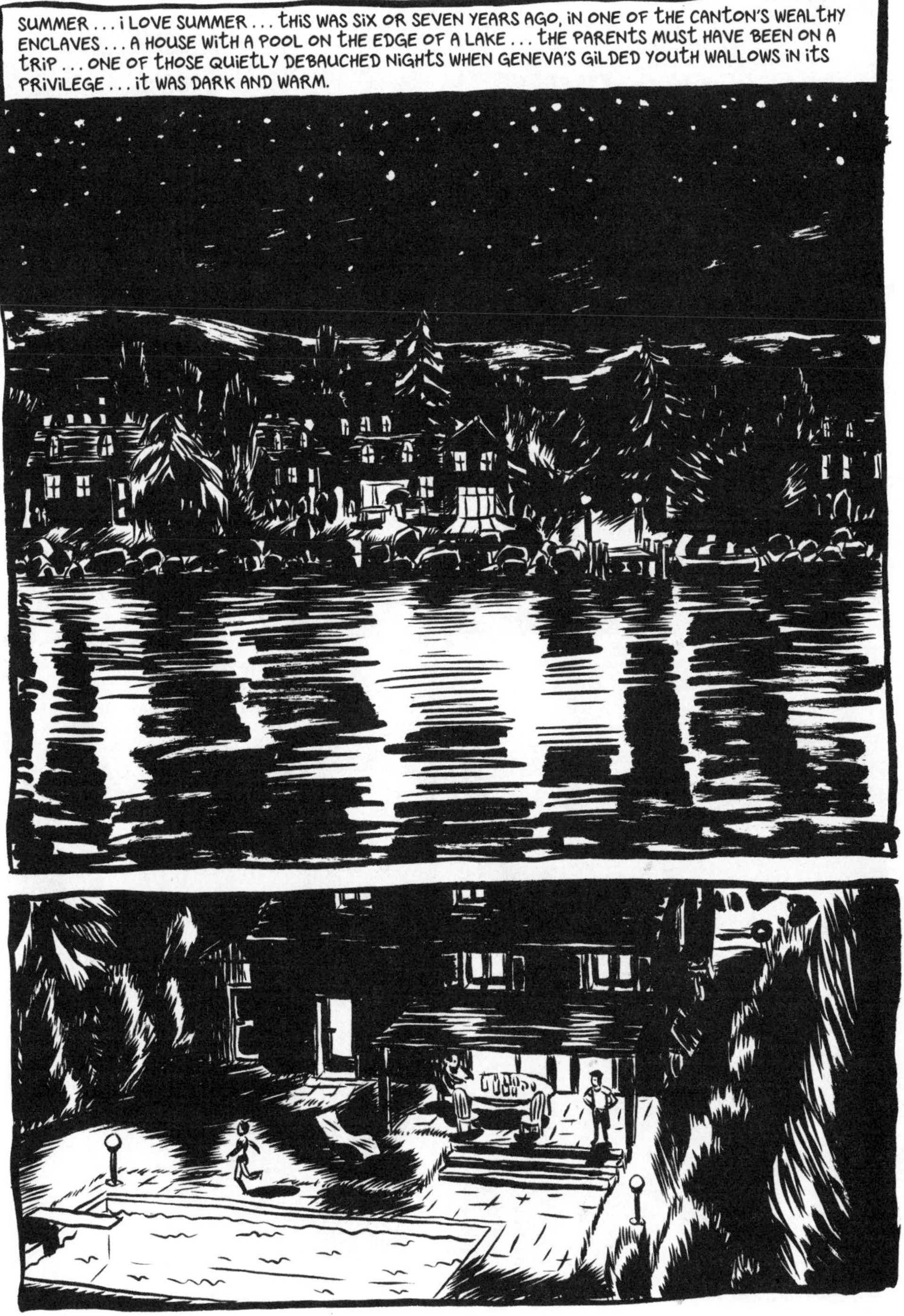
SUMMER . . . i LOVE SUMMER . . . tHiS WAS SiX OR SEVEN YEARS AGO, iN ONE OF tHE CANtON'S WEALtHY ENCLAVES . . . A HOUSE WitH A POOL ON tHE EDGE OF A LAKE . . . tHE PARENtS MUSt HAVE BEEN ON A tRiP . . . ONE OF tHOSE QUiEtLY DEBAUCHED NiGHtS WHEN GENEVA'S GiLDED YOUtH WALLOWS iN itS PRiViLEGE . . . it WAS DARK AND WARM.

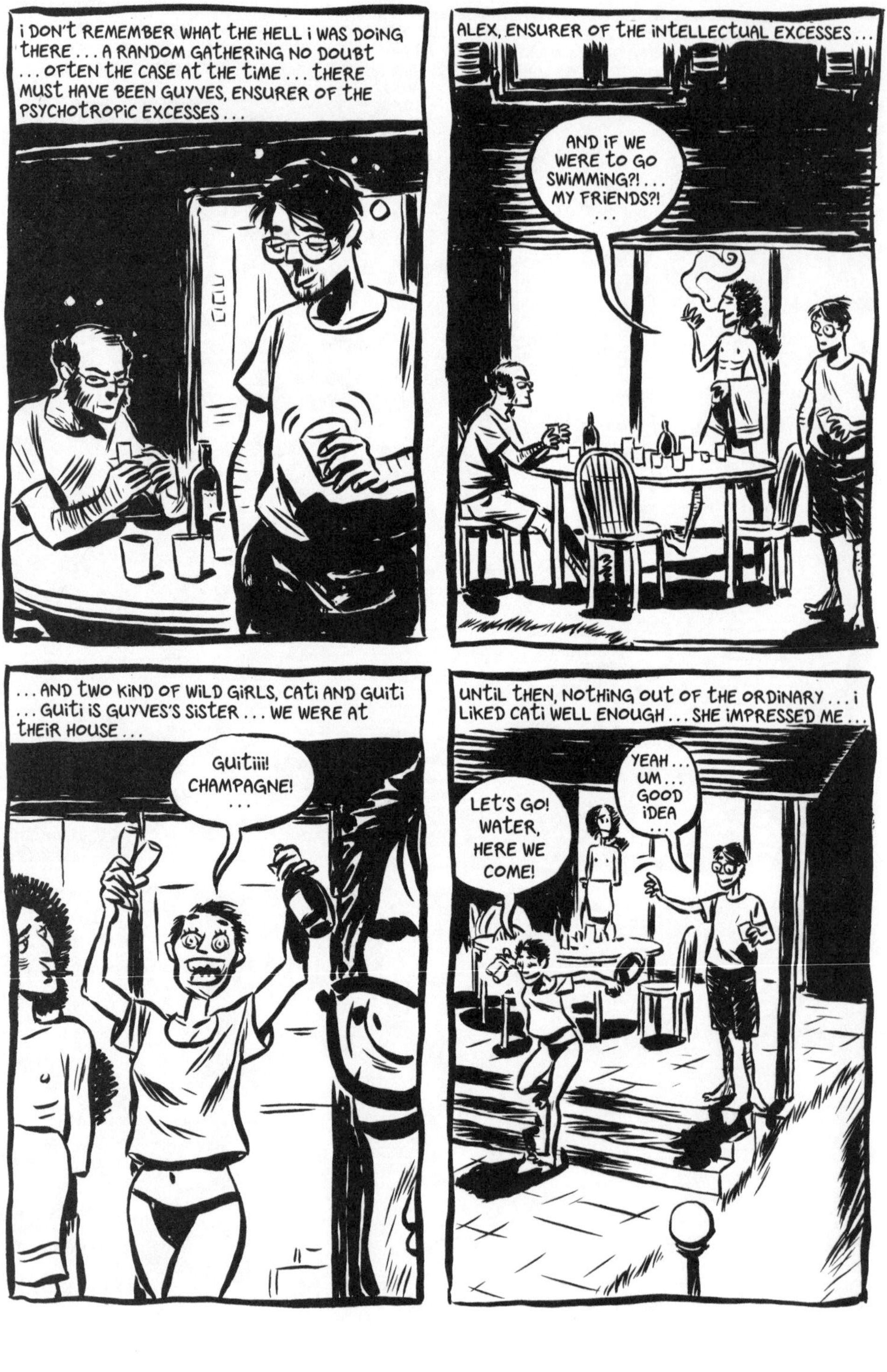
i DON'T REMEMBER WHAT THE HELL i WAS DOiNG THERE . . . A RANDOM GATHERiNG NO DOUBT . . . OFTEN THE CASE AT THE TiME . . . THERE MUST HAVE BEEN GUYVES, ENSURER OF THE PSYCHOTROPiC EXCESSES . . .
ALEX, ENSURER OF THE iNTELLECTUAL EXCESSES . . .
AND iF WE WERE TO GO SWiMMiNG?! . . . MY FRiENDS?! . . .
. . . AND TWO KiND OF WiLD GiRLS, CATi AND GUiTi . . . GUiTi iS GUYVES'S SiSTER . . . WE WERE AT THEiR HOUSE . . .
GUiTiii! CHAMPAGNE! . . .
UNTiL THEN, NOTHiNG OUT OF THE ORDiNARY . . . i LiKED CATi WELL ENOUGH . . . SHE iMPRESSED ME . . .
LET'S GO! WATER, HERE WE COME!
YEAH . . . UM . . . GOOD iDEA . . .

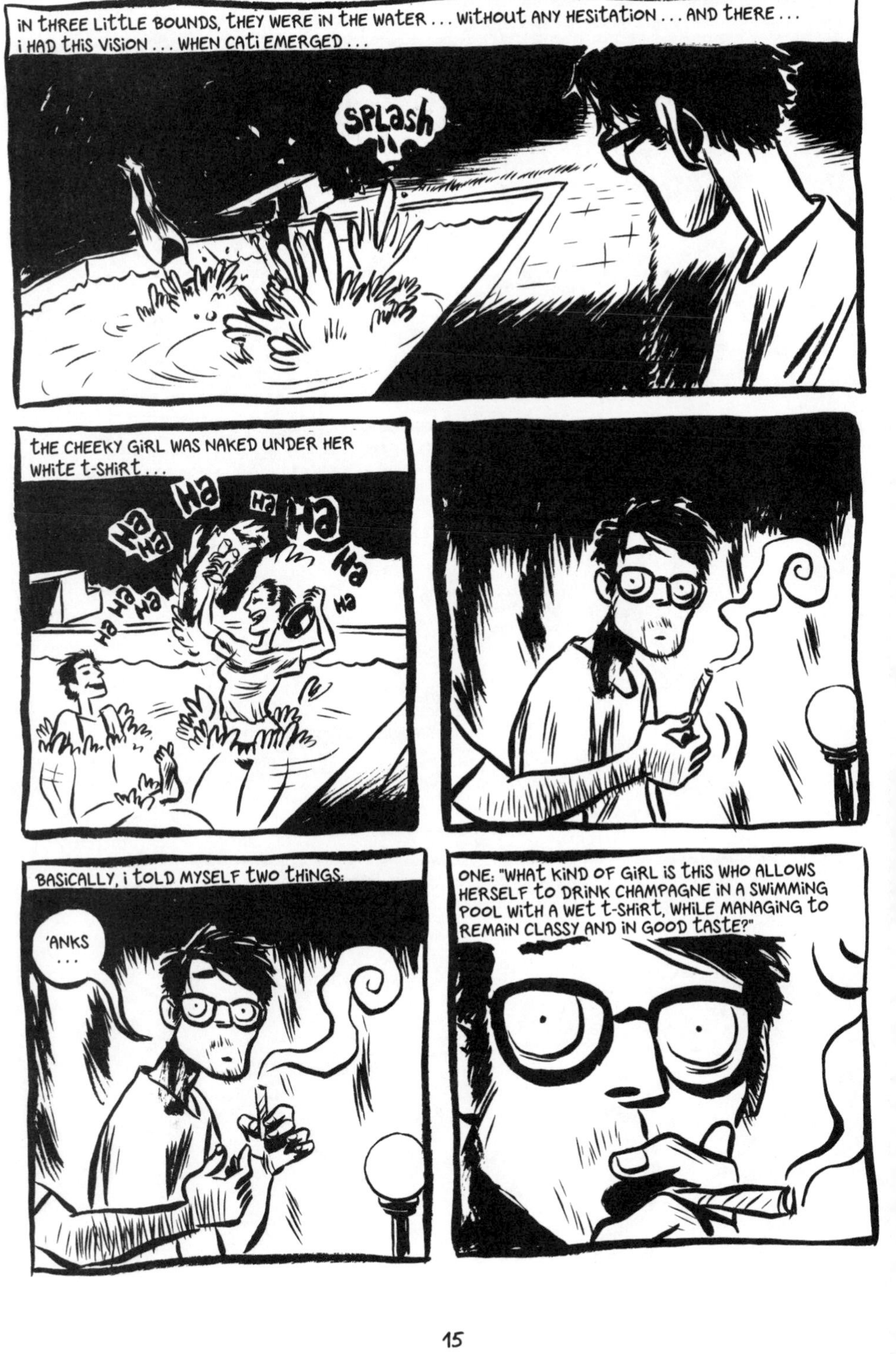
IN THREE LITTLE BOUNDS, THEY WERE IN THE WATER . . . WITHOUT ANY HESITATION . . . AND THERE . . .
I HAD THIS VISION . . . WHEN CATI EMERGED . . .
SPLASH
THE CHEEKY GIRL WAS NAKED UNDER HER WHITE T-SHIRT . . .
HA HA HA HA HA HA HA HA HA HA HA HA
BASICALLY, I TOLD MYSELF TWO THINGS:
'ANKS . . .
ONE: "WHAT KIND OF GIRL IS THIS WHO ALLOWS HERSELF TO DRINK CHAMPAGNE IN A SWIMMING POOL WITH A WET T-SHIRT, WHILE MANAGING TO REMAIN CLASSY AND IN GOOD TASTE?"

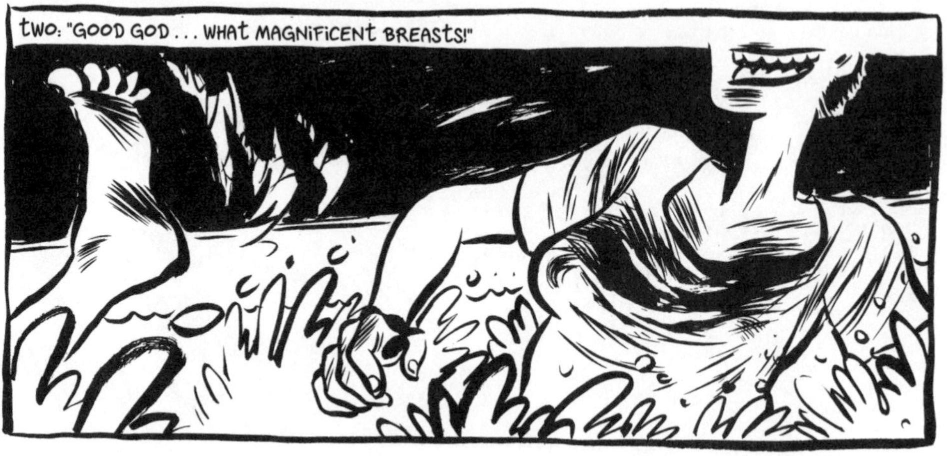
two: "GOOD GOD . . . WHAT MAGNIFICENT BREASTS!"

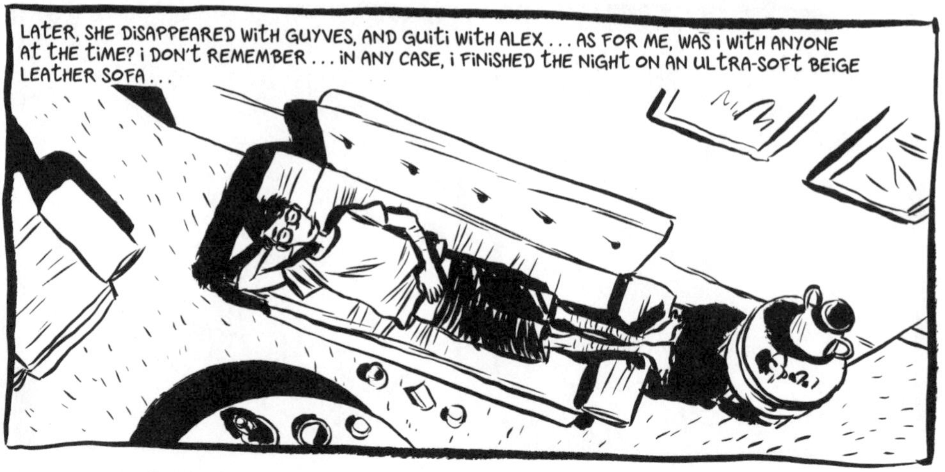
LATER, SHE DISAPPEARED WITH GUYVES, AND GUITI WITH ALEX . . . AS FOR ME, WAS I WITH ANYONE AT THE TIME? I DON'T REMEMBER . . . IN ANY CASE, I FINISHED THE NIGHT ON AN ULTRA-SOFT BEIGE LEATHER SOFA . . .

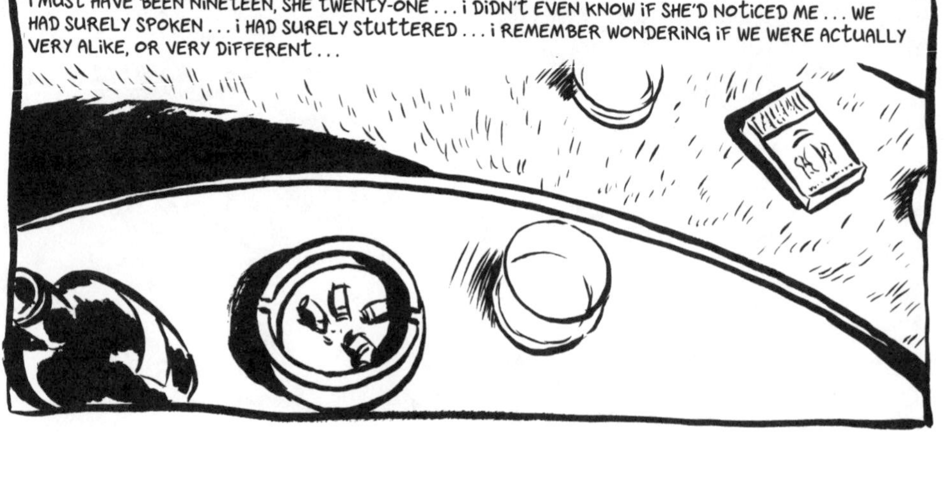
I MUST HAVE BEEN NINETEEN, SHE TWENTY-ONE . . . I DIDN'T EVEN KNOW IF SHE'D NOTICED ME . . . WE HAD SURELY SPOKEN . . . I HAD SURELY STUTTERED . . . I REMEMBER WONDERING IF WE WERE ACTUALLY VERY ALIKE, OR VERY DIFFERENT . . .

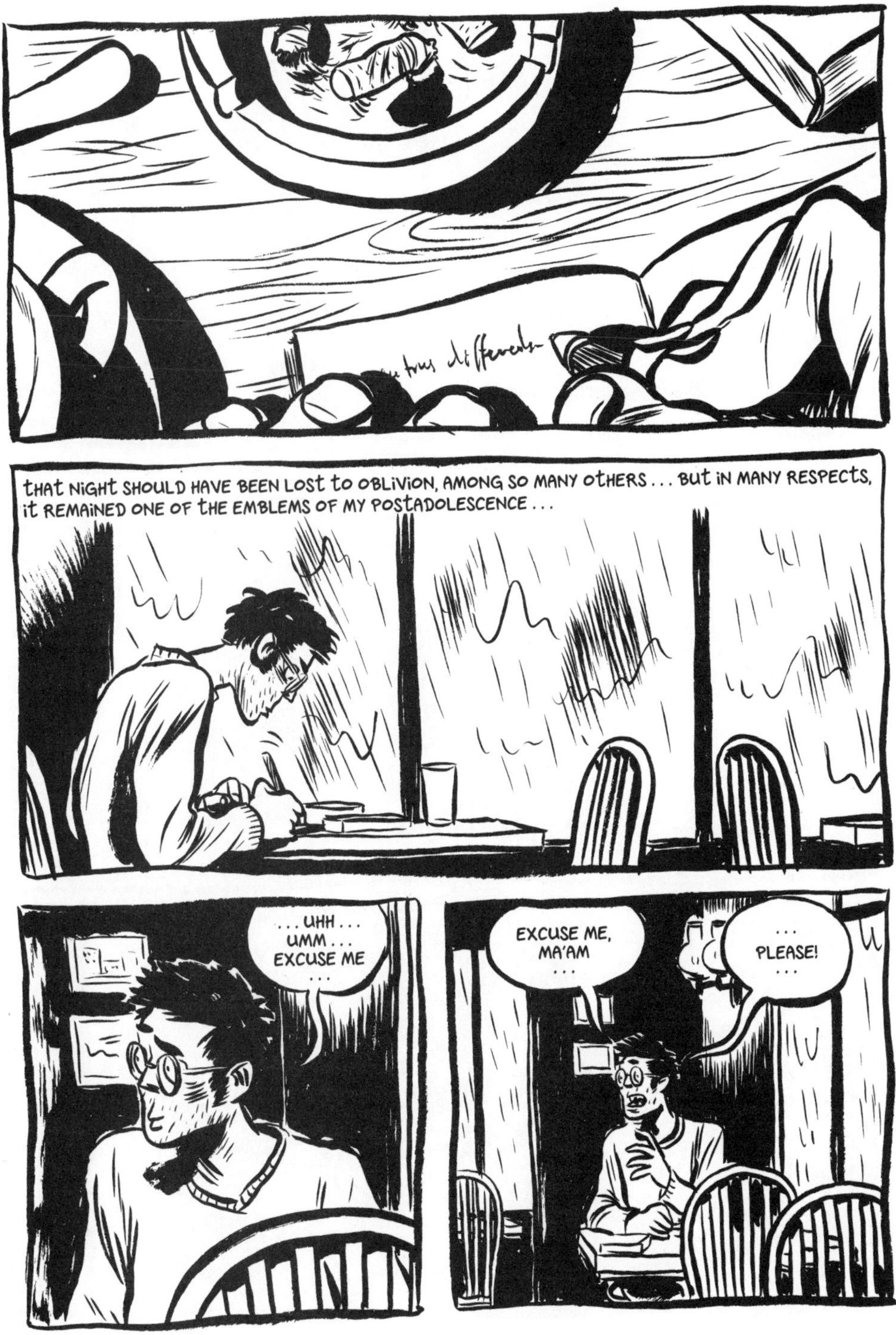
THAT NIGHT SHOULD HAVE BEEN LOST TO OBLIVION, AMONG SO MANY OTHERS . . . BUT IN MANY RESPECTS, IT REMAINED ONE OF THE EMBLEMS OF MY POSTADOLESCENCE . . .
. . . UHH . . . UMM . . . EXCUSE ME . . .
EXCUSE ME, MA'AM . . .
. . . PLEASE! . . .

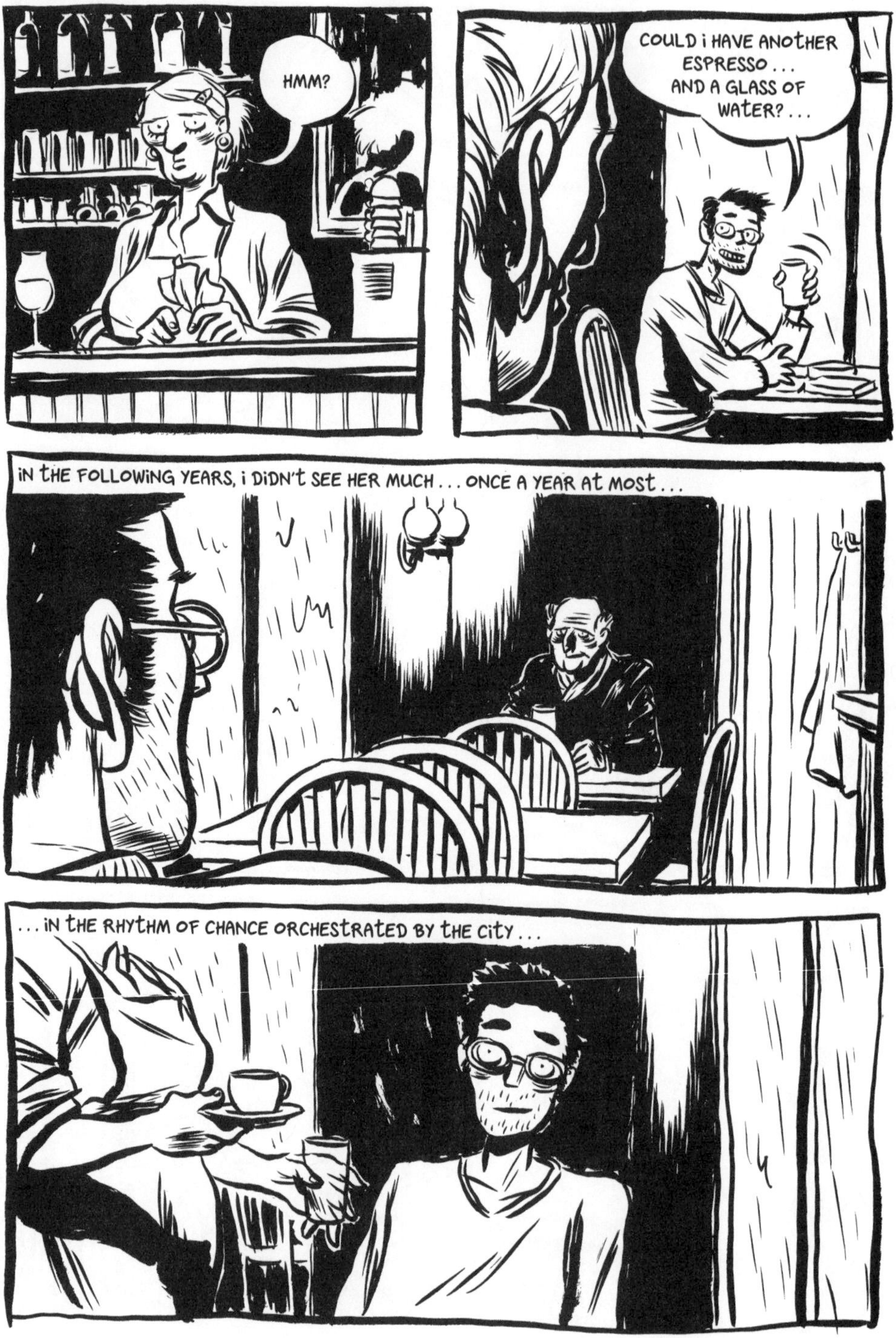
HMM?
COULD i HAVE ANOTHER ESPRESSO . . . AND A GLASS OF WATER? . . .
iN THE FOLLOWiNG YEARS, i DiDN'T SEE HER MUCH . . . ONCE A YEAR AT MOST . . .
. . . iN THE RHYTHM OF CHANCE ORCHESTRATED BY THE CiTY . . .

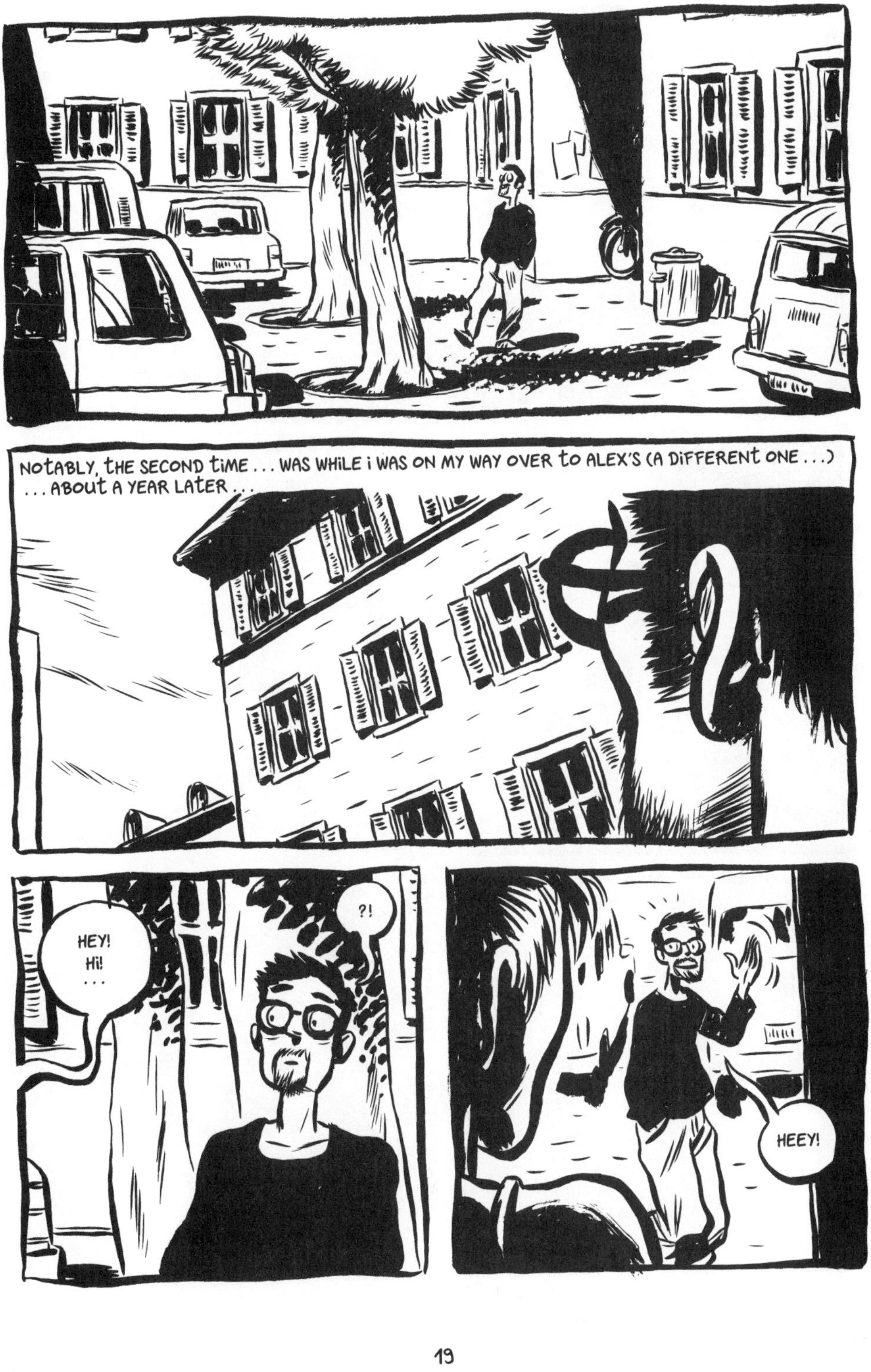
NOTABLY, THE SECOND TIME . . . WAS WHILE I WAS ON MY WAY OVER TO ALEX'S (A DIFFERENT ONE . . .)
. . . ABOUT A YEAR LATER . . .
HEY!
HI!
. . .
?!
HEEY!

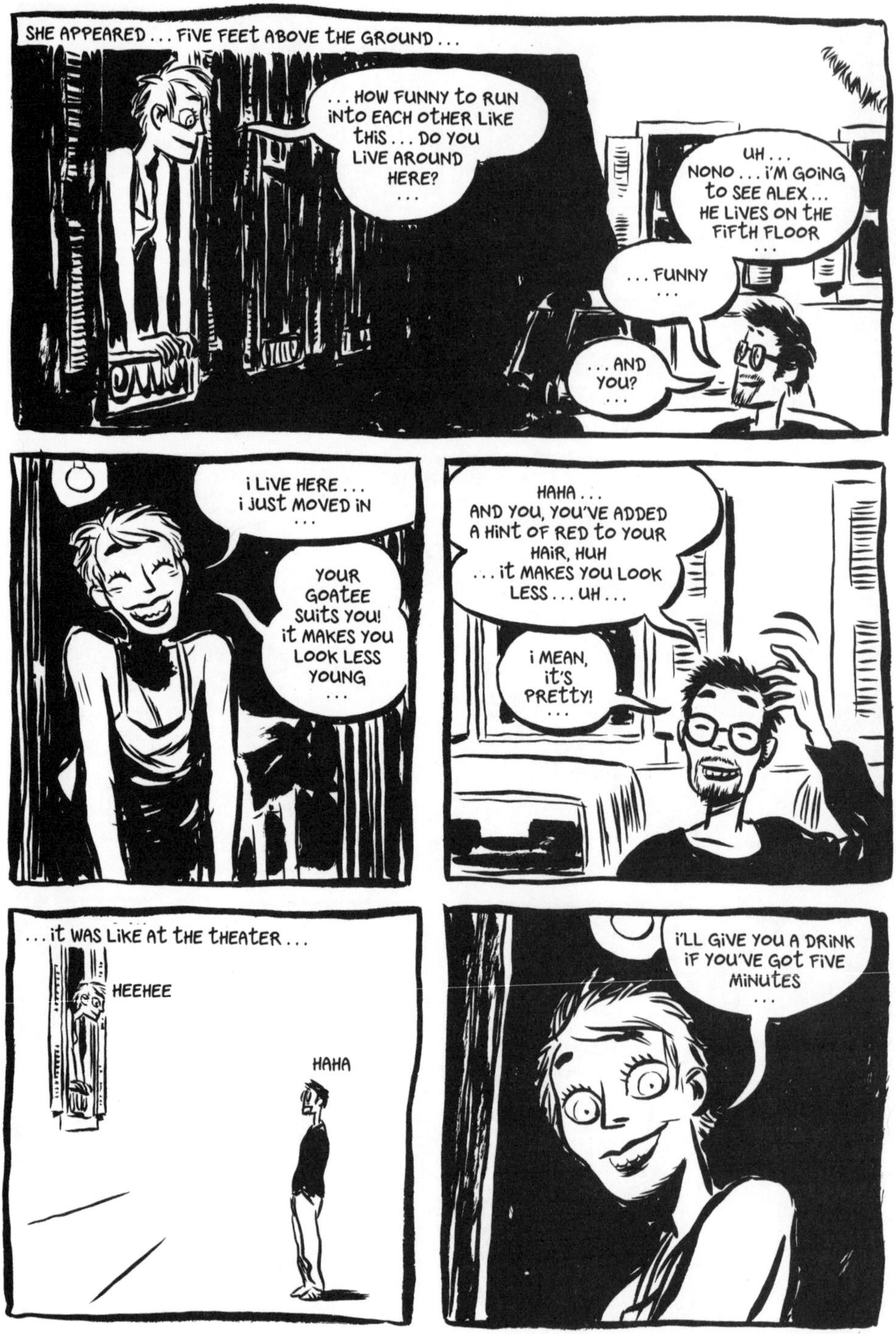
SHE APPEARED . . . FIVE FEET ABOVE THE GROUND . . .
. . . HOW FUNNY TO RUN INTO EACH OTHER LIKE THIS . . . DO YOU LIVE AROUND HERE? . . .
UH . . . NONO . . . I'M GOING TO SEE ALEX . . . HE LIVES ON THE FIFTH FLOOR . . .
. . . FUNNY . . .
. . . AND YOU? . . .
I LIVE HERE . . . I JUST MOVED IN . . .
YOUR GOATEE SUITS YOU! IT MAKES YOU LOOK LESS YOUNG . . .
HAHA . . . AND YOU, YOU'VE ADDED A HINT OF RED TO YOUR HAIR, HUH . . . IT MAKES YOU LOOK LESS . . . UH . . .
I MEAN, IT'S PRETTY! . . .
. . . IT WAS LIKE AT THE THEATER . . .
HEEHEE
HAHA
I'LL GIVE YOU A DRINK IF YOU'VE GOT FIVE MINUTES . . .

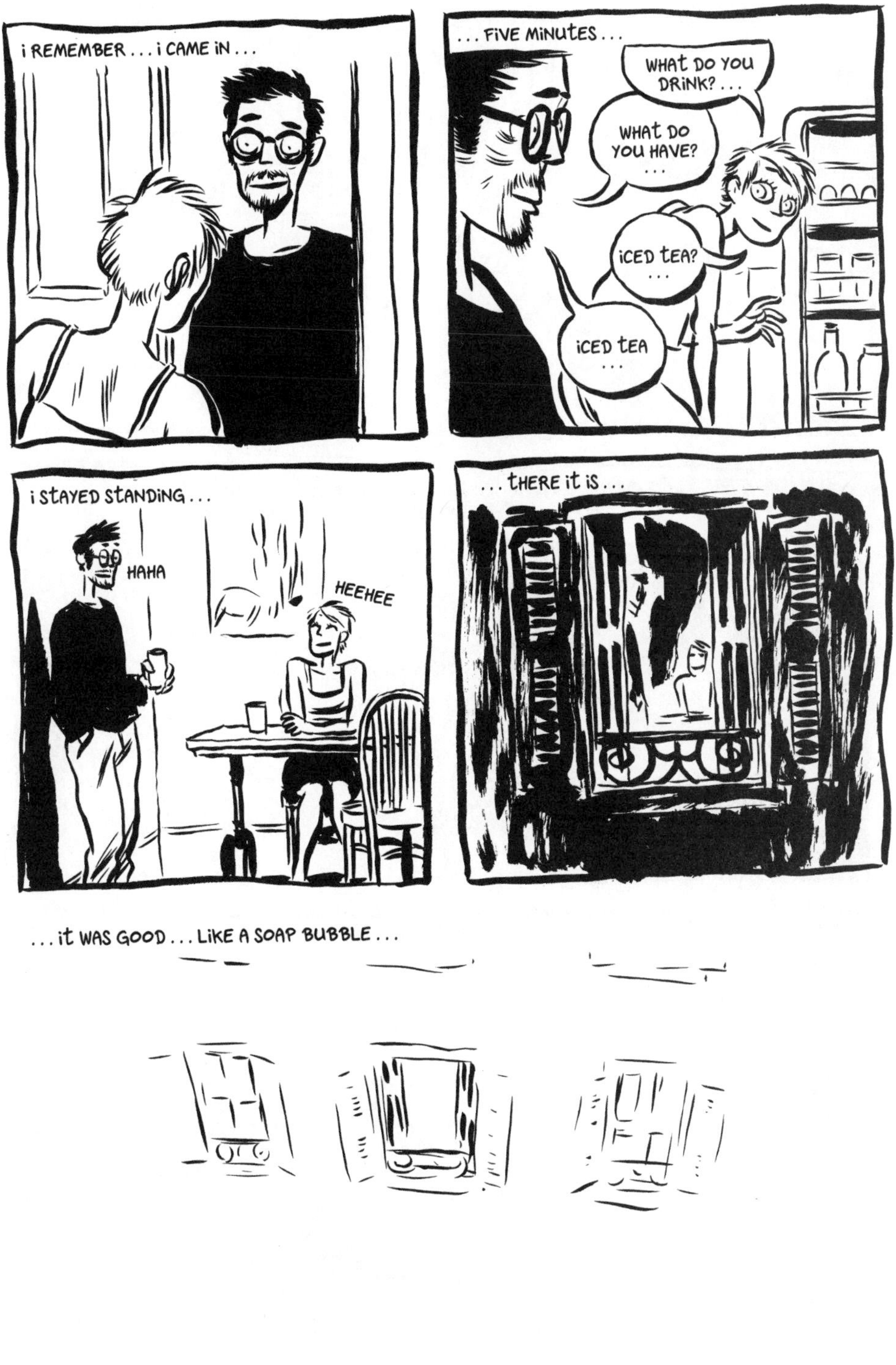
i REMEMBER . . . i CAME iN . . .
. . . FiVE MiNUtES . . .
WHAt DO YOU DRiNK? . . .
WHAt DO YOU HAVE? . . .
iCED tEA? . . .
iCED tEA . . .
i StAYED StANDiNG . . .
HAHA
HEEHEE
. . . tHERE it iS . . .
. . . it WAS GOOD . . . LiKE A SOAP BUBBLE . . .

During the years that followed, i learned that she got married, that she became a mother ... she moved to the fourth floor of the same building ... just below Alex's apartment ...

i ran into her again at the end of the summer of '99 ... i remember because i was extremely closed, in a terrible mood ... a bad period ...

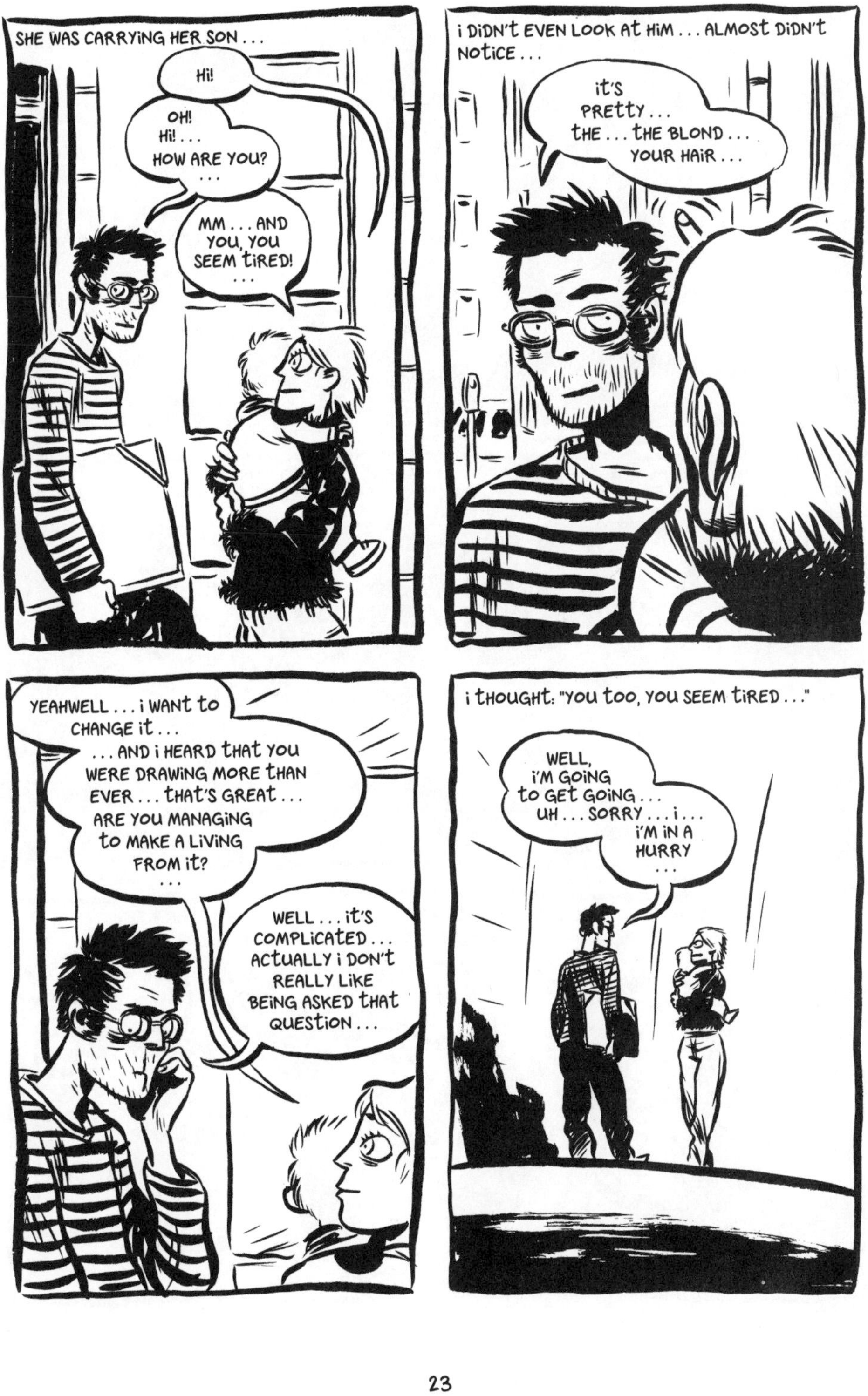
SHE WAS CARRYING HER SON . . .
Hi!
OH! Hi! . . . HOW ARE YOU? . . .
MM . . . AND YOU, YOU SEEM tiRED! . . .
i DIDN'T EVEN LOOK At HiM . . . ALMOSt DiDN't NOtiCE . . .
it's PREtty . . . tHE . . . tHE BLOND . . . YOUR HAiR . . .
YEAHWELL . . . i WANt to CHANGE it . . . . . . AND i HEARD tHAt YOU WERE DRAWiNG MORE tHAN EVER . . . tHAt'S GREAt . . . ARE YOU MANAGiNG to MAKE A LiViNG FROM it? . . .
WELL . . . it's COMPLiCAtED . . . ACtUALLY i DON't REALLY LiKE BEiNG ASKED tHAt QUEStiON . . .
i tHOUGHt: "YOU tOO, YOU SEEM tiRED . . ."
WELL, i'M GOiNG to GEt GOiNG . . . UH . . . SORRY . . . i . . . i'M iN A HURRY . . .

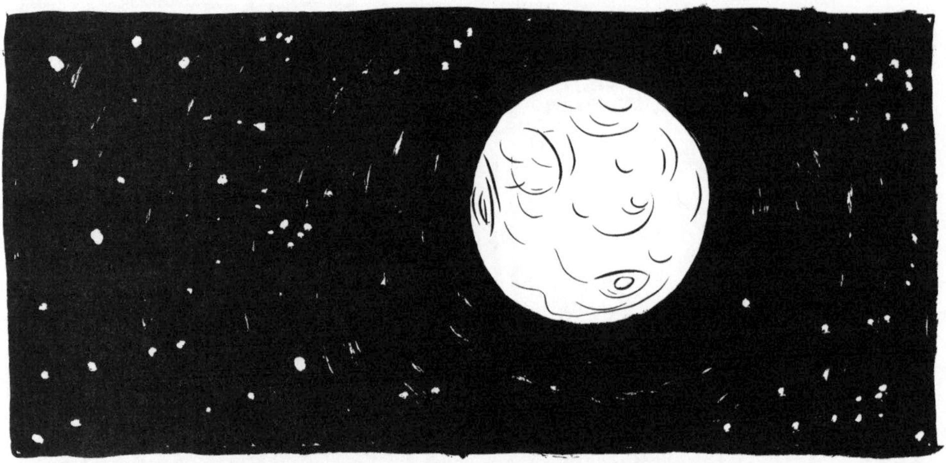

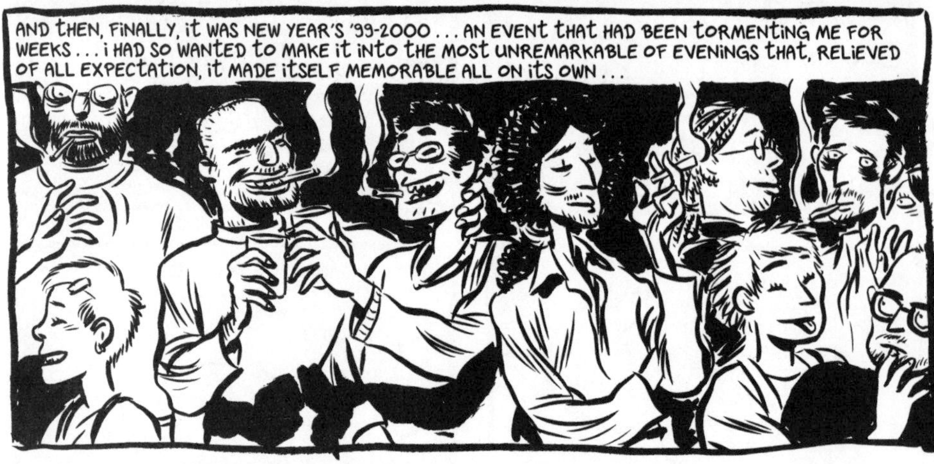
AND THEN, FINALLY, IT WAS NEW YEAR'S '99-2000 . . . AN EVENT THAT HAD BEEN TORMENTING ME FOR WEEKS . . . I HAD SO WANTED TO MAKE IT INTO THE MOST UNREMARKABLE OF EVENINGS THAT, RELIEVED OF ALL EXPECTATION, IT MADE ITSELF MEMORABLE ALL ON ITS OWN . . .

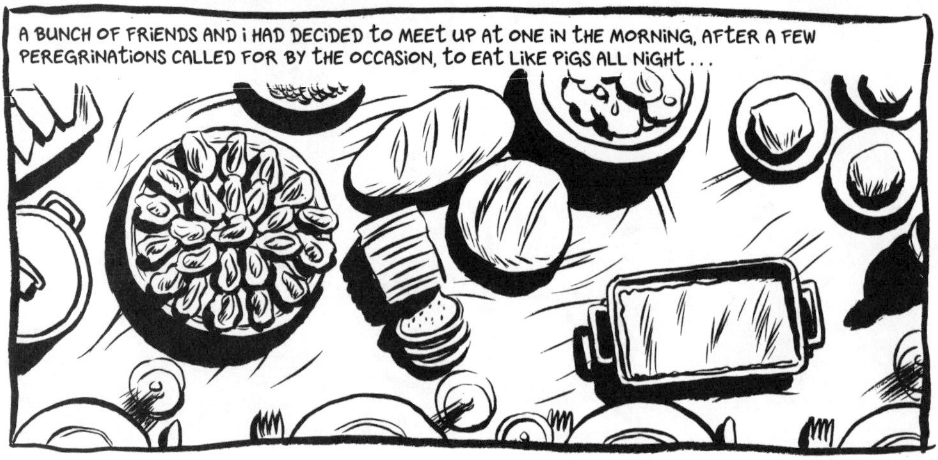
A BUNCH OF FRIENDS AND I HAD DECIDED TO MEET UP AT ONE IN THE MORNING, AFTER A FEW PEREGRINATIONS CALLED FOR BY THE OCCASION, TO EAT LIKE PIGS ALL NIGHT . . .

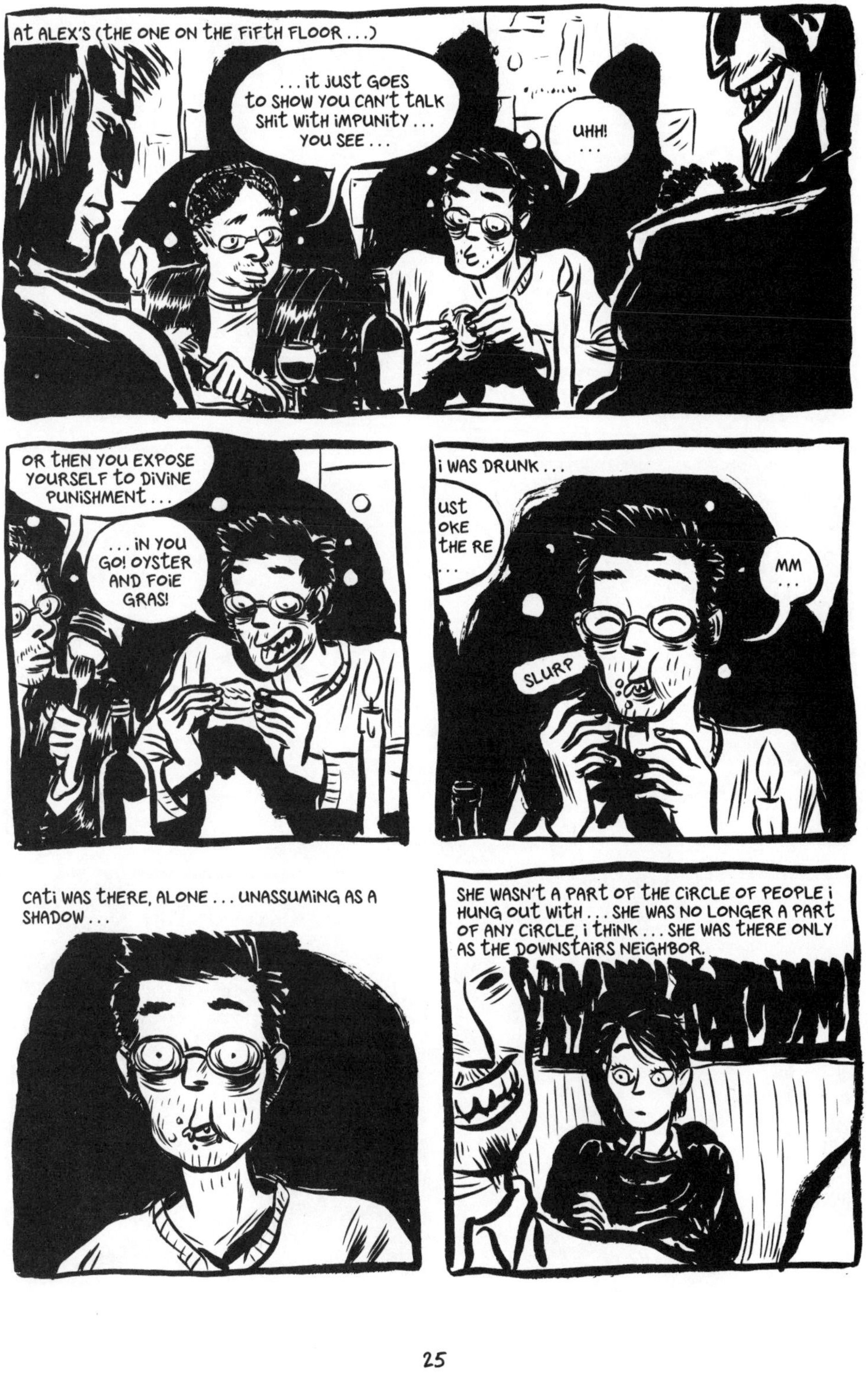
AT ALEX'S (THE ONE ON THE FIFTH FLOOR . . .)
. . . IT JUST GOES TO SHOW YOU CAN'T TALK SHIT WITH IMPUNITY . . . YOU SEE . . .
UHH! . . .
OR THEN YOU EXPOSE YOURSELF TO DIVINE PUNISHMENT . . .
. . . IN YOU GO! OYSTER AND FOIE GRAS!
I WAS DRUNK . . .
UST OKE THE RE . . .
MM . . .
SLURP
CATI WAS THERE, ALONE . . . UNASSUMING AS A SHADOW . . .
SHE WASN'T A PART OF THE CIRCLE OF PEOPLE I HUNG OUT WITH . . . SHE WAS NO LONGER A PART OF ANY CIRCLE, I THINK . . . SHE WAS THERE ONLY AS THE DOWNSTAIRS NEIGHBOR.

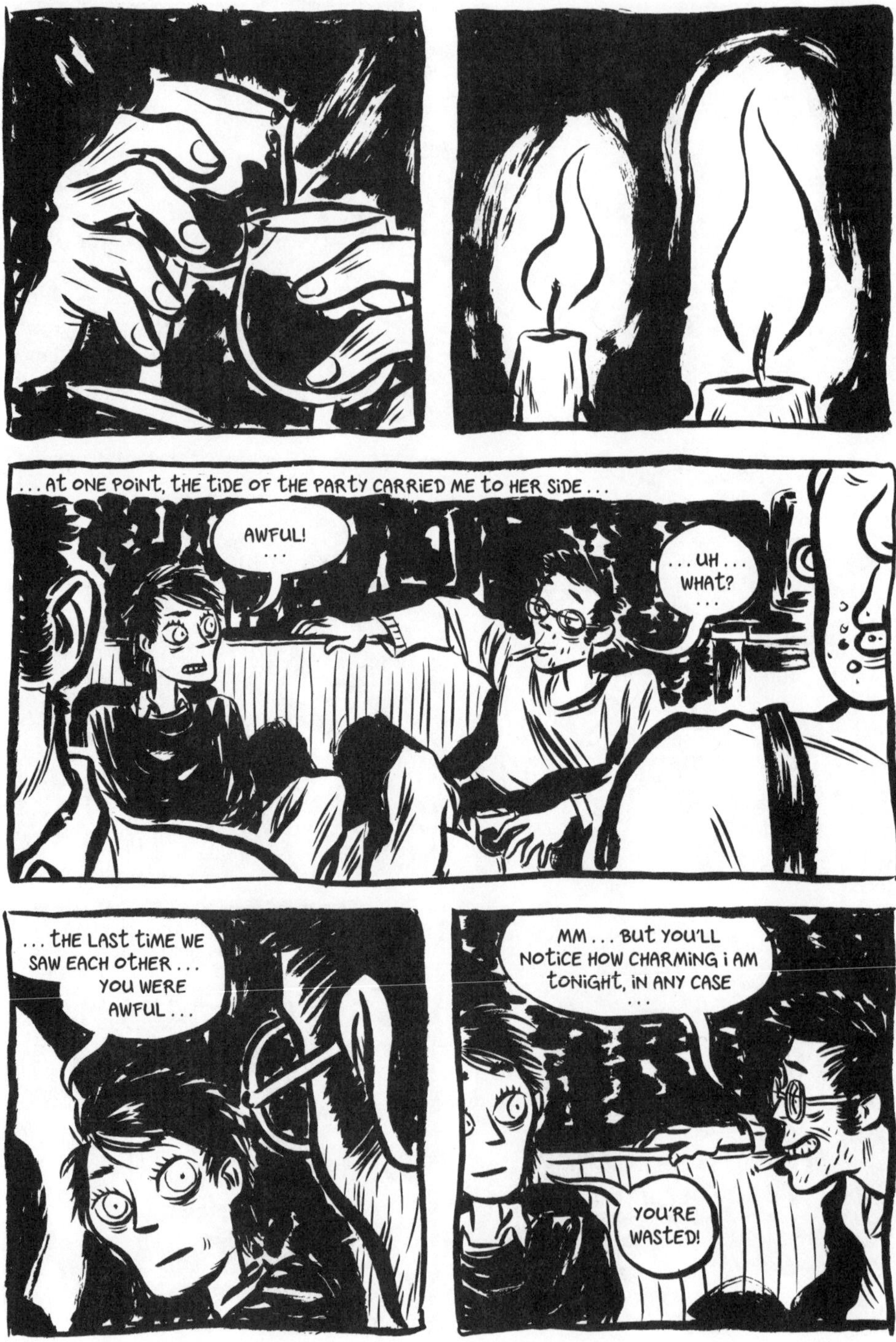

...AT ONE POINT, THE TIDE OF THE PARTY CARRIED ME TO HER SIDE...
AWFUL! ...
...UH... WHAT? ...
...THE LAST TIME WE SAW EACH OTHER... YOU WERE AWFUL...
MM... BUT YOU'LL NOTICE HOW CHARMING I AM TONIGHT, IN ANY CASE ...
YOU'RE WASTED!

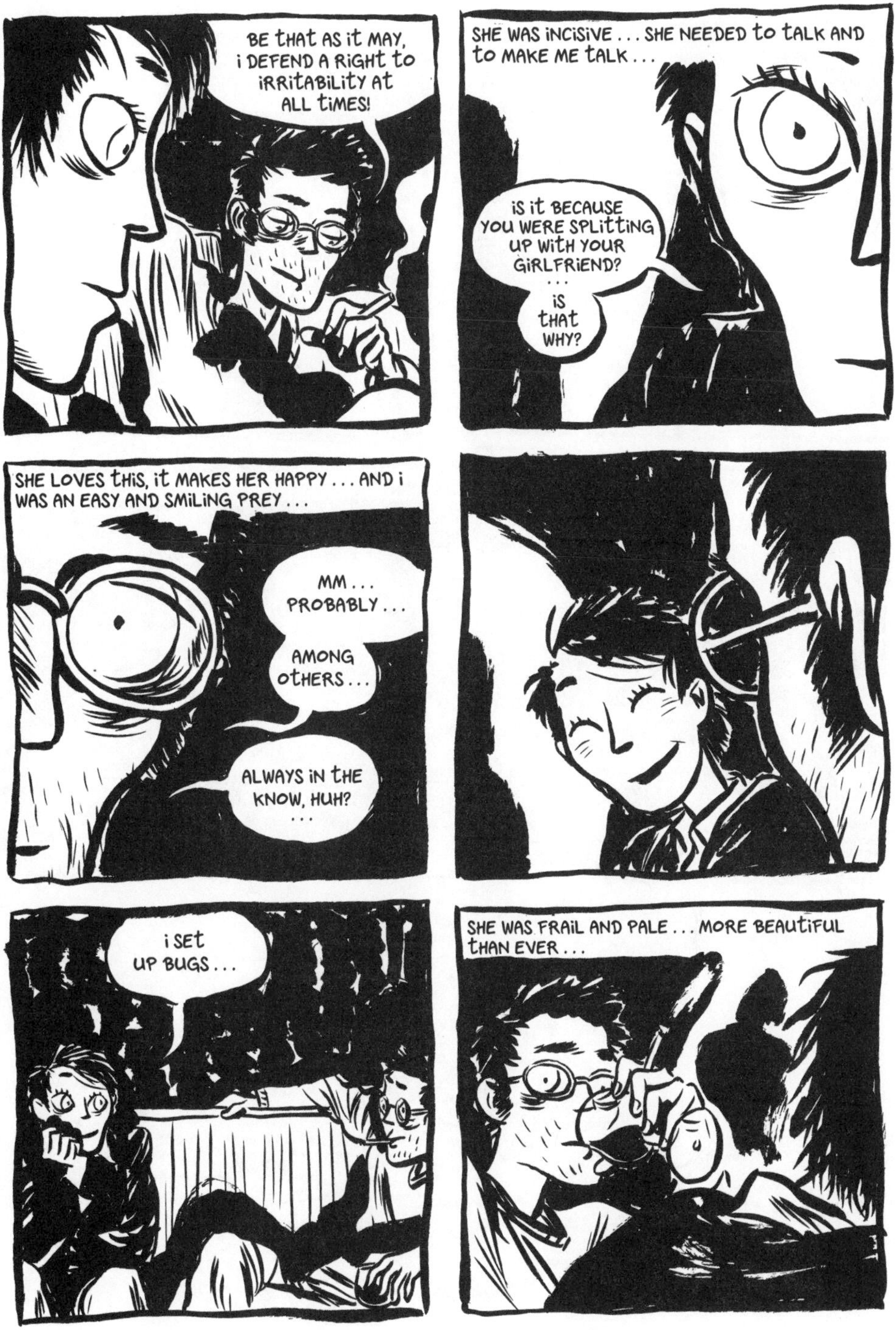

BE THAT AS IT MAY, I DEFEND A RIGHT TO IRRITABILITY AT ALL TIMES!
SHE WAS INCISIVE . . . SHE NEEDED TO TALK AND TO MAKE ME TALK . . .
IS IT BECAUSE YOU WERE SPLITTING UP WITH YOUR GIRLFRIEND? . . .
IS THAT WHY?
SHE LOVES THIS, IT MAKES HER HAPPY . . . AND I WAS AN EASY AND SMILING PREY . . .
MM . . . PROBABLY . . .
AMONG OTHERS . . .
ALWAYS IN THE KNOW, HUH? . . .
I SET UP BUGS . . .
SHE WAS FRAIL AND PALE . . . MORE BEAUTIFUL THAN EVER . . .

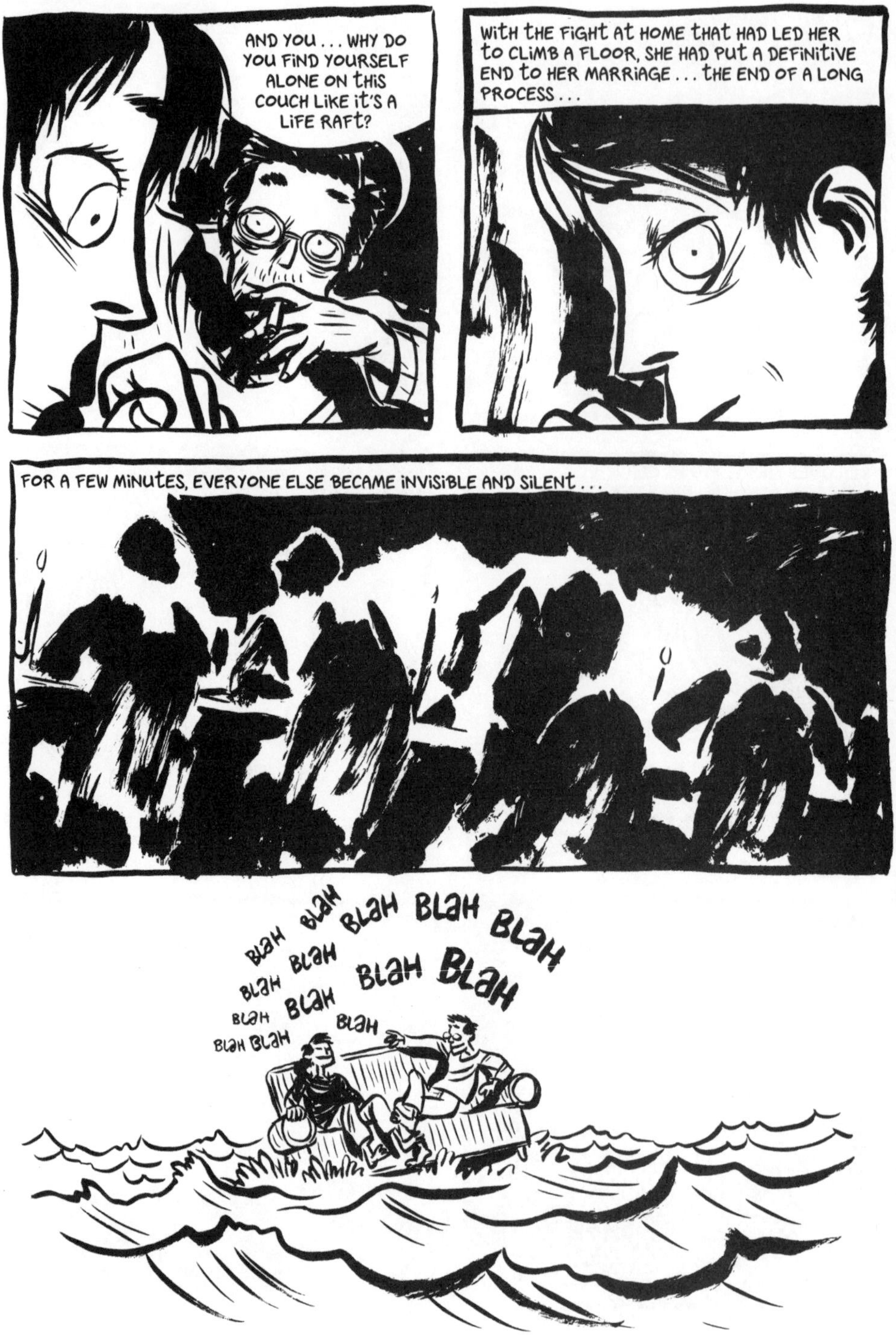

AND YOU . . . WHY DO YOU FIND YOURSELF ALONE ON THIS COUCH LIKE IT'S A LIFE RAFT?
WITH THE FIGHT AT HOME THAT HAD LED HER TO CLIMB A FLOOR, SHE HAD PUT A DEFINITIVE END TO HER MARRIAGE . . . THE END OF A LONG PROCESS . . .
FOR A FEW MINUTES, EVERYONE ELSE BECAME INVISIBLE AND SILENT . . .
BLAH BLAH BLAH BLAH BLAH
BLAH BLAH BLAH BLAH
BLAH BLAH BLAH
BLAH BLAH

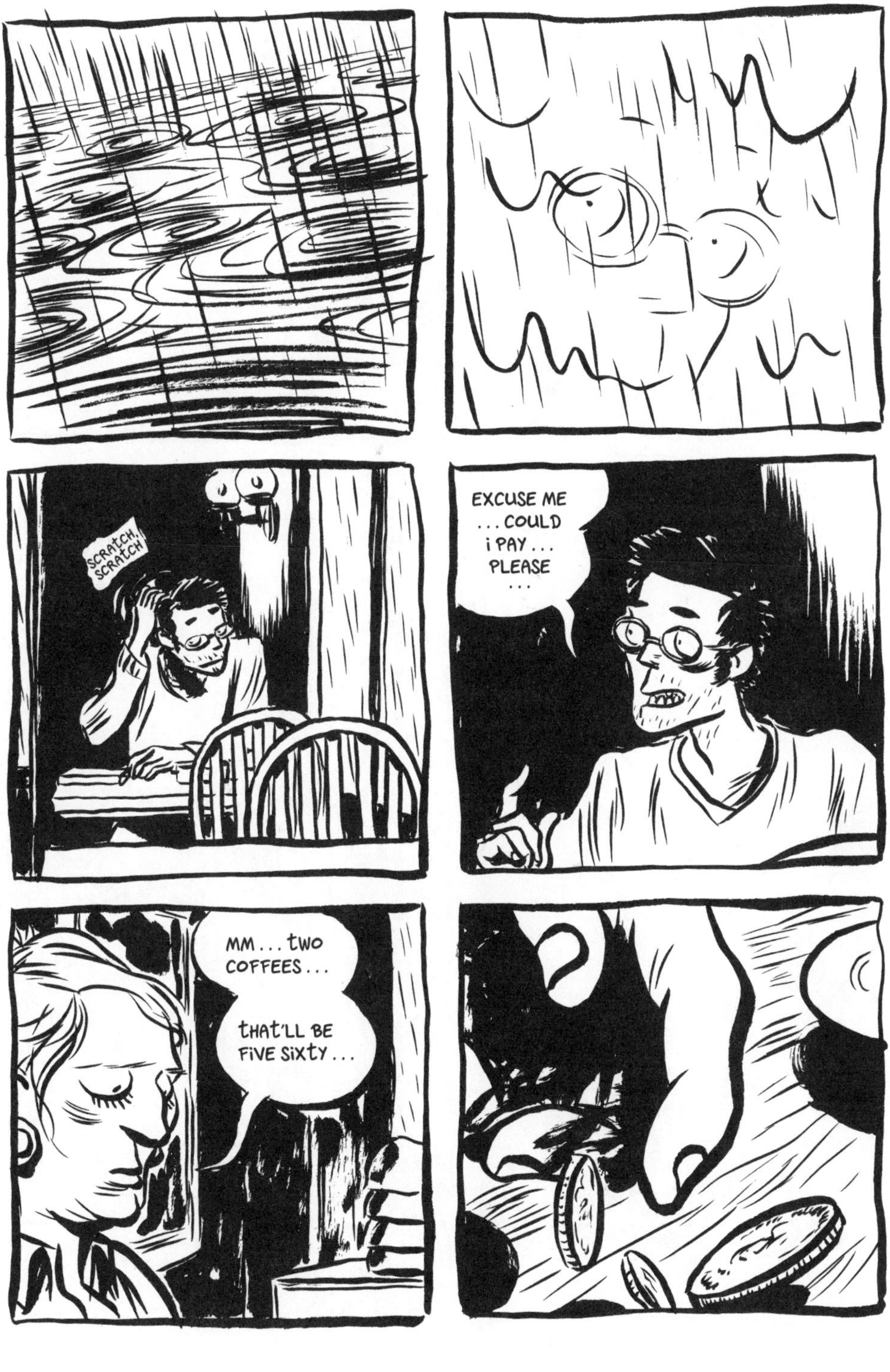
SCRATCH SCRATCH
EXCUSE ME ...COULD i PAY ... PLEASE ...
MM ... two COFFEES ...
that'll BE FiVE SiXty ...

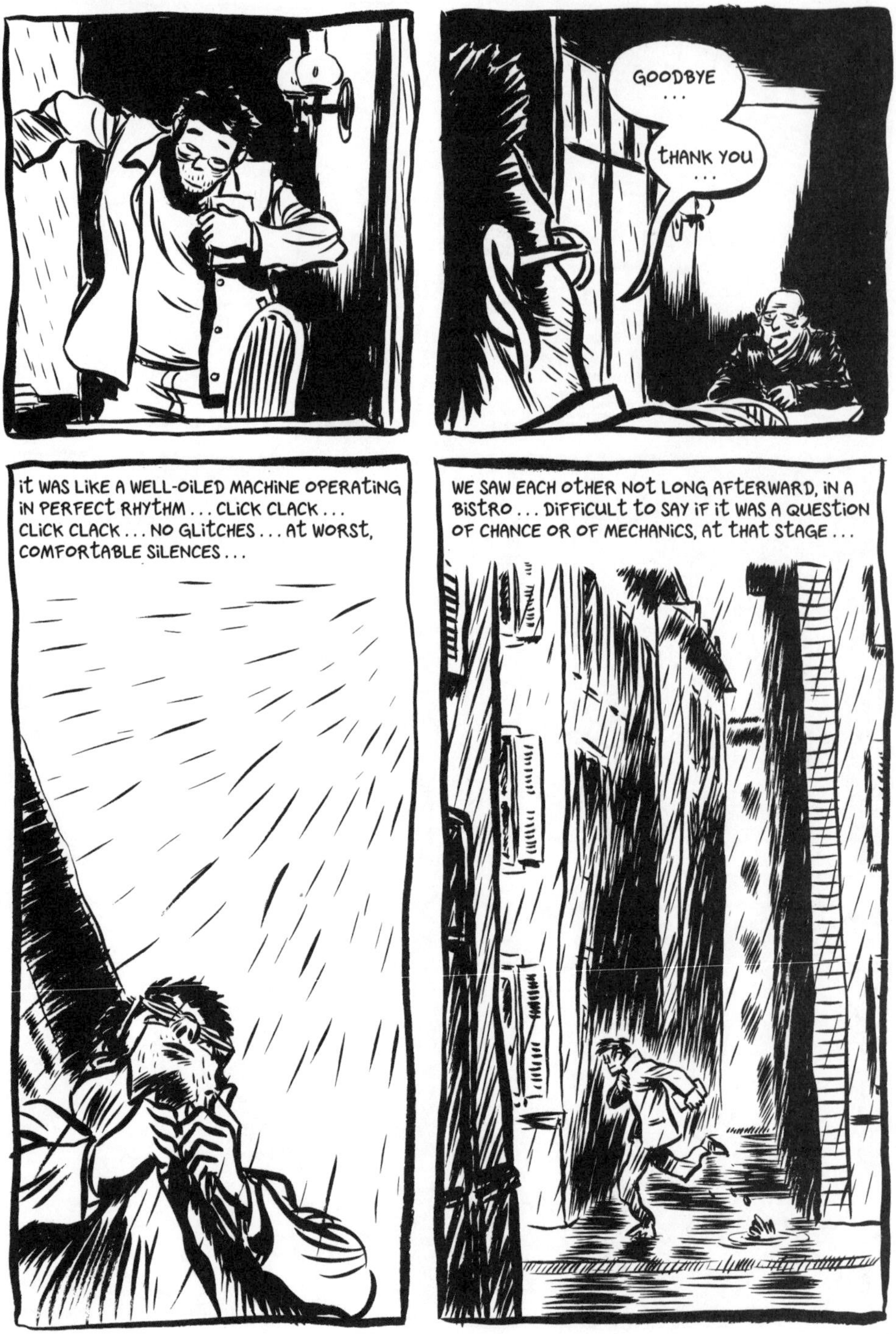
GOODBYE ...
THANK YOU ...
IT WAS LIKE A WELL-OILED MACHINE OPERATING IN PERFECT RHYTHM ... CLICK CLACK ... CLICK CLACK ... NO GLITCHES ... AT WORST, COMFORTABLE SILENCES ...
WE SAW EACH OTHER NOT LONG AFTERWARD, IN A BISTRO ... DIFFICULT TO SAY IF IT WAS A QUESTION OF CHANCE OR OF MECHANICS, AT THAT STAGE ...

...MOVIES...A GRIM FILM...ATOM EGOYAN, I BELIEVE...

...PROVOCATIONS...ALLUSIONS...CLICK...CLACK...CLICK...CLACK...

BLAH BLAH BLAH BLAH BLAH BLAH BLAH BLAH BLAH BLAH BLAH BLAH BLAH BLAH BLAH BLAH BLAH BLAH BLAH

...AND, SINCE IT WAS REQUIRED THAT ALL THIS LEAD SOMEWHERE, AN INTIMATE MEAL AT MY PLACE...

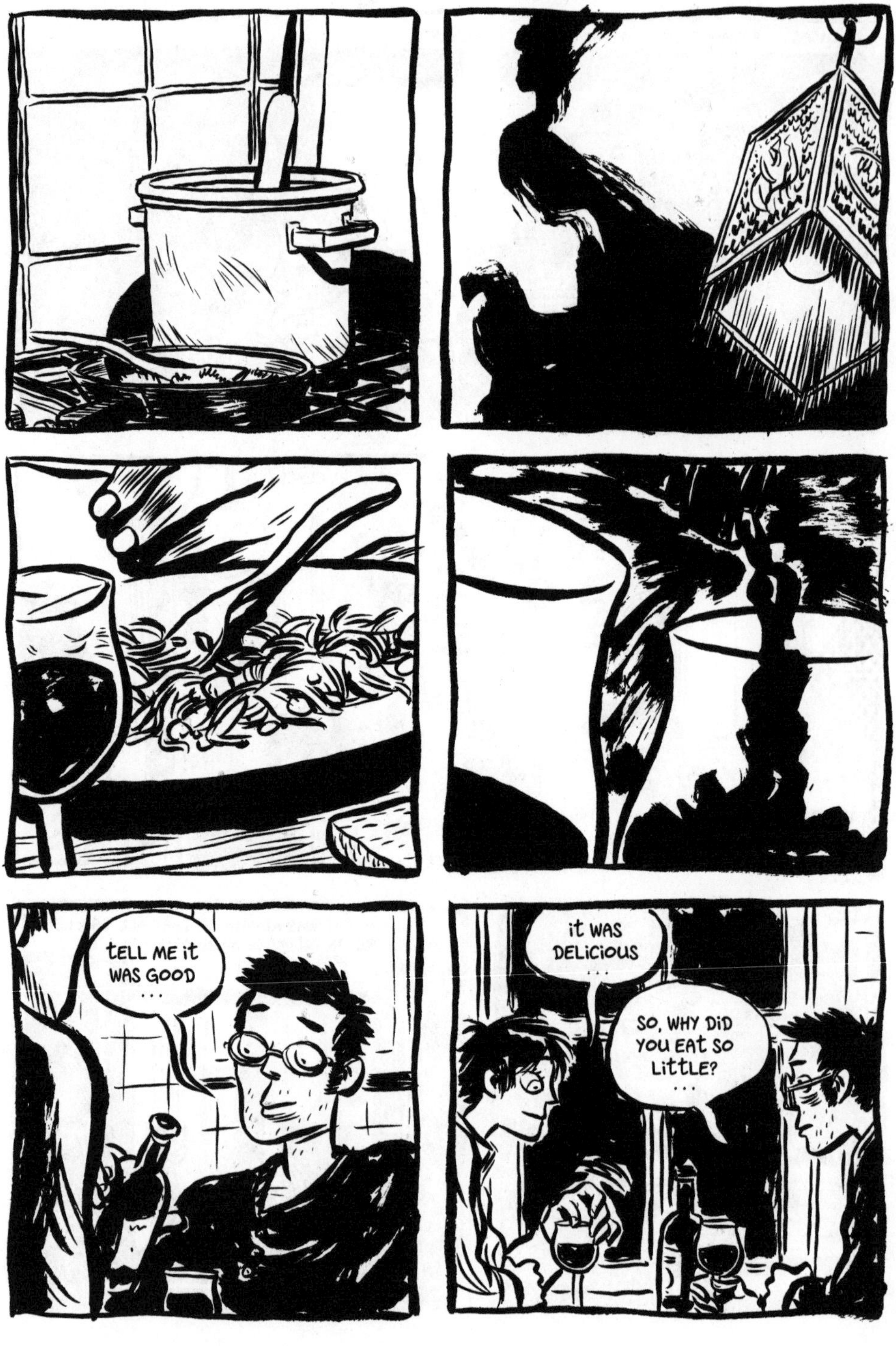

TELL ME IT WAS GOOD . . .
IT WAS DELICIOUS . . .
SO, WHY DID YOU EAT SO LITTLE? . . .

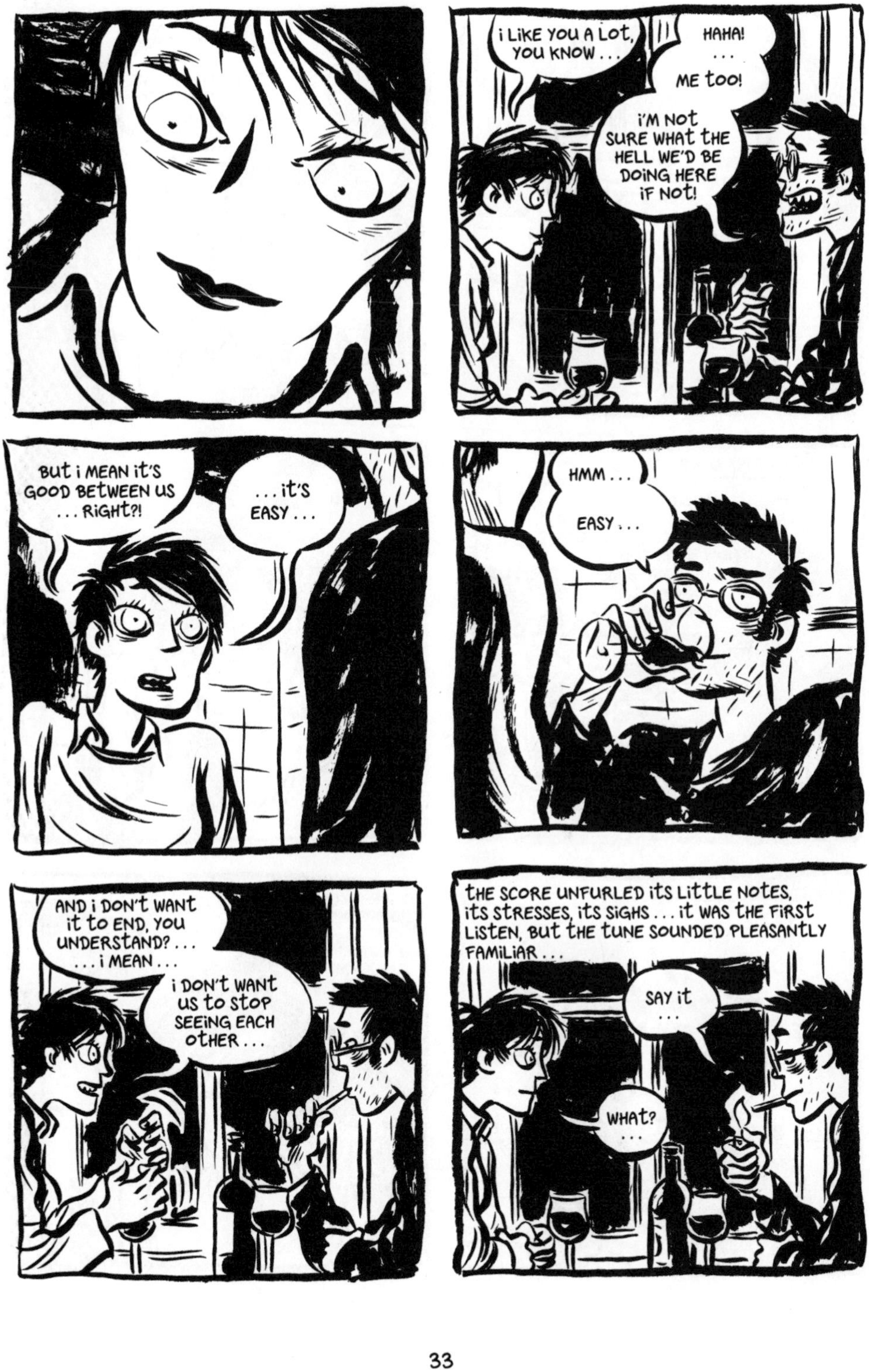
i LiKE YOU A Lot, YOU KNOW . . .
HAHA! . . .
ME too!
i'M NOt SURE WHAt tHE HELL WE'D BE DOiNG HERE iF NOt!
But i MEAN it's GOOD BETWEEN US . . . RiGHt?!
. . . it's EASY . . .
HMM . . .
EASY . . .
AND i DON'T WANT it to END, YOU UNDERSTAND? . . . . . . i MEAN . . .
i DON'T WANT US to StOP SEEiNG EACH OtHER . . .
tHE SCORE UNFURLED itS LittLE NOTES, itS StRESSES, itS SiGHS . . . it WAS tHE FiRSt LiStEN, BUt tHE tUNE SOUNDED PLEASANTLY FAMiLiAR . . .
SAY it . . .
WHAt? . . .

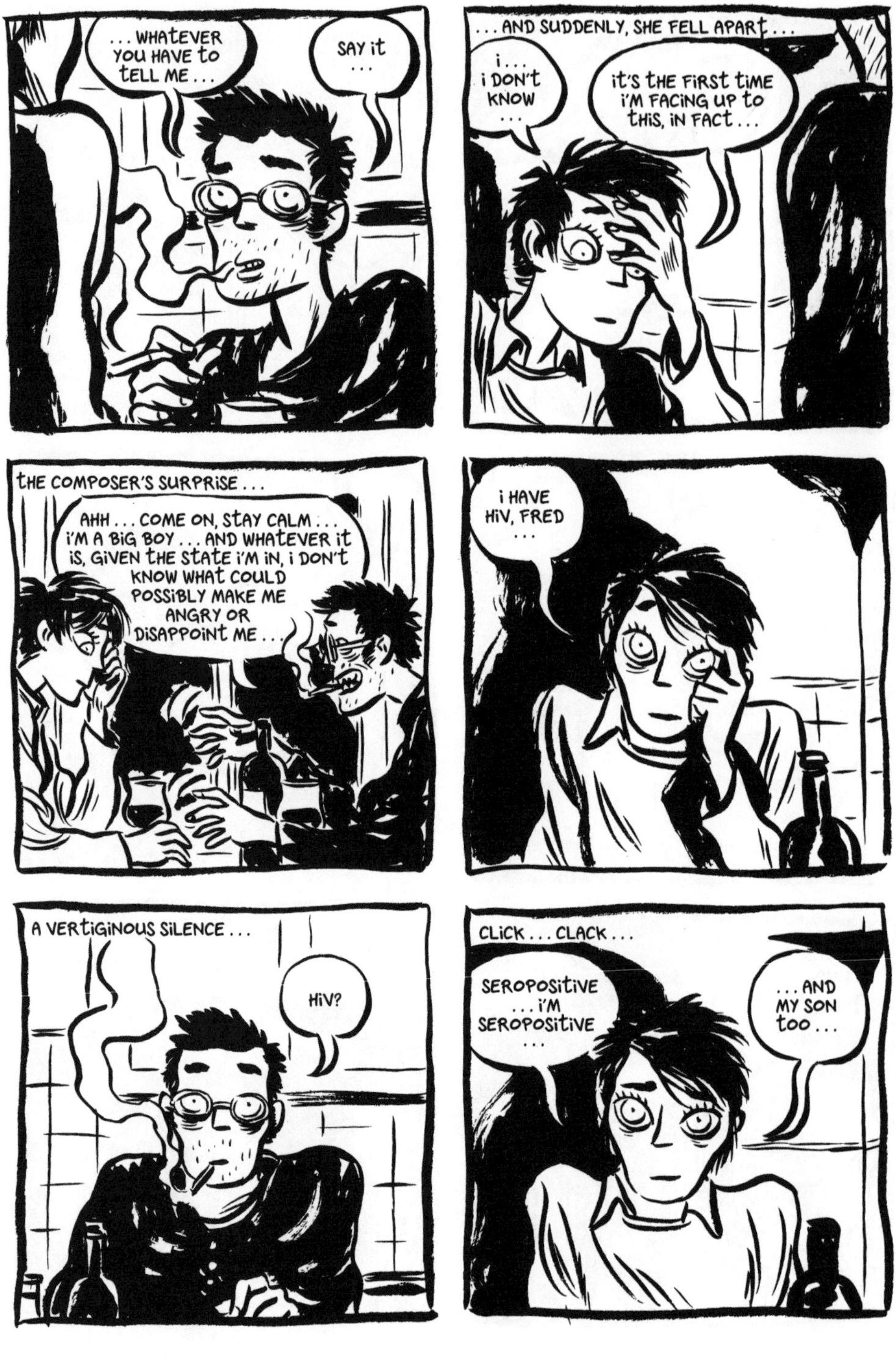
... WHATEVER YOU HAVE TO TELL ME ...
SAY IT ...
... AND SUDDENLY, SHE FELL APART ...
I ... I DON'T KNOW ...
IT'S THE FIRST TIME I'M FACING UP TO THIS, IN FACT ...
THE COMPOSER'S SURPRISE ...
AHH ... COME ON, STAY CALM ... I'M A BIG BOY ... AND WHATEVER IT IS, GIVEN THE STATE I'M IN, I DON'T KNOW WHAT COULD POSSIBLY MAKE ME ANGRY OR DISAPPOINT ME ...
I HAVE HIV, FRED ...
A VERTIGINOUS SILENCE ...
HIV?
CLICK ... CLACK ...
SEROPOSITIVE ... I'M SEROPOSITIVE ...
... AND MY SON TOO ...

I GAVE OVER ONE FULL SECOND, IN MY HEAD AND MY HEART, TO ALL MY MOST EXTREME FEELINGS...

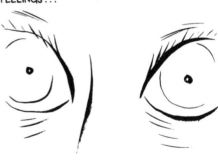

CLICK...

passion PITY desire

CLACK...

flight rejection discussion possession PITY punishment sadness abuse

CLICK...

flight rape pod

THE SCORE PICKED UP AGAIN VERY QUICKLY, EVEN IF THE INSTRUMENTS STAYED OUT OF TUNE A MOMENT...

...DEAR GOD, I HAVE THE FEELING THAT MY LIFE HAS JUST STARTED OVER...OR THAT IT'S JUST CHANGED FOREVER... I DON'T KNOW...

I PLAYED THE GUY WHO'S ON TOP OF THINGS, WHO HOLDS IT TOGETHER, WHO KNOWS WHAT HE'S STEPPING INTO...

...DO YOU WANT ME TO GO?

...I...I... AM GOING TO LEAVE I THINK...

...SHH... ARE YOU CRAZY OR WHAT?...

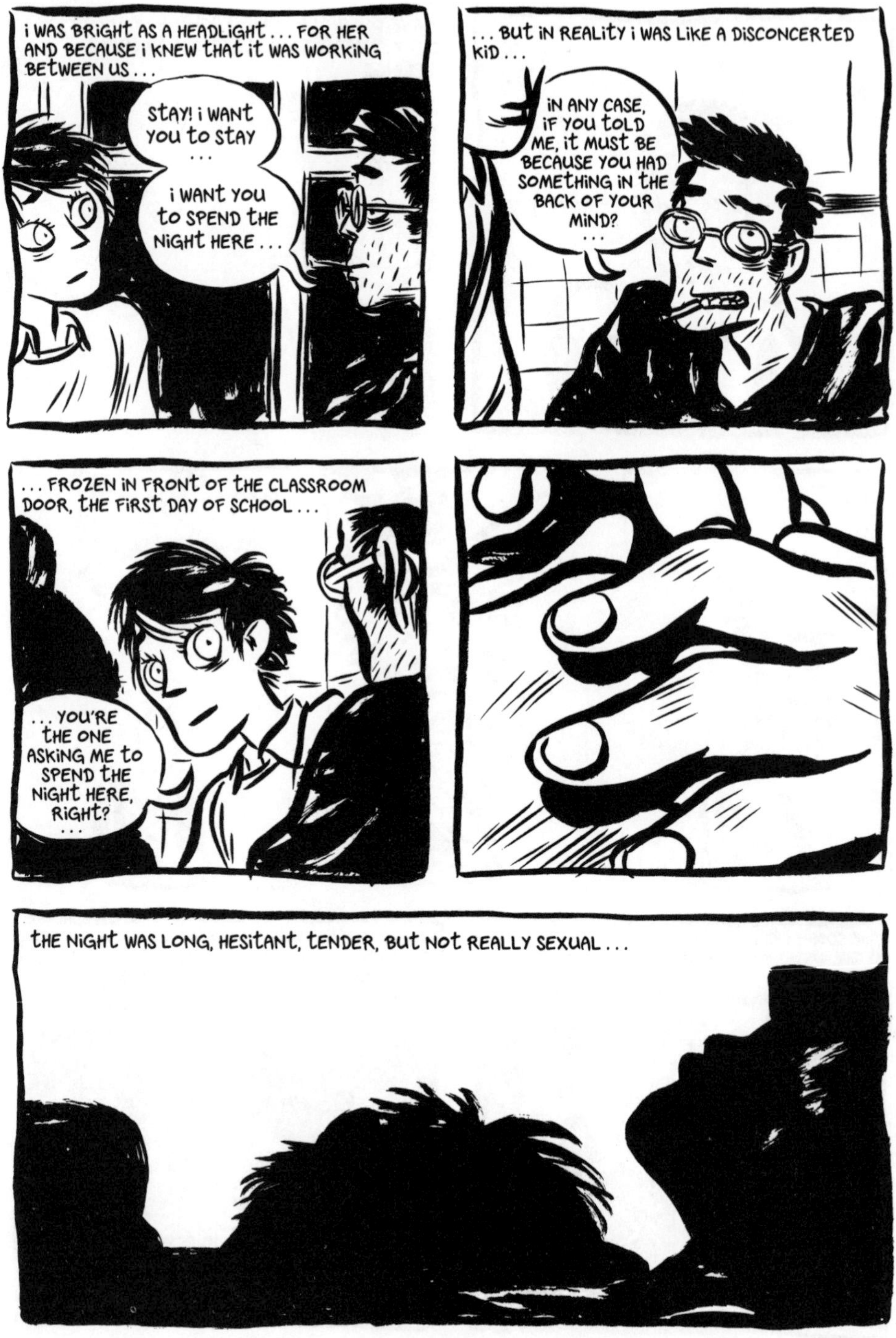
i WAS BRiGHt AS A HEADLiGHt . . . FOR HER AND BECAUSE i KNEW tHAt it WAS WORKiNG BEtWEEN US . . .
StAY! i WANt YOU tO StAY . . .
i WANt YOU tO SPEND tHE NiGHt HERE . . .
. . . BUt iN REALitY i WAS LiKE A DiSCONCERtED KiD . . .
iN ANY CASE, iF YOU tOLD ME, it MUSt BE BECAUSE YOU HAD SOMEtHiNG iN tHE BACK OF YOUR MiND? . . .
. . . FROZEN iN FRONt OF tHE CLASSROOM DOOR, tHE FiRSt DAY OF SCHOOL . . .
. . . YOU'RE tHE ONE ASKiNG ME tO SPEND tHE NiGHt HERE, RiGHt? . . .
tHE NiGHt WAS LONG, HESitANt, tENDER, BUt NOt REALLY SEXUAL . . .

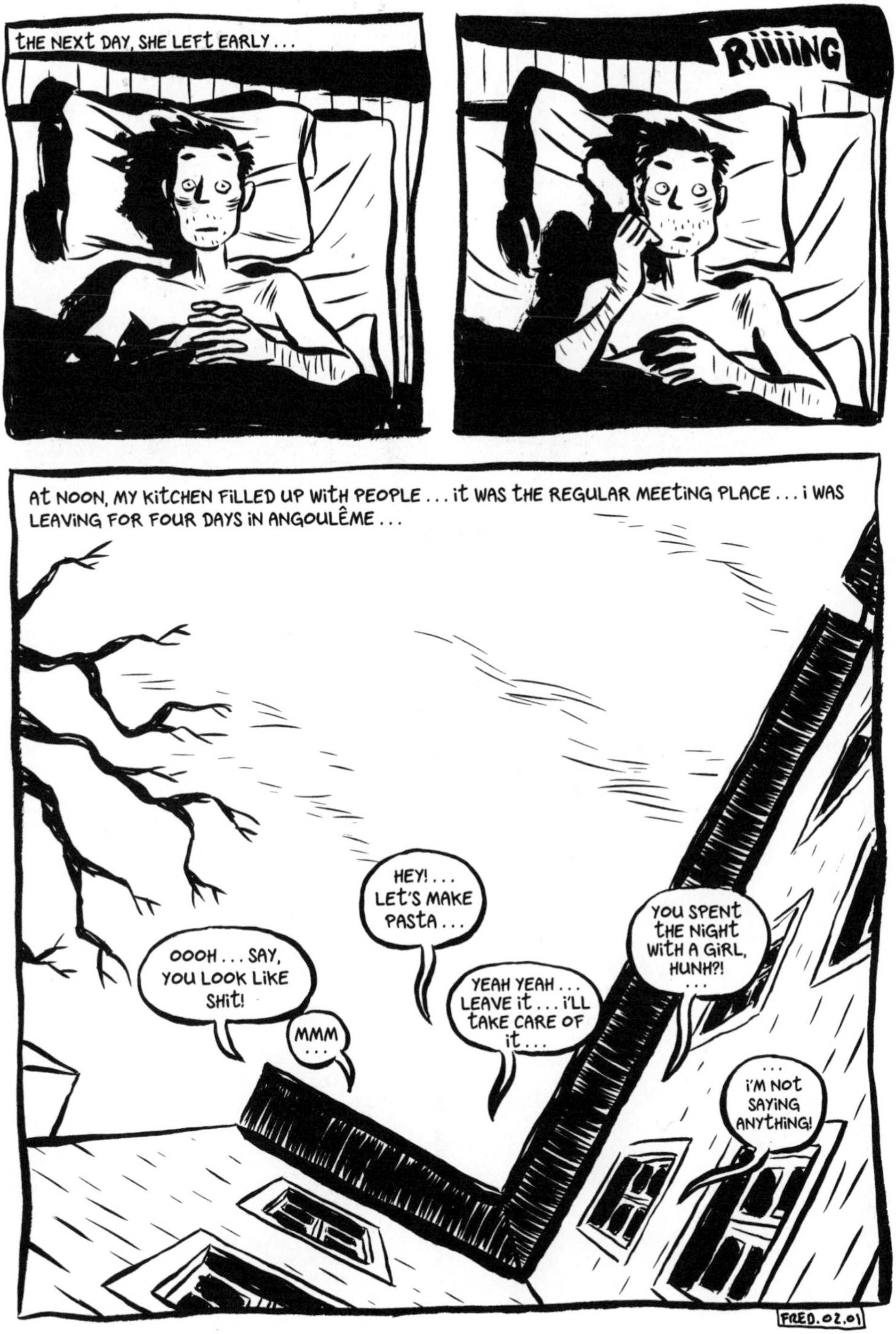
THE NEXT DAY, SHE LEFT EARLY . . .
RIIIING
AT NOON, MY KITCHEN FILLED UP WITH PEOPLE . . . IT WAS THE REGULAR MEETING PLACE . . . I WAS LEAVING FOR FOUR DAYS IN ANGOULÊME . . .
OOOH . . . SAY, YOU LOOK LIKE SHIT!
MMM . . .
HEY! . . . LET'S MAKE PASTA . . .
YEAH YEAH . . . LEAVE IT . . . I'LL TAKE CARE OF IT . . .
YOU SPENT THE NIGHT WITH A GIRL, HUNH?! . . .
. . . I'M NOT SAYING ANYTHING!
FRED. 02.01

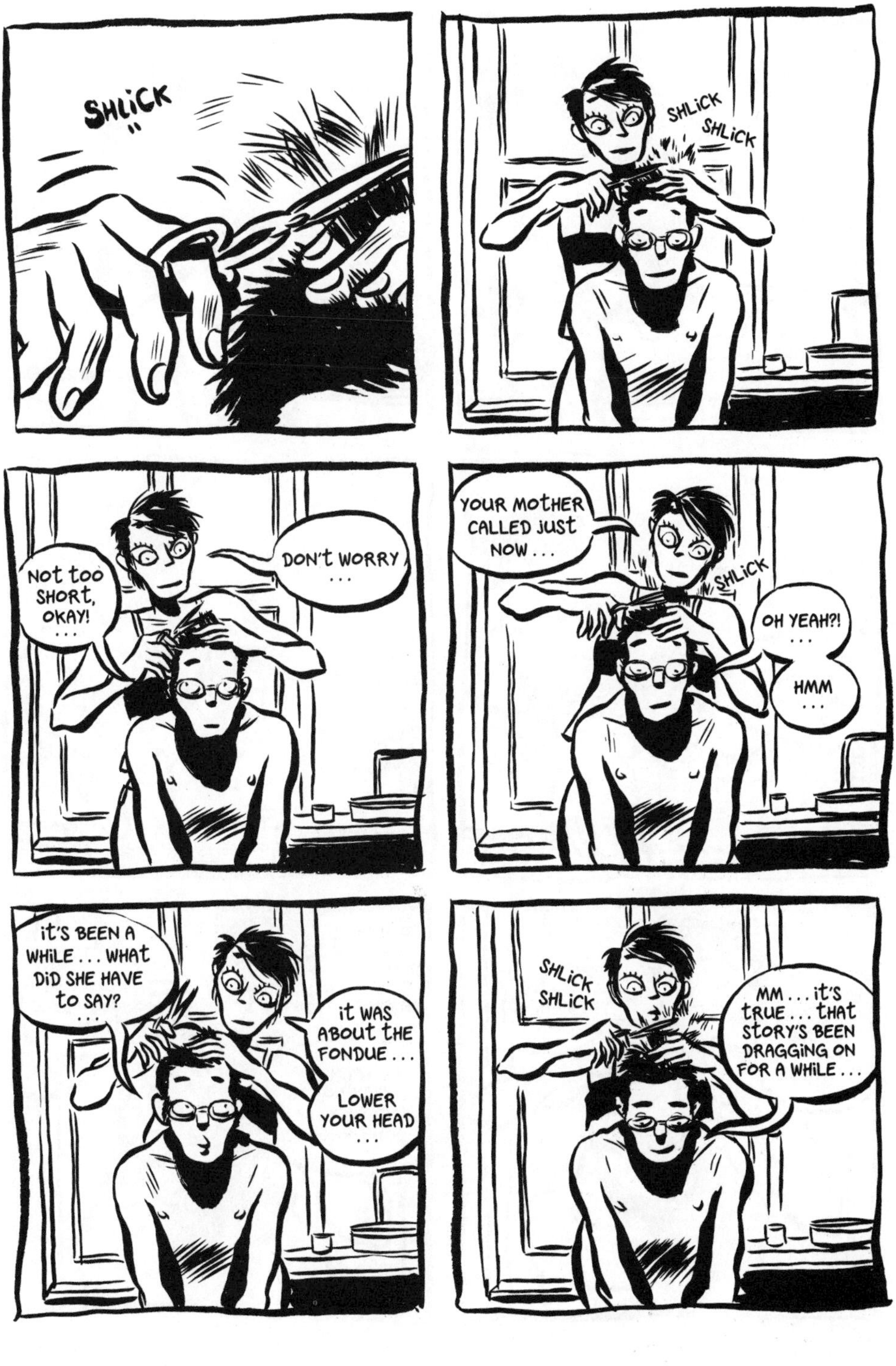
SHLiCK
SHLiCK
SHLiCK
Not too SHORT, OKAY! . . .
DON'T WORRY . . .
YOUR MOTHER CALLED JUST NOW . . .
SHLiCK
OH YEAH?! . . .
HMM . . .
iT'S BEEN A WHiLE . . . WHAT DiD SHE HAVE TO SAY? . . .
iT WAS ABOUT THE FONDUE . . .
LOWER YOUR HEAD . . .
SHLiCK
SHLiCK
MM . . . iT'S TRUE . . . THAT STORY'S BEEN DRAGGiNG ON FOR A WHiLE . . .

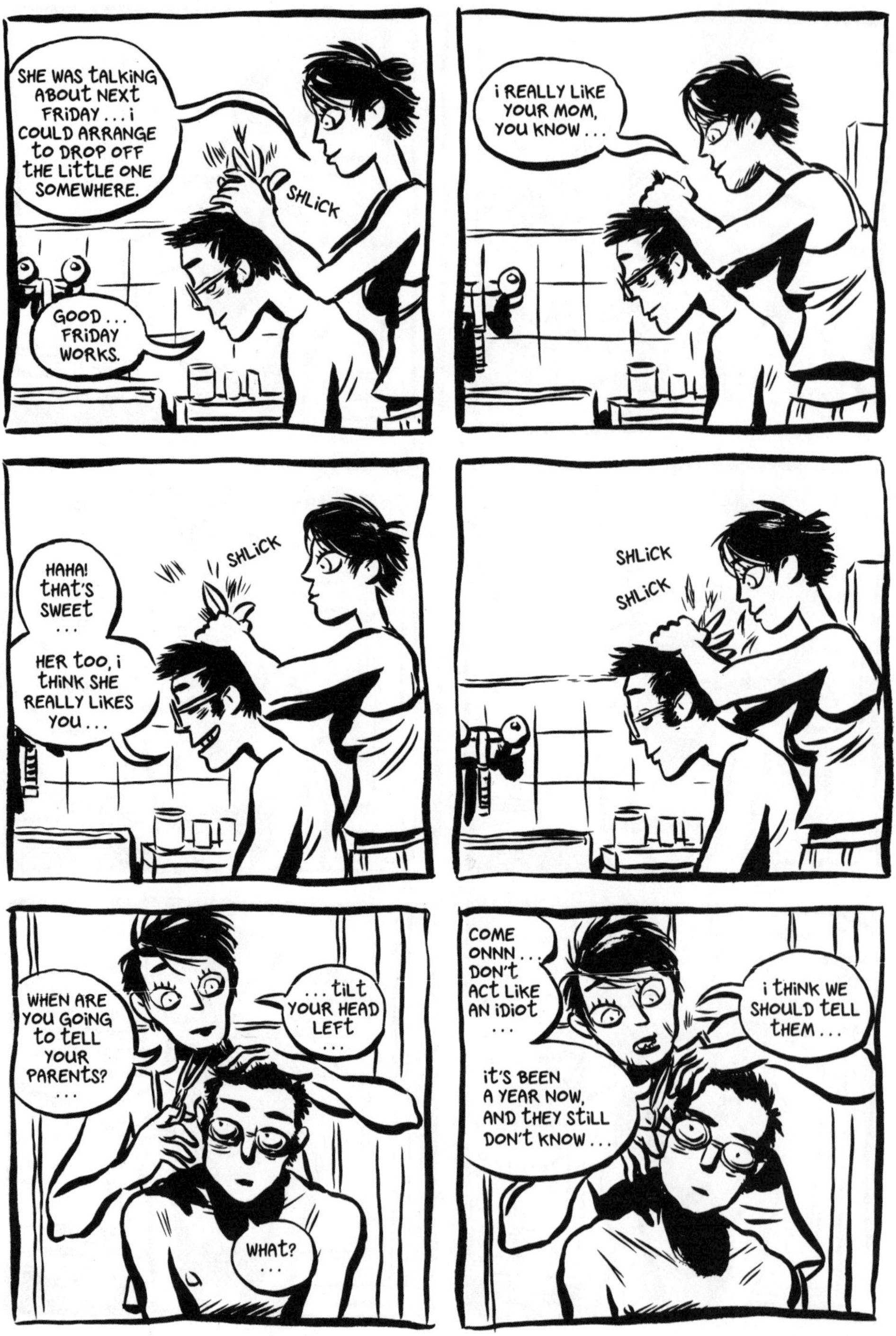
SHE WAS tALkiNG ABOut NEXt FRiDAY . . . i COULD ARRANGE to DROP OFF thE LittLE ONE SOMEWHERE.
SHLiCK
GOOD . . . FRiDAY WORKS.
i REALLY LiKE YOUR MOM, YOU KNOW . . .
SHLiCK
HAHA! thAt'S SWEEt . . .
HER too, i thiNK SHE REALLY LiKES YOU . . .
SHLiCK
SHLiCK
WHEN ARE YOU GOiNG to tELL YOUR PARENtS? . . .
. . . tiLt YOUR HEAD LEFt . . .
WHAt? . . .
COME ONNN . . . DON'T ACt LiKE AN iDiot . . .
it'S BEEN A YEAR NOW, AND tHEY Still DON'T KNOW . . .
i thiNK WE SHOULD tELL tHEM . . .

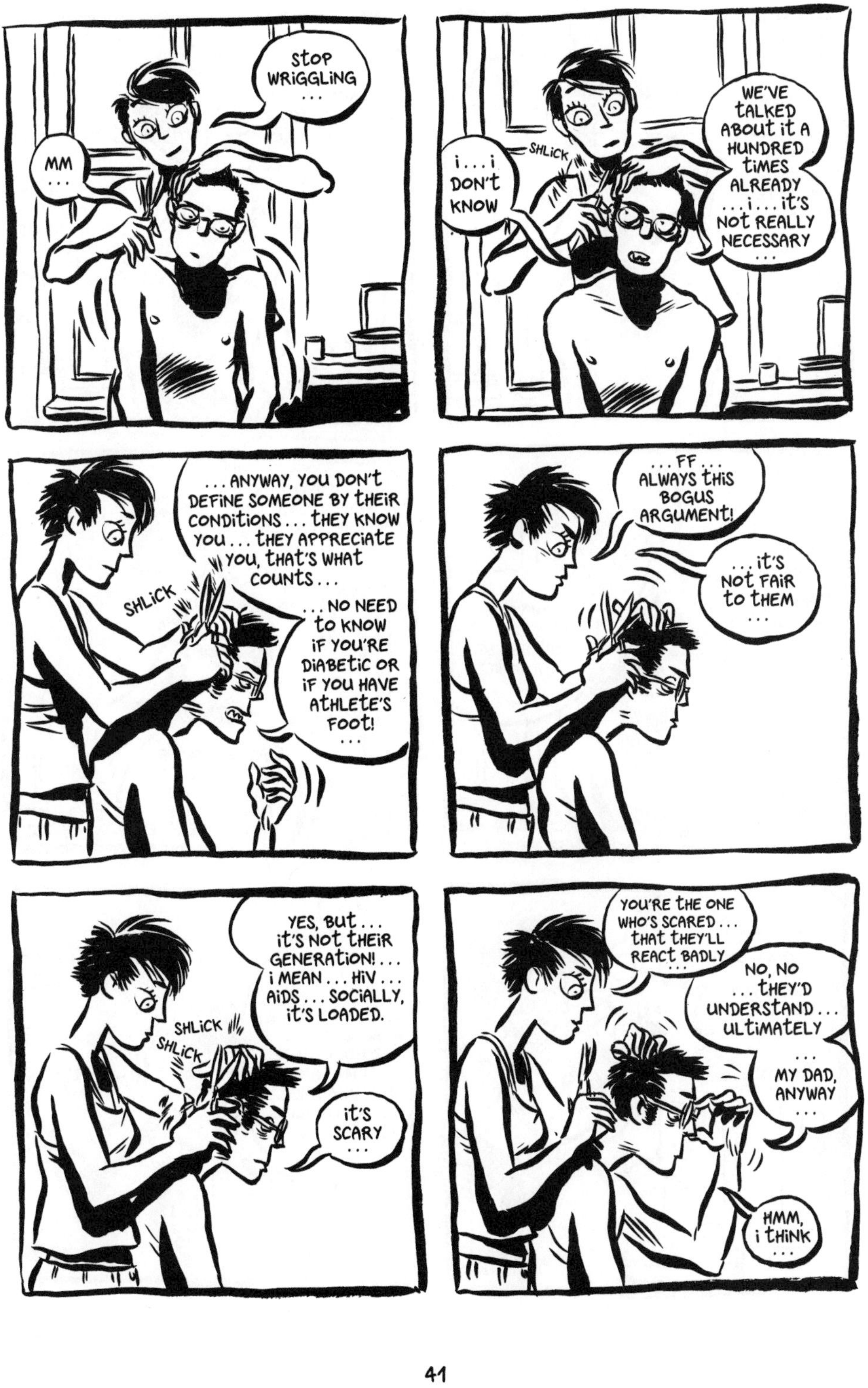
MM . . .
STOP WRIGGLING . . .
SHLICK
i . . . i DON'T KNOW
WE'VE TALKED ABOUT IT A HUNDRED TIMES ALREADY . . . i . . . it's NOT REALLY NECESSARY . . .
. . . ANYWAY, YOU DON'T DEFINE SOMEONE BY THEIR CONDITIONS . . . THEY KNOW YOU . . . THEY APPRECIATE YOU, THAT'S WHAT COUNTS . . .
SHLICK
. . . NO NEED TO KNOW IF YOU'RE DIABETIC OR IF YOU HAVE ATHLETE'S FOOT! . . .
. . . FF . . . ALWAYS THIS BOGUS ARGUMENT!
. . . it's NOT FAIR TO THEM . . .
YES, BUT . . . it's NOT THEIR GENERATION! . . . i MEAN . . . HiV . . . AiDS . . . SOCiALLY, it's LOADED.
SHLICK
SHLICK
it's SCARY . . .
YOU'RE THE ONE WHO'S SCARED . . . THAT THEY'LL REACT BADLY . . .
NO, NO . . . THEY'D UNDERSTAND . . . ULTiMATELY . . .
MY DAD, ANYWAY . . .
HMM, i THiNK . . .

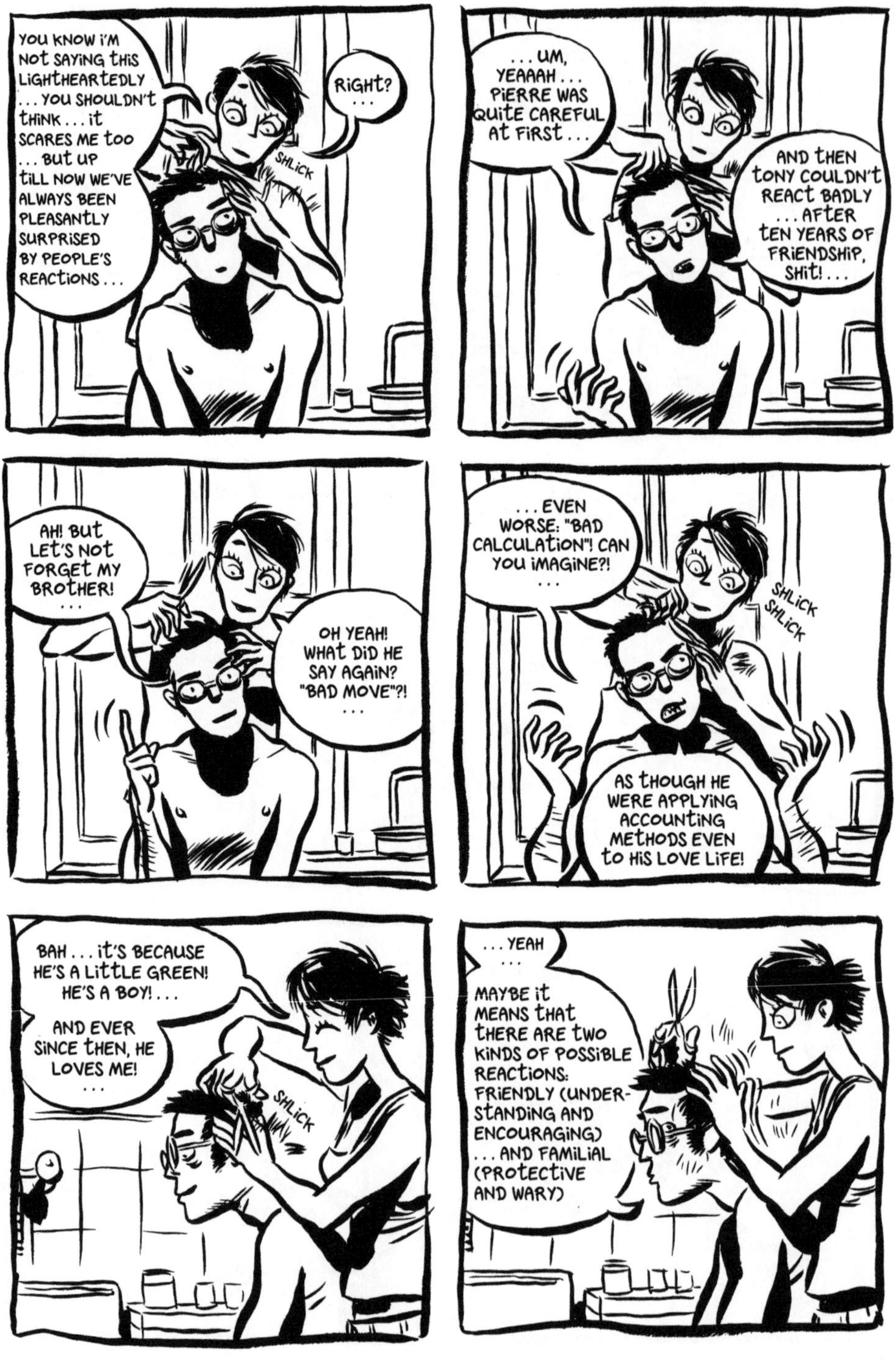
YOU KNOW I'M NOT SAYING THIS LIGHTHEARTEDLY . . . YOU SHOULDN'T THINK . . . IT SCARES ME TOO . . . BUT UP TILL NOW WE'VE ALWAYS BEEN PLEASANTLY SURPRISED BY PEOPLE'S REACTIONS . . .
SHLICK
RIGHT? . . .
. . . UM, YEAAAH . . . PIERRE WAS QUITE CAREFUL AT FIRST . . .
AND THEN TONY COULDN'T REACT BADLY . . . AFTER TEN YEARS OF FRIENDSHIP, SHIT! . . .
AH! BUT LET'S NOT FORGET MY BROTHER! . . .
OH YEAH! WHAT DID HE SAY AGAIN? "BAD MOVE"?! . . .
. . . EVEN WORSE: "BAD CALCULATION"! CAN YOU IMAGINE?! . . .
SHLICK SHLICK
AS THOUGH HE WERE APPLYING ACCOUNTING METHODS EVEN TO HIS LOVE LIFE!
BAH . . . IT'S BECAUSE HE'S A LITTLE GREEN! HE'S A BOY! . . .
AND EVER SINCE THEN, HE LOVES ME! . . .
SHLICK
. . . YEAH . . .
MAYBE IT MEANS THAT THERE ARE TWO KINDS OF POSSIBLE REACTIONS: FRIENDLY (UNDER-STANDING AND ENCOURAGING) . . . AND FAMILIAL (PROTECTIVE AND WARY)

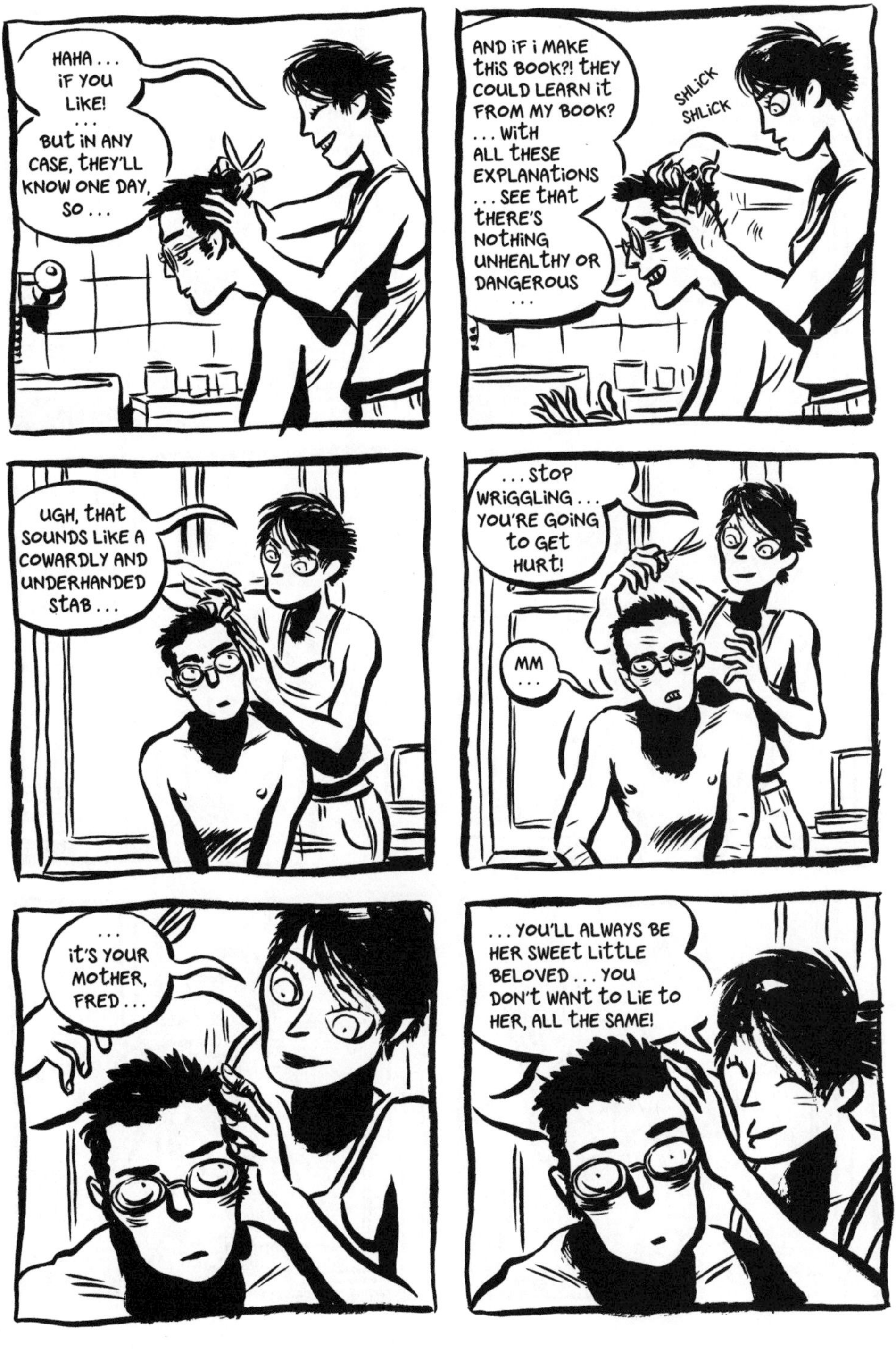
HAHA . . . iF YOU LiKE! . . . But iN ANY CASE, tHEY'LL KNOW ONE DAY, SO . . .
AND iF i MAKE tHiS BOOK?! tHEY COULD LEARN it FROM MY BOOK? . . . WitH ALL tHESE EXPLANAtiONS . . . SEE tHAt tHERE'S NOtHiNG UNHEALtHY OR DANGEROUS . . .
SHLiCK
SHLiCK
UGH, tHAt SOUNDS LiKE A COWARDLY AND UNDERHANDED StAB . . .
. . . StOP WRiGGLiNG . . . YOU'RE GOiNG tO GEt HURt!
MM . . .
. . . it'S YOUR MOtHER, FRED . . .
. . . YOU'LL ALWAYS BE HER SWEEt LittLE BELOVED . . . YOU DON'T WANt tO LiE tO HER, ALL tHE SAME!

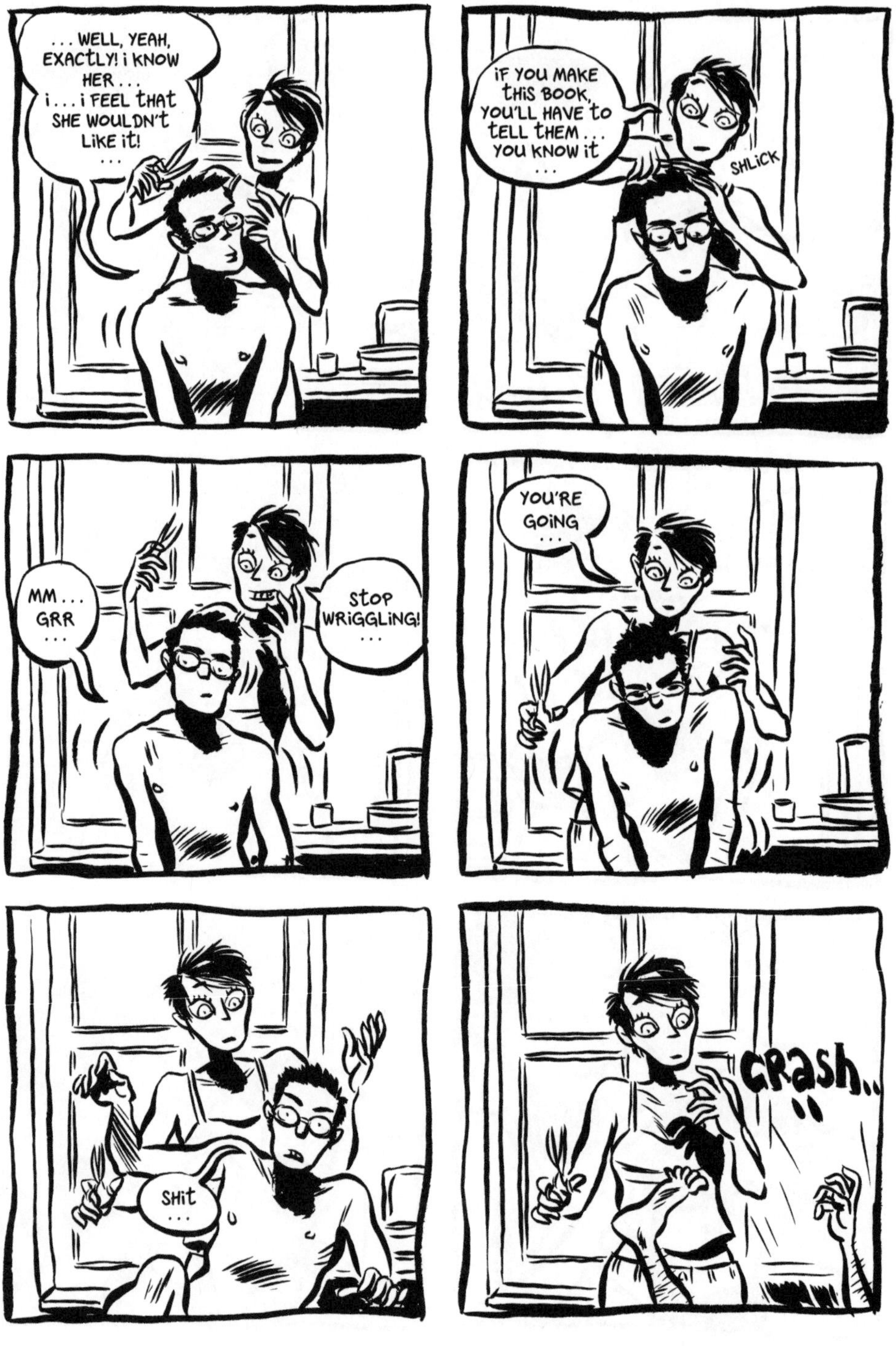
. . . WELL, YEAH, EXACTLY! i KNOW HER . . . i . . . i FEEL THAT SHE WOULDN'T LIKE iT! . . .
iF YOU MAKE THiS BOOK, YOU'LL HAVE TO TELL THEM . . . YOU KNOW iT . . .
SHLiCK
MM . . . GRR . . .
STOP WRiGGLiNG! . . .
YOU'RE GOiNG . . .
SHiT . . .
CRASH..

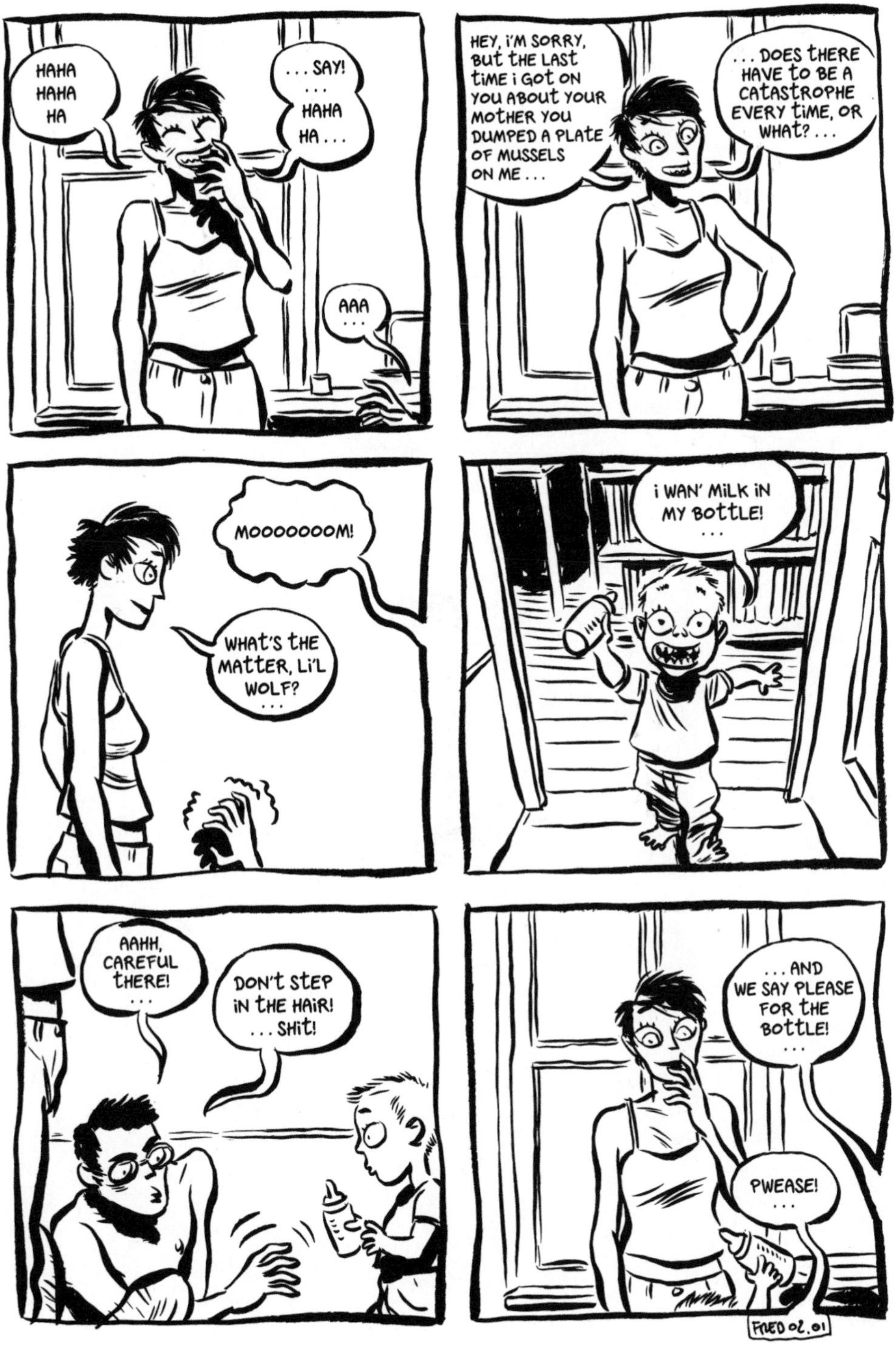
HAHA HAHA HA
. . . SAY! . . . HAHA HA . . .
AAA . . .
HEY, I'M SORRY, BUT THE LAST TIME I GOT ON YOU ABOUT YOUR MOTHER YOU DUMPED A PLATE OF MUSSELS ON ME . . .
. . . DOES THERE HAVE TO BE A CATASTROPHE EVERY TIME, OR WHAT? . . .
MOOOOOOOM!
WHAT'S THE MATTER, LI'L WOLF? . . .
I WAN' MILK IN MY BOTTLE! . . .
AAHH, CAREFUL THERE! . . .
DON'T STEP IN THE HAIR! . . . SHIT!
. . . AND WE SAY PLEASE FOR THE BOTTLE! . . .
PWEASE! . . .
FRED 02.01

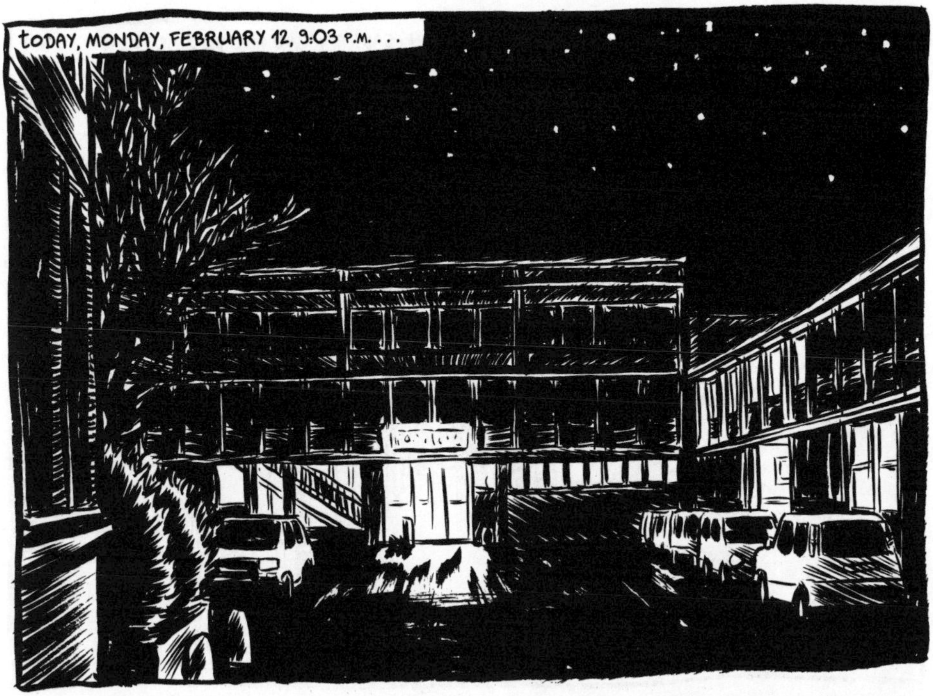
TODAY, MONDAY, FEBRUARY 12, 9:03 P.M. . . .

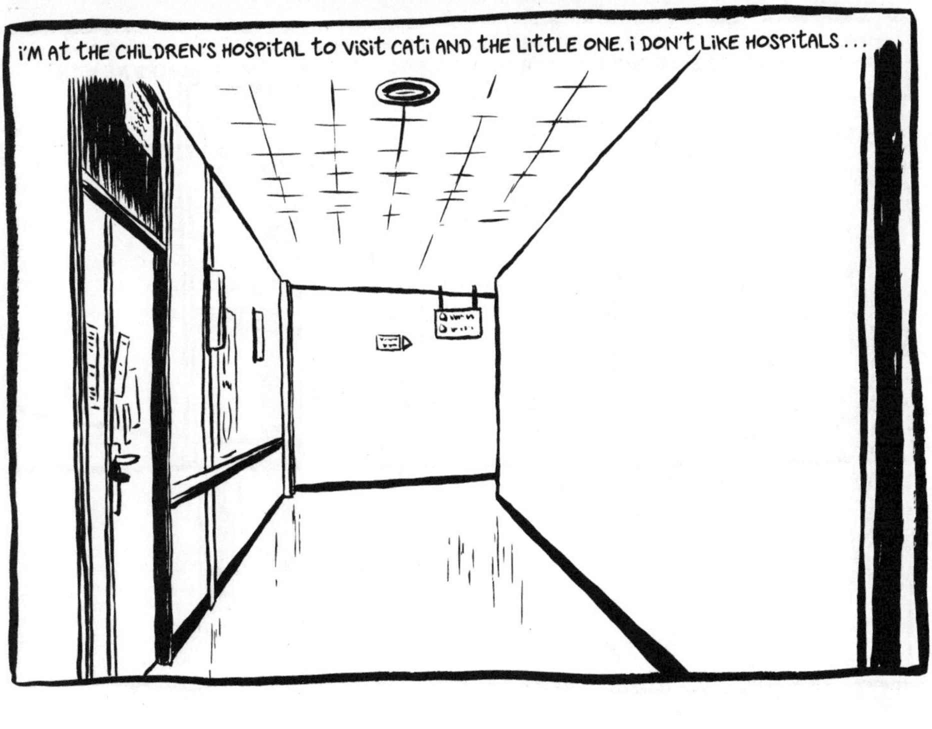
I'M AT THE CHILDREN'S HOSPITAL TO VISIT CATI AND THE LITTLE ONE. I DON'T LIKE HOSPITALS . . .

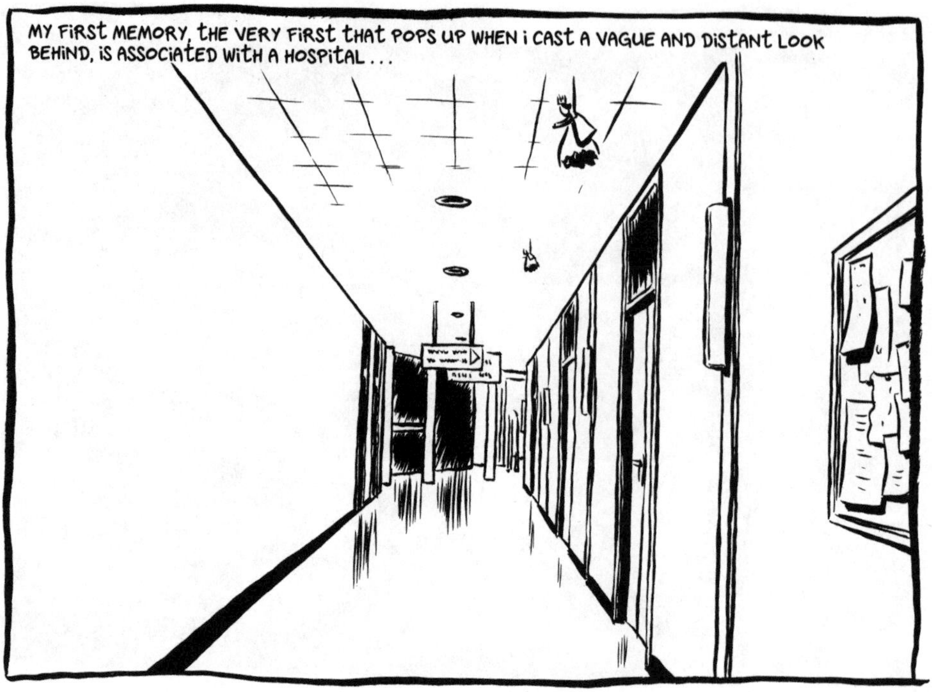
MY FIRST MEMORY, THE VERY FIRST THAT POPS UP WHEN I CAST A VAGUE AND DISTANT LOOK BEHIND, IS ASSOCIATED WITH A HOSPITAL . . .

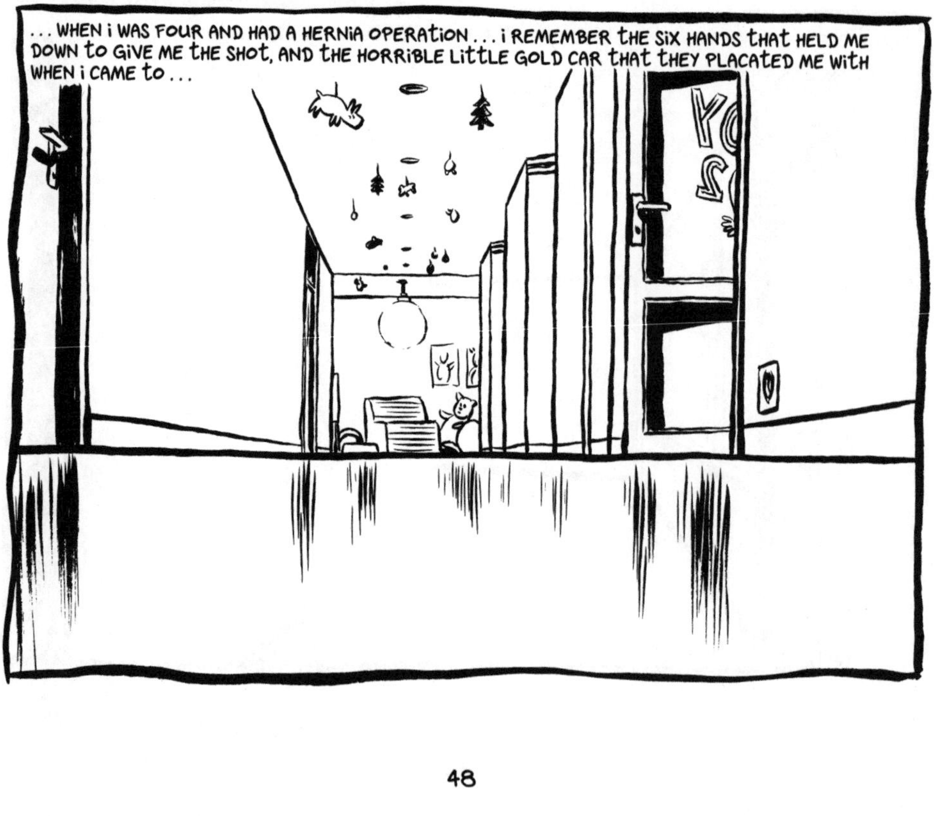
. . . WHEN I WAS FOUR AND HAD A HERNIA OPERATION . . . I REMEMBER THE SIX HANDS THAT HELD ME DOWN TO GIVE ME THE SHOT, AND THE HORRIBLE LITTLE GOLD CAR THAT THEY PLACATED ME WITH WHEN I CAME TO . . .

TODAY, THE LITTLE ONE JUST TURNED FOUR ... THE HALLWAYS SMELL LIKE OLD FORMALIN, THE FURNITURE MUST DATE FROM THE SOVIET ERA, THE CURTAINS ARE A DIRTY ORANGE, THE NURSES ARE UGLY AND KIND ...

HE AND CATI ARRIVED AT 6 P.M. ... THEY'RE GOING TO SPEND THE NIGHT IN THIS ROOM, AND THEY'LL LEAVE AROUND 6 P.M. THE NEXT DAY ...

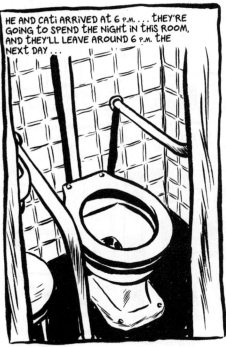

OBVIOUSLY, IT'S NOTHING SERIOUS ... THEY HAVE TO OPERATE ON HIS TEETH, BECAUSE HE HAS A LOT OF "BABY-BOTTLE CAVITIES" ... TOMORROW MORNING, UNDER GENERAL ANESTHESIA ...

49

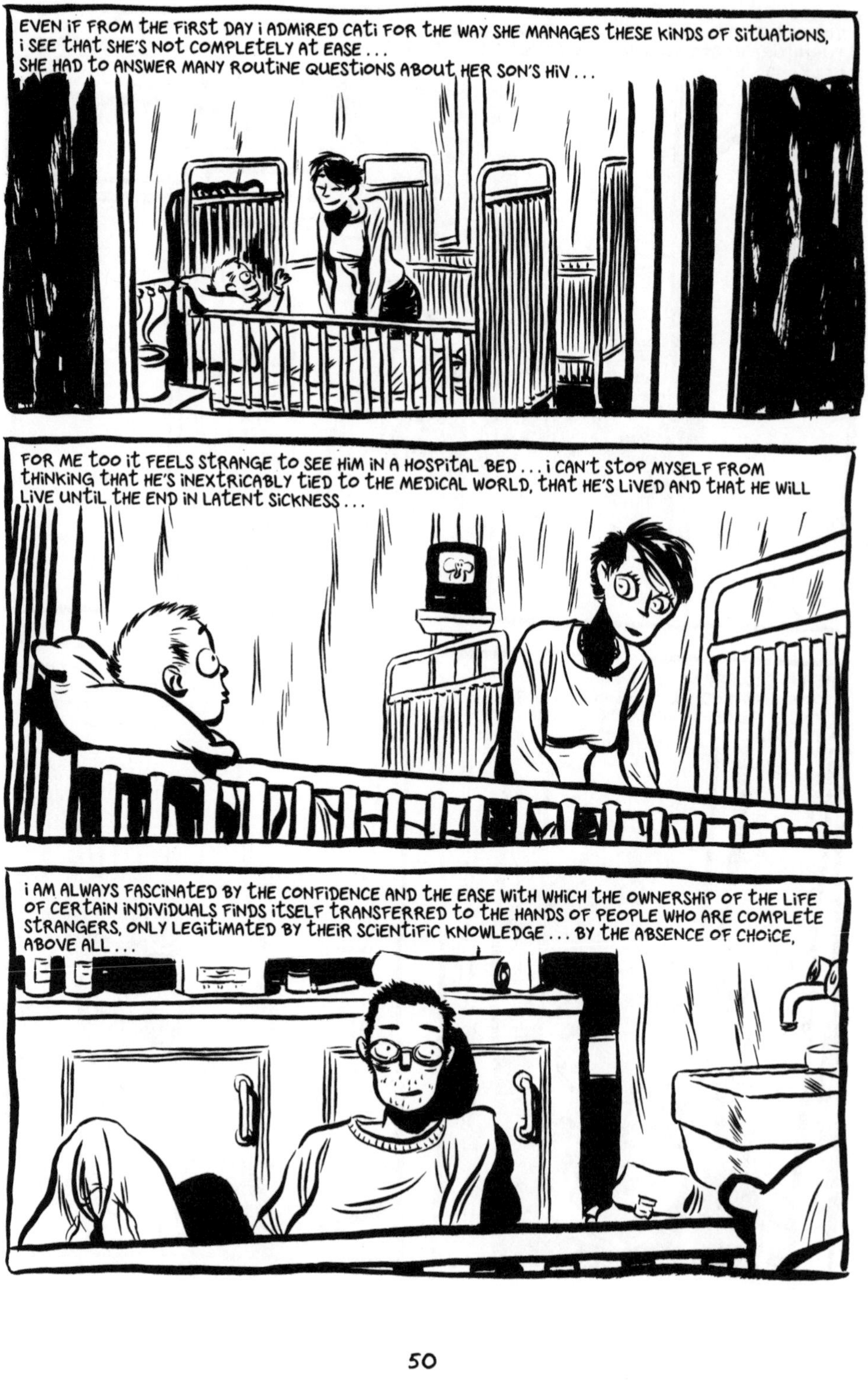
EVEN iF FROM THE FiRST DAY i ADMiRED CATi FOR THE WAY SHE MANAGES THESE KiNDS OF SiTUATiONS, i SEE THAT SHE'S NOT COMPLETELY AT EASE . . .
SHE HAD TO ANSWER MANY ROUTiNE QUESTiONS ABOUT HER SON'S HiV . . .
FOR ME TOO iT FEELS STRANGE TO SEE HiM iN A HOSPiTAL BED . . . i CAN'T STOP MYSELF FROM THiNKiNG THAT HE'S iNEXTRiCABLY TiED TO THE MEDiCAL WORLD, THAT HE'S LiVED AND THAT HE WiLL LiVE UNTiL THE END iN LATENT SiCKNESS . . .
i AM ALWAYS FASCiNATED BY THE CONFiDENCE AND THE EASE WiTH WHiCH THE OWNERSHiP OF THE LiFE OF CERTAiN iNDiViDUALS FiNDS iTSELF TRANSFERRED TO THE HANDS OF PEOPLE WHO ARE COMPLETE STRANGERS, ONLY LEGiTiMATED BY THEiR SCiENTiFiC KNOWLEDGE . . . BY THE ABSENCE OF CHOiCE, ABOVE ALL . . .

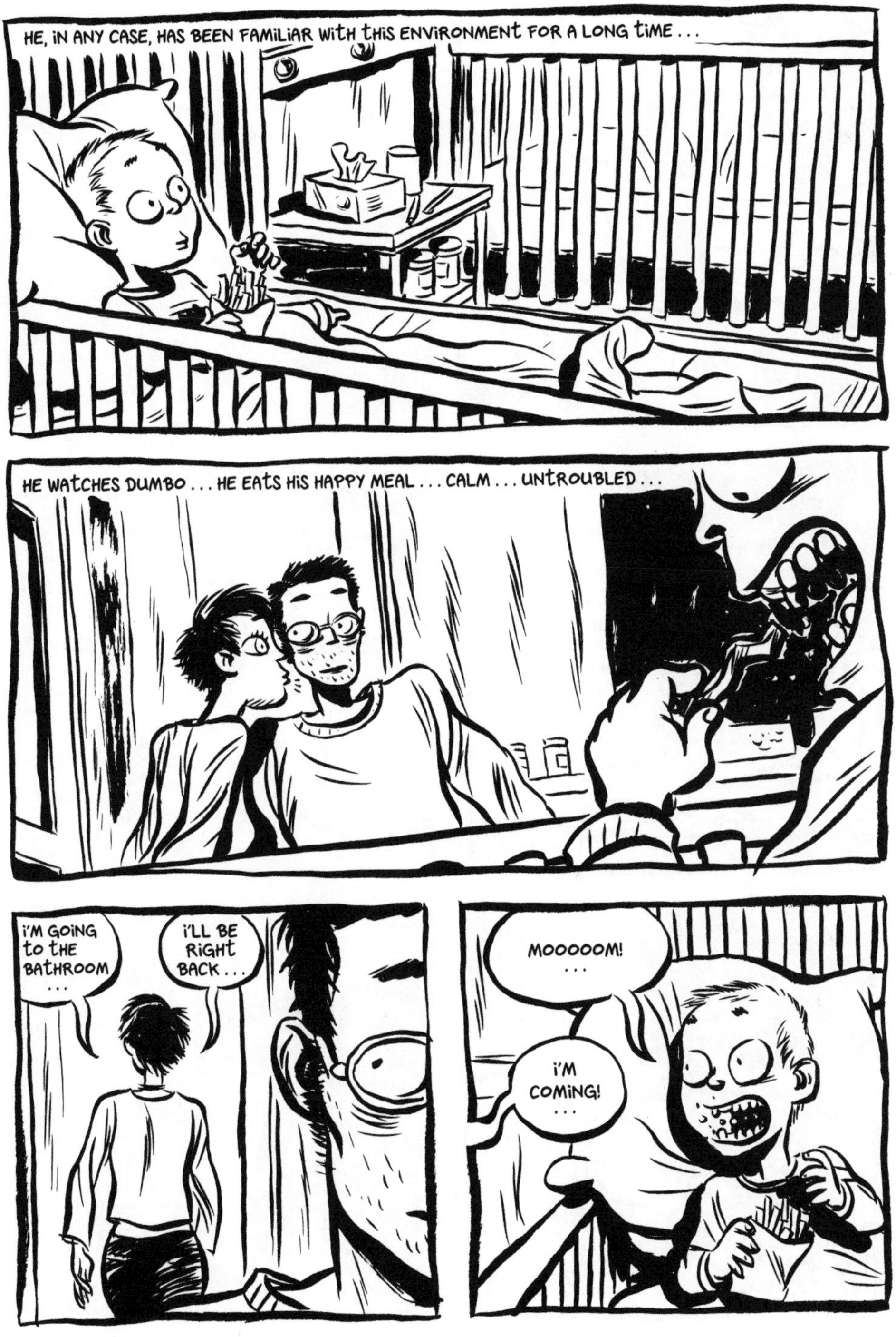
HE, iN ANY CASE, HAS BEEN FAMiLiAR WitH tHiS ENViRONMENt FOR A LONG tiME . . .
HE WAtCHES DUMBO . . . HE EAtS HiS HAPPY MEAL . . . CALM . . . UNtROUBLED . . .
i'M GOiNG to tHE BATHROOM . . .
i'LL BE RiGHt BACK . . .
MOOOOOM! . . .
i'M COMiNG! . . .

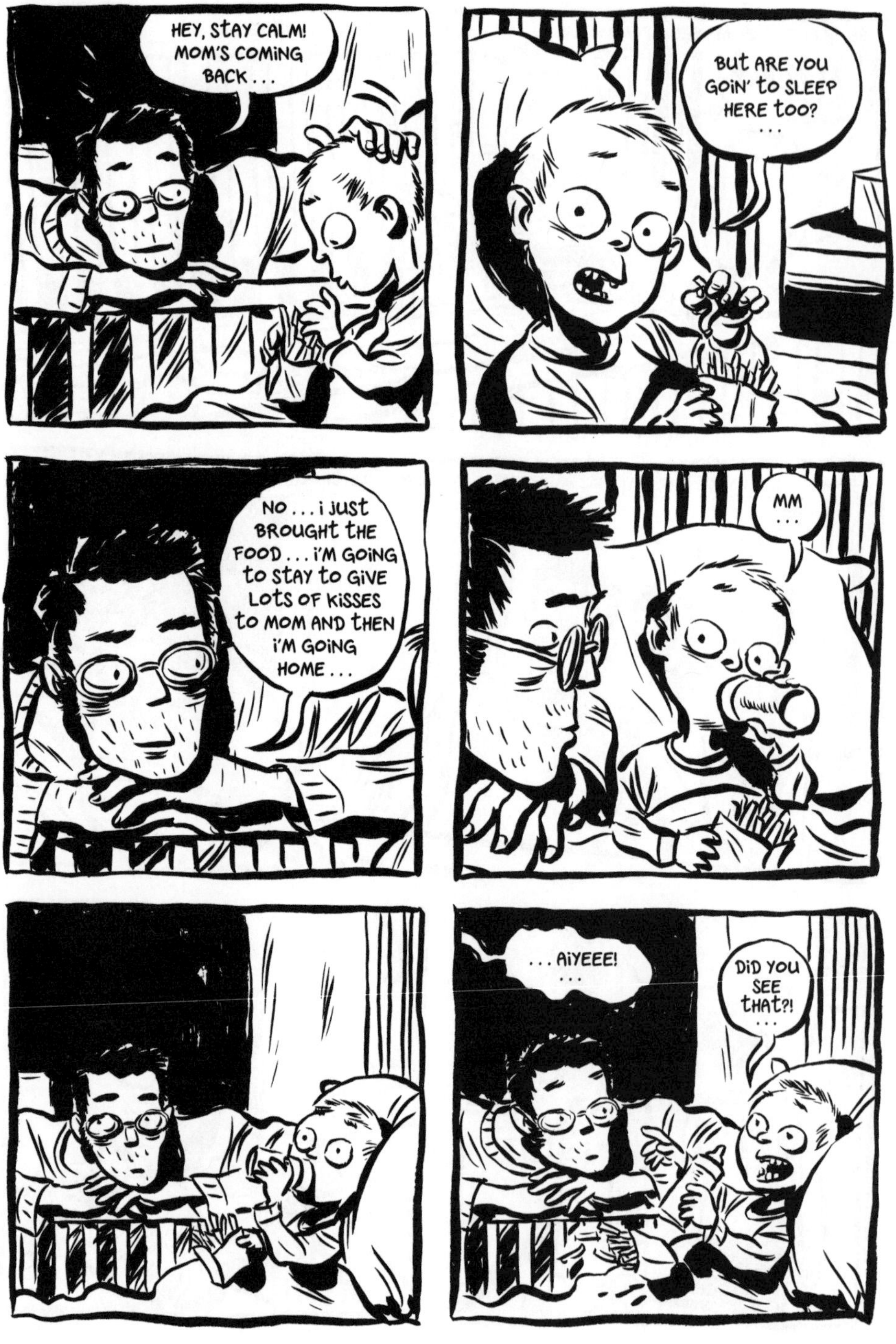
HEY, StAY CALM! MOM'S COMiNG BACK . . .
But ARE YOU GOiN' tO SLEEP HERE tOO? . . .
NO . . . i JUSt BROUGHt tHE FOOD . . . i'M GOiNG tO StAY tO GiVE LOtS OF KiSSES tO MOM AND tHEN i'M GOiNG HOME . . .
MM . . .
. . . AiYEEE! . . .
DiD YOU SEE tHAt?! . . .

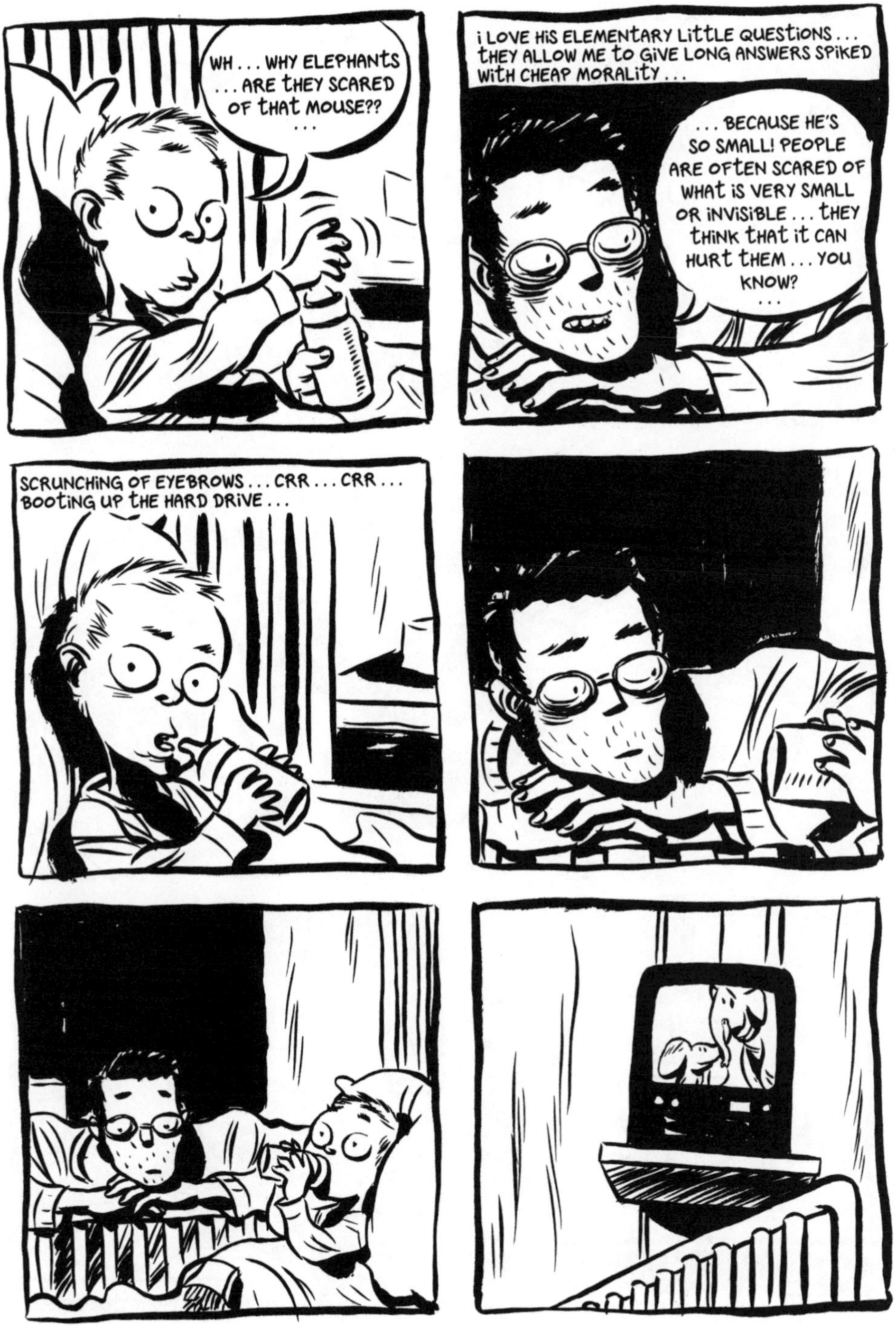
WH . . . WHY ELEPHANTS . . . ARE THEY SCARED OF THAT MOUSE?? . . .
I LOVE HIS ELEMENTARY LITTLE QUESTIONS . . . THEY ALLOW ME TO GIVE LONG ANSWERS SPIKED WITH CHEAP MORALITY . . .
. . . BECAUSE HE'S SO SMALL! PEOPLE ARE OFTEN SCARED OF WHAT IS VERY SMALL OR INVISIBLE . . . THEY THINK THAT IT CAN HURT THEM . . . YOU KNOW? . . .
SCRUNCHING OF EYEBROWS . . . CRR . . . CRR . . . BOOTING UP THE HARD DRIVE . . .

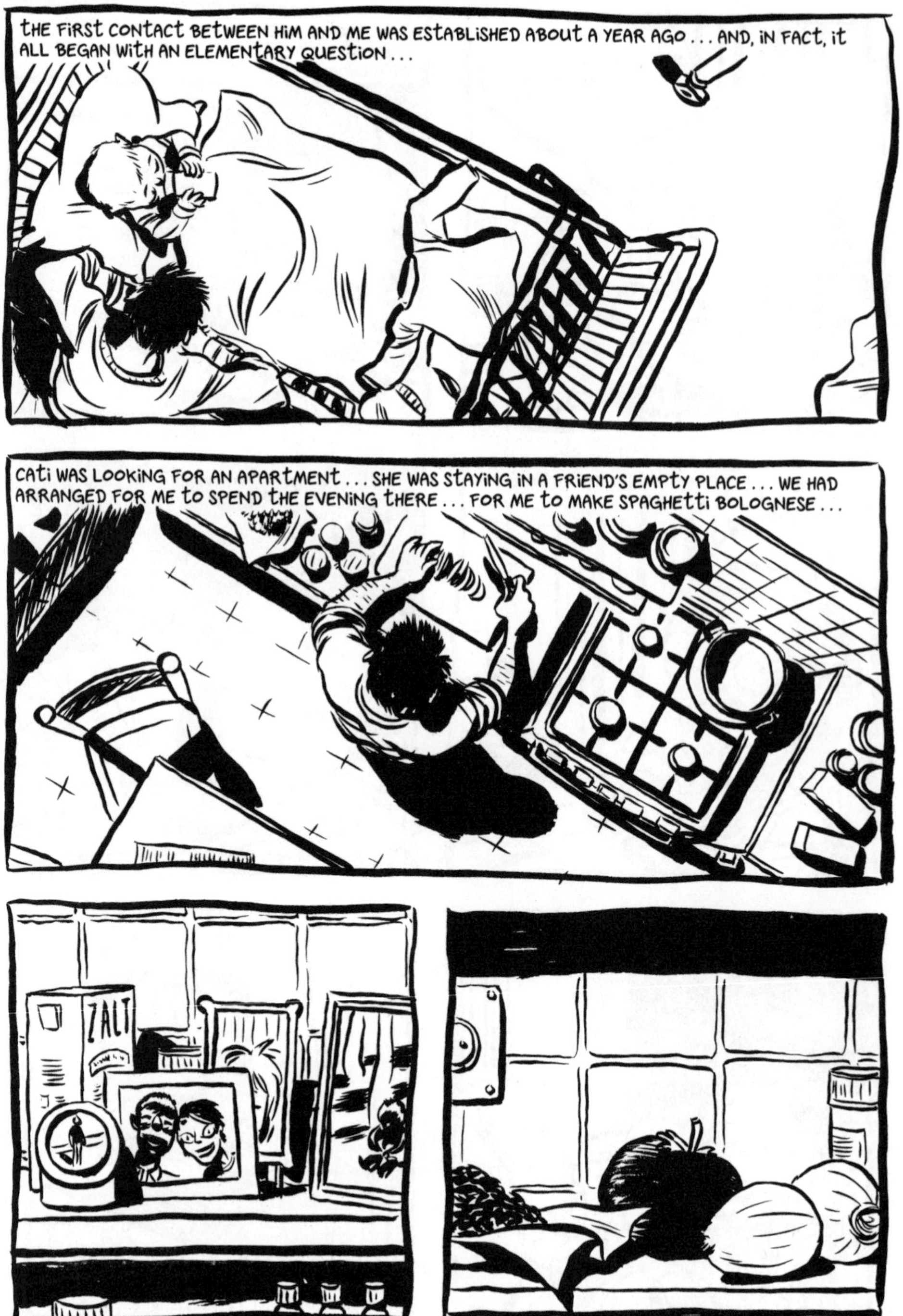
THE FIRST CONTACT BETWEEN HIM AND ME WAS ESTABLISHED ABOUT A YEAR AGO . . . AND, IN FACT, IT ALL BEGAN WITH AN ELEMENTARY QUESTION . . .
CATI WAS LOOKING FOR AN APARTMENT . . . SHE WAS STAYING IN A FRIEND'S EMPTY PLACE . . . WE HAD ARRANGED FOR ME TO SPEND THE EVENING THERE . . . FOR ME TO MAKE SPAGHETTI BOLOGNESE . . .
ZALT

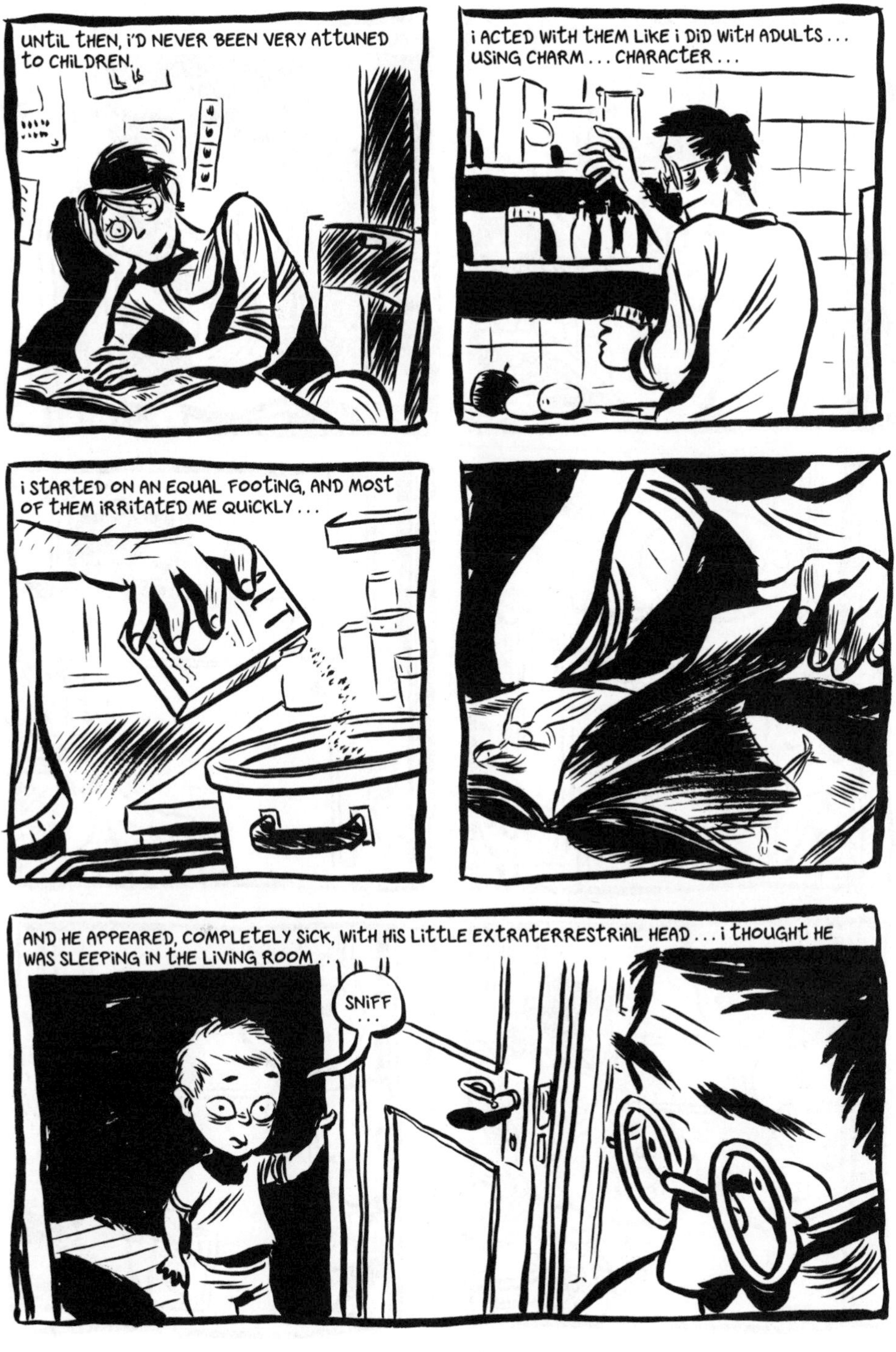
UNTIL THEN, I'D NEVER BEEN VERY ATTUNED TO CHILDREN.
I ACTED WITH THEM LIKE I DID WITH ADULTS . . . USING CHARM . . . CHARACTER . . .
I STARTED ON AN EQUAL FOOTING, AND MOST OF THEM IRRITATED ME QUICKLY . . .
AND HE APPEARED, COMPLETELY SICK, WITH HIS LITTLE EXTRATERRESTRIAL HEAD . . . I THOUGHT HE WAS SLEEPING IN THE LIVING ROOM . . .
SNIFF . . .

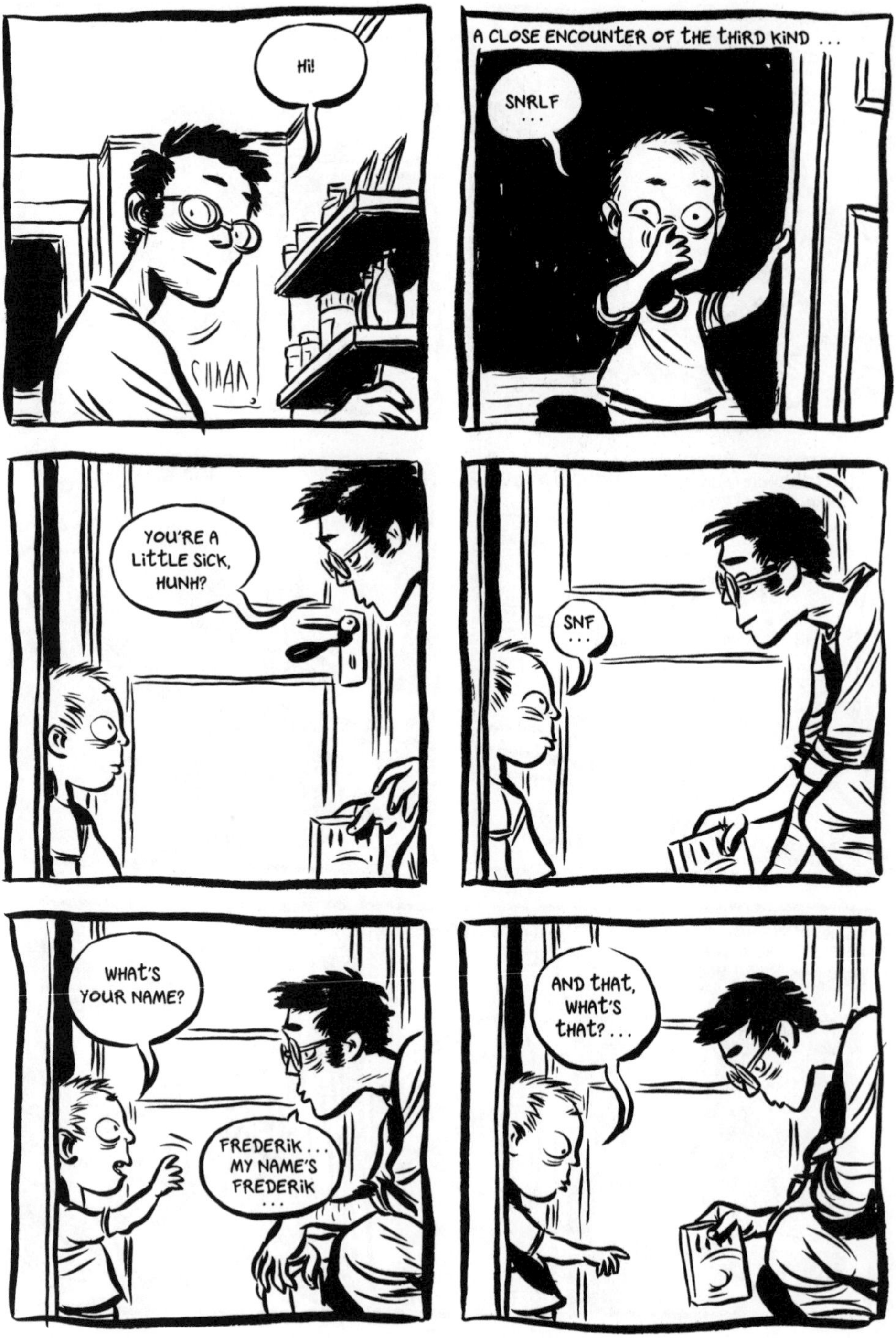
Hi!
SHAAN
A CLOSE ENCOUNTER OF THE THIRD KIND . . .
SNRLF . . .
YOU'RE A LITTLE SICK, HUNH?
SNF . . .
WHAT'S YOUR NAME?
FREDERIK . . . MY NAME'S FREDERIK . . .
AND THAT, WHAT'S THAT? . . .

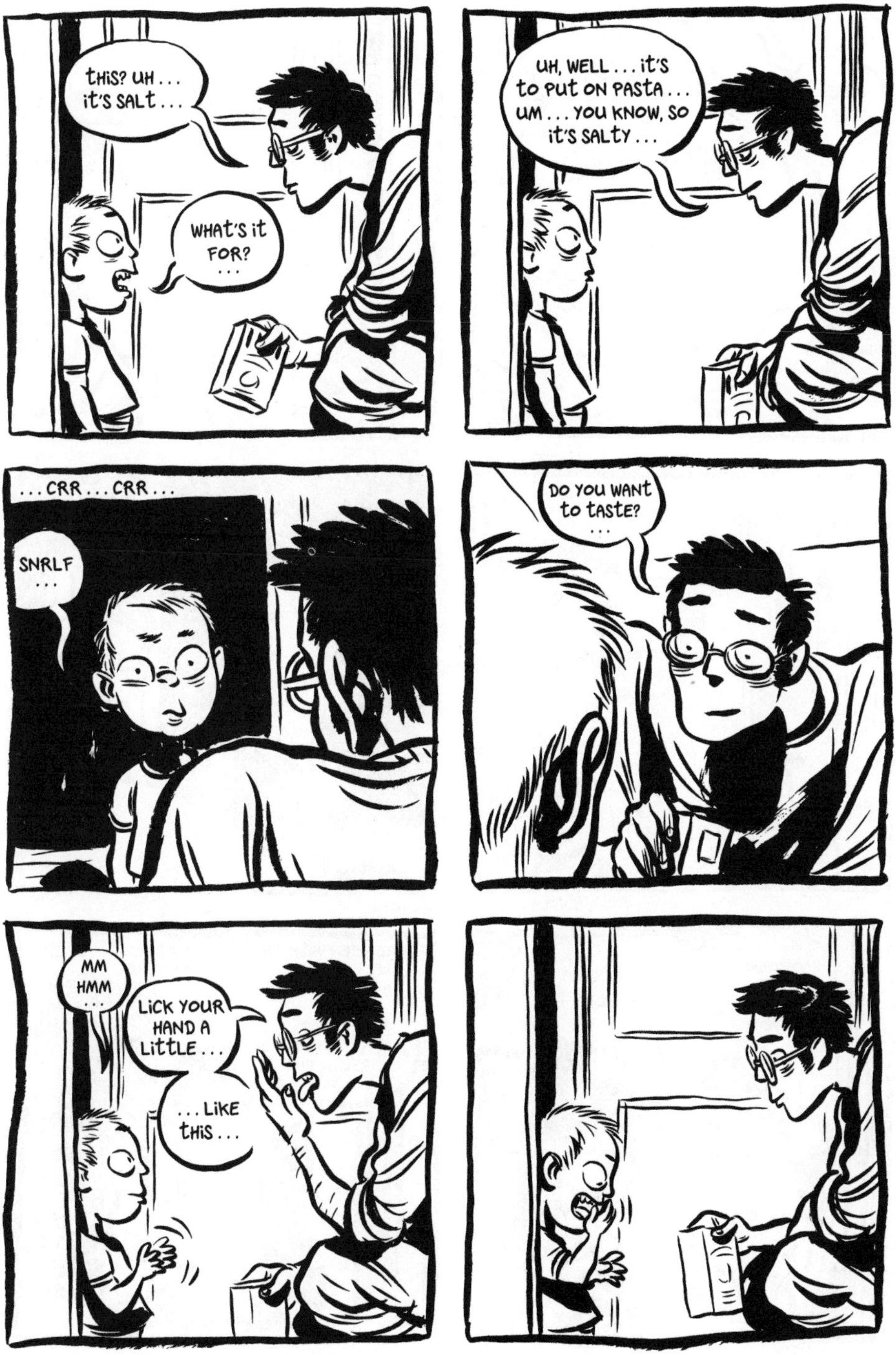
tHiS? UH . . .
it's SALt . . .
WHAt'S it FOR? . . .
UH, WELL . . . it's to Put ON PAStA . . . UM . . . YOU KNOW, SO it's SALtY . . .
. . . CRR . . . CRR . . .
SNRLF . . .
DO YOU WANt to tAStE? . . .
MM HMM . . .
LiCK YOUR HAND A LittLE . . .
. . . LiKE tHiS . . .

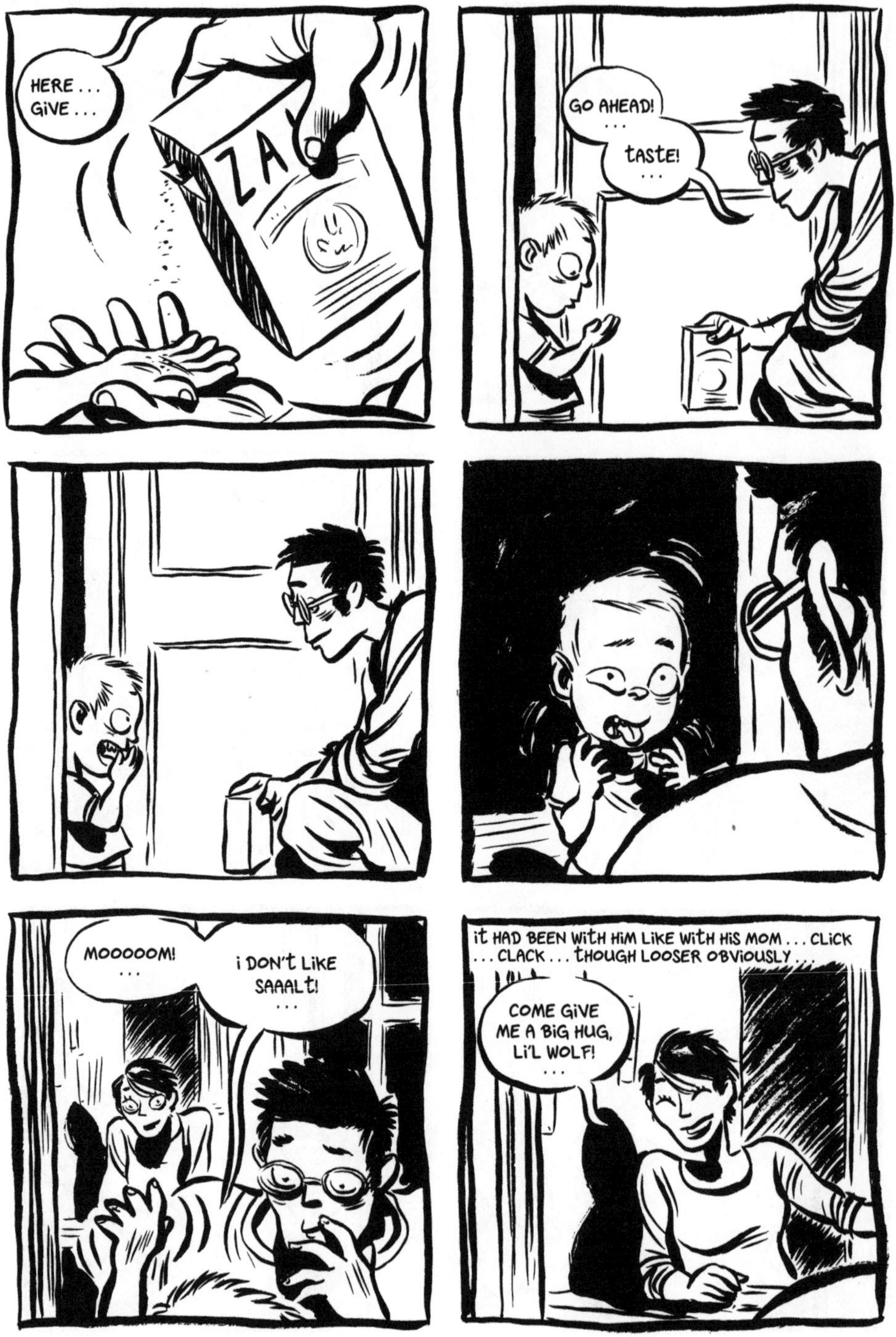
HERE . . .
GiVE . . .
ZA
GO AHEAD! . . .
taste! . . .
MOOOOOM! . . .
i DON'T LiKE SAAALt! . . .
it HAD BEEN WitH HiM LiKE WitH HiS MOM . . . CLiCK . . . CLACK . . . tHOUGH LOOSER OBViOUSLY . . .
COME GiVE ME A BiG HUG, Li'L WOLF! . . .

I KNEW VERY EARLY THAT IT WAS GOING TO WORK... BUT AT THAT MOMENT I DIDN'T KNOW WHAT SHAPE IT WOULD TAKE...

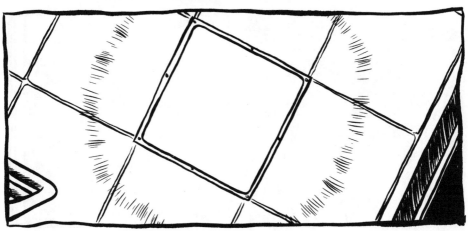

...EVEN TODAY FOR THAT MATTER...

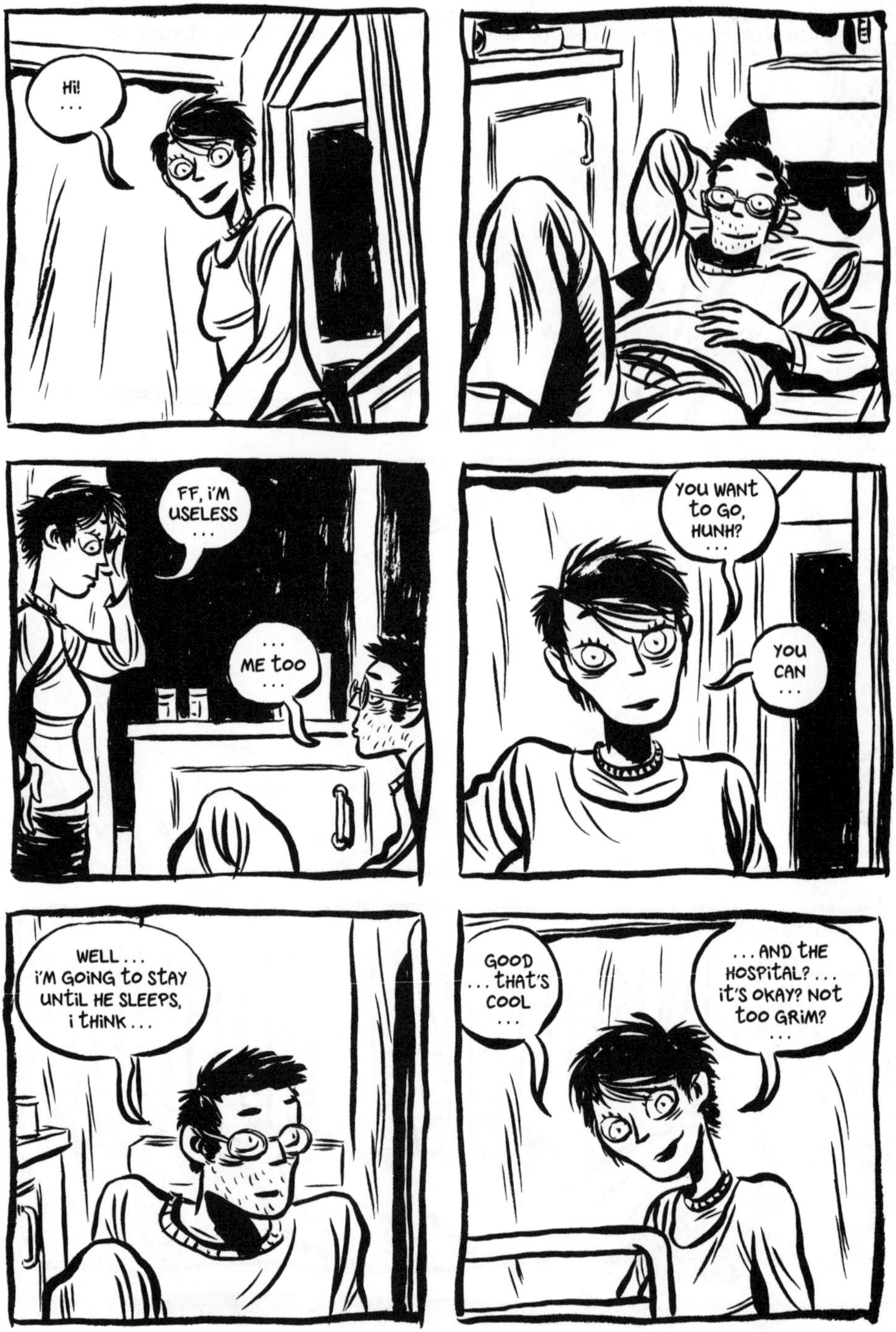
Hi!
...
FF, i'M USELESS
...
...
ME too
...
YOU WANT to GO, HUNH?
...
YOU CAN
...
WELL...
i'M GOiNG to STAY UNTiL HE SLEEPS, i THiNK...
GOOD ...THAT'S COOL
...
...AND THE HOSPiTAL?... iT'S OKAY? NOT too GRiM?
...

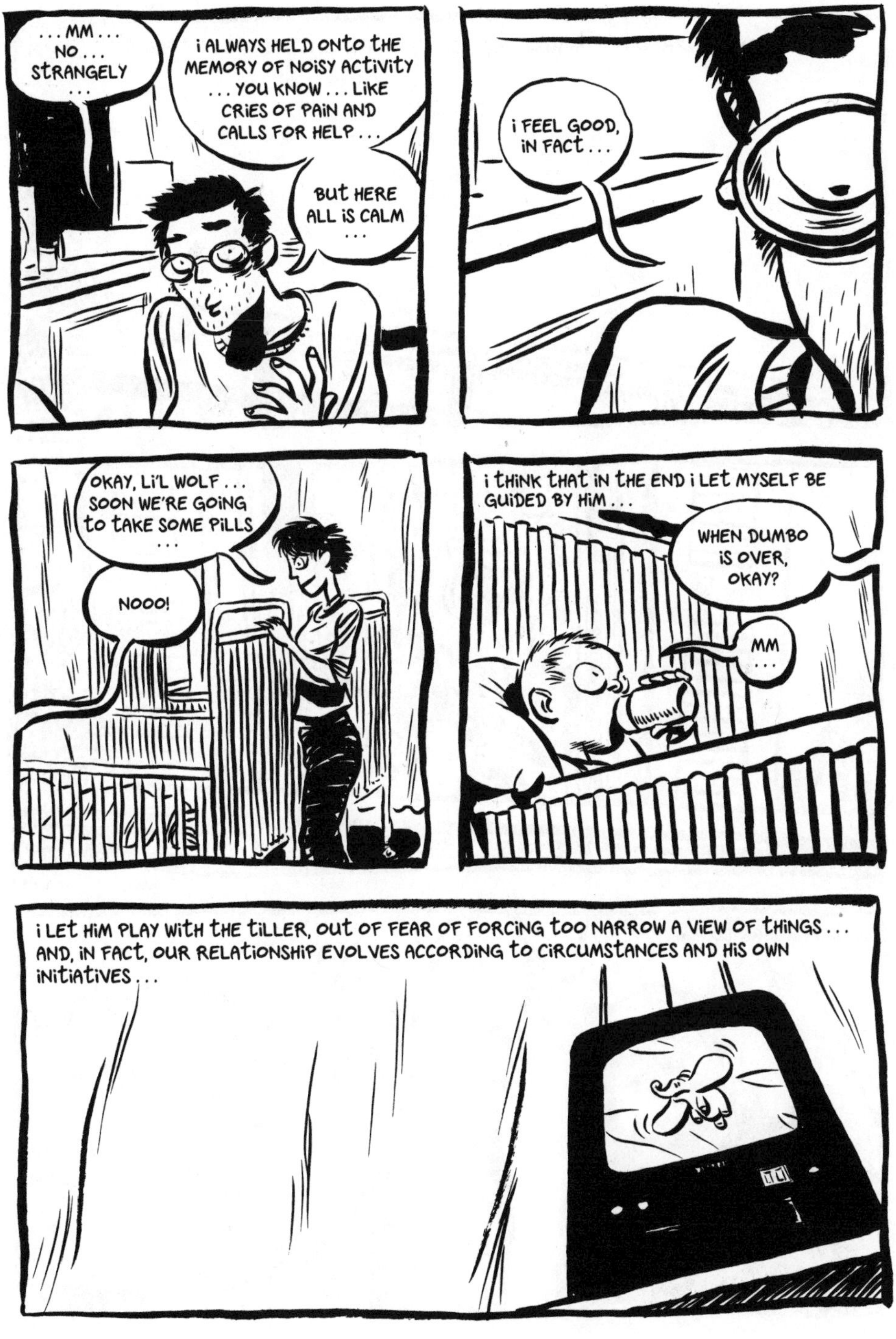

. . . MM . . . NO . . . STRANGELY . . .
i ALWAYS HELD ONtO tHE MEMORY OF NOiSY ACtiVitY . . . YOU KNOW . . . LiKE CRiES OF PAiN AND CALLS FOR HELP . . .
BUt HERE ALL iS CALM . . .
i FEEL GOOD, iN FACt . . .
OKAY, Li'L WOLF . . . SOON WE'RE GOiNG tO tAKE SOME PiLLS . . .
NOOO!
i tHiNK tHAt iN tHE END i LEt MYSELF BE GUiDED BY HiM . . .
WHEN DUMBO iS OVER, OKAY?
MM . . .
i LEt HiM PLAY WitH tHE tiLLER, OUt OF FEAR OF FORCiNG tOO NARROW A ViEW OF tHiNGS . . . AND, iN FACt, OUR RELAtiONSHiP EVOLVES ACCORDiNG tO CiRCUMStANCES AND HiS OWN iNitiAtiVES . . .

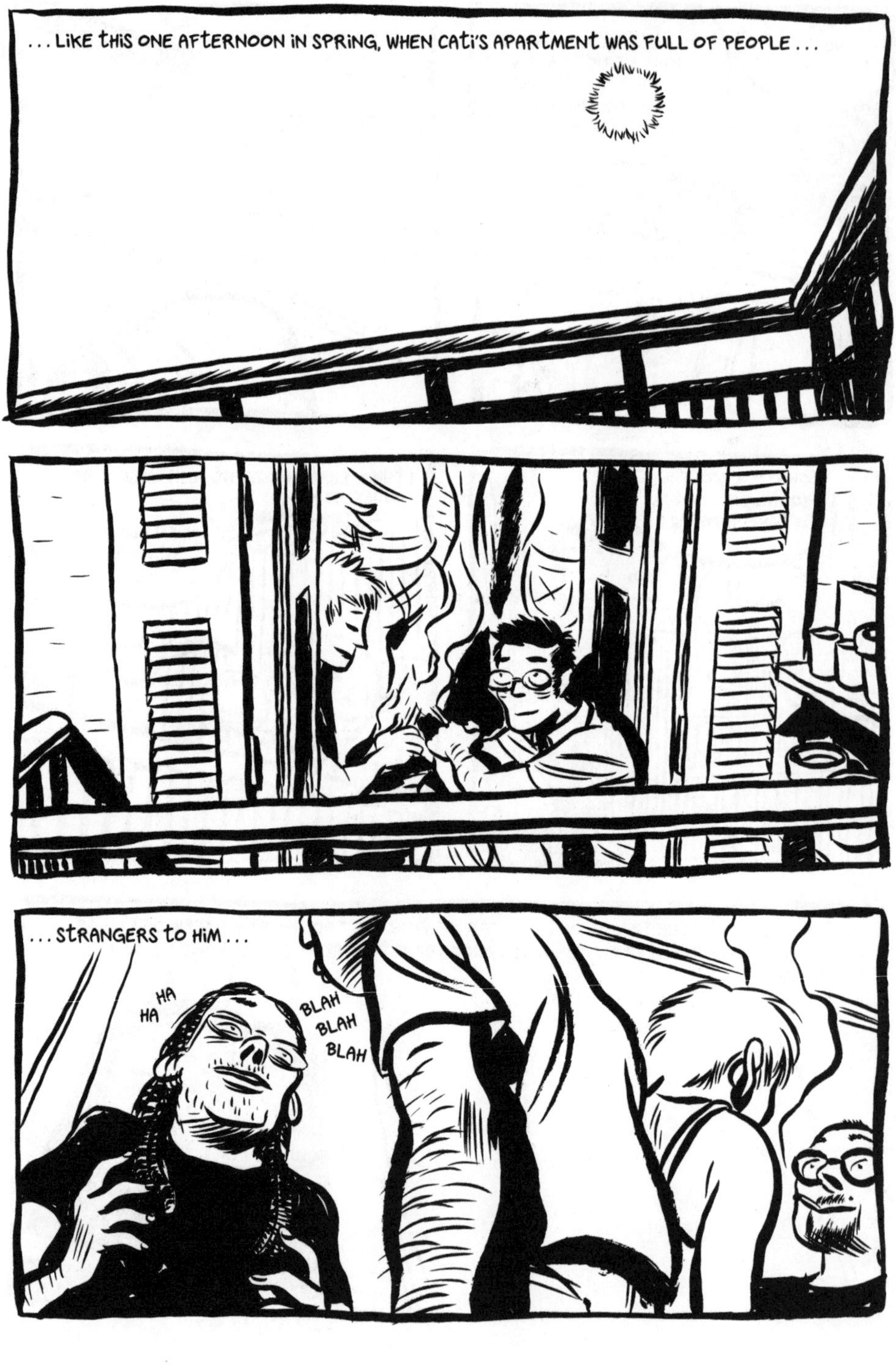
...LIKE THIS ONE AFTERNOON IN SPRING, WHEN CATI'S APARTMENT WAS FULL OF PEOPLE...
...STRANGERS TO HIM...
HA HA
BLAH BLAH BLAH

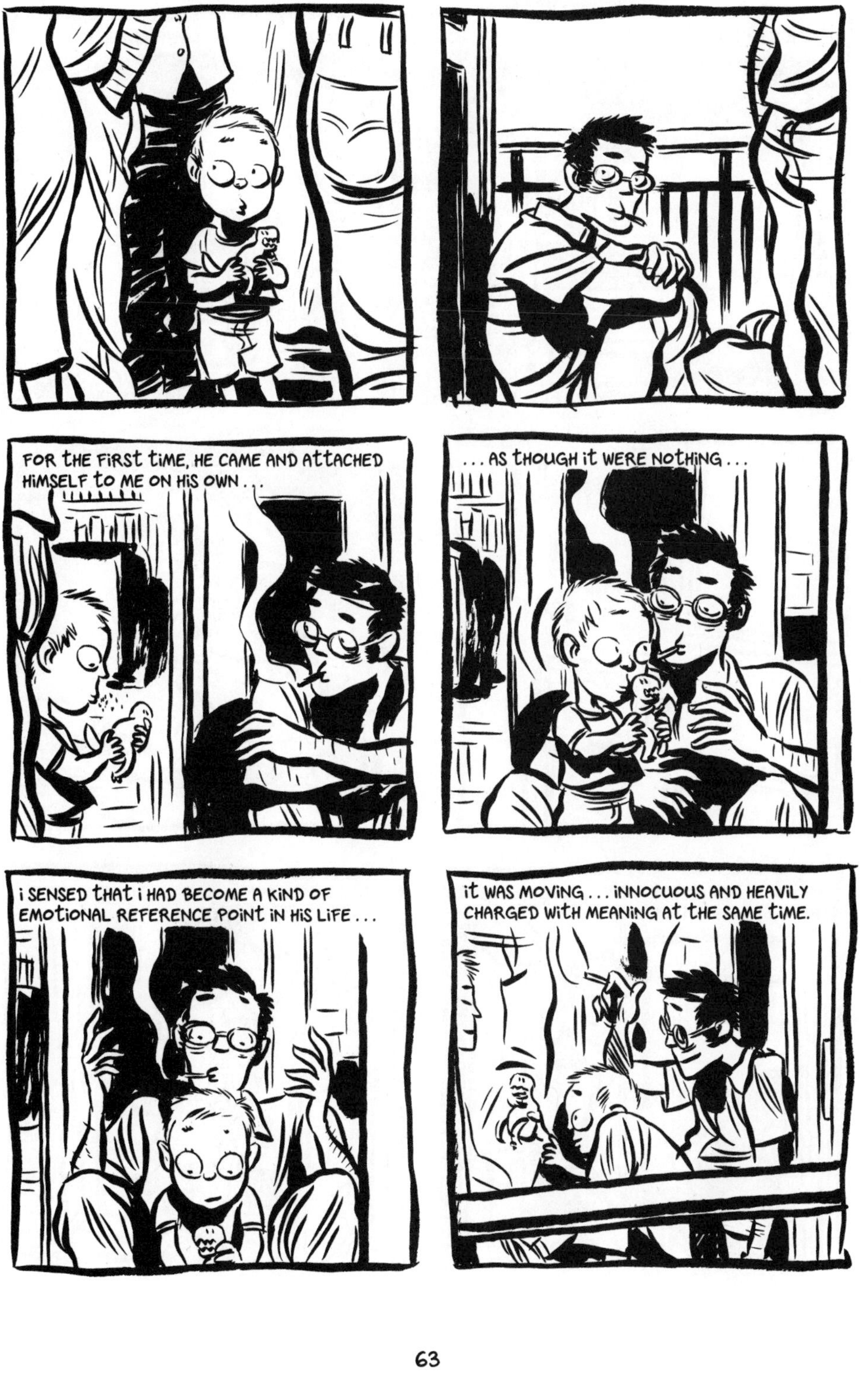
FOR THE FIRST TIME, HE CAME AND ATTACHED HIMSELF TO ME ON HIS OWN . . .
. . . AS THOUGH IT WERE NOTHING . . .
I SENSED THAT I HAD BECOME A KIND OF EMOTIONAL REFERENCE POINT IN HIS LIFE . . .
IT WAS MOVING . . . INNOCUOUS AND HEAVILY CHARGED WITH MEANING AT THE SAME TIME.

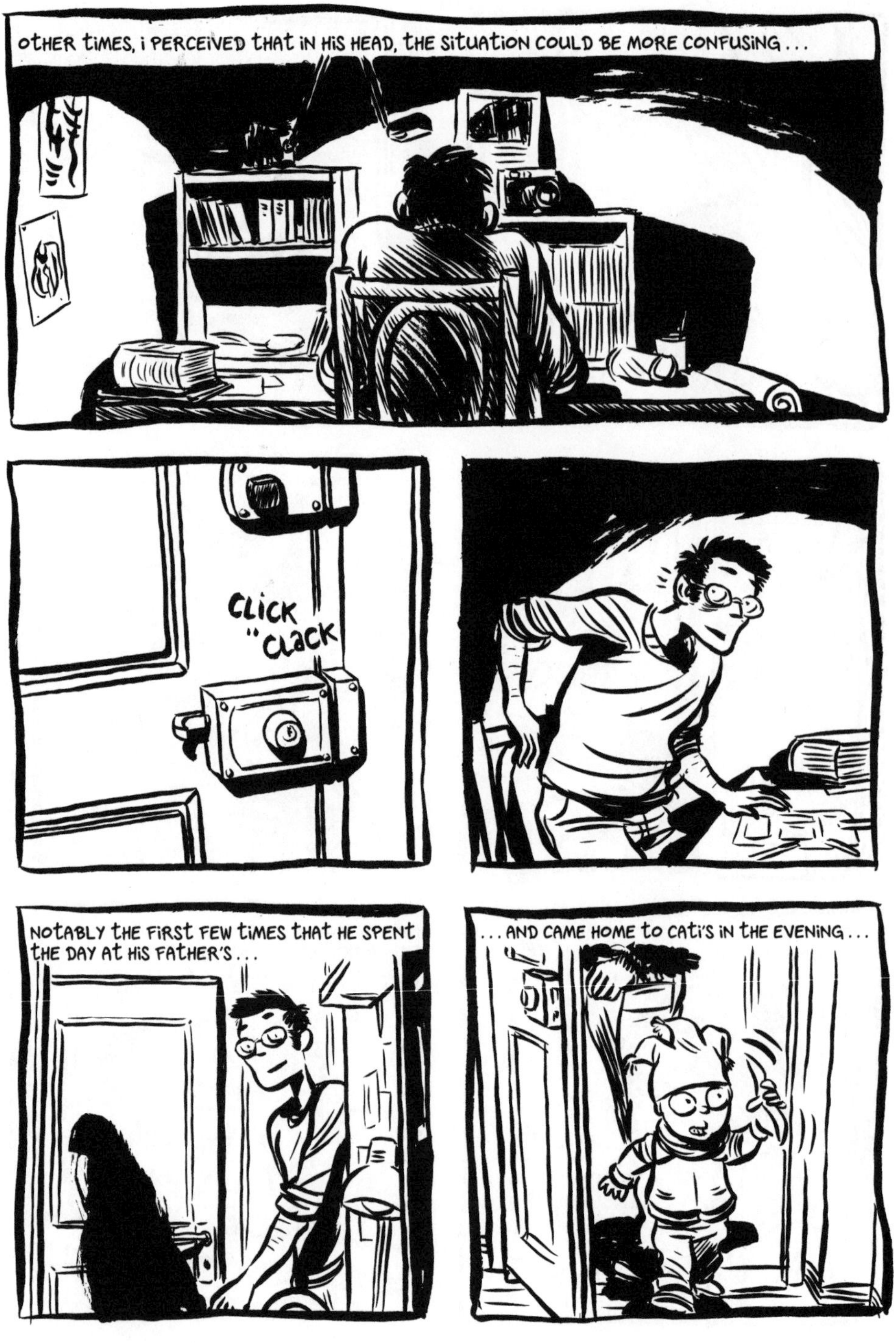
OTHER TIMES, I PERCEIVED THAT IN HIS HEAD, THE SITUATION COULD BE MORE CONFUSING . . .
CLICK
CLACK
NOTABLY THE FIRST FEW TIMES THAT HE SPENT THE DAY AT HIS FATHER'S . . .
. . . AND CAME HOME TO CATI'S IN THE EVENING . . .

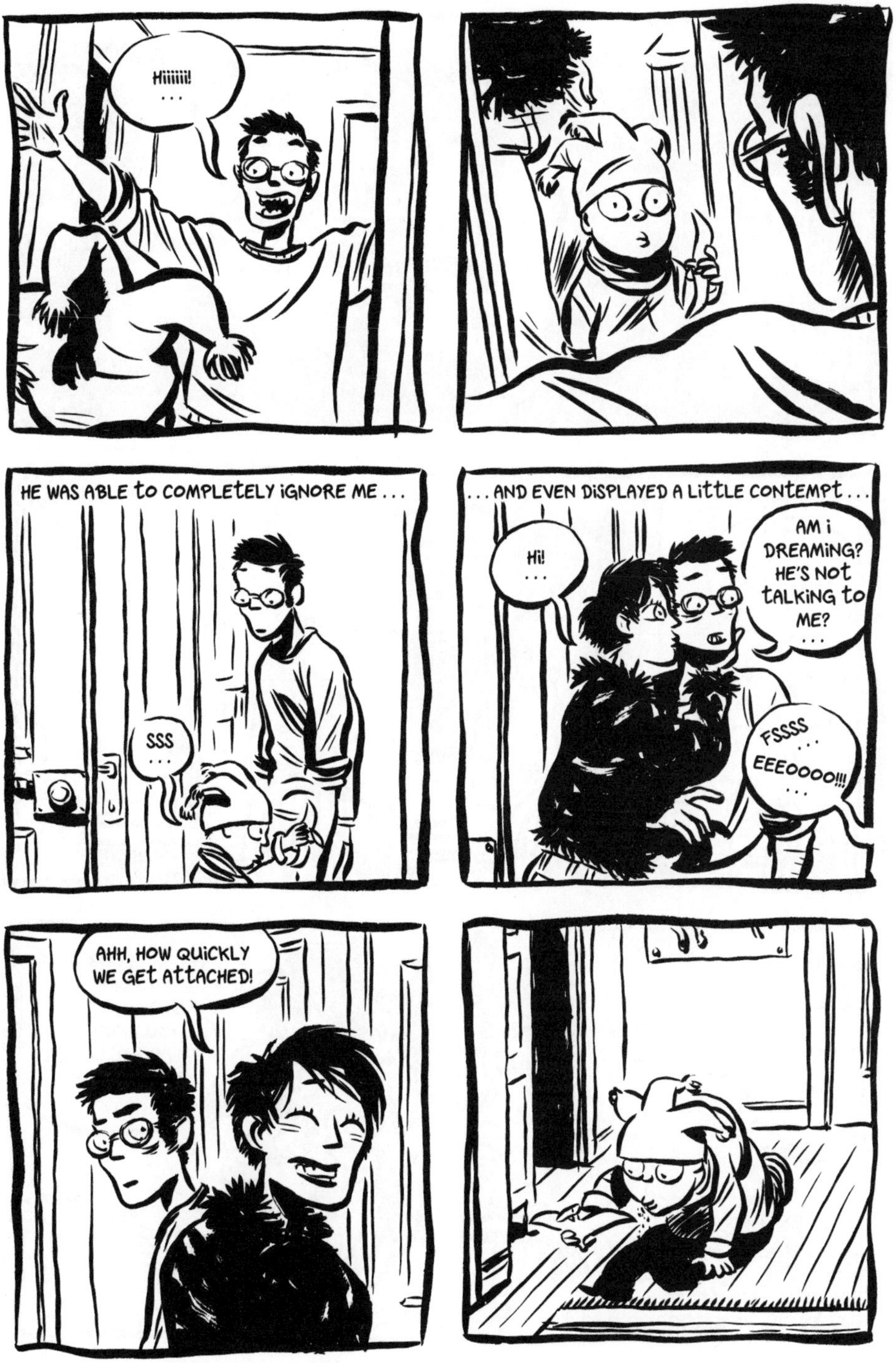
Hiiiiii!
. . .
HE WAS ABLE TO COMPLETELY IGNORE ME . . .
SSS
. . .
. . . AND EVEN DISPLAYED A LITTLE CONTEMPT . . .
Hi!
. . .
AM I DREAMING? HE'S NOT TALKING TO ME?
. . .
FSSSS
. . .
EEEOOOO!!!
. . .
AHH, HOW QUICKLY WE GET ATTACHED!

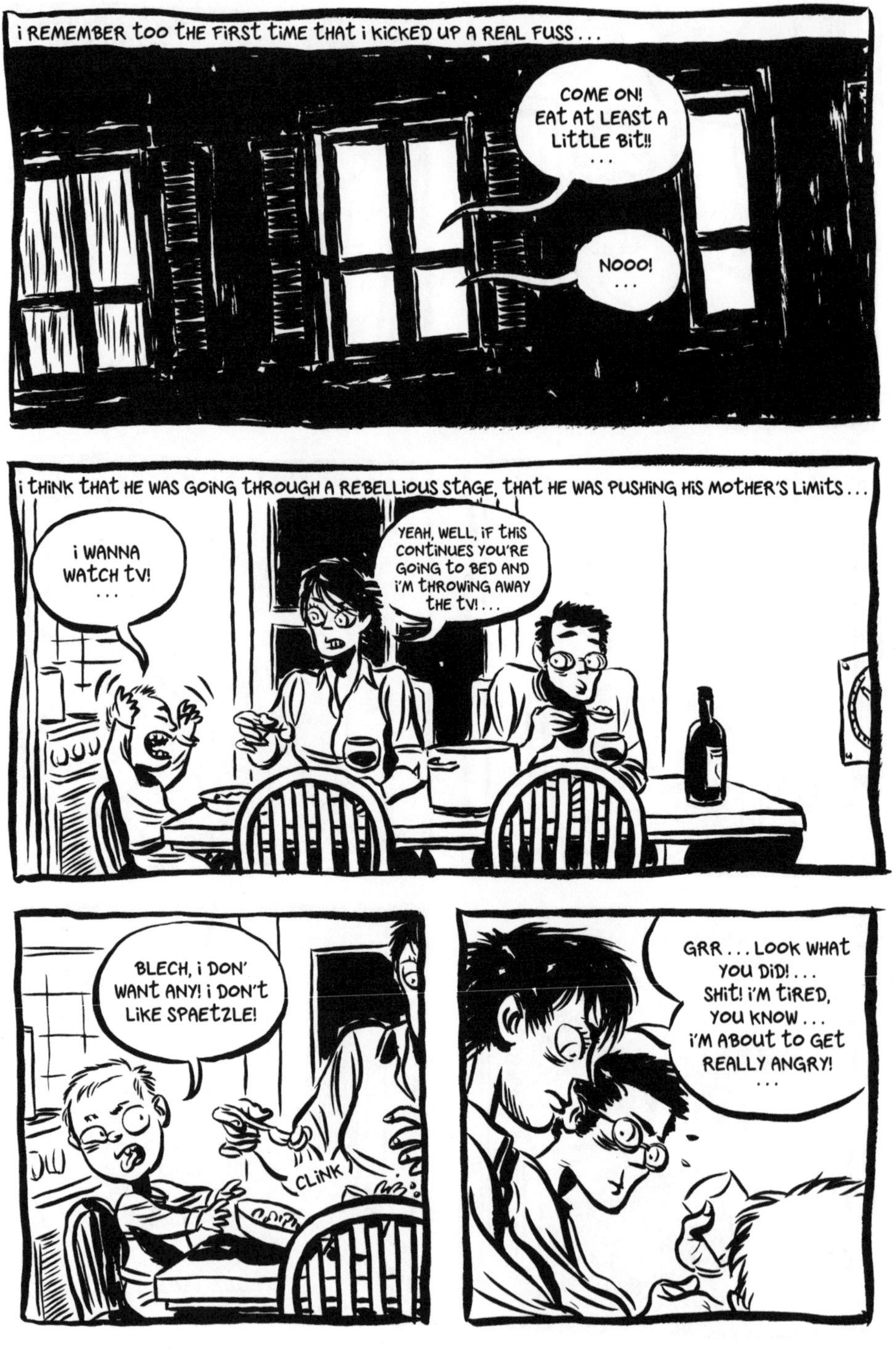
i REMEMBER too THE FIRST time THAT i KICKED UP A REAL FUSS . . .
COME ON! EAt At LEASt A LittLE Bit!! . . .
NOOO! . . .
i tHiNK tHAt HE WAS GOiNG tHROUGH A REBELLiOUS StAGE, tHAt HE WAS PUSHiNG HiS MOtHER'S LiMitS . . .
i WANNA WAtCH tV! . . .
YEAH, WELL, iF tHiS CONtiNUES YOU'RE GOiNG tO BED AND i'M tHROWiNG AWAY tHE tV! . . .
BLECH, i DON' WANt ANY! i DON't LiKE SPAEtZLE!
CLiNK
GRR . . . LOOK WHAt YOU DiD! . . . SHit! i'M tiRED, YOU KNOW . . . i'M ABOUt tO GEt REALLY ANGRY! . . .

NO!
...

WHEN HE LOOKED LIKE HE WAS GOING TO HIT HER, I LEAPT UP...

UH-UH, WHAT IS THAT?!
...

...AND I WATCHED MYSELF REACT...

...NOW THAT IS NOT ACCEPTABLE! FOR GOD'S SAKE!

LET'S GO! TO BED!
...

WAAAA!
...

WE DON'T HIT PEOPLE, DO YOU HEAR?

...IT IS NOT OKAY!
...

AND CERTAINLY NOT YOUR MOM!

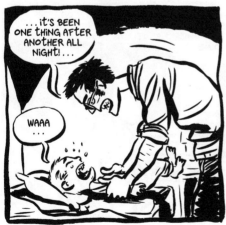

...IT'S BEEN ONE THING AFTER ANOTHER ALL NIGHT!...

WAAA
...

MOM IS NICE TO YOU...SO YOU WILL COME OUT OF YOUR ROOM WHEN YOU CAN BE NICE TOO! IS THAT UNDERSTOOD?
...

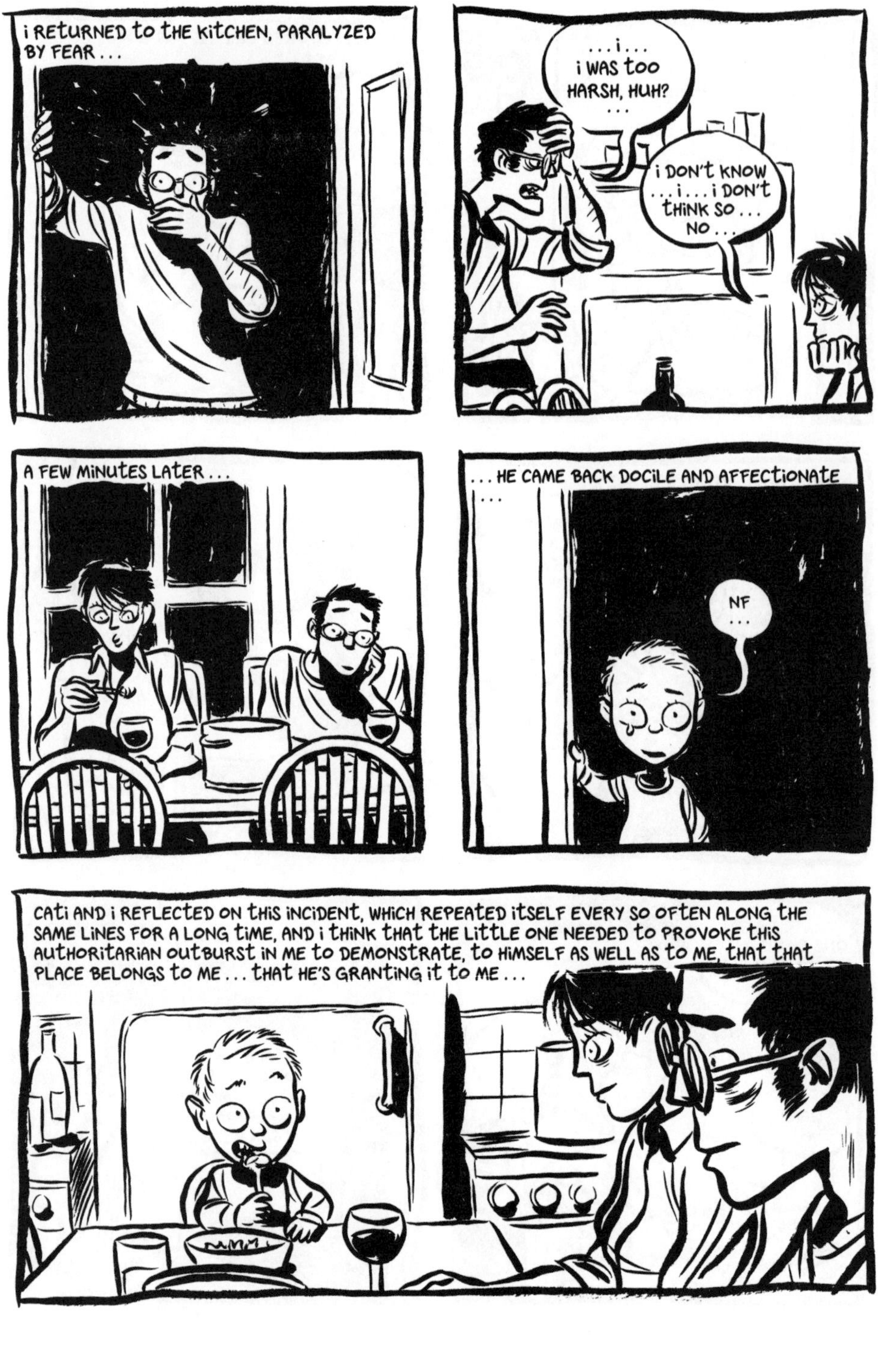

i RETURNED to THE KitCHEN, PARALYZED BY FEAR . . .
. . . i . . . i WAS too HARSH, HUH? . . .
i DON'T KNOW . . . i . . . i DON'T tHiNK SO . . . NO . . .
A FEW MiNUtES LAtER . . .
. . . HE CAME BACK DOCiLE AND AFFECtiONAtE . . .
NF . . .
CAti AND i REFLECtED ON tHiS iNCiDENt, WHiCH REPEAtED itSELF EVERY SO OftEN ALONG tHE SAME LiNES FOR A LONG tiME, AND i tHiNK tHAt tHE LittLE ONE NEEDED to PROVOKE tHiS AUtHORitARiAN OUtBURSt iN ME to DEMONStRAtE, to HiMSELF AS WELL AS to ME, tHAt tHAt PLACE BELONGS to ME . . . tHAt HE'S GRANtiNG it to ME . . .

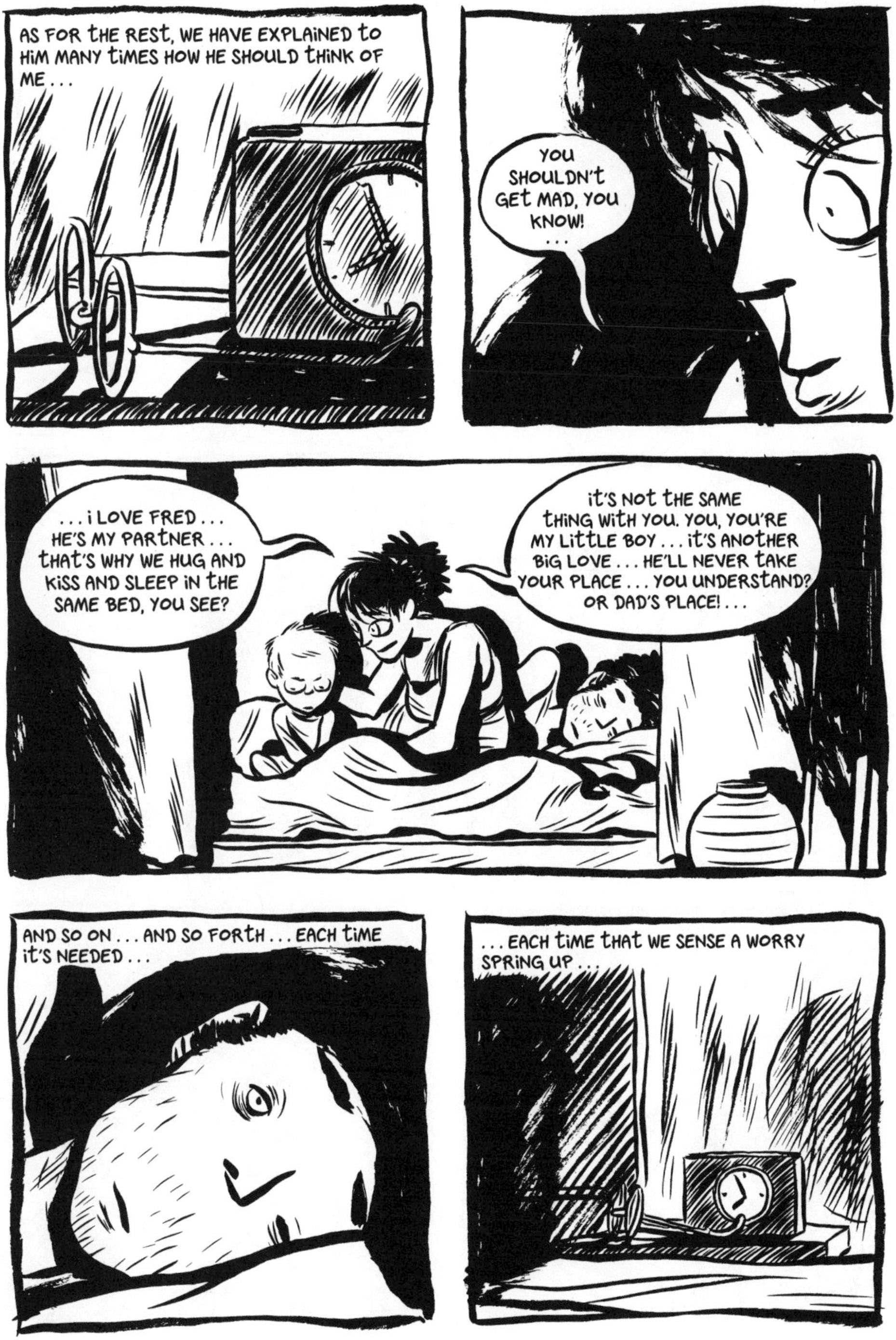
AS FOR THE REST, WE HAVE EXPLAINED TO HIM MANY TIMES HOW HE SHOULD THINK OF ME . . .
YOU SHOULDN'T GET MAD, YOU KNOW! . . .
. . . I LOVE FRED . . . HE'S MY PARTNER . . . THAT'S WHY WE HUG AND KISS AND SLEEP IN THE SAME BED, YOU SEE?
IT'S NOT THE SAME THING WITH YOU. YOU, YOU'RE MY LITTLE BOY . . . IT'S ANOTHER BIG LOVE . . . HE'LL NEVER TAKE YOUR PLACE . . . YOU UNDERSTAND? OR DAD'S PLACE! . . .
AND SO ON . . . AND SO FORTH . . . EACH TIME IT'S NEEDED . . .
. . . EACH TIME THAT WE SENSE A WORRY SPRING UP . . .

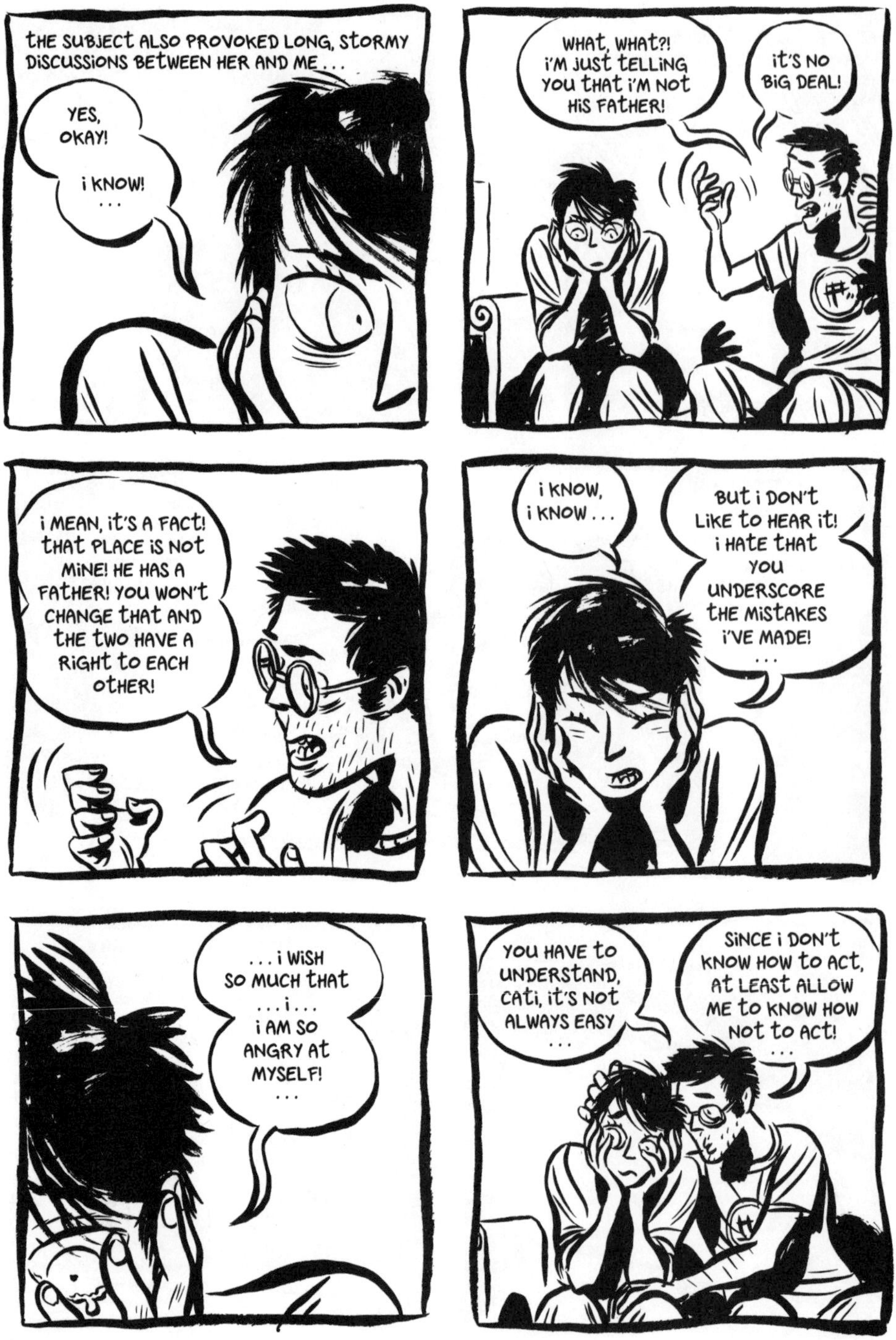
THE SUBJECT ALSO PROVOKED LONG, STORMY DISCUSSIONS BETWEEN HER AND ME . . .
YES, OKAY! I KNOW! . . .
WHAT, WHAT?! I'M JUST TELLING YOU THAT I'M NOT HIS FATHER!
IT'S NO BIG DEAL!
I MEAN, IT'S A FACT! THAT PLACE IS NOT MINE! HE HAS A FATHER! YOU WON'T CHANGE THAT AND THE TWO HAVE A RIGHT TO EACH OTHER!
I KNOW, I KNOW . . .
BUT I DON'T LIKE TO HEAR IT! I HATE THAT YOU UNDERSCORE THE MISTAKES I'VE MADE! . . .
. . . I WISH SO MUCH THAT . . . I . . . I AM SO ANGRY AT MYSELF! . . .
YOU HAVE TO UNDERSTAND, CATI, IT'S NOT ALWAYS EASY . . .
SINCE I DON'T KNOW HOW TO ACT, AT LEAST ALLOW ME TO KNOW HOW NOT TO ACT! . . .

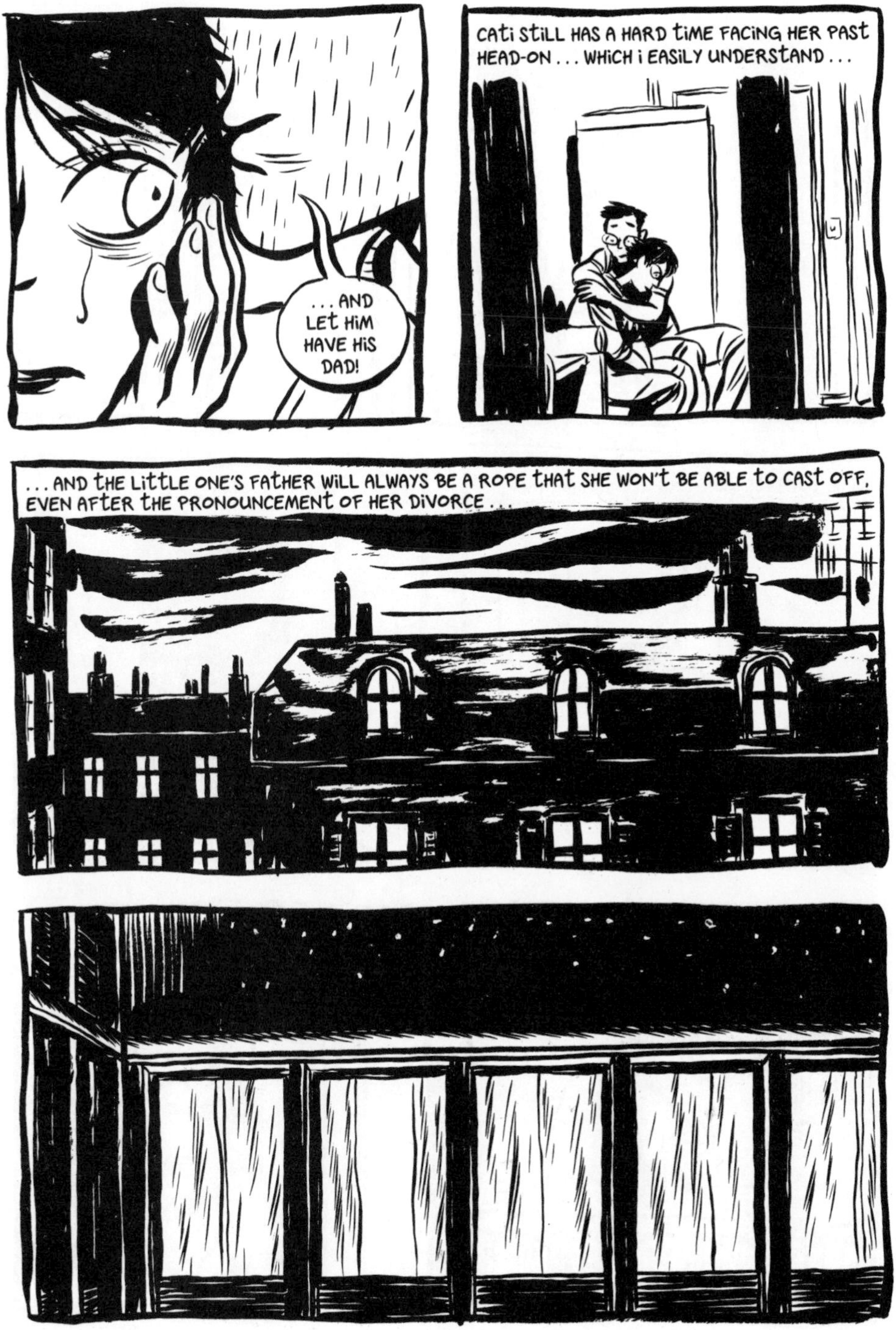
...AND LET HIM HAVE HIS DAD!
CATI STILL HAS A HARD TIME FACING HER PAST HEAD-ON... WHICH I EASILY UNDERSTAND...
...AND THE LITTLE ONE'S FATHER WILL ALWAYS BE A ROPE THAT SHE WON'T BE ABLE TO CAST OFF, EVEN AFTER THE PRONOUNCEMENT OF HER DIVORCE...

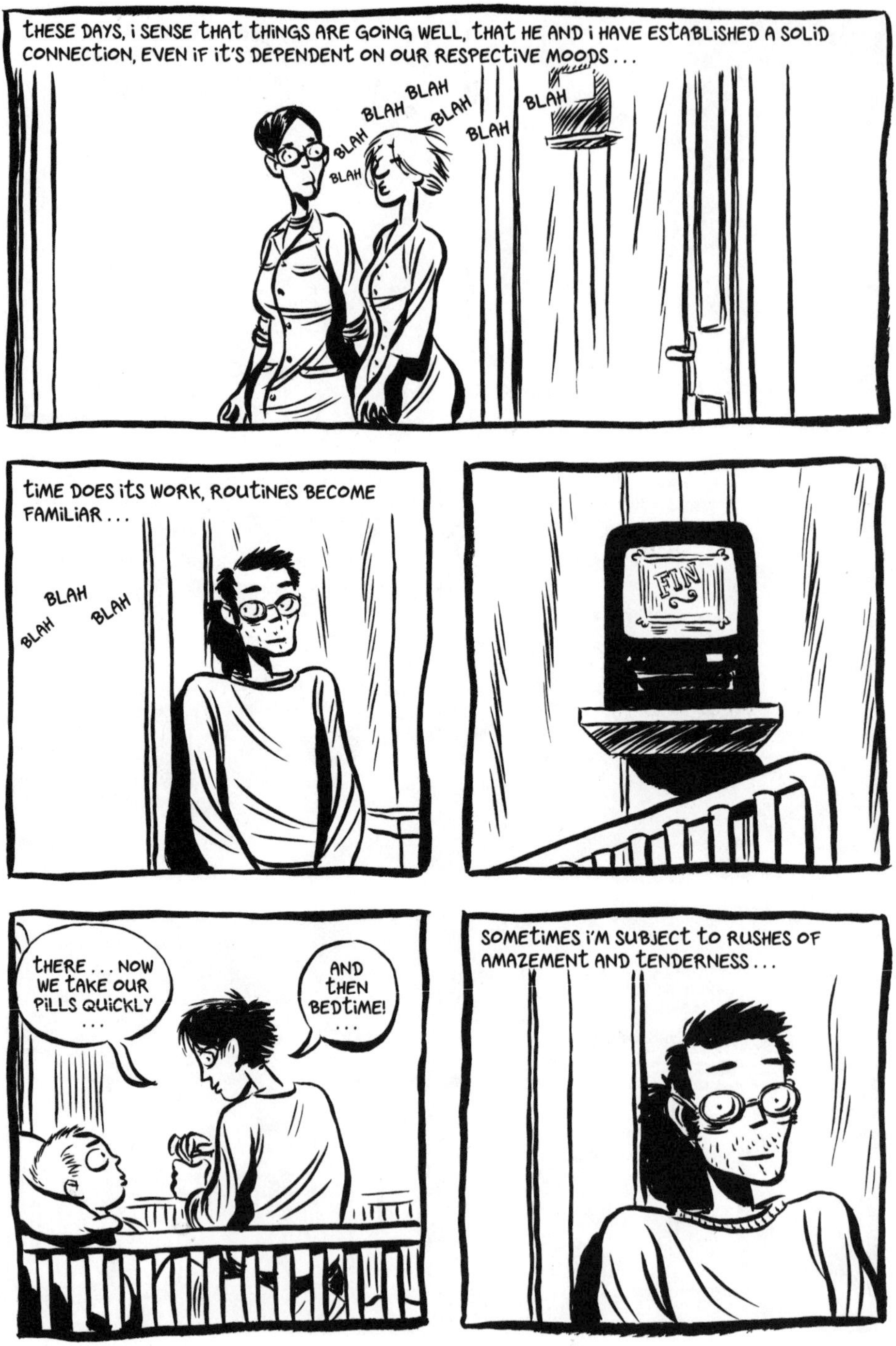
THESE DAYS, I SENSE THAT THINGS ARE GOING WELL, THAT HE AND I HAVE ESTABLISHED A SOLID CONNECTION, EVEN IF IT'S DEPENDENT ON OUR RESPECTIVE MOODS . . .
BLAH BLAH BLAH BLAH BLAH BLAH BLAH
TIME DOES ITS WORK, ROUTINES BECOME FAMILIAR . . .
BLAH BLAH BLAH
FIN
THERE . . . NOW WE TAKE OUR PILLS QUICKLY . . .
AND THEN BEDTIME! . . .
SOMETIMES I'M SUBJECT TO RUSHES OF AMAZEMENT AND TENDERNESS . . .

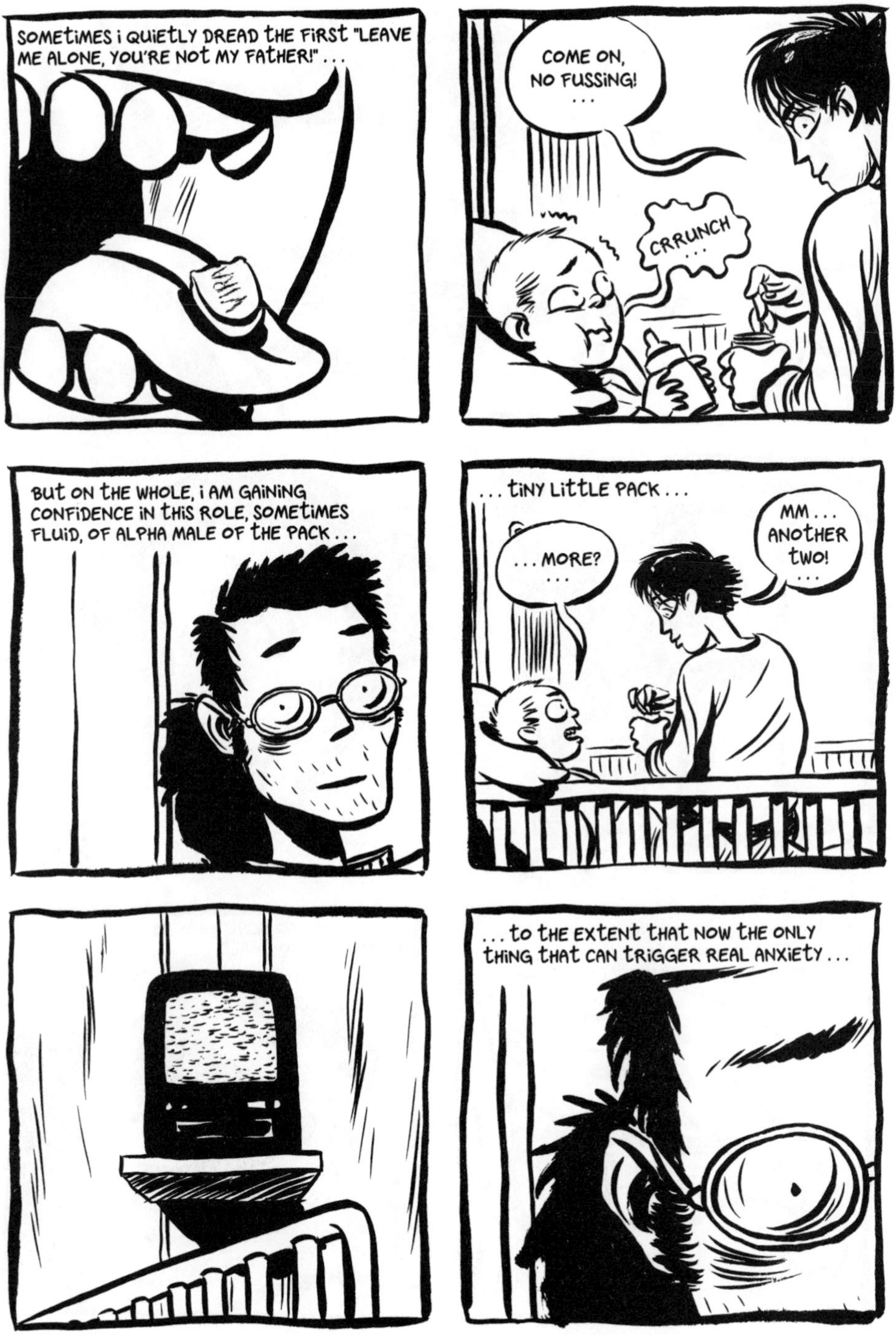
SOMETIMES i QUIETLY DREAD THE FIRST "LEAVE ME ALONE, YOU'RE NOT MY FATHER!" . . .
COME ON, NO FUSSING! . . .
CRRUNCH . . .
BUT ON THE WHOLE, i AM GAINING CONFIDENCE IN THIS ROLE, SOMETIMES FLUID, OF ALPHA MALE OF THE PACK . . .
. . . TINY LITTLE PACK . . .
. . . MORE? . . .
MM . . . ANOTHER TWO! . . .
. . . TO THE EXTENT THAT NOW THE ONLY THING THAT CAN TRIGGER REAL ANXIETY . . .

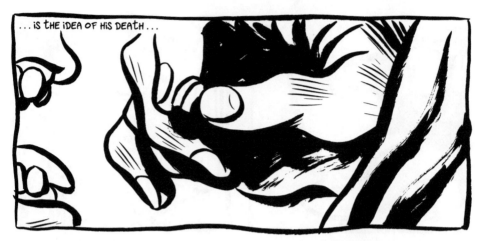
...IS THE IDEA OF HIS DEATH...

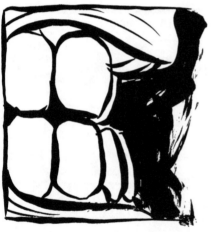

One day Cati told me that in her entire existence, the worst thing that she'd endured was the discovery of her son's HIV...

...and the moment when he had to begin his antiretrovirals...

FOR SOME TIME, CATI AND HE HAVE BEEN MEDI-CALLY MONITORED... EVERY THREE MONTHS, A BLOOD TEST ALLOWS THEM TO MEASURE THE VIRUS'S EVOLUTION AND THE STATE OF THEIR HEALTH... A SHORT ENOUGH TIME LAPSE FOR THEM TO ACT IN CASE OF DETERIORATION...

THE LITTLE ONE WAS ALWAYS FRAIL AND SUBJECT TO AN ARRAY OF ILLNESSES... BUT IN SPRING 2000, THE SITUATION BECAME DISTURBING AND THE ANALYSES SHOWED THAT THE VIRUS HAD INDEED BECOME ACTIVE AND HAD BEGUN A RAMPANT MULTIPLICATION...

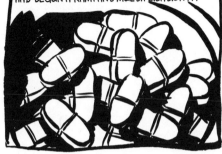

INEVITABLY, A DECISION WAS THEREFORE MADE TO BEGIN AN INTENSIVE TREATMENT... CATI WAS SHATTERED...

FIRST, THE NEWS PLUNGED HER INTO THE DEPTHS OF HER GUILT... IN HER MIND, SHE WAS RESPONSIBLE FOR THE INFECTION OF HER SON AND SHE THEREFORE DESERVED TO FALL SICK BEFORE HIM... MEANING, TO PUT IT MORE SYMBOLICALLY, TO DIE SO THAT HE COULD LIVE LONGER...

AND THEN, THE SIDE EFFECTS OF THESE POWERFUL TREATMENTS, ALREADY POORLY UNDERSTOOD FOR ADULTS, BECAME DOWN-RIGHT UNPREDICTABLE WHEN IT CAME TO A THREE-YEAR-OLD CHILD, ESPECIALLY IN TERMS OF YEARS OR DECADES.

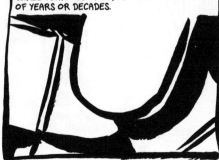

WITHOUT SCIENTIFIC ADVANCEMENT, THIS CHILD WILL BE PLUNGED UNTIL THE END OF HIS LIFE INTO A KIND OF VITAL DRUG ADDICTION, UNDER HIS MOTHER'S ADMINISTRATION... WITH NO POSSIBLE CHOICE, NOTHING BUT FEARS AND QUESTIONS...

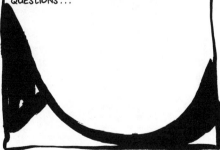

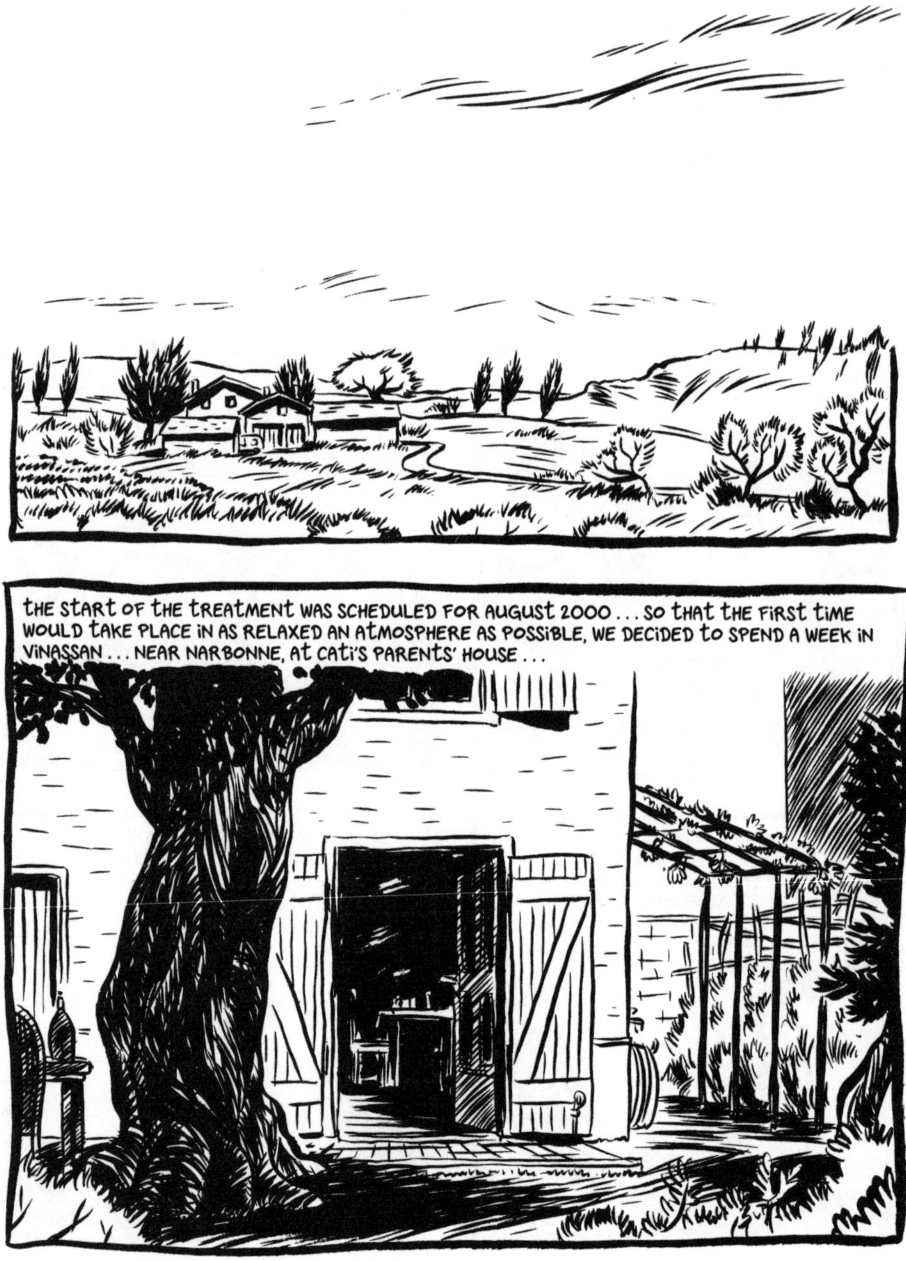
THE START OF THE TREATMENT WAS SCHEDULED FOR AUGUST 2000 . . . SO THAT THE FIRST TIME WOULD TAKE PLACE IN AS RELAXED AN ATMOSPHERE AS POSSIBLE, WE DECIDED TO SPEND A WEEK IN VINASSAN . . . NEAR NARBONNE, AT CATI'S PARENTS' HOUSE . . .

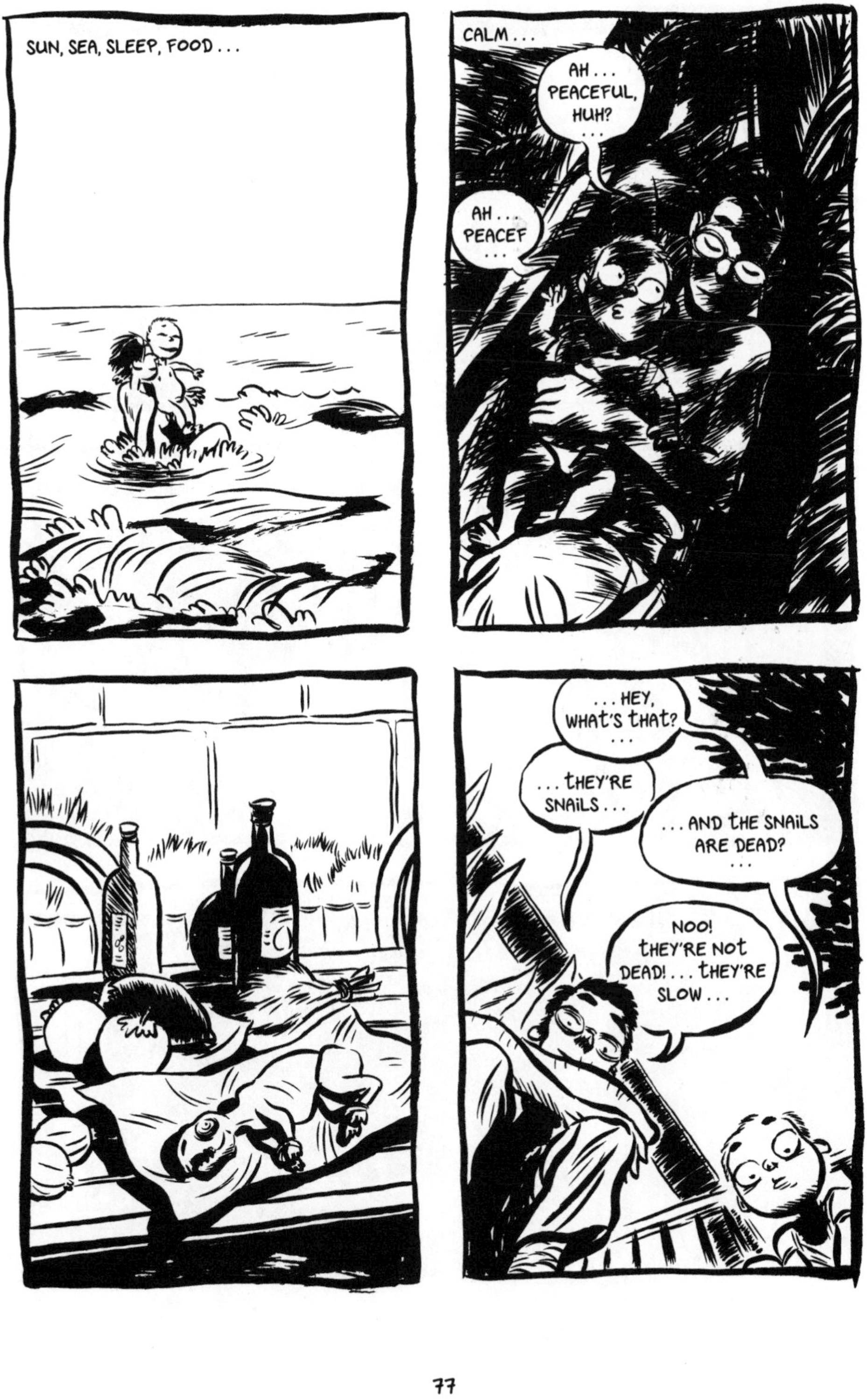
SUN, SEA, SLEEP, FOOD . . .
CALM . . .
AH . . . PEACEFUL, HUH? . . .
AH . . . PEACEF . . .
. . . HEY, WHAT'S THAT? . . .
. . . THEY'RE SNAILS . . .
. . . AND THE SNAILS ARE DEAD? . . .
NOO! THEY'RE NOT DEAD! . . . THEY'RE SLOW . . .

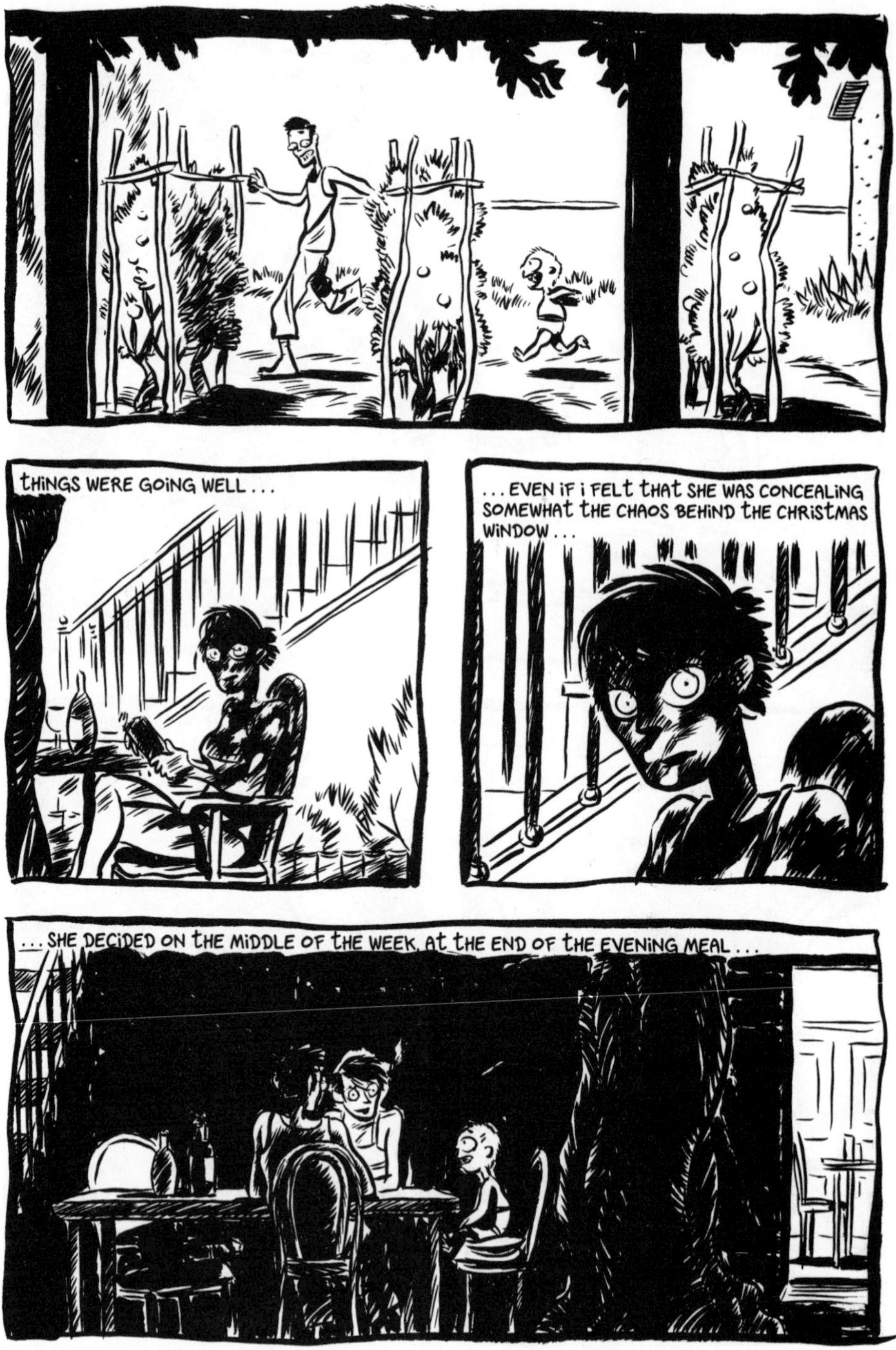
THINGS WERE GOING WELL . . .
. . . EVEN IF I FELT THAT SHE WAS CONCEALING SOMEWHAT THE CHAOS BEHIND THE CHRISTMAS WINDOW . . .
. . . SHE DECIDED ON THE MIDDLE OF THE WEEK, AT THE END OF THE EVENING MEAL . . .

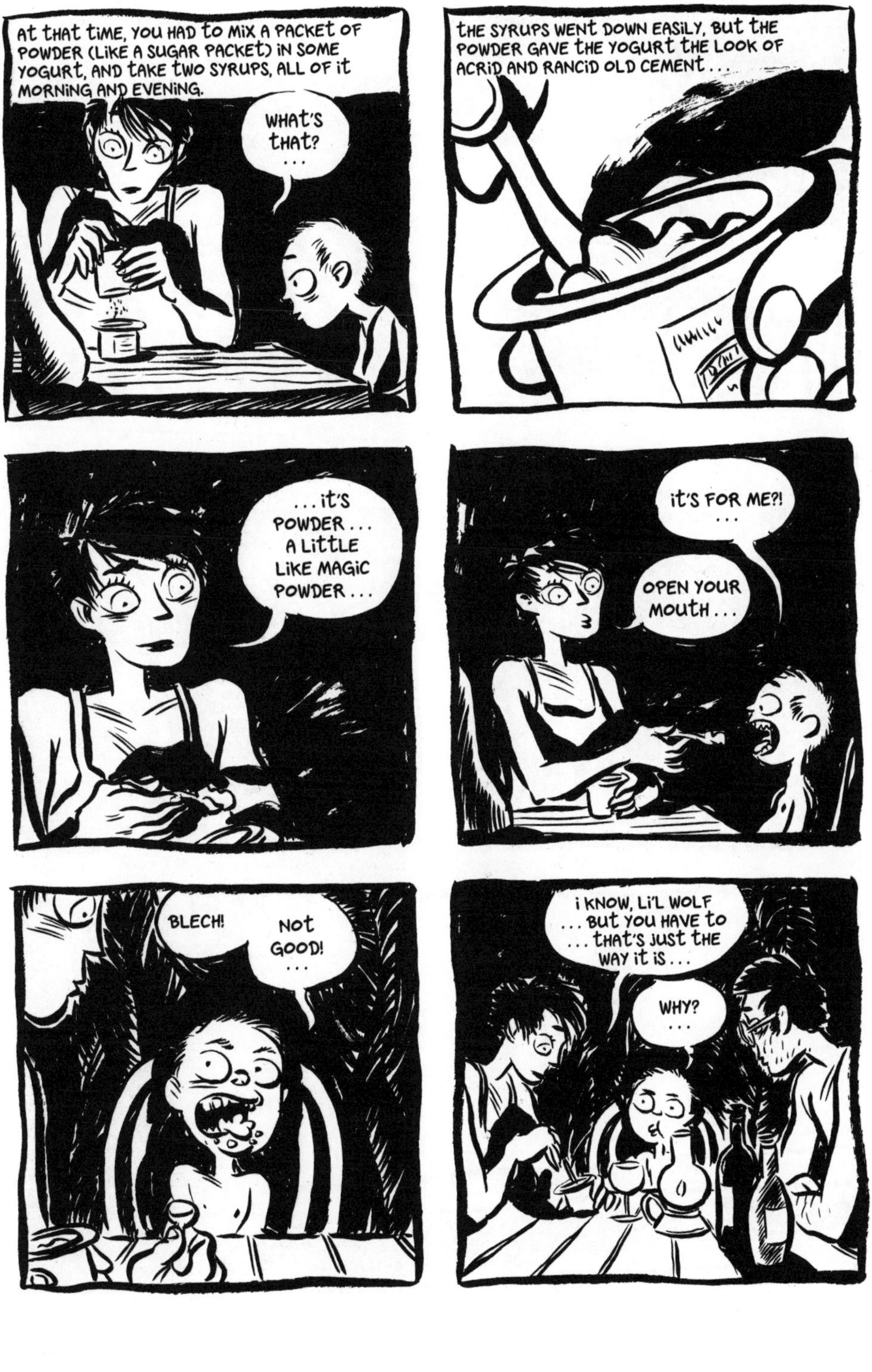

AT THAT TIME, YOU HAD TO MIX A PACKET OF POWDER (LIKE A SUGAR PACKET) IN SOME YOGURT, AND TAKE TWO SYRUPS, ALL OF IT MORNING AND EVENING.
WHAT'S THAT? . . .
THE SYRUPS WENT DOWN EASILY, BUT THE POWDER GAVE THE YOGURT THE LOOK OF ACRID AND RANCID OLD CEMENT . . .
. . . IT'S POWDER . . . A LITTLE LIKE MAGIC POWDER . . .
IT'S FOR ME?! . . .
OPEN YOUR MOUTH . . .
BLECH!
NOT GOOD! . . .
I KNOW, LI'L WOLF . . . BUT YOU HAVE TO . . . THAT'S JUST THE WAY IT IS . . .
WHY? . . .

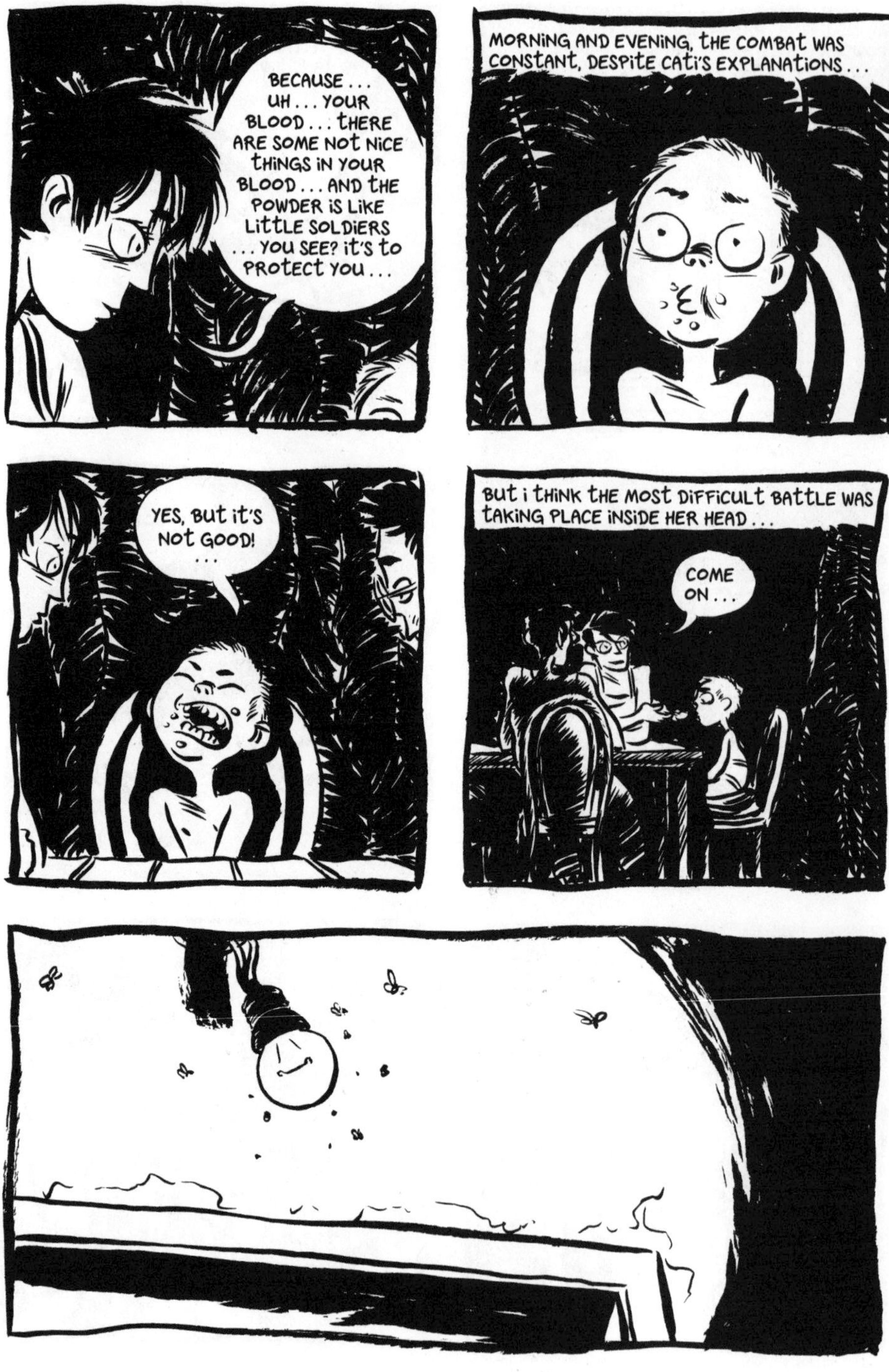
BECAUSE . . . UH . . . YOUR BLOOD . . . THERE ARE SOME NOT NICE THINGS IN YOUR BLOOD . . . AND THE POWDER IS LIKE LITTLE SOLDIERS . . . YOU SEE? IT'S TO PROTECT YOU . . .
MORNING AND EVENING, THE COMBAT WAS CONSTANT, DESPITE CATI'S EXPLANATIONS . . .
YES, BUT IT'S NOT GOOD! . . .
BUT I THINK THE MOST DIFFICULT BATTLE WAS TAKING PLACE INSIDE HER HEAD . . .
COME ON . . .

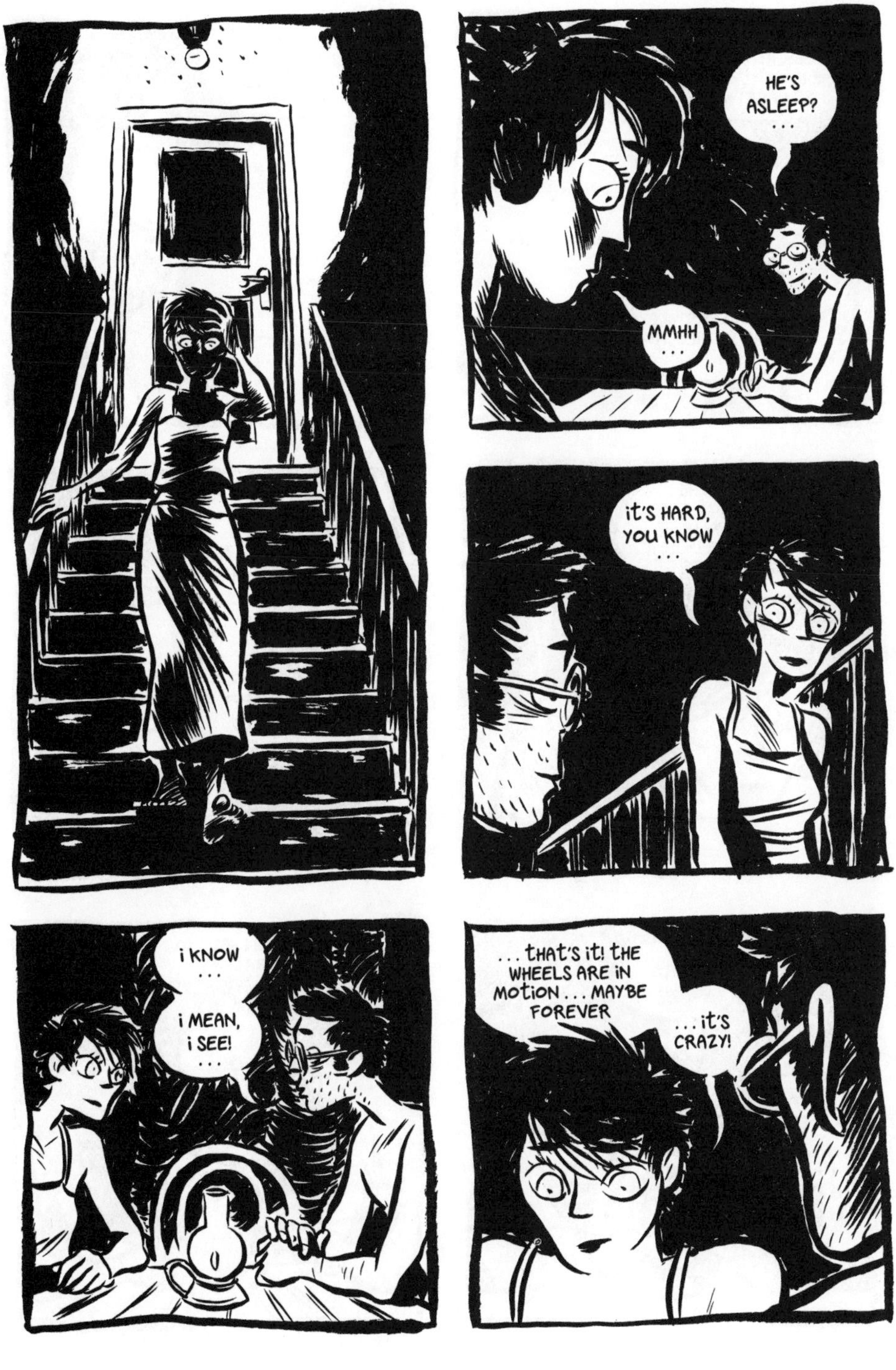
HE'S ASLEEP? . . .
MMHH . . .
it'S HARD, YOU KNOW . . .
i KNOW . . .
i MEAN, i SEE! . . .
. . . THAT'S it! THE WHEELS ARE iN MOTiON . . . MAYBE FOREVER
. . . it'S CRAZY!

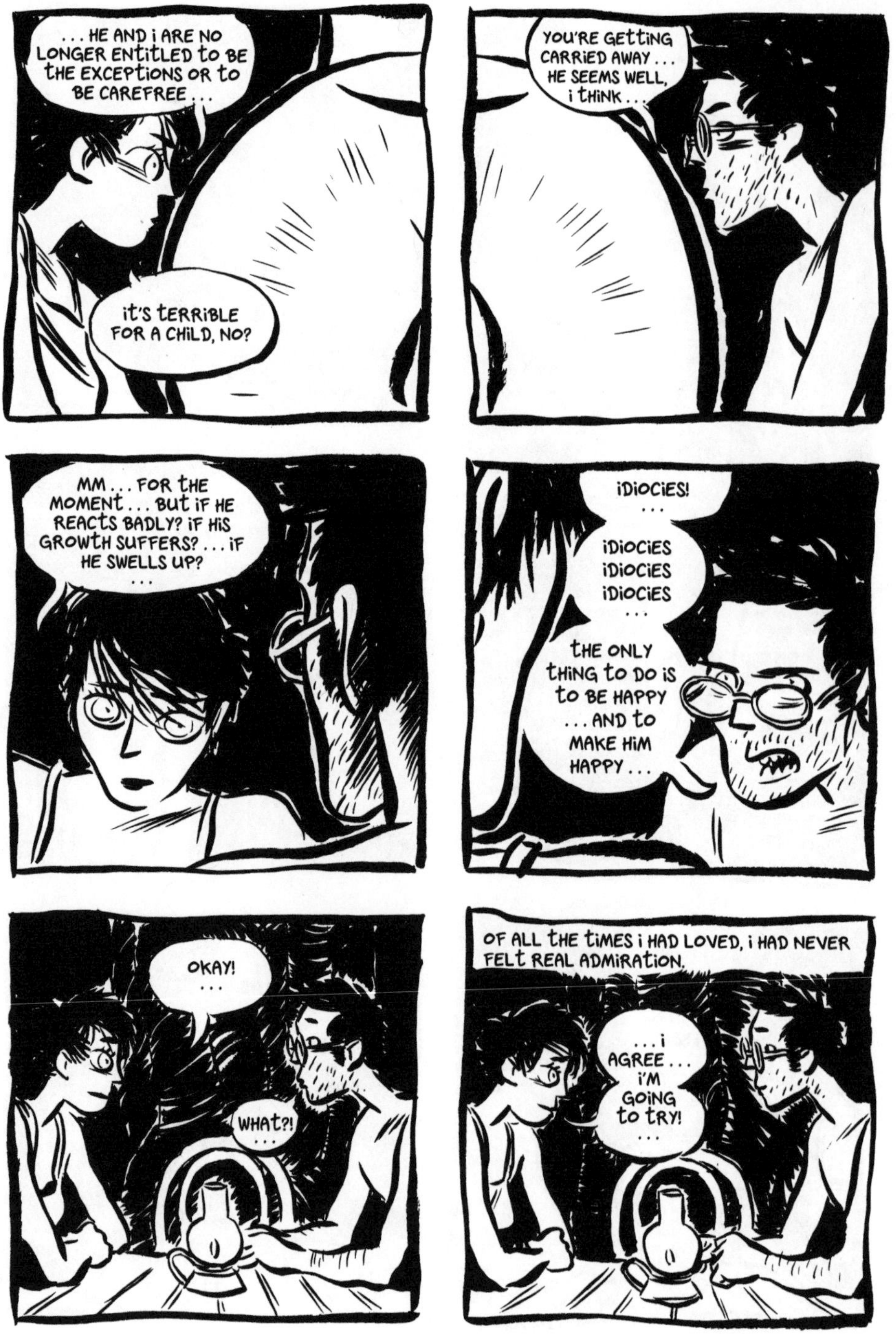

. . . HE AND i ARE NO LONGER ENTitLED to BE tHE EXCEPtiONS OR to BE CAREFREE . . .
it'S tERRiBLE FOR A CHiLD, NO?
YOU'RE GEttiNG CARRiED AWAY . . . HE SEEMS WELL, i tHiNK . . .
MM . . . FOR tHE MOMENt . . . But iF HE REACtS BADLY? iF HiS GROWtH SUFFERS? . . . iF HE SWELLS UP? . . .
iDiOCiES! . . .
iDiOCiES iDiOCiES iDiOCiES . . .
tHE ONLY tHiNG to DO iS to BE HAPPY . . . AND to MAKE HiM HAPPY . . .
OKAY! . . .
WHAt?! . . .
OF ALL tHE tiMES i HAD LOVED, i HAD NEVER FELt REAL ADMiRAtiON.
. . . i AGREE . . . i'M GOiNG to tRY! . . .

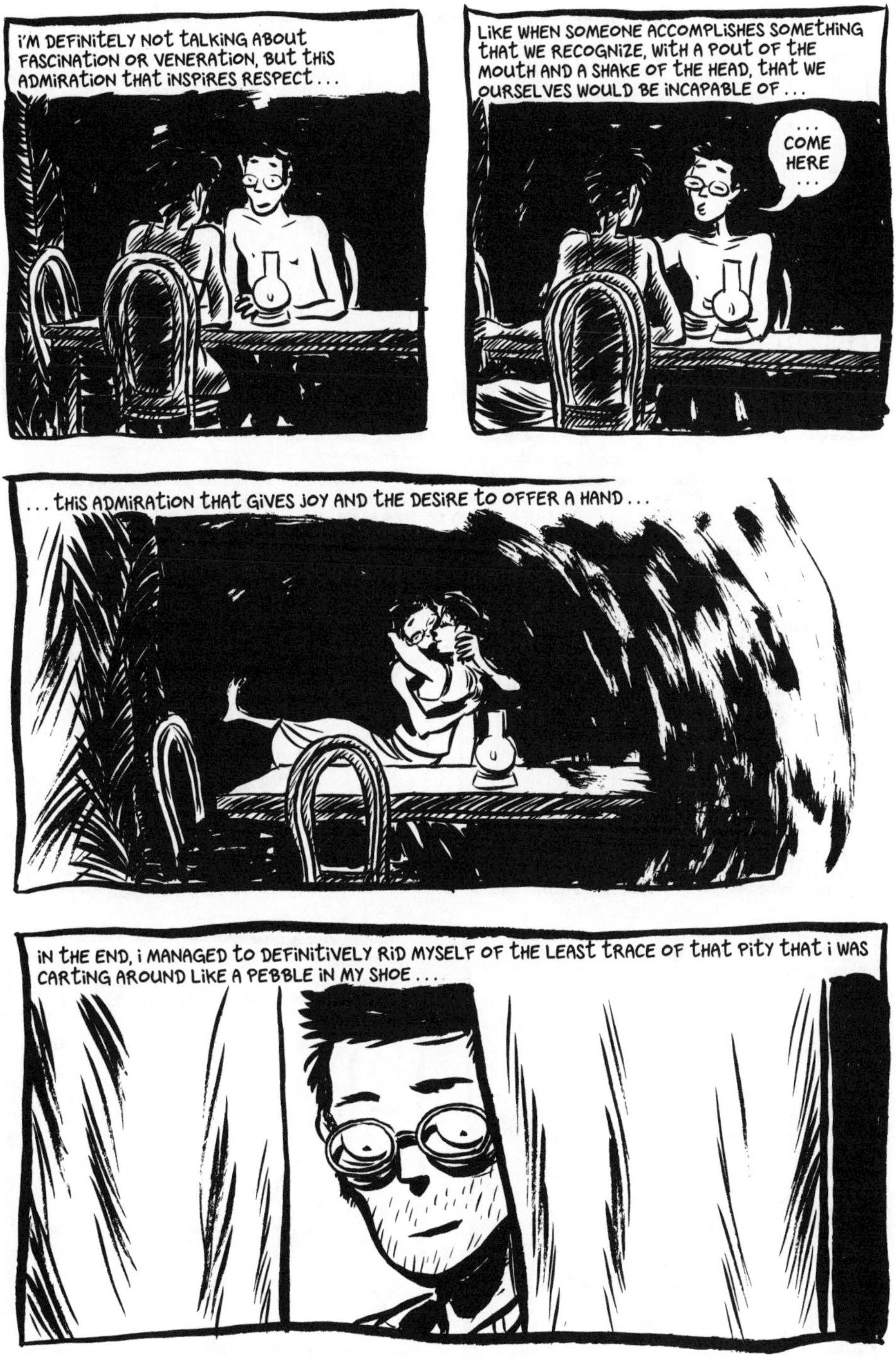
I'M DEFINITELY NOT TALKING ABOUT FASCINATION OR VENERATION, BUT THIS ADMIRATION THAT INSPIRES RESPECT . . .
LIKE WHEN SOMEONE ACCOMPLISHES SOMETHING THAT WE RECOGNIZE, WITH A POUT OF THE MOUTH AND A SHAKE OF THE HEAD, THAT WE OURSELVES WOULD BE INCAPABLE OF . . .
. . . COME HERE . . .
. . . THIS ADMIRATION THAT GIVES JOY AND THE DESIRE TO OFFER A HAND . . .
IN THE END, I MANAGED TO DEFINITIVELY RID MYSELF OF THE LEAST TRACE OF THAT PITY THAT I WAS CARTING AROUND LIKE A PEBBLE IN MY SHOE . . .

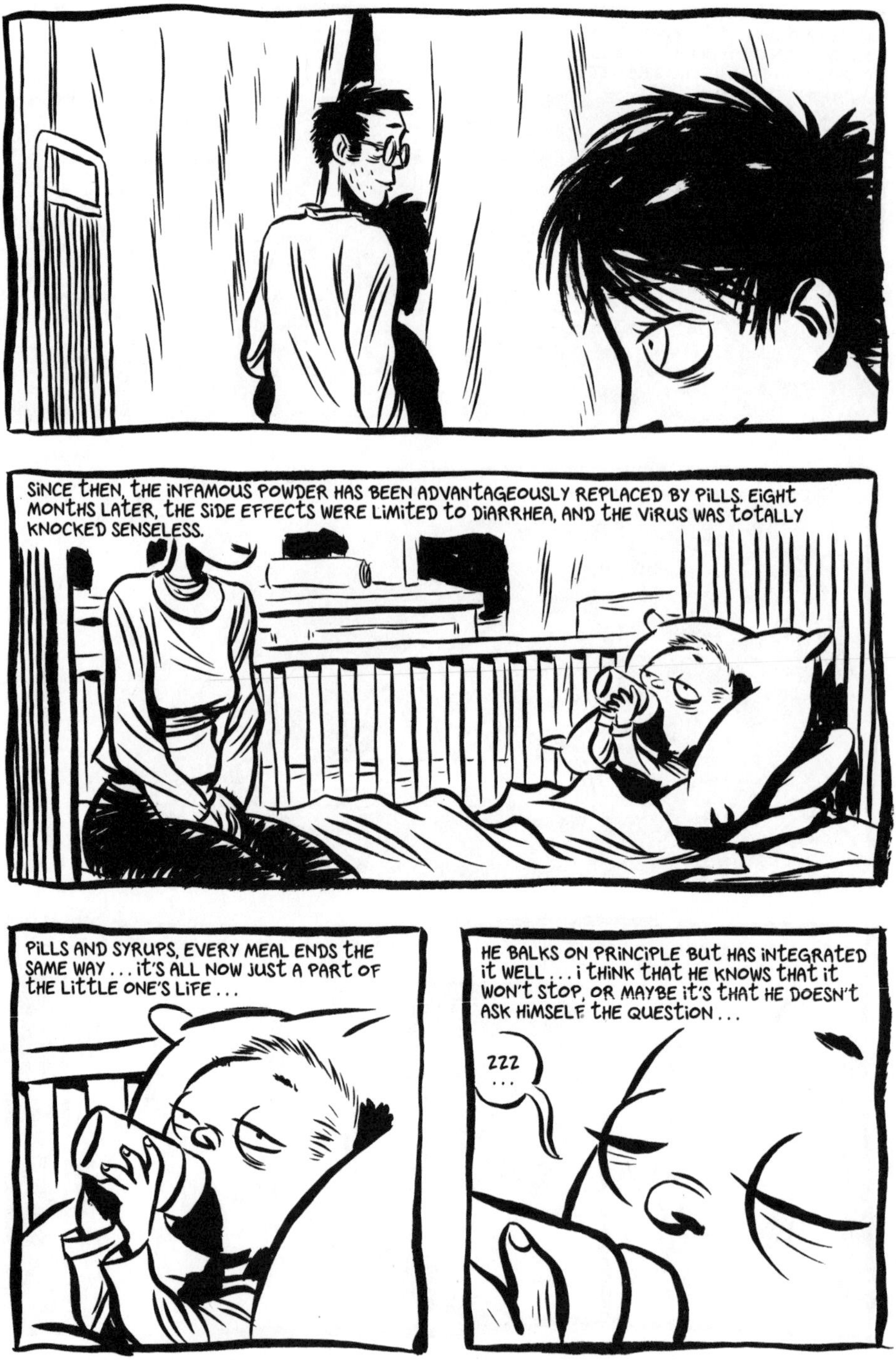
SINCE THEN, THE INFAMOUS POWDER HAS BEEN ADVANTAGEOUSLY REPLACED BY PILLS. EIGHT MONTHS LATER, THE SIDE EFFECTS WERE LIMITED TO DIARRHEA, AND THE VIRUS WAS TOTALLY KNOCKED SENSELESS.
PILLS AND SYRUPS, EVERY MEAL ENDS THE SAME WAY . . . IT'S ALL NOW JUST A PART OF THE LITTLE ONE'S LIFE . . .
HE BALKS ON PRINCIPLE BUT HAS INTEGRATED IT WELL . . . I THINK THAT HE KNOWS THAT IT WON'T STOP, OR MAYBE IT'S THAT HE DOESN'T ASK HIMSELF THE QUESTION . . .
ZZZ
. . .

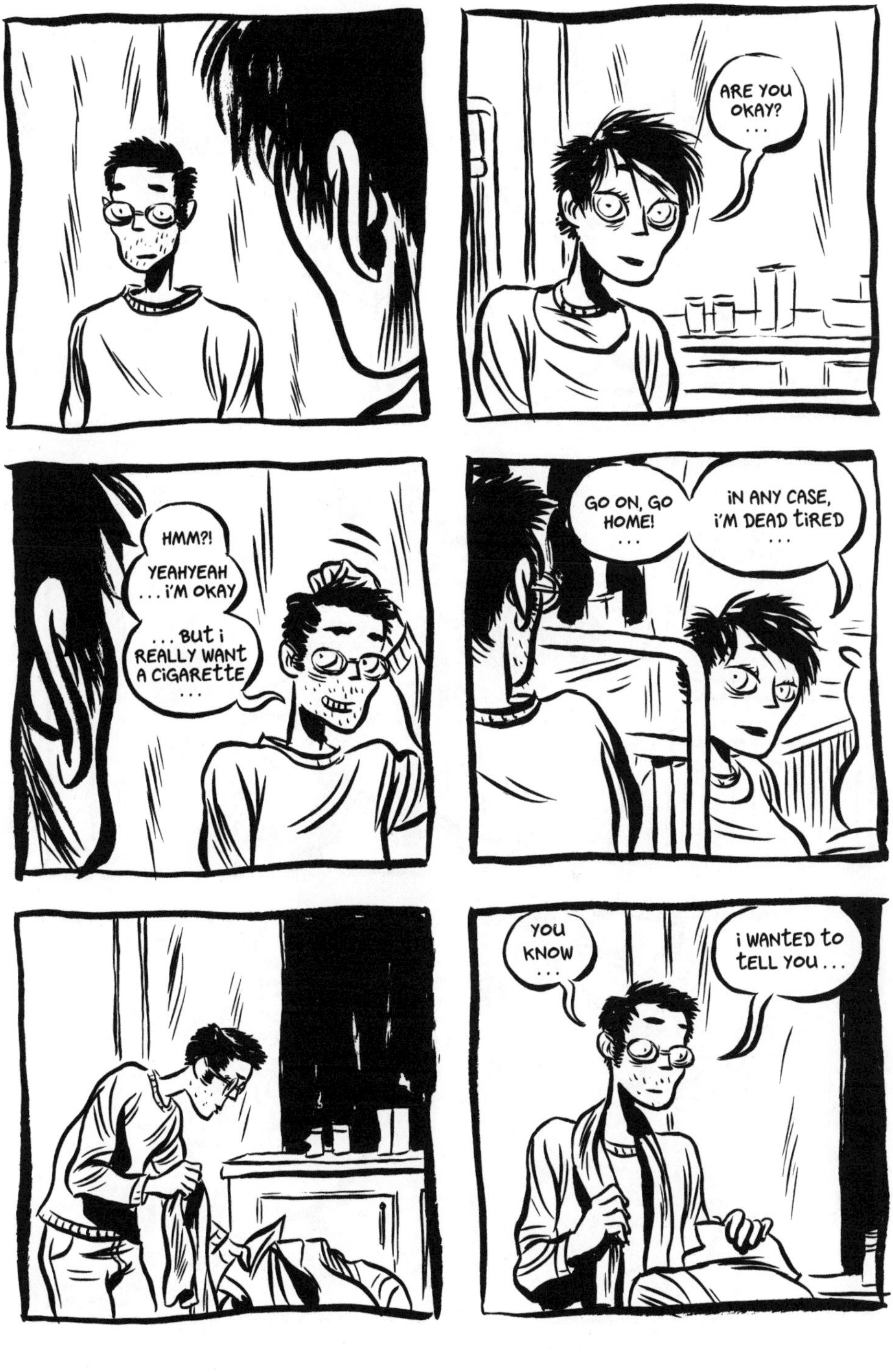
ARE YOU OKAY? . . .
HMM?!
YEAHYEAH . . . i'M OKAY
. . . But i REALLY WANT A CiGARETTE . . .
GO ON, GO HOME! . . .
iN ANY CASE, i'M DEAD TiRED . . .
YOU KNOW . . .
i WANTED to TELL YOU . . .

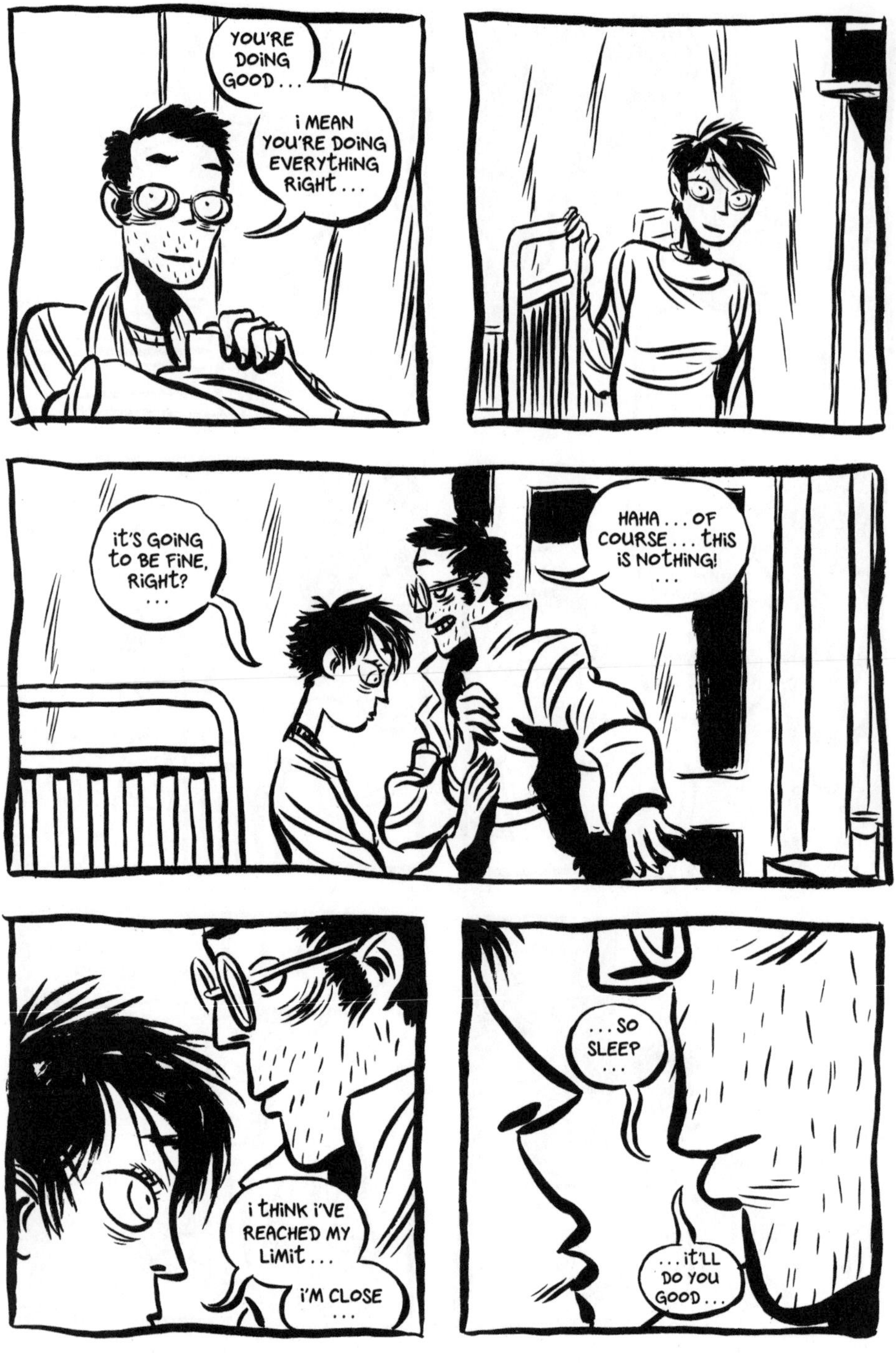
YOU'RE DOING GOOD . . .
i MEAN YOU'RE DOiNG EVERYthiNG RiGHt . . .
it'S GOiNG to BE FiNE, RiGHt? . . .
HAHA . . . OF COURSE . . . thiS iS NOthiNG! . . .
i thiNK i'VE REACHED MY LiMit . . .
i'M CLOSE . . .
. . . SO SLEEP . . .
. . . it'LL DO YOU GOOD . . .

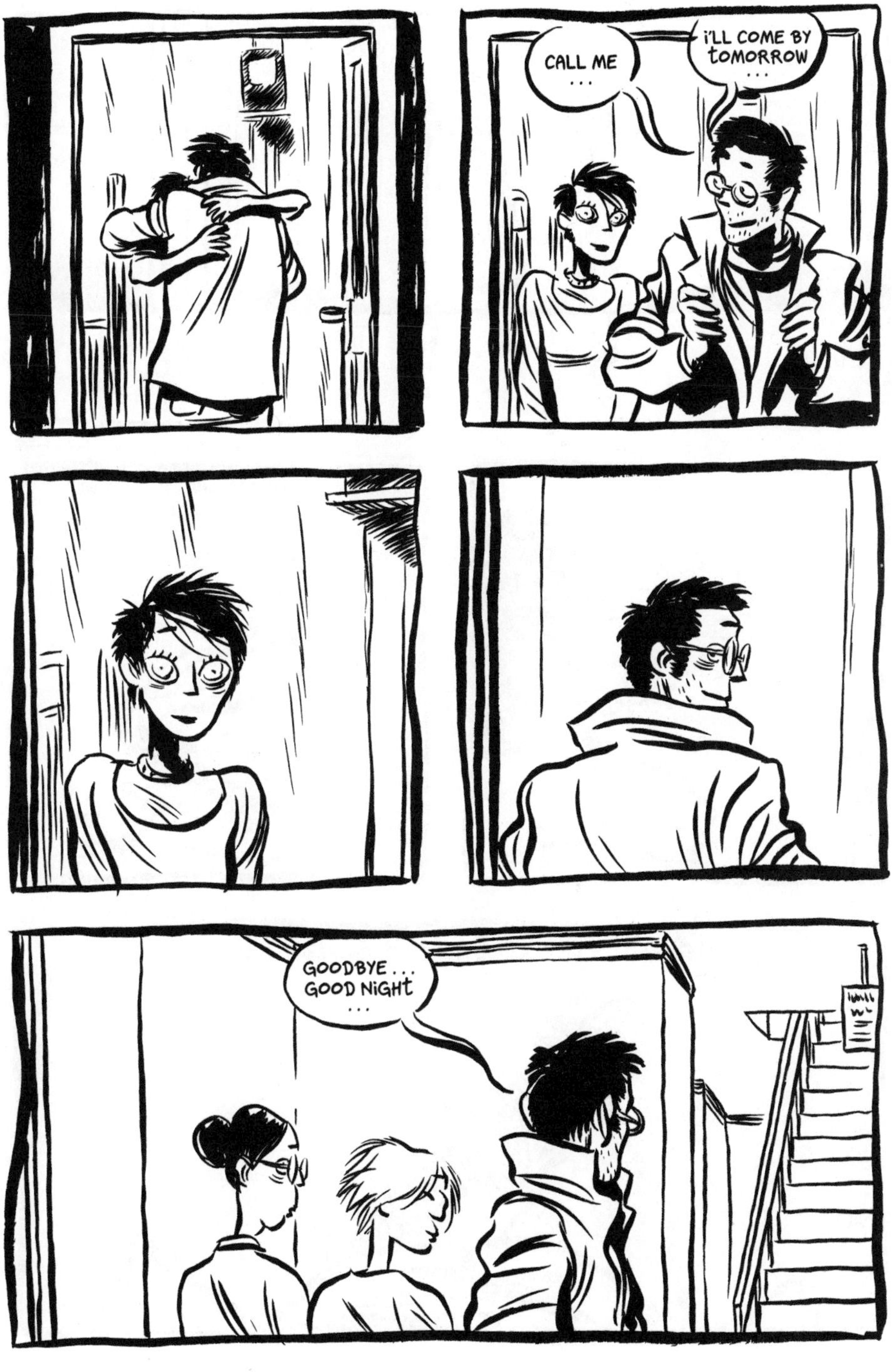
CALL ME . . .
i'LL COME BY tOMORROW . . .
GOODBYE . . . GOOD NiGHt . . .

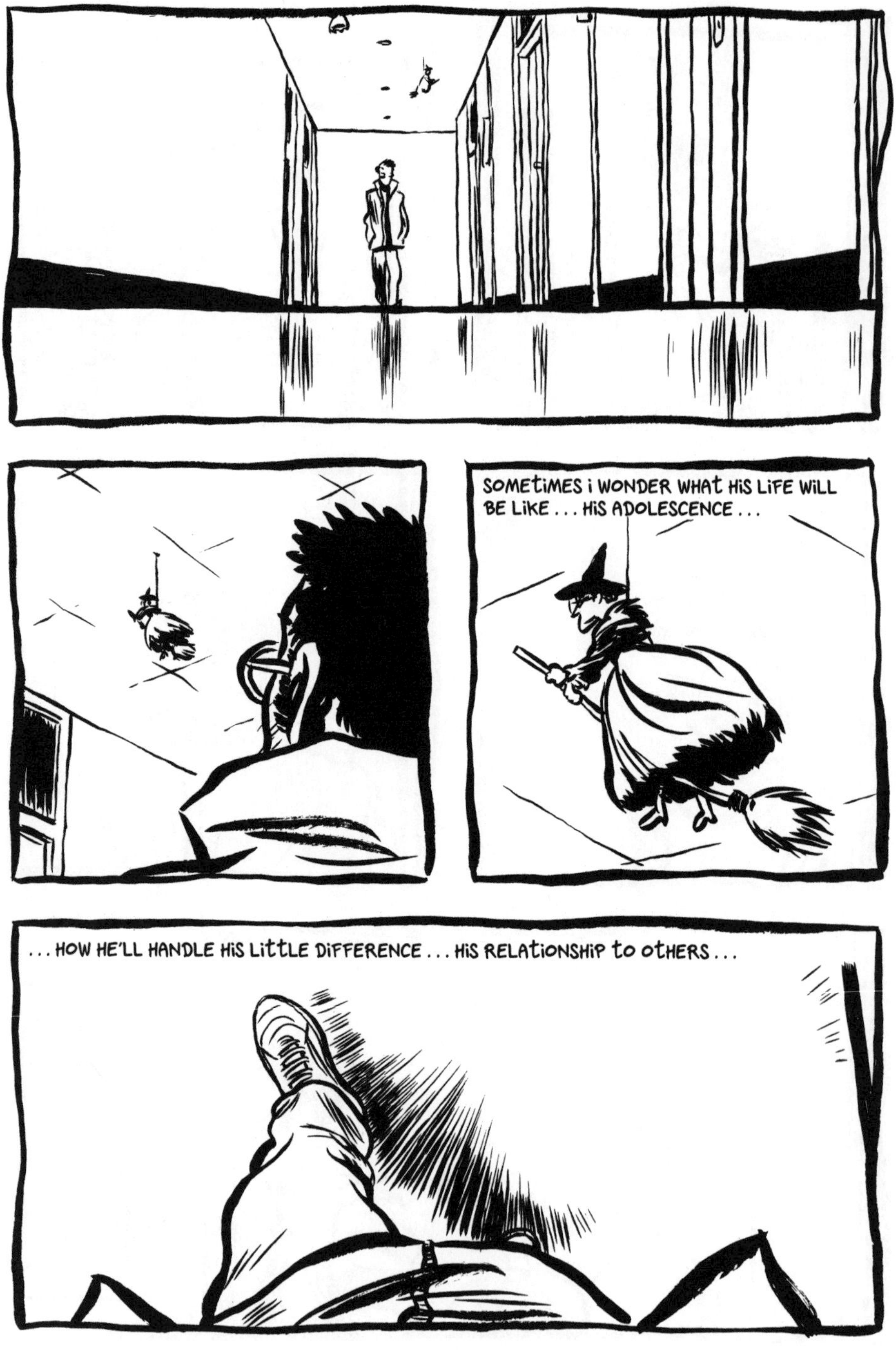
SOMETIMES I WONDER WHAT HIS LIFE WILL BE LIKE . . . HIS ADOLESCENCE . . .
. . . HOW HE'LL HANDLE HIS LITTLE DIFFERENCE . . . HIS RELATIONSHIP TO OTHERS . . .

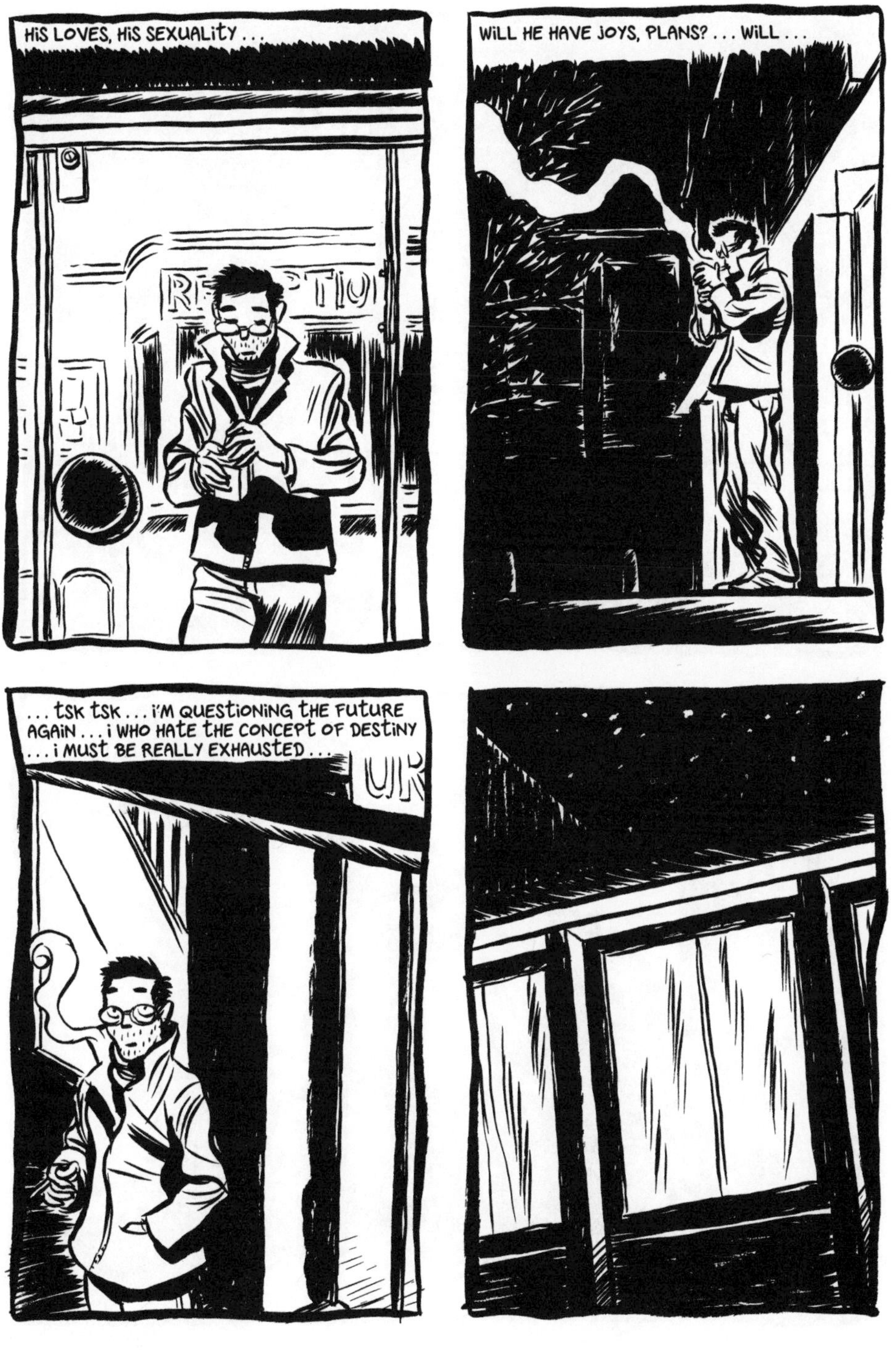
HiS LOVES, HiS SEXUALity . . .
WiLL HE HAVE JOYS, PLANS? . . . WiLL . . .
. . . tsk tsk . . . i'M QUEStiONiNG tHE FUtURE AGAiN . . . i WHO HAtE tHE CONCEPt OF DEStiNY . . . i MUSt BE REALLY EXHAUStED . . .

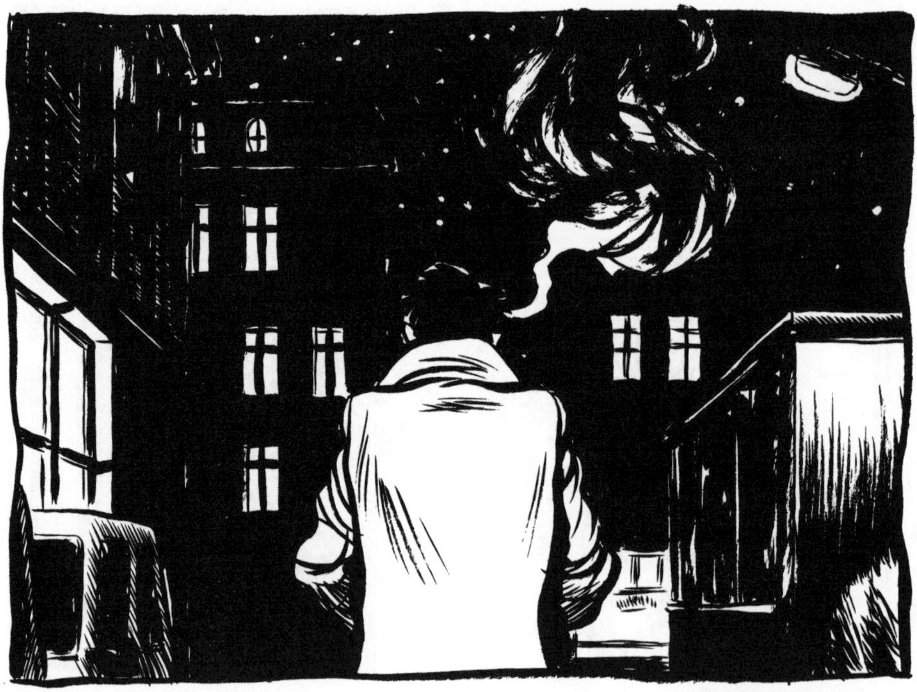

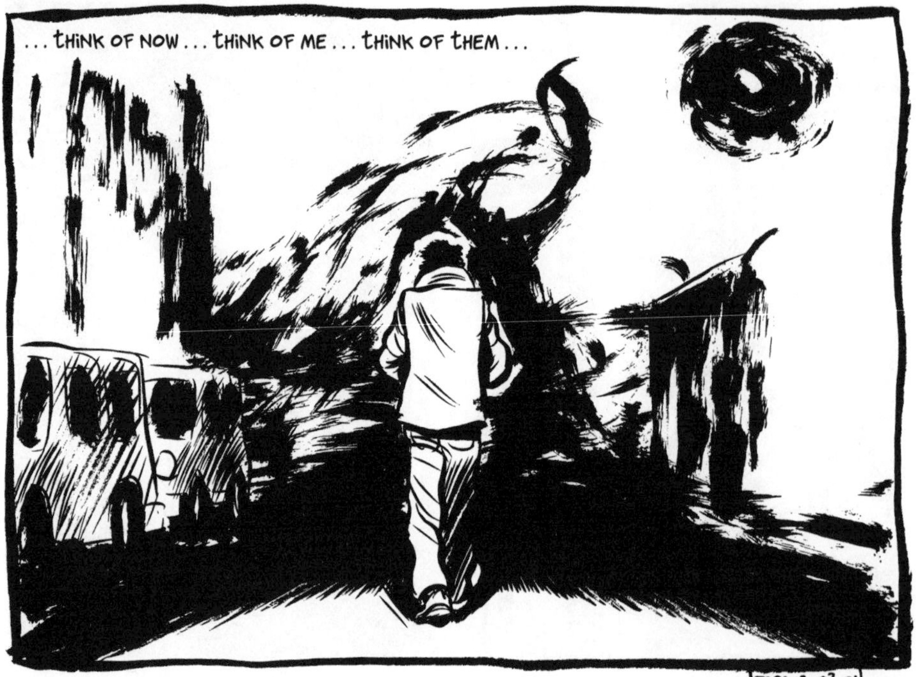
. . . THINK OF NOW . . . THINK OF ME . . . THINK OF THEM . . .

FRED 02-03.01

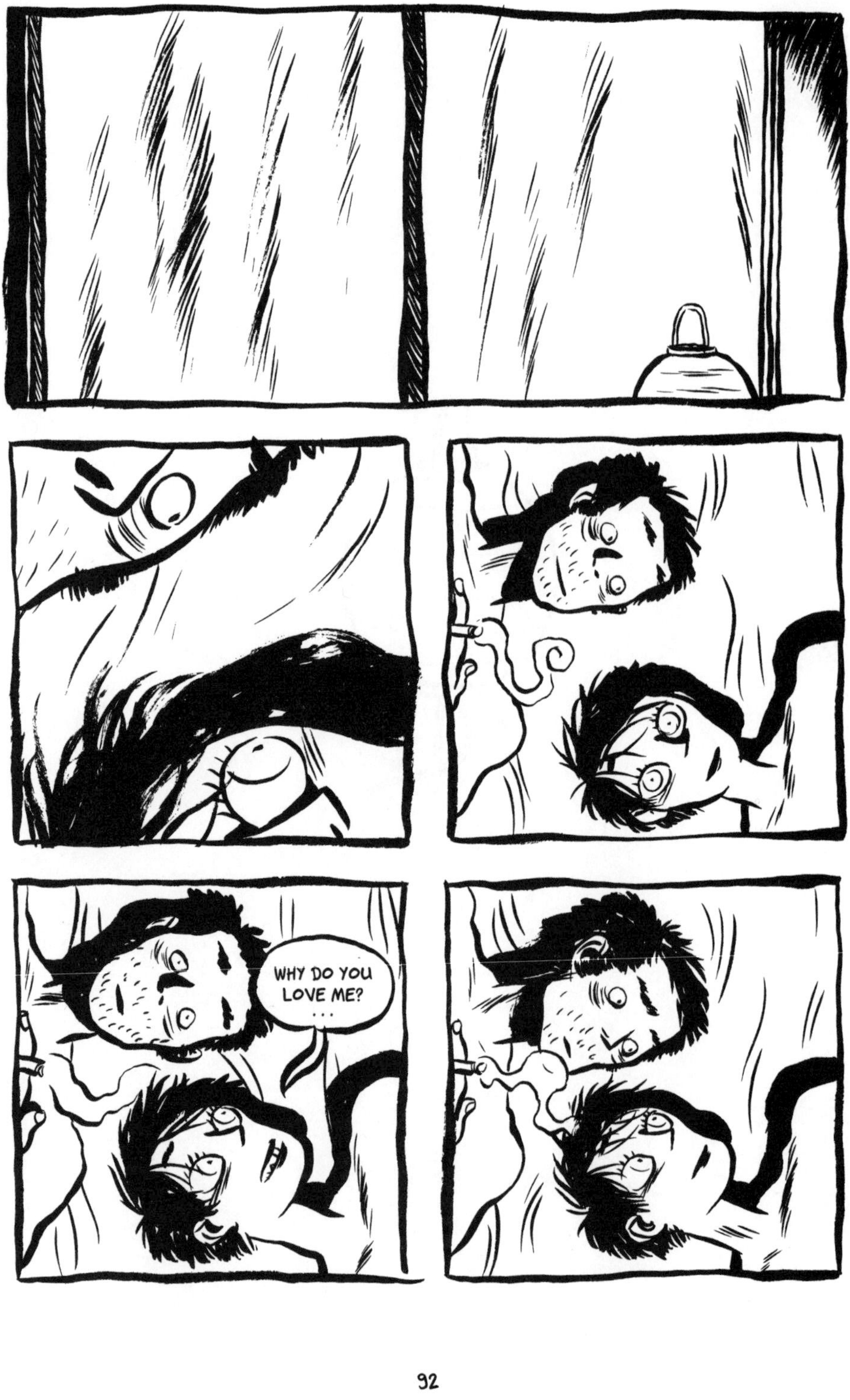
WHY DO YOU LOVE ME?
. . .

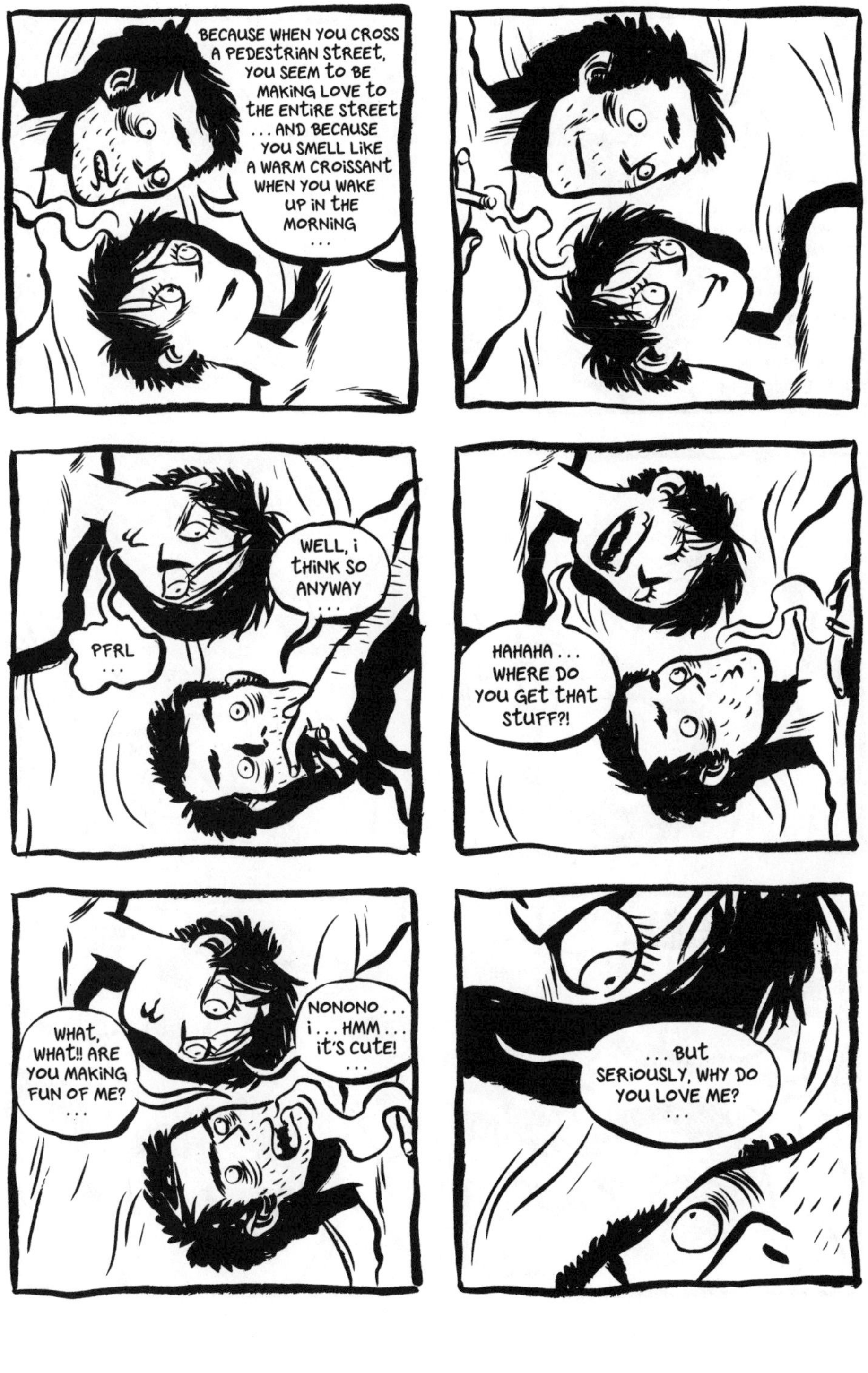
BECAUSE WHEN YOU CROSS A PEDESTRIAN STREET, YOU SEEM TO BE MAKING LOVE TO THE ENTIRE STREET . . . AND BECAUSE YOU SMELL LIKE A WARM CROISSANT WHEN YOU WAKE UP IN THE MORNING . . .
WELL, I THINK SO ANYWAY . . .
PFRL . . .
HAHAHA . . . WHERE DO YOU GET THAT STUFF?!
WHAT, WHAT!! ARE YOU MAKING FUN OF ME? . . .
NONONO . . . I . . . HMM . . . IT'S CUTE! . . .
. . . BUT SERIOUSLY, WHY DO YOU LOVE ME? . . .

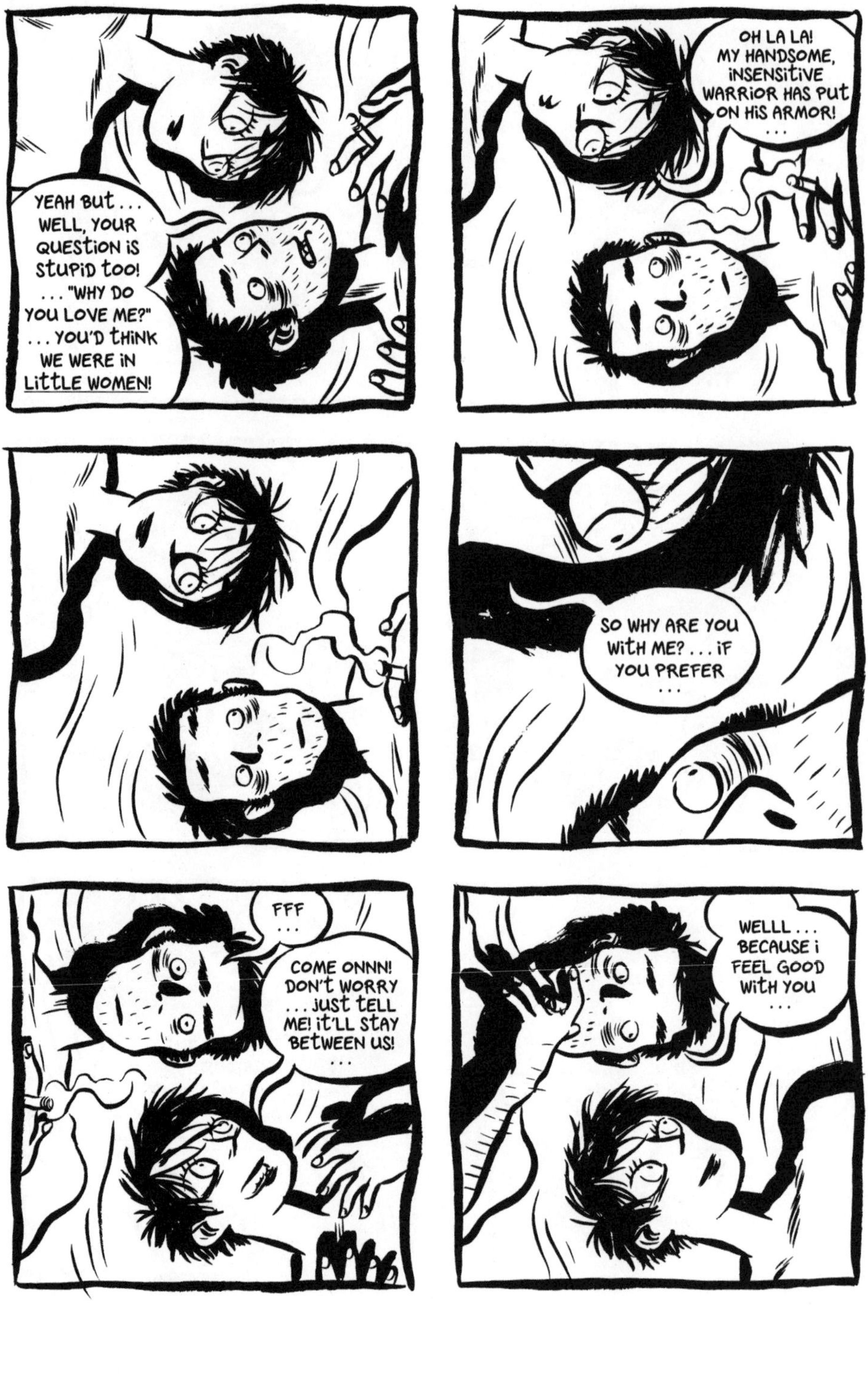
YEAH BUT . . . WELL, YOUR QUESTION IS STUPID TOO! . . . "WHY DO YOU LOVE ME?" . . . YOU'D THINK WE WERE IN LITTLE WOMEN!
OH LA LA! MY HANDSOME, INSENSITIVE WARRIOR HAS PUT ON HIS ARMOR! . . .
SO WHY ARE YOU WITH ME? . . . IF YOU PREFER . . .
FFF . . .
COME ONNN! DON'T WORRY . . . JUST TELL ME! IT'LL STAY BETWEEN US! . . .
WELLL . . . BECAUSE I FEEL GOOD WITH YOU . . .

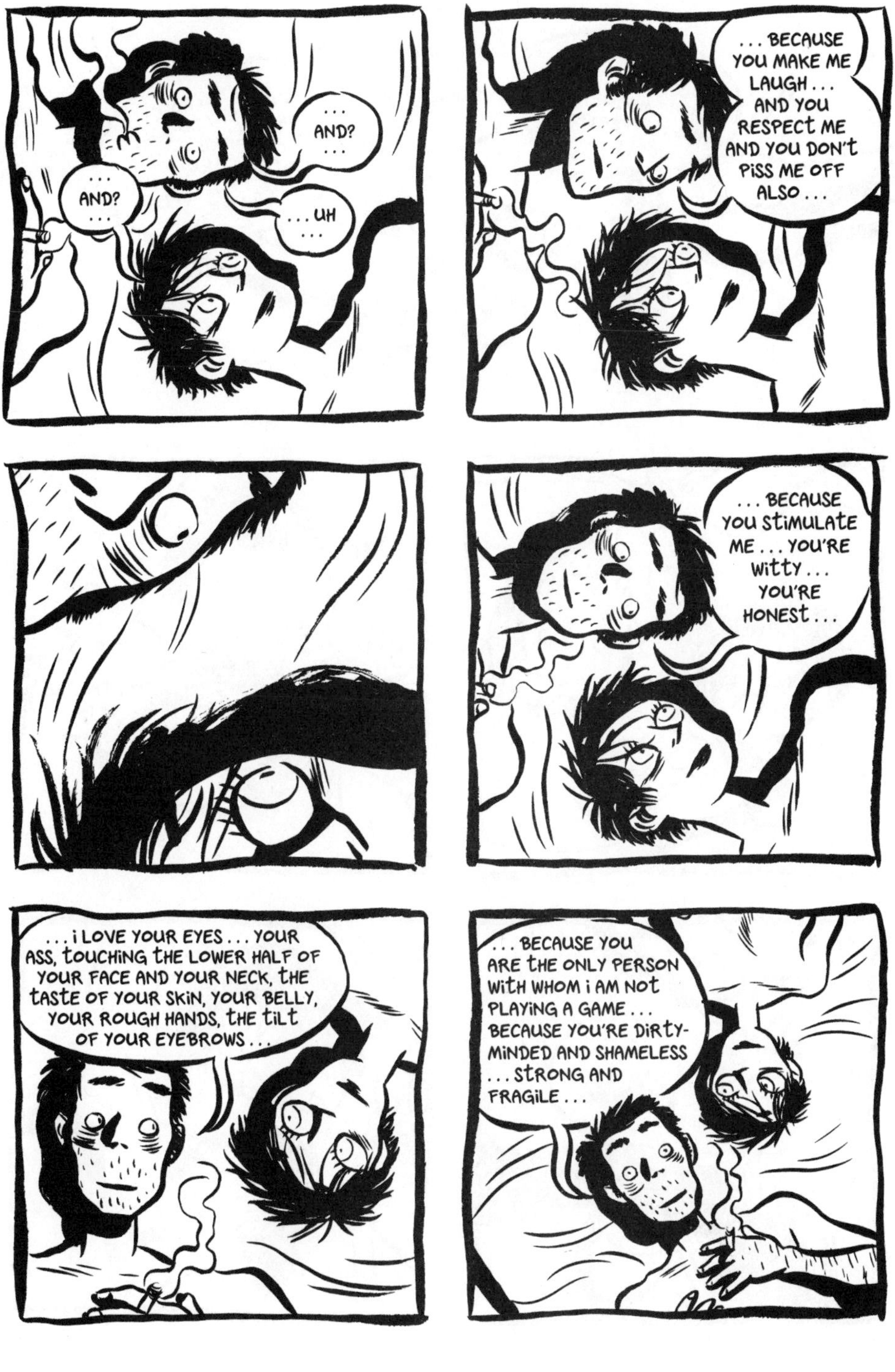
. . . AND? . . .
. . . UH . . .
. . . AND? . . .
. . . BECAUSE YOU MAKE ME LAUGH . . . AND YOU RESPECT ME AND YOU DON'T PISS ME OFF ALSO . . .
. . . BECAUSE YOU STIMULATE ME . . . YOU'RE WITTY . . . YOU'RE HONEST . . .
. . . I LOVE YOUR EYES . . . YOUR ASS, TOUCHING THE LOWER HALF OF YOUR FACE AND YOUR NECK, THE TASTE OF YOUR SKIN, YOUR BELLY, YOUR ROUGH HANDS, THE TILT OF YOUR EYEBROWS . . .
. . . BECAUSE YOU ARE THE ONLY PERSON WITH WHOM I AM NOT PLAYING A GAME . . . BECAUSE YOU'RE DIRTY-MINDED AND SHAMELESS . . . STRONG AND FRAGILE . . .

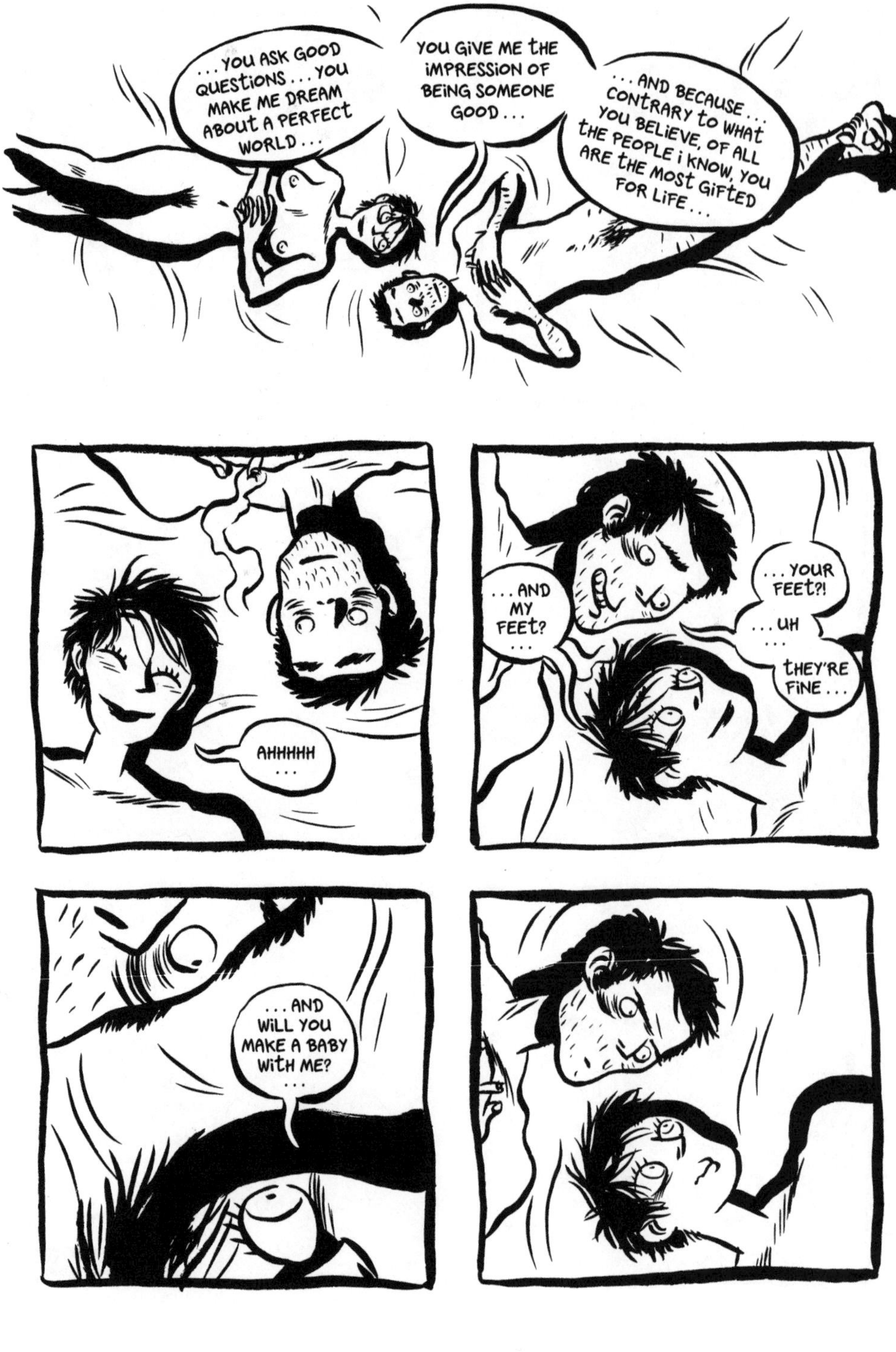
...YOU ASK GOOD QUESTIONS...YOU MAKE ME DREAM ABOUT A PERFECT WORLD...
YOU GIVE ME THE IMPRESSION OF BEING SOMEONE GOOD...
...AND BECAUSE... CONTRARY TO WHAT YOU BELIEVE, OF ALL THE PEOPLE I KNOW, YOU ARE THE MOST GIFTED FOR LIFE...
AHHHHH...
...AND MY FEET?...
...YOUR FEET?!
...UH...
THEY'RE FINE...
...AND WILL YOU MAKE A BABY WITH ME?...

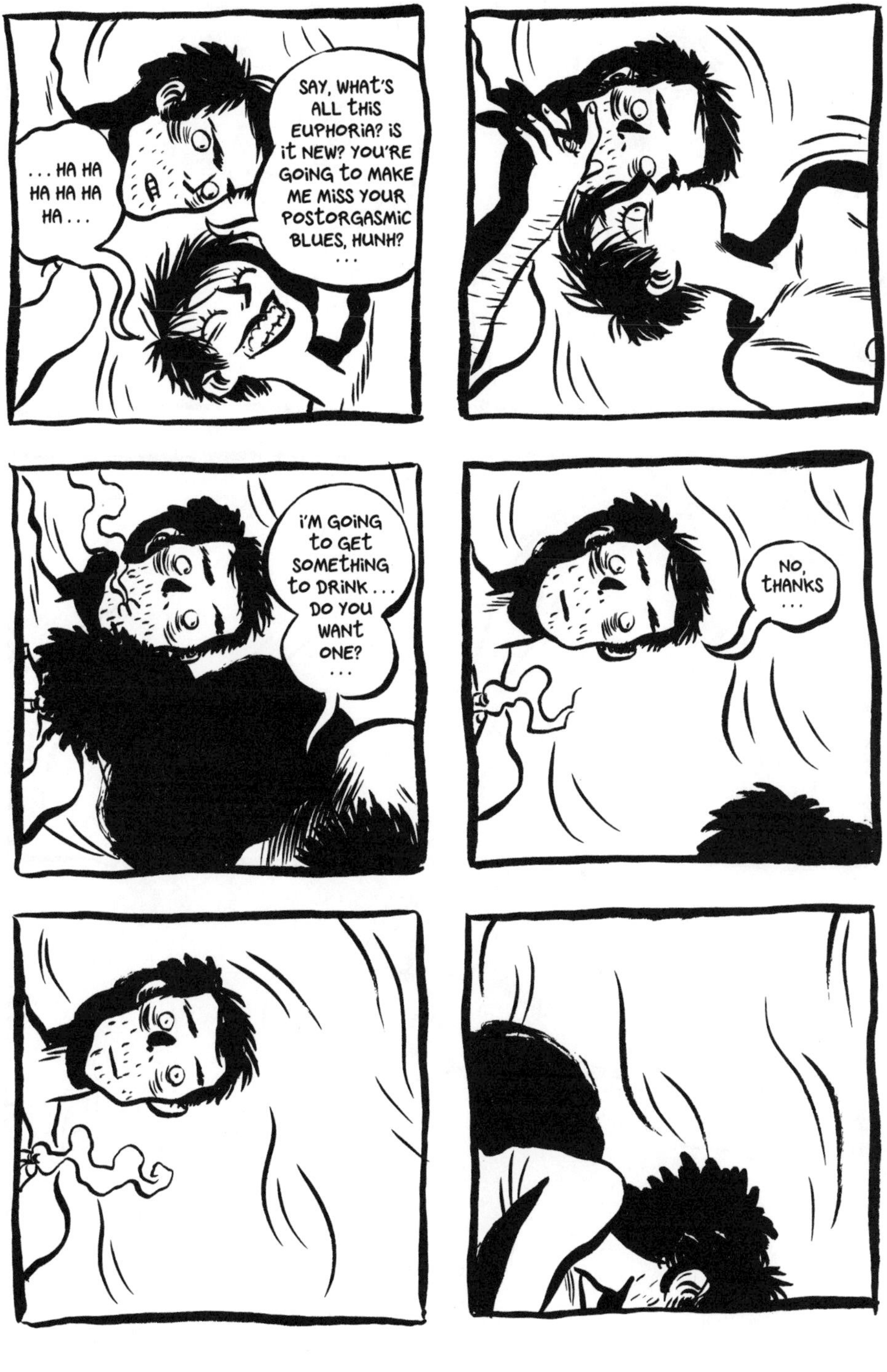

... HA HA HA HA HA HA ...
SAY, WHAT'S ALL THIS EUPHORIA? IS IT NEW? YOU'RE GOING TO MAKE ME MISS YOUR POSTORGASMIC BLUES, HUNH? ...
I'M GOING TO GET SOMETHING TO DRINK ... DO YOU WANT ONE? ...
NO, THANKS ...

FALEO 03.01

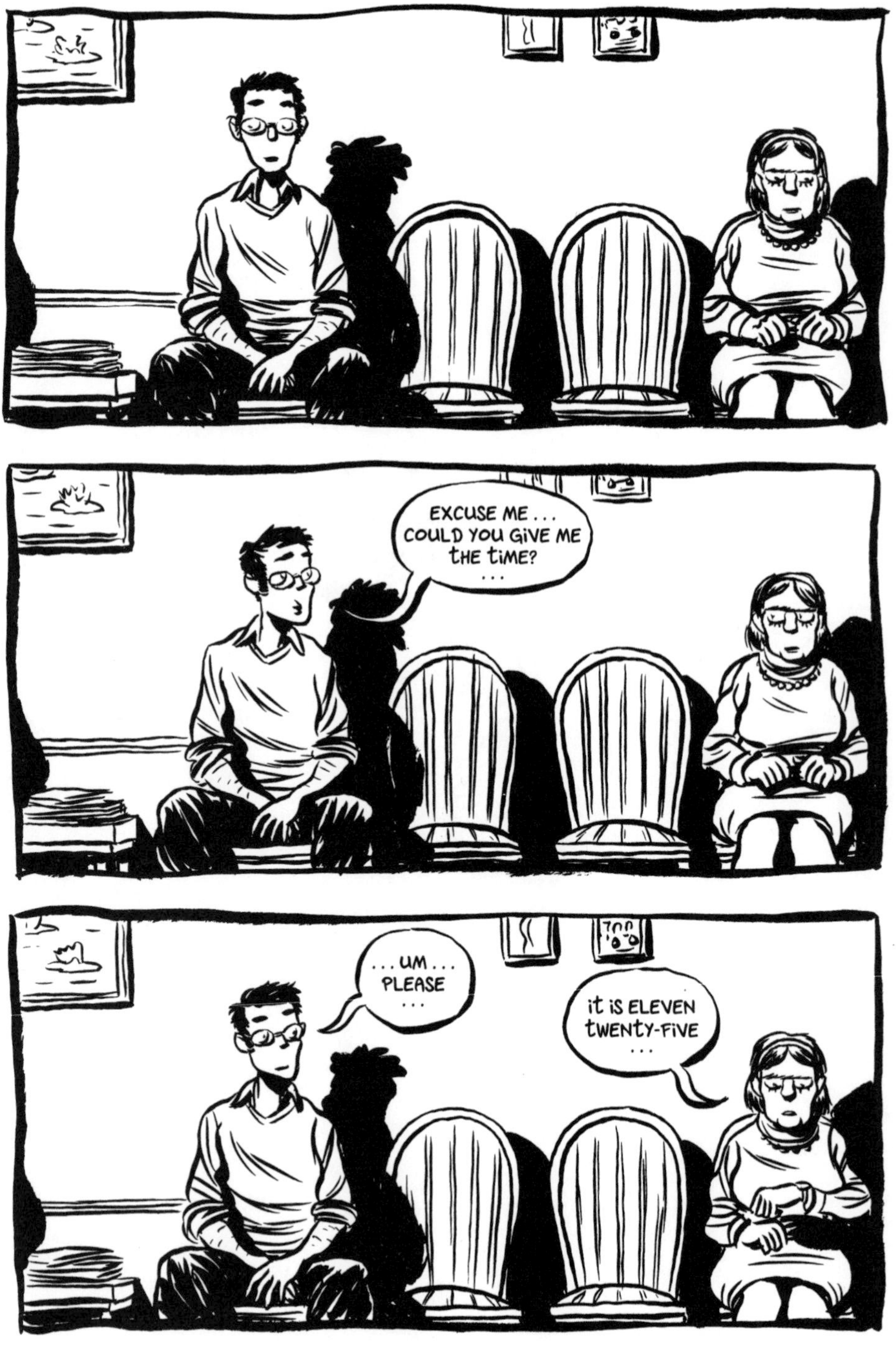
EXCUSE ME . . . COULD YOU GIVE ME THE TIME? . . .
. . . UM . . . PLEASE . . .
IT IS ELEVEN TWENTY-FIVE . . .

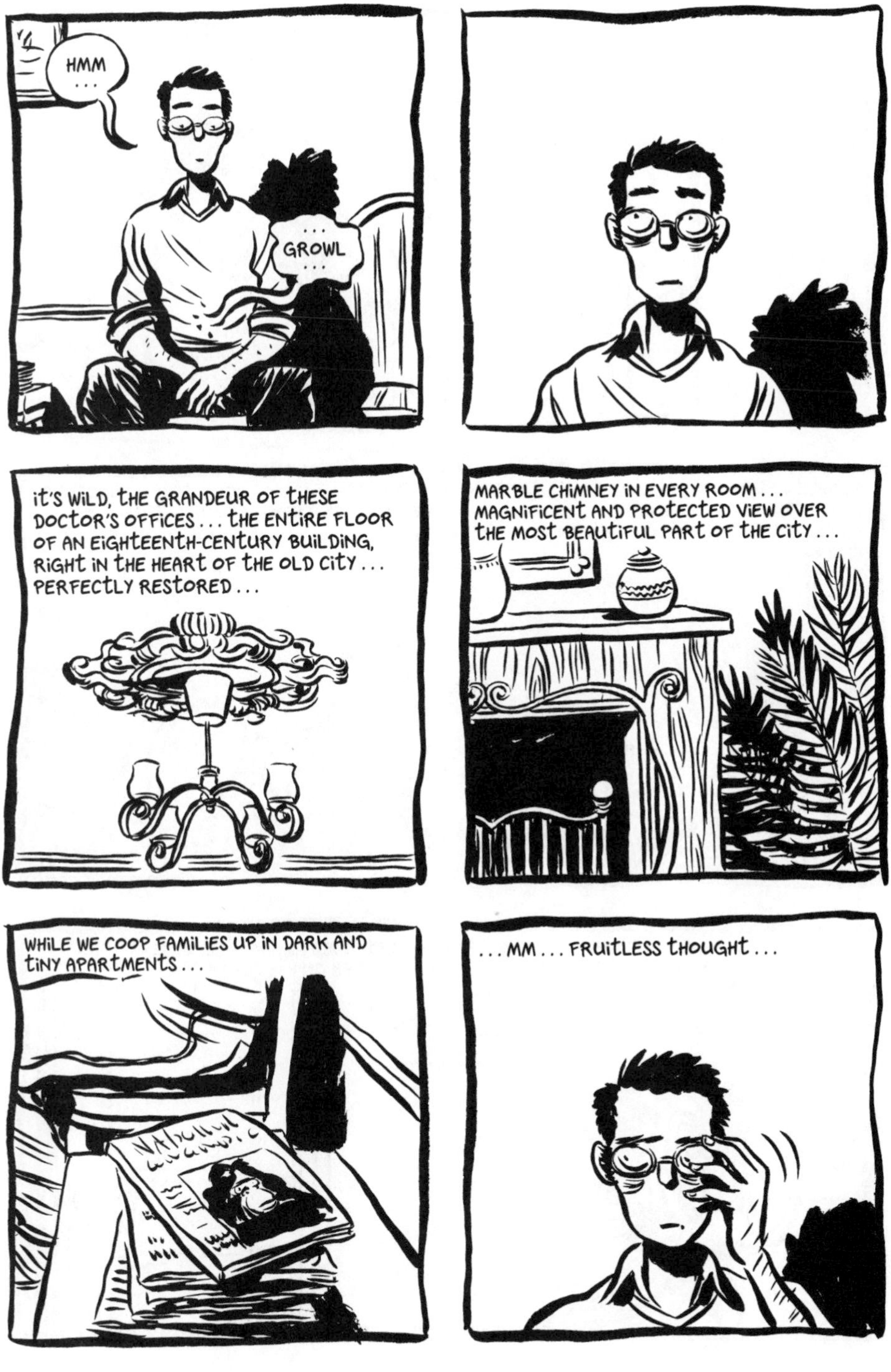
HMM . . .
. . . GROWL . . .
it'S WiLD, THE GRANDEUR OF THESE DOCTOR'S OFFiCES . . . THE ENtiRE FLOOR OF AN EiGHtEENtH-CENTURY BUiLDiNG, RiGHt iN THE HEARt OF tHE OLD City . . . PERFECtLY RESTORED . . .
MARBLE CHiMNEY iN EVERY ROOM . . . MAGNiFiCENt AND PROTECTED ViEW OVER THE MOST BEAUtiFUL PARt OF THE City . . .
WHiLE WE COOP FAMiLiES UP iN DARK AND tiNY APARtMENtS . . .
. . . MM . . . FRUitLESS tHOUGHt . . .

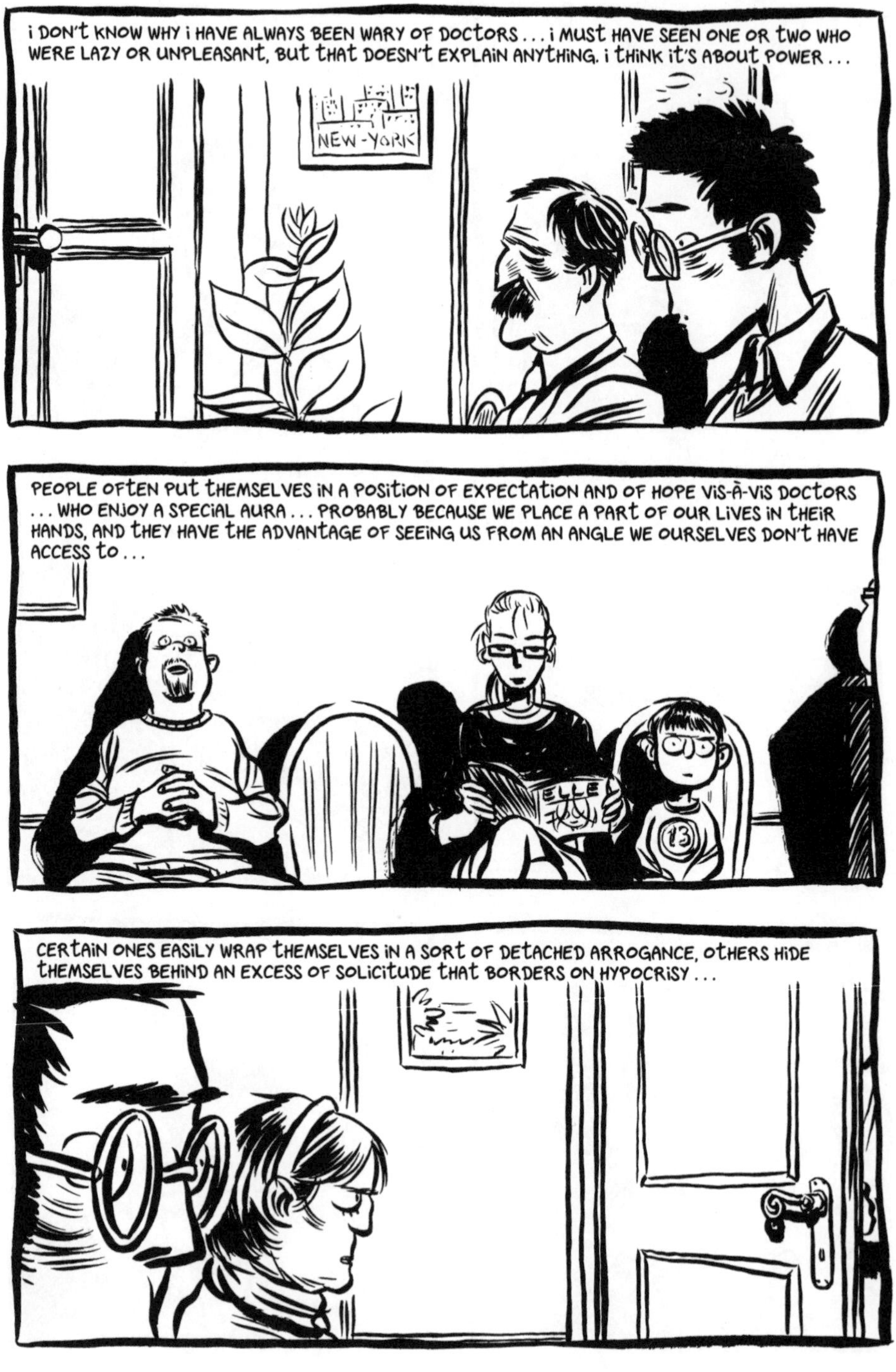
I DON'T KNOW WHY I HAVE ALWAYS BEEN WARY OF DOCTORS . . . I MUST HAVE SEEN ONE OR TWO WHO WERE LAZY OR UNPLEASANT, BUT THAT DOESN'T EXPLAIN ANYTHING. I THINK IT'S ABOUT POWER . . .
NEW-YORK
PEOPLE OFTEN PUT THEMSELVES IN A POSITION OF EXPECTATION AND OF HOPE VIS-À-VIS DOCTORS . . . WHO ENJOY A SPECIAL AURA . . . PROBABLY BECAUSE WE PLACE A PART OF OUR LIVES IN THEIR HANDS, AND THEY HAVE THE ADVANTAGE OF SEEING US FROM AN ANGLE WE OURSELVES DON'T HAVE ACCESS TO . . .
ELLE
13
CERTAIN ONES EASILY WRAP THEMSELVES IN A SORT OF DETACHED ARROGANCE, OTHERS HIDE THEMSELVES BEHIND AN EXCESS OF SOLICITUDE THAT BORDERS ON HYPOCRISY . . .

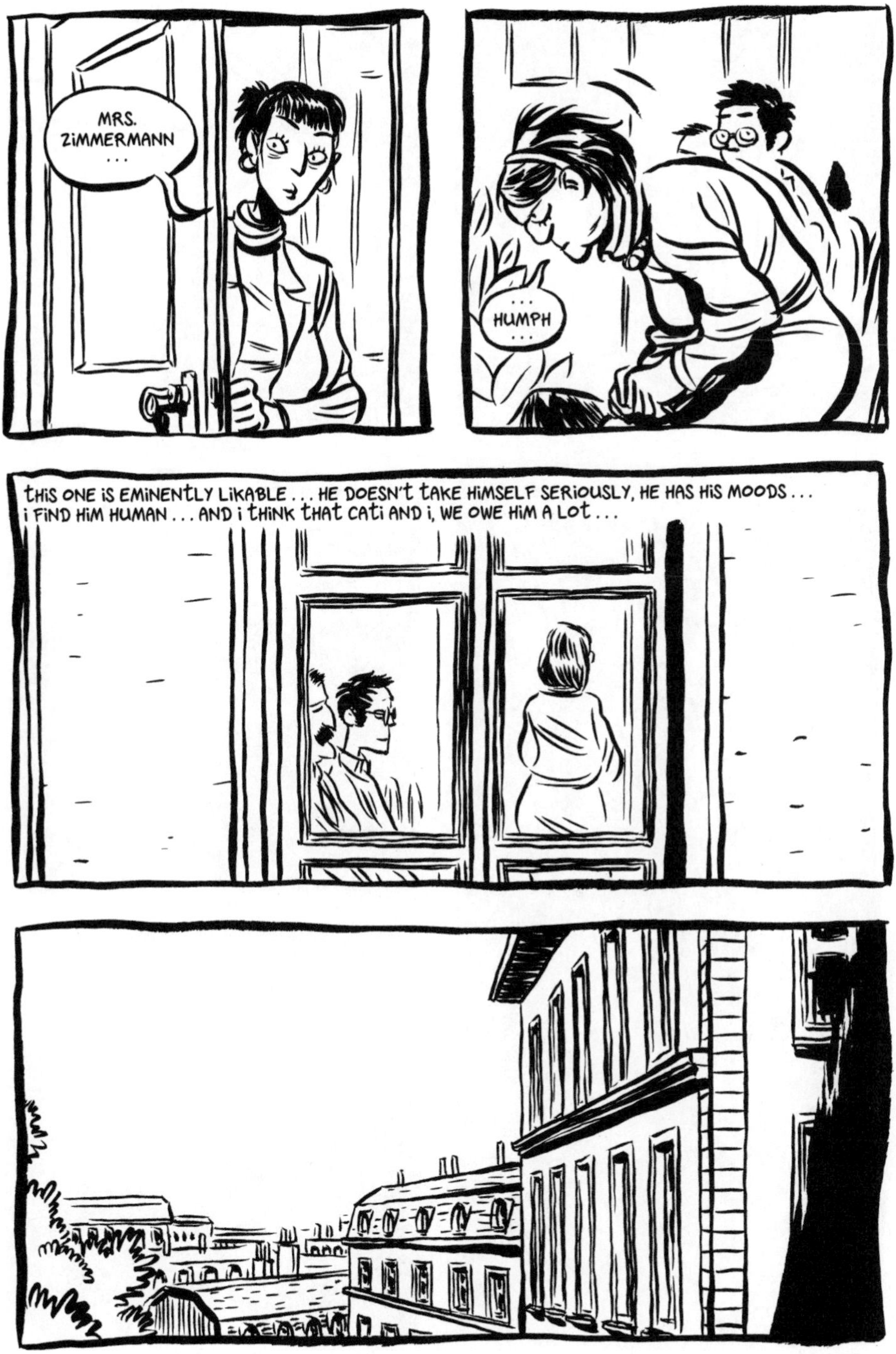
MRS. ZIMMERMANN . . .
. . . HUMPH . . .
THIS ONE IS EMINENTLY LIKABLE . . . HE DOESN'T TAKE HIMSELF SERIOUSLY, HE HAS HIS MOODS . . . I FIND HIM HUMAN . . . AND I THINK THAT CATI AND I, WE OWE HIM A LOT . . .

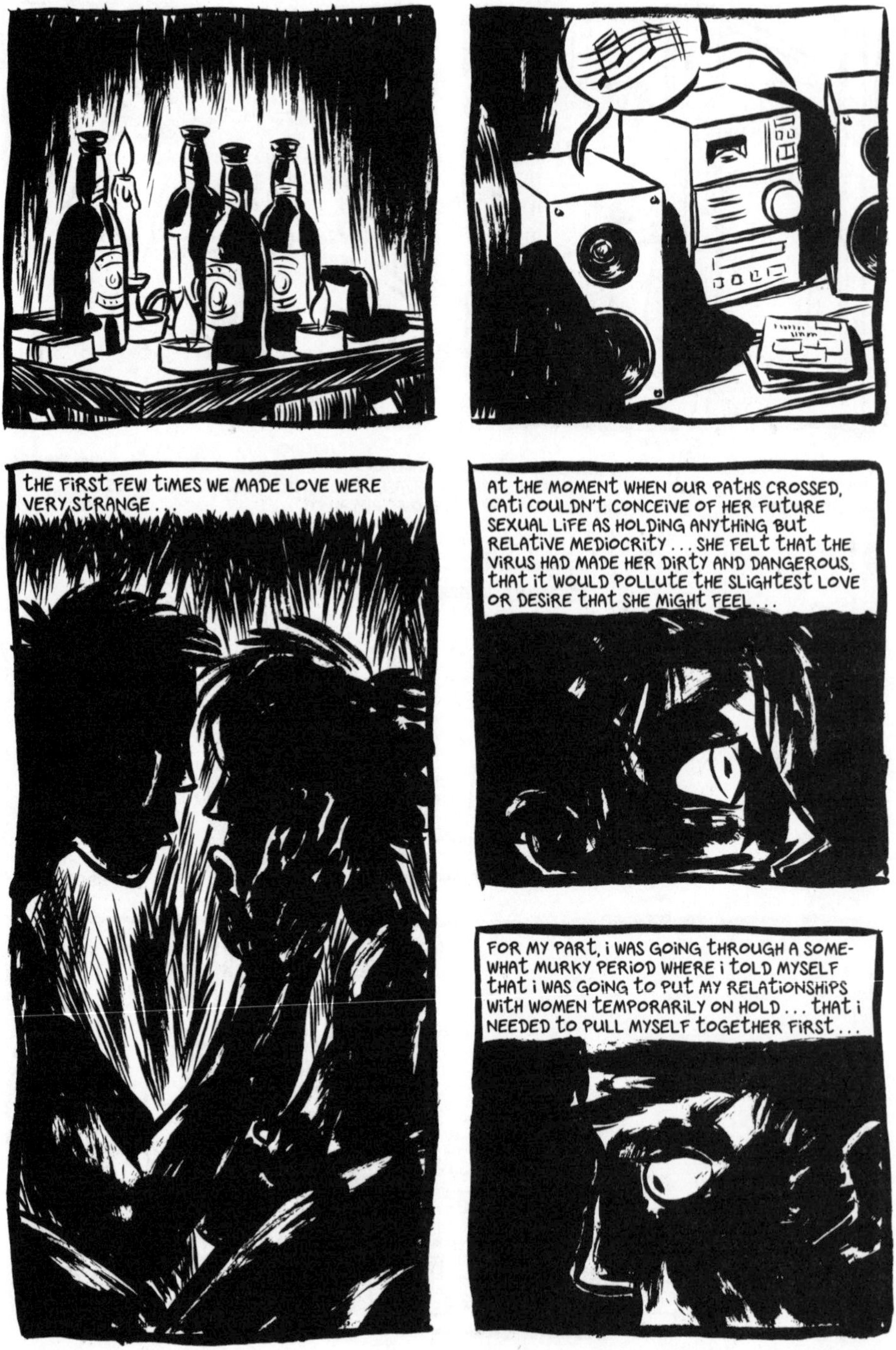
THE FIRST FEW TIMES WE MADE LOVE WERE VERY STRANGE . . .
AT THE MOMENT WHEN OUR PATHS CROSSED, CATI COULDN'T CONCEIVE OF HER FUTURE SEXUAL LIFE AS HOLDING ANYTHING BUT RELATIVE MEDIOCRITY . . . SHE FELT THAT THE VIRUS HAD MADE HER DIRTY AND DANGEROUS, THAT IT WOULD POLLUTE THE SLIGHTEST LOVE OR DESIRE THAT SHE MIGHT FEEL . . .
FOR MY PART, I WAS GOING THROUGH A SOME-WHAT MURKY PERIOD WHERE I TOLD MYSELF THAT I WAS GOING TO PUT MY RELATIONSHIPS WITH WOMEN TEMPORARILY ON HOLD . . . THAT I NEEDED TO PULL MYSELF TOGETHER FIRST . . .

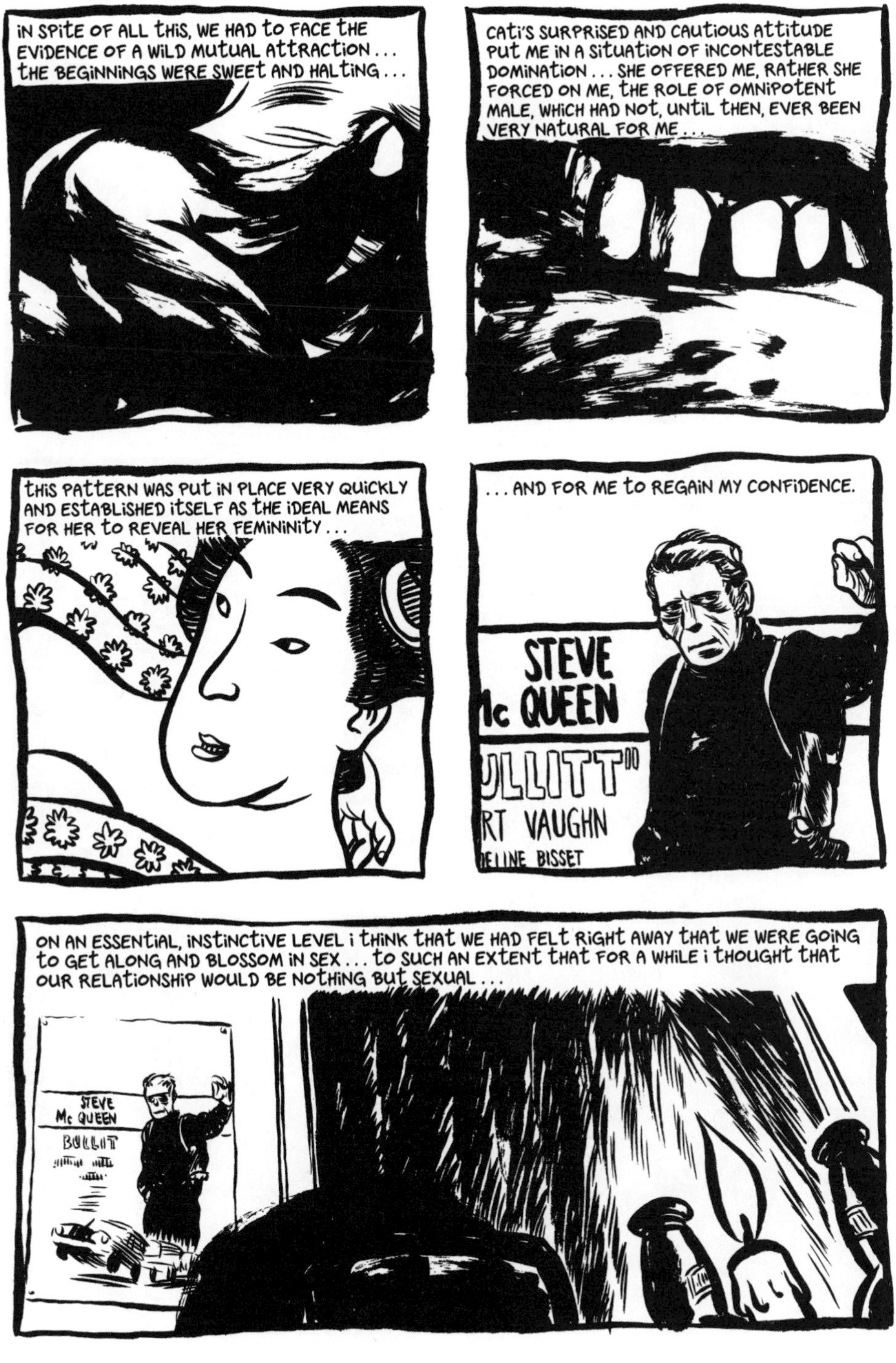
IN SPITE OF ALL THIS, WE HAD TO FACE THE EVIDENCE OF A WILD MUTUAL ATTRACTION . . . THE BEGINNINGS WERE SWEET AND HALTING . . .
CATI'S SURPRISED AND CAUTIOUS ATTITUDE PUT ME IN A SITUATION OF INCONTESTABLE DOMINATION . . . SHE OFFERED ME, RATHER SHE FORCED ON ME, THE ROLE OF OMNIPOTENT MALE, WHICH HAD NOT, UNTIL THEN, EVER BEEN VERY NATURAL FOR ME . . .
THIS PATTERN WAS PUT IN PLACE VERY QUICKLY AND ESTABLISHED ITSELF AS THE IDEAL MEANS FOR HER TO REVEAL HER FEMININITY . . .
. . . AND FOR ME TO REGAIN MY CONFIDENCE.
STEVE
Mc QUEEN
ULLITT"
RT VAUGHN
ELINE BISSET
ON AN ESSENTIAL, INSTINCTIVE LEVEL I THINK THAT WE HAD FELT RIGHT AWAY THAT WE WERE GOING TO GET ALONG AND BLOSSOM IN SEX . . . TO SUCH AN EXTENT THAT FOR A WHILE I THOUGHT THAT OUR RELATIONSHIP WOULD BE NOTHING BUT SEXUAL . . .
STEVE
Mc QUEEN
BULLIT

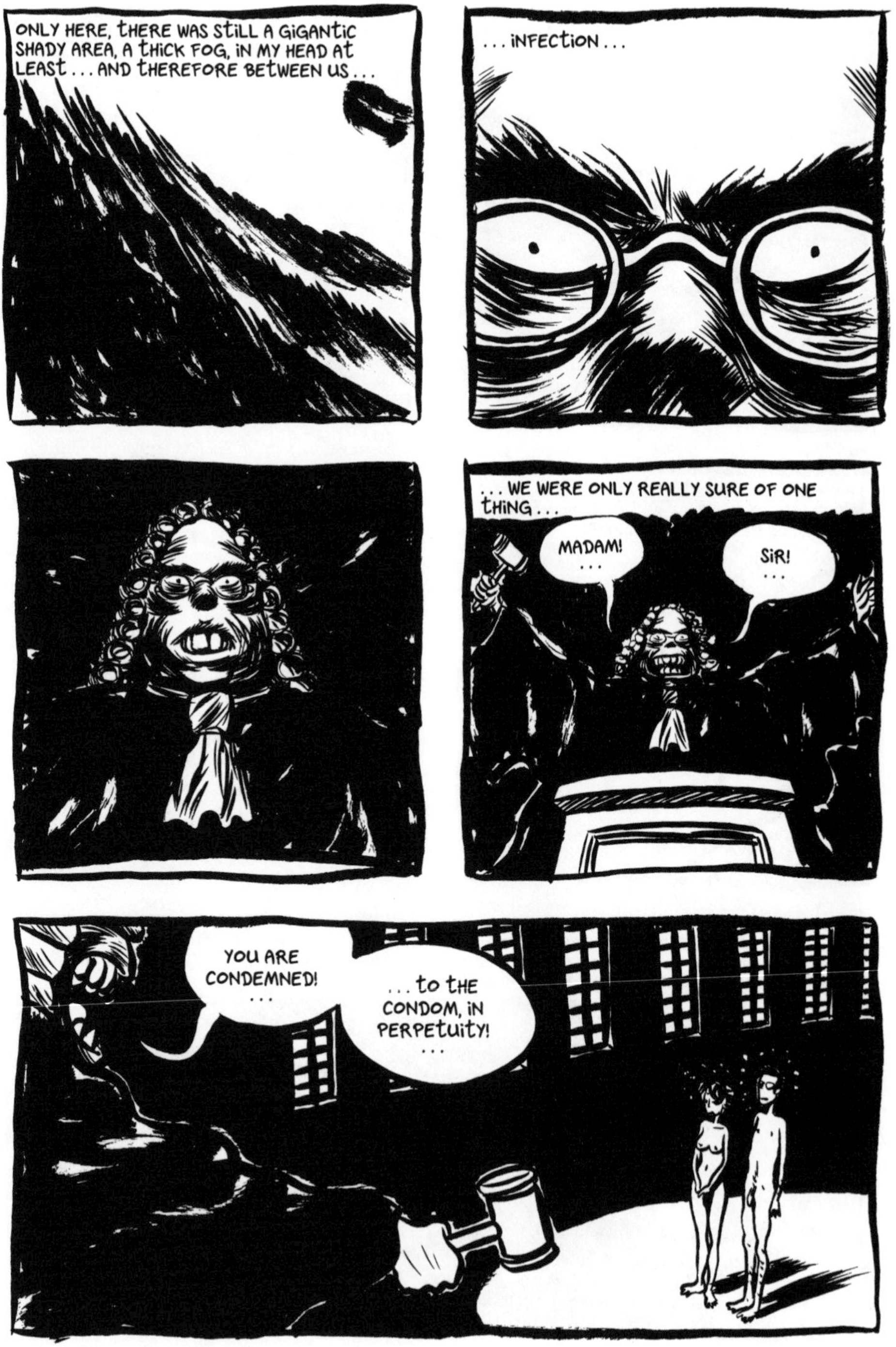
ONLY HERE, THERE WAS STILL A GIGANTIC SHADY AREA, A THICK FOG, IN MY HEAD AT LEAST . . . AND THEREFORE BETWEEN US . . .
. . . INFECTION . . .
. . . WE WERE ONLY REALLY SURE OF ONE THING . . .
MADAM! . . .
SIR! . . .
YOU ARE CONDEMNED! . . .
. . . TO THE CONDOM, IN PERPETUITY! . . .

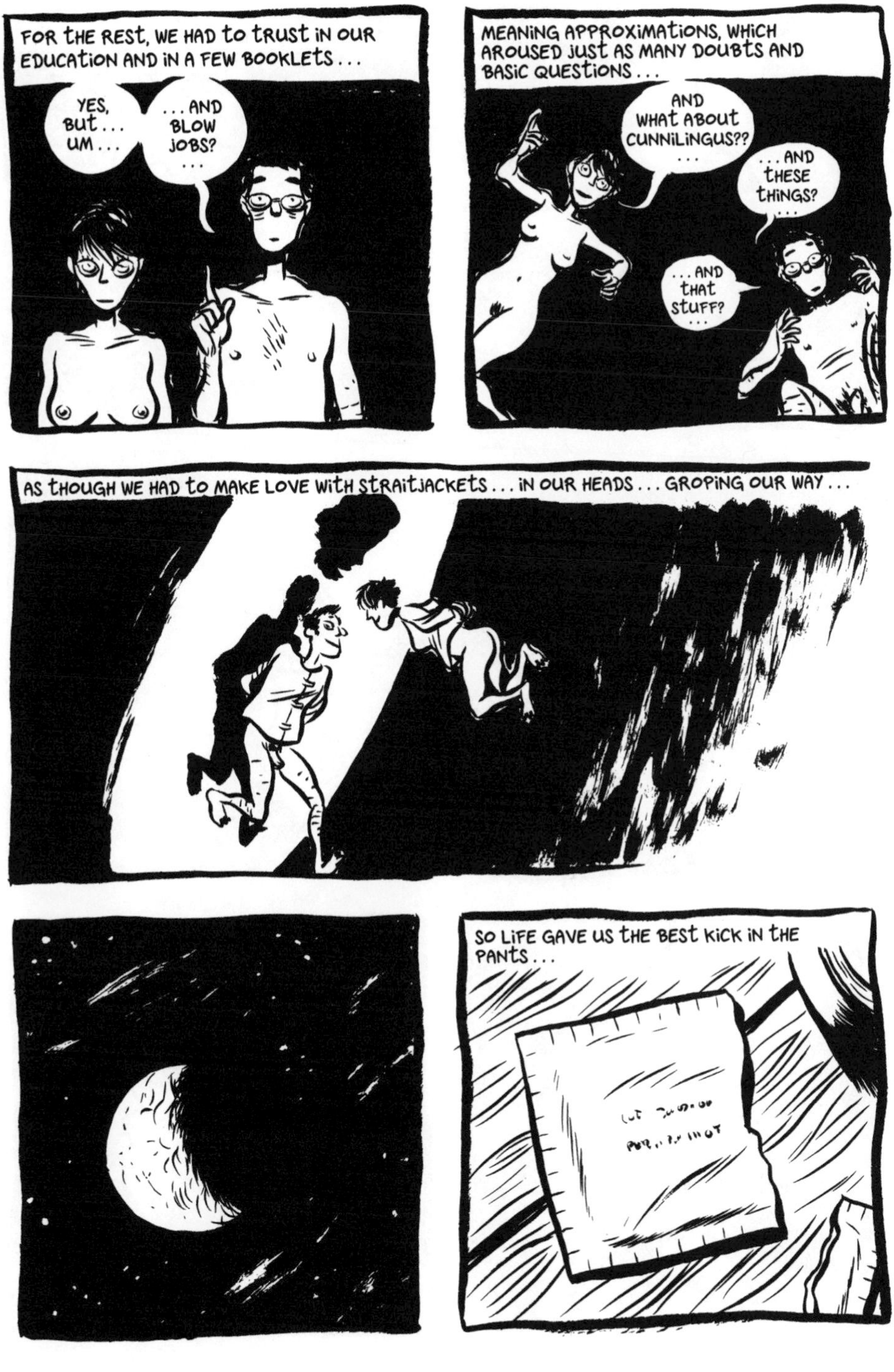
FOR THE REST, WE HAD TO TRUST IN OUR EDUCATION AND IN A FEW BOOKLETS . . .
YES, BUT . . . UM . . .
. . . AND BLOW JOBS? . . .
MEANING APPROXIMATIONS, WHICH AROUSED JUST AS MANY DOUBTS AND BASIC QUESTIONS . . .
AND WHAT ABOUT CUNNILINGUS?? . . .
. . . AND THESE THINGS? . . .
. . . AND THAT STUFF? . . .
AS THOUGH WE HAD TO MAKE LOVE WITH STRAITJACKETS . . . IN OUR HEADS . . . GROPING OUR WAY . . .
SO LIFE GAVE US THE BEST KICK IN THE PANTS . . .

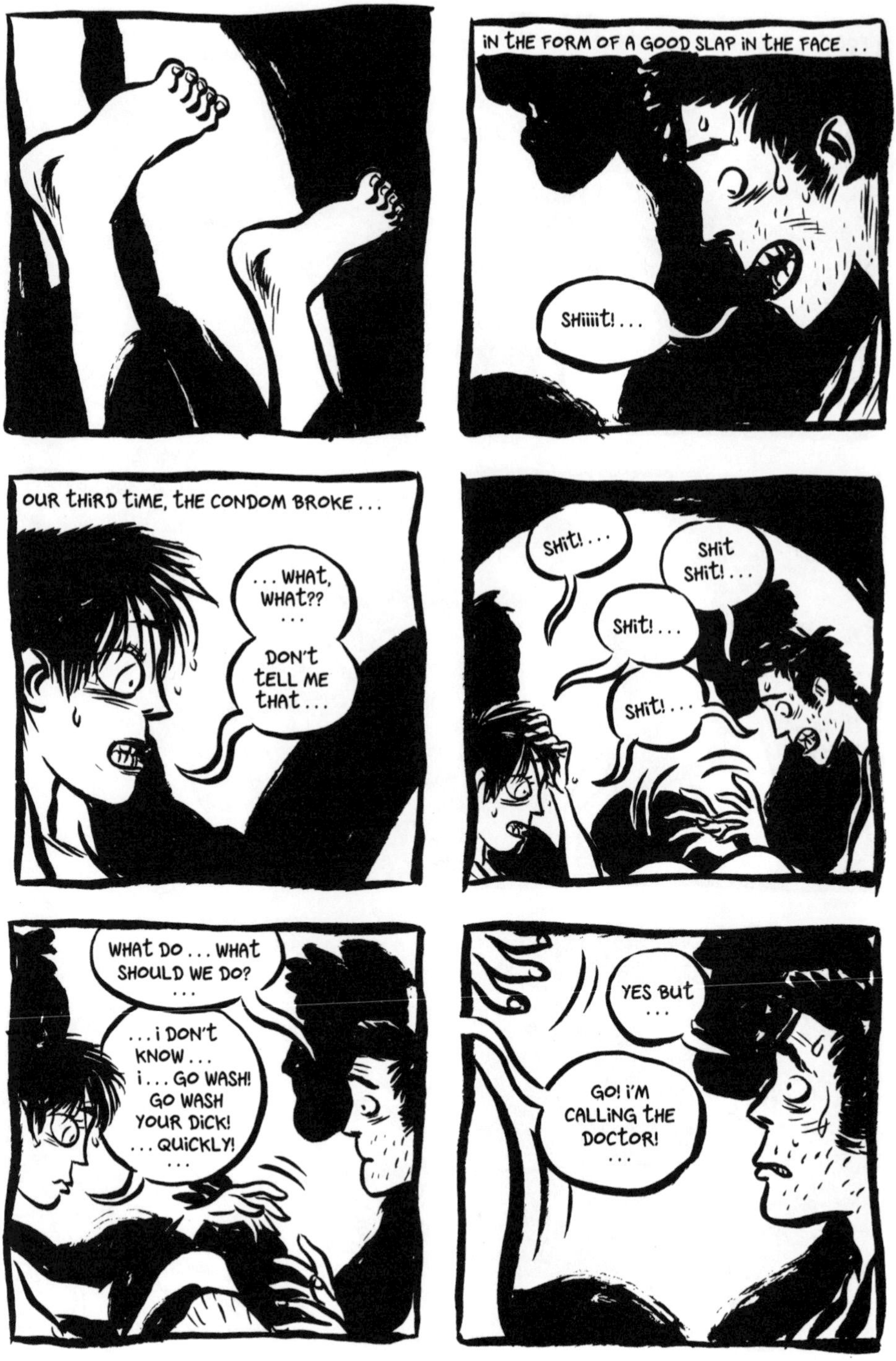
IN THE FORM OF A GOOD SLAP IN THE FACE . . .
SHiiiit! . . .
OUR THIRD TIME, THE CONDOM BROKE . . .
. . . WHAT, WHAT?? . . .
DON'T TELL ME THAT . . .
SHit! . . .
SHit SHit! . . .
SHit! . . .
SHit! . . .
WHAT DO . . . WHAT SHOULD WE DO? . . .
. . . i DON'T KNOW . . . i . . . GO WASH! GO WASH YOUR DiCK! . . . QUiCKLY! . . .
YES BUT . . .
GO! i'M CALLiNG THE DOCTOR! . . .

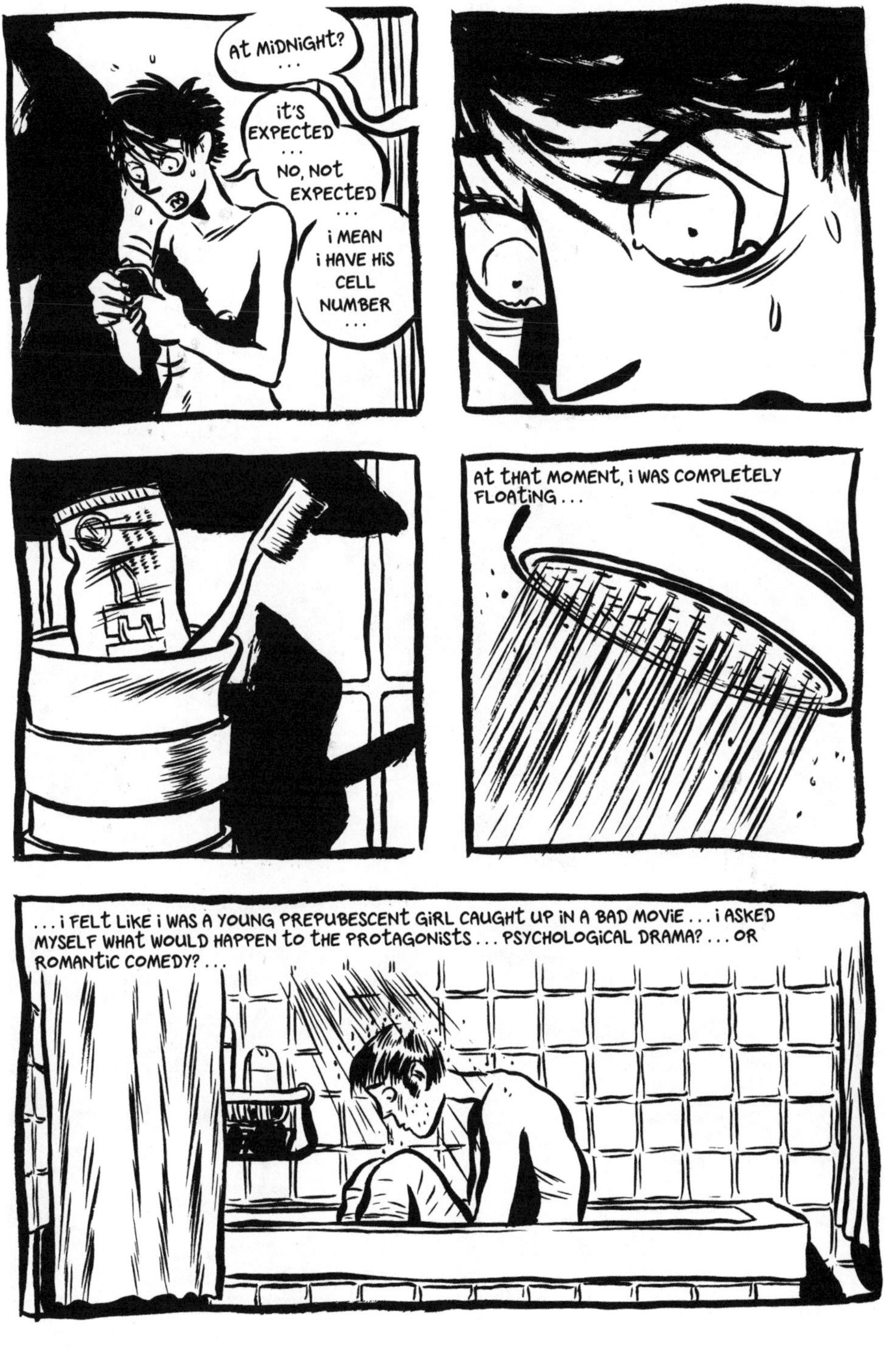
At MiDNiGHt?
. . .
it's EXPECTED
. . .
NO, NOt EXPECTED
. . .
i MEAN i HAVE HiS CELL NUMBER
. . .
At tHAt MOMENT, i WAS COMPLETELY FLOAtiNG . . .
. . . i FELt LiKE i WAS A YOUNG PREPUBESCENt GiRL CAUGHt UP iN A BAD MOViE . . . i ASKED MYSELF WHAt WOULD HAPPEN to tHE PROtAGONiStS . . . PSYCHOLOGiCAL DRAMA? . . . OR ROMANtiC COMEDY? . . .

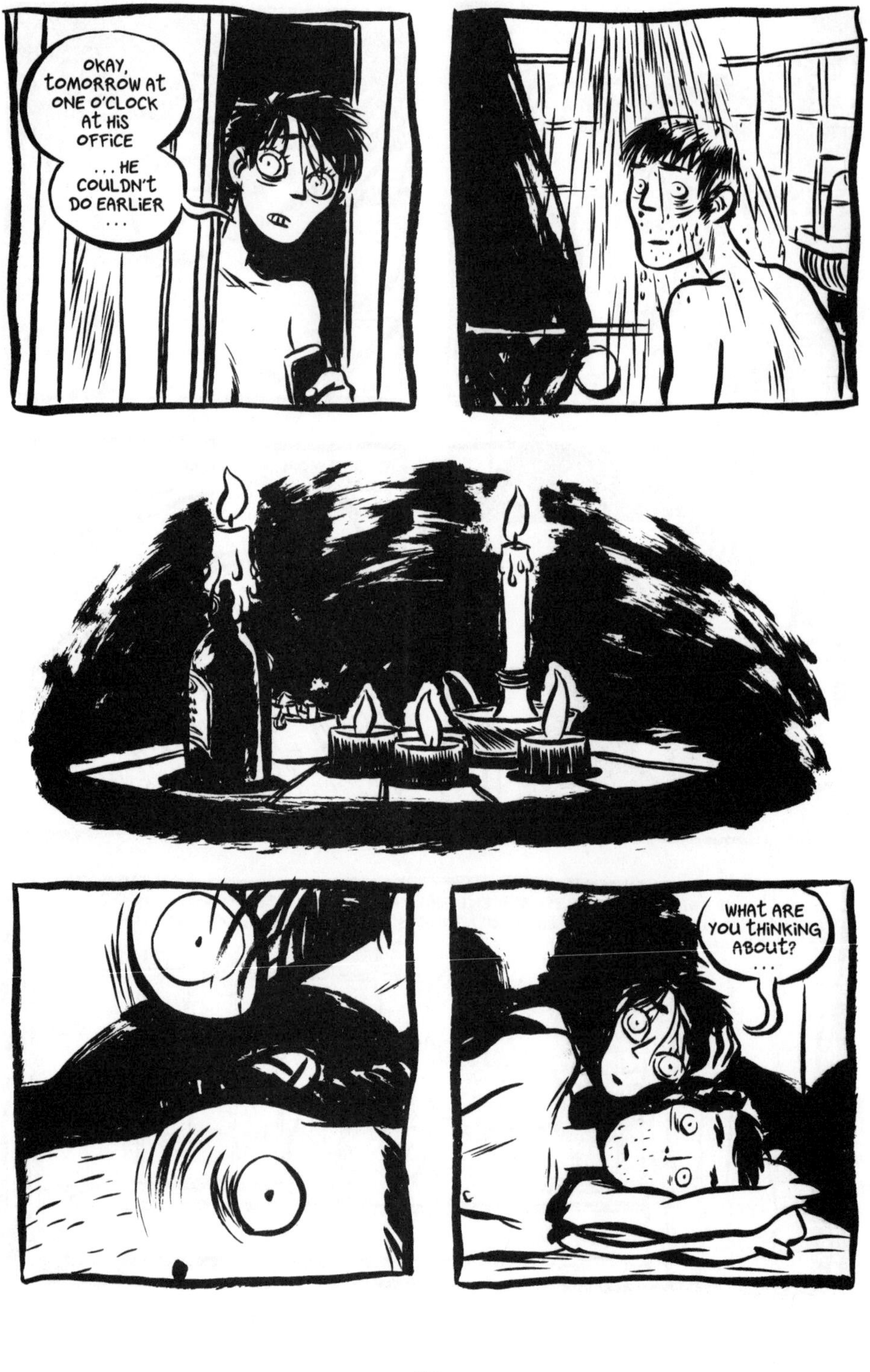
OKAY, TOMORROW AT ONE O'CLOCK AT HIS OFFICE
. . . HE COULDN'T DO EARLIER . . .
WHAT ARE YOU THINKING ABOUT? . . .

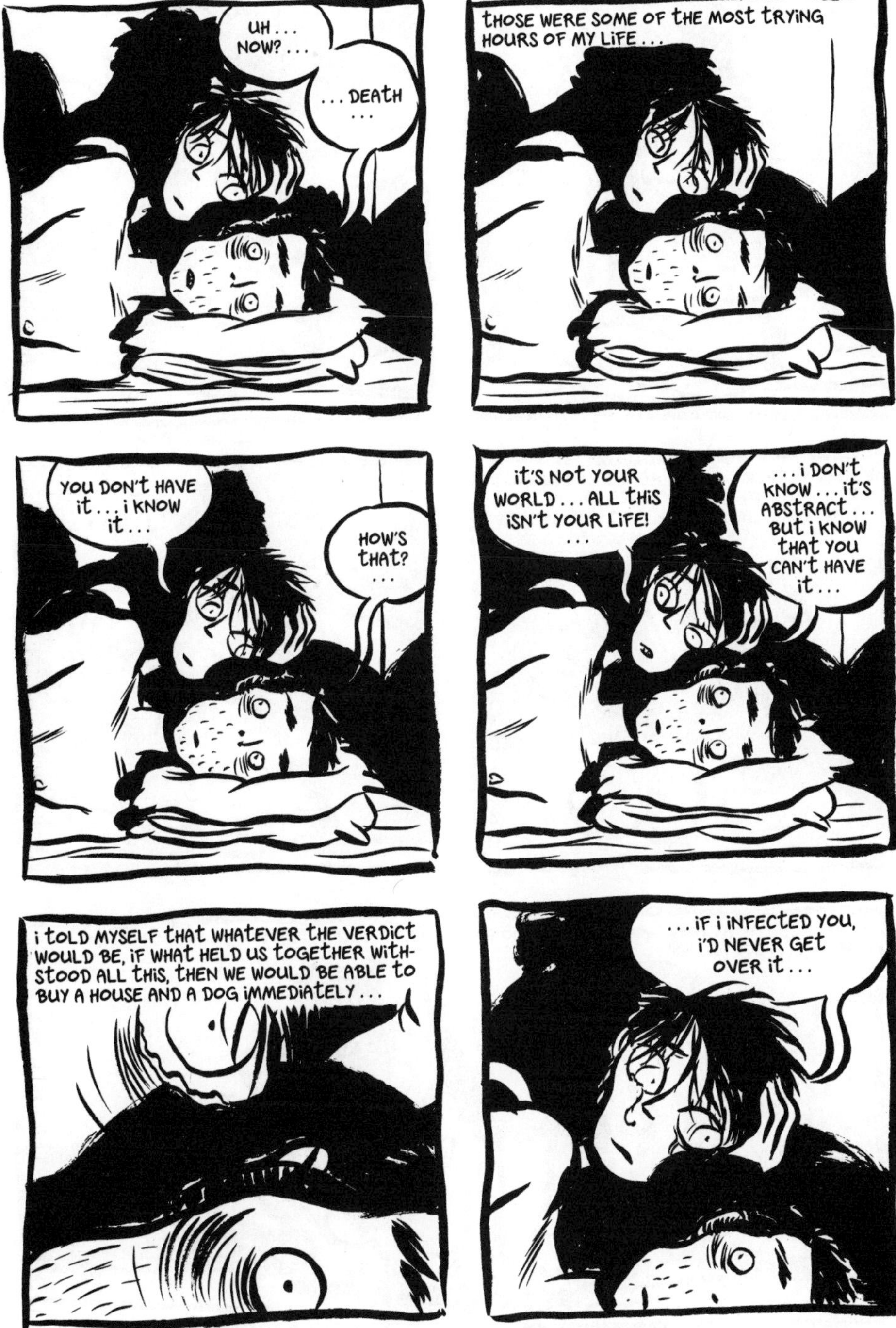
UH . . . NOW? . . .
. . . DEATH . . .
THOSE WERE SOME OF THE MOST TRYING HOURS OF MY LIFE . . .
YOU DON'T HAVE it . . . i KNOW it . . .
HOW'S THAT? . . .
it'S NOT YOUR WORLD . . . ALL THIS iSN'T YOUR LiFE! . . .
. . . i DON'T KNOW . . . it'S ABSTRACT . . . But i KNOW THAT YOU CAN'T HAVE it . . .
i TOLD MYSELF THAT WHATEVER THE VERDICT WOULD BE, iF WHAT HELD US TOGETHER WITH-STOOD ALL THIS, THEN WE WOULD BE ABLE TO BUY A HOUSE AND A DOG iMMEDiATELY . . .
. . . iF i iNFECTED YOU, i'D NEVER GET OVER it . . .

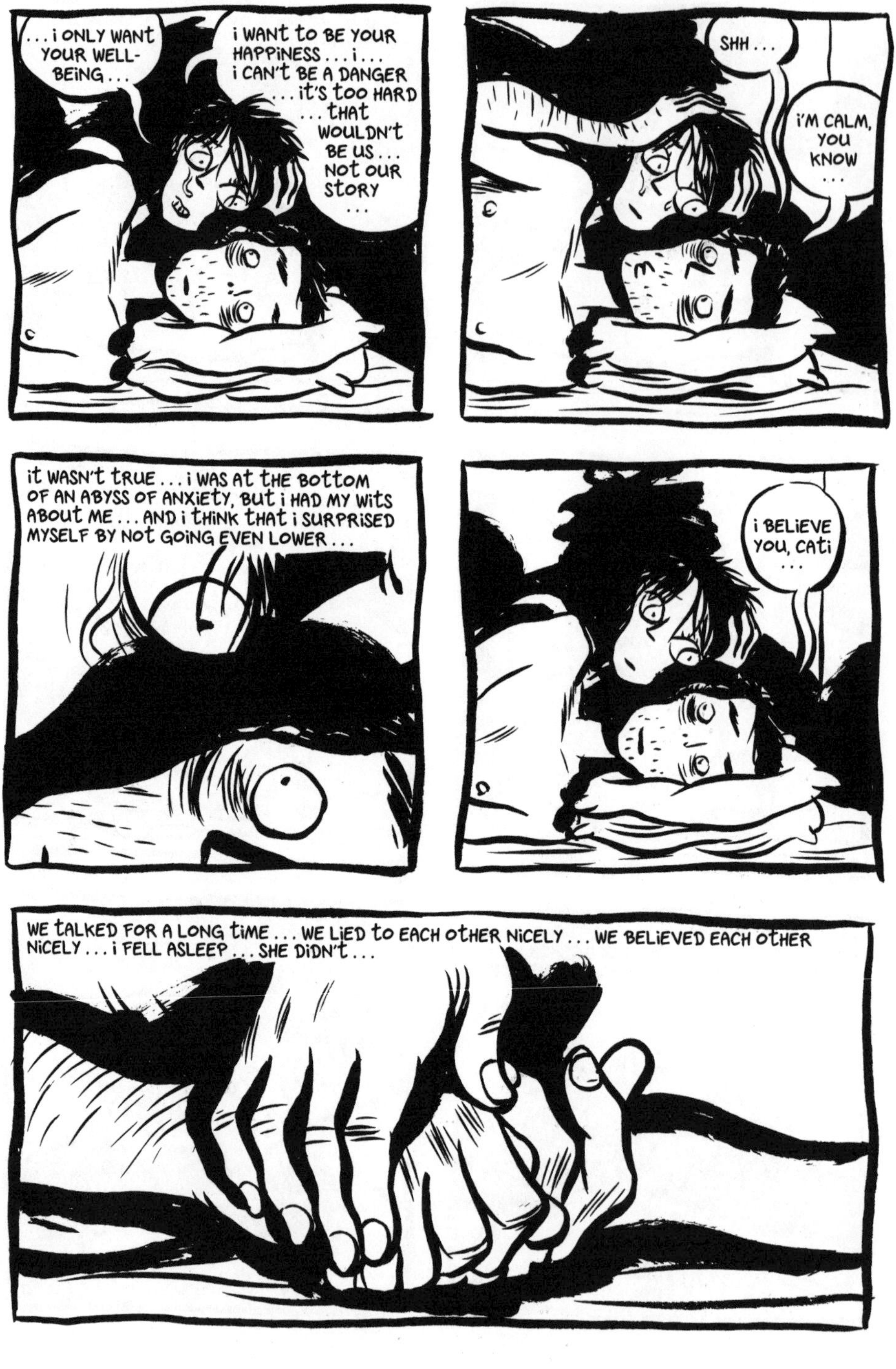

. . . i ONLY WANT YOUR WELL-BEiNG . . .
i WANT to BE YOUR HAPPiNESS . . . i . . . i CAN'T BE A DANGER . . . it'S too HARD . . . tHAt WOULDN'T BE US . . . NOt OUR StORY . . .
SHH . . .
i'M CALM, YOU KNOW . . .
it WASN't tRUE . . . i WAS At tHE BOttOM OF AN ABYSS OF ANXiEtY, BUt i HAD MY WitS ABOUt ME . . . AND i tHiNK tHAt i SURPRiSED MYSELF BY NOt GOiNG EVEN LOWER . . .
i BELiEVE YOU, CAti . . .
WE tALKED FOR A LONG tiME . . . WE LiED to EACH OtHER NiCELY . . . WE BELiEVED EACH OtHER NiCELY . . . i FELL ASLEEP . . . SHE DiDN't . . .

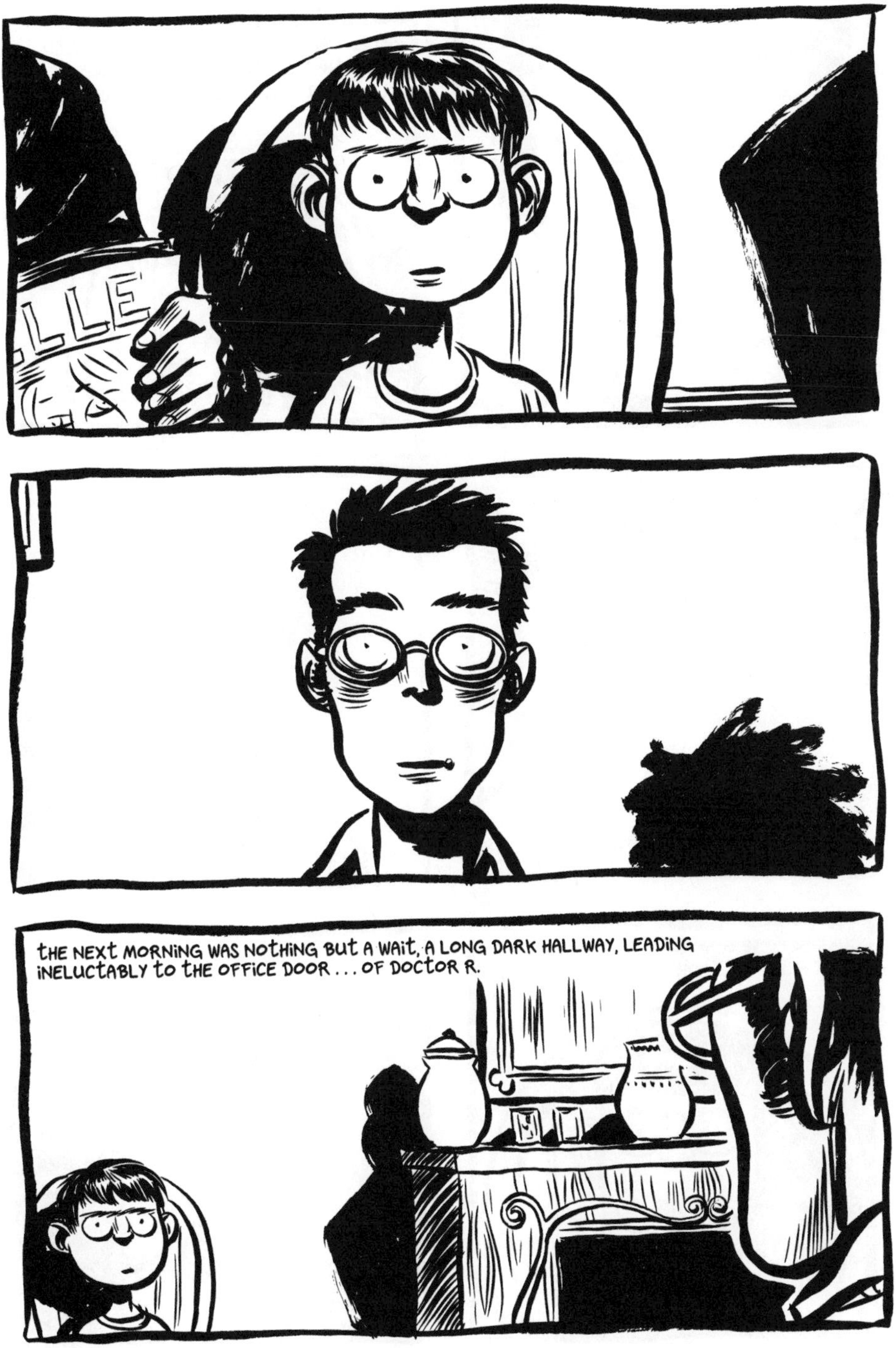
THE NEXT MORNING WAS NOTHING BUT A WAIT, A LONG DARK HALLWAY, LEADING INELUCTABLY TO THE OFFICE DOOR . . . OF DOCTOR R.

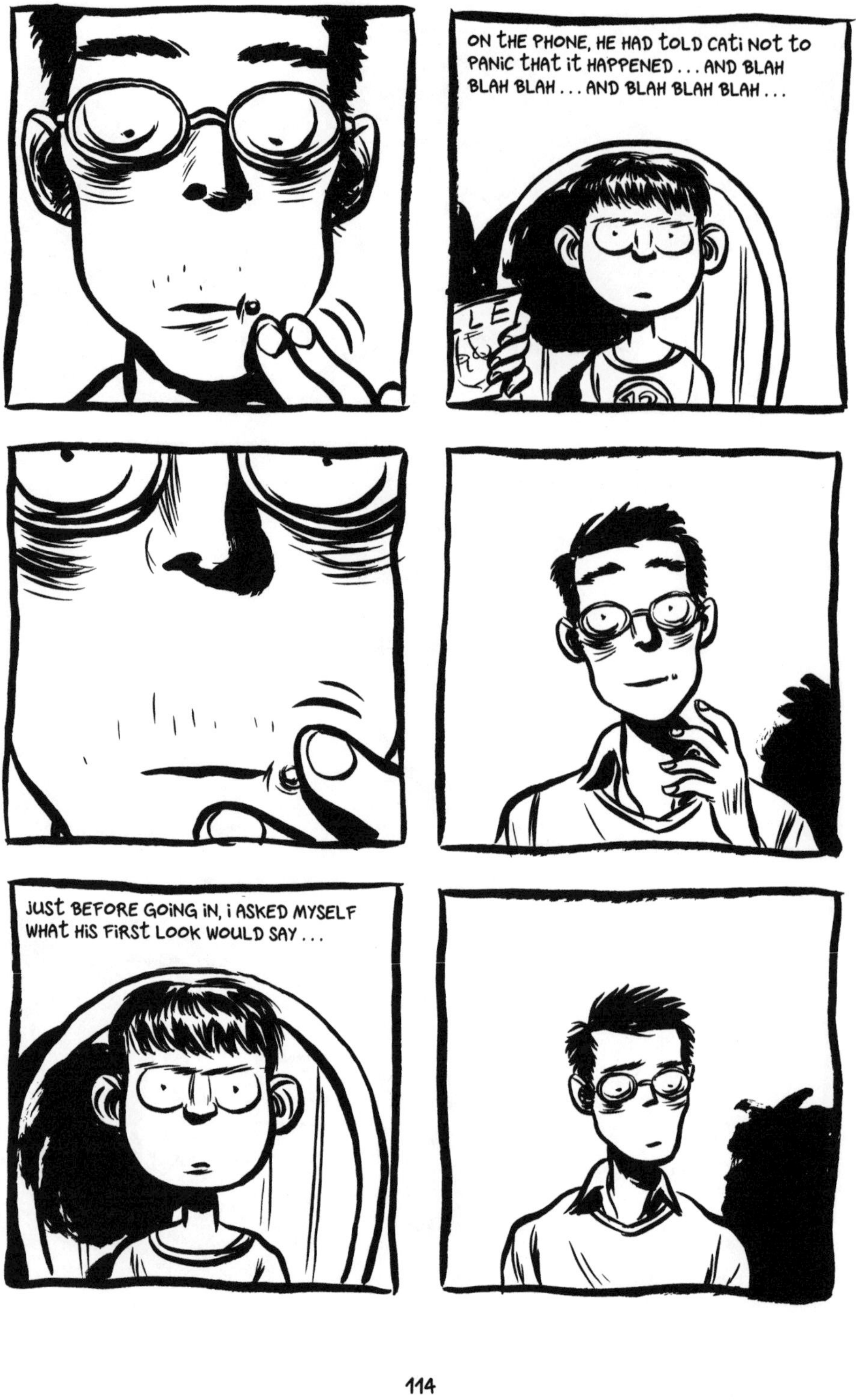
ON THE PHONE, HE HAD TOLD CATI NOT TO PANIC THAT IT HAPPENED . . . AND BLAH BLAH BLAH . . . AND BLAH BLAH BLAH . . .
JUST BEFORE GOING IN, I ASKED MYSELF WHAT HIS FIRST LOOK WOULD SAY . . .

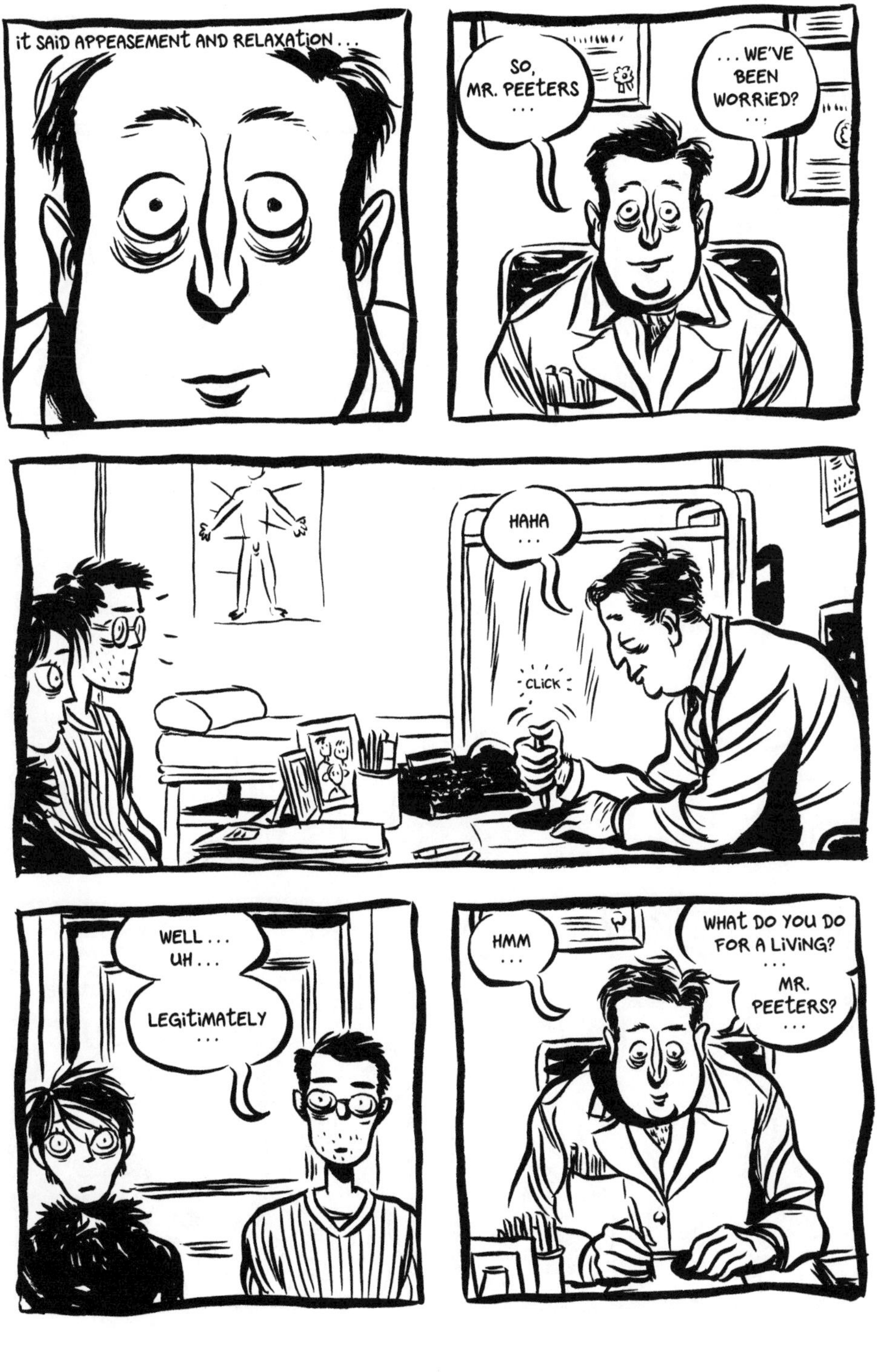
it SAiD APPEASEMENT AND RELAXAtiON . . .
SO, MR. PEEtERS . . .
. . . WE'VE BEEN WORRiED? . . .
HAHA . . .
CLiCK
WELL . . . UH . . .
LEGitiMATELY . . .
HMM . . .
WHAt DO YOU DO FOR A LiViNG? . . .
MR. PEEtERS? . . .

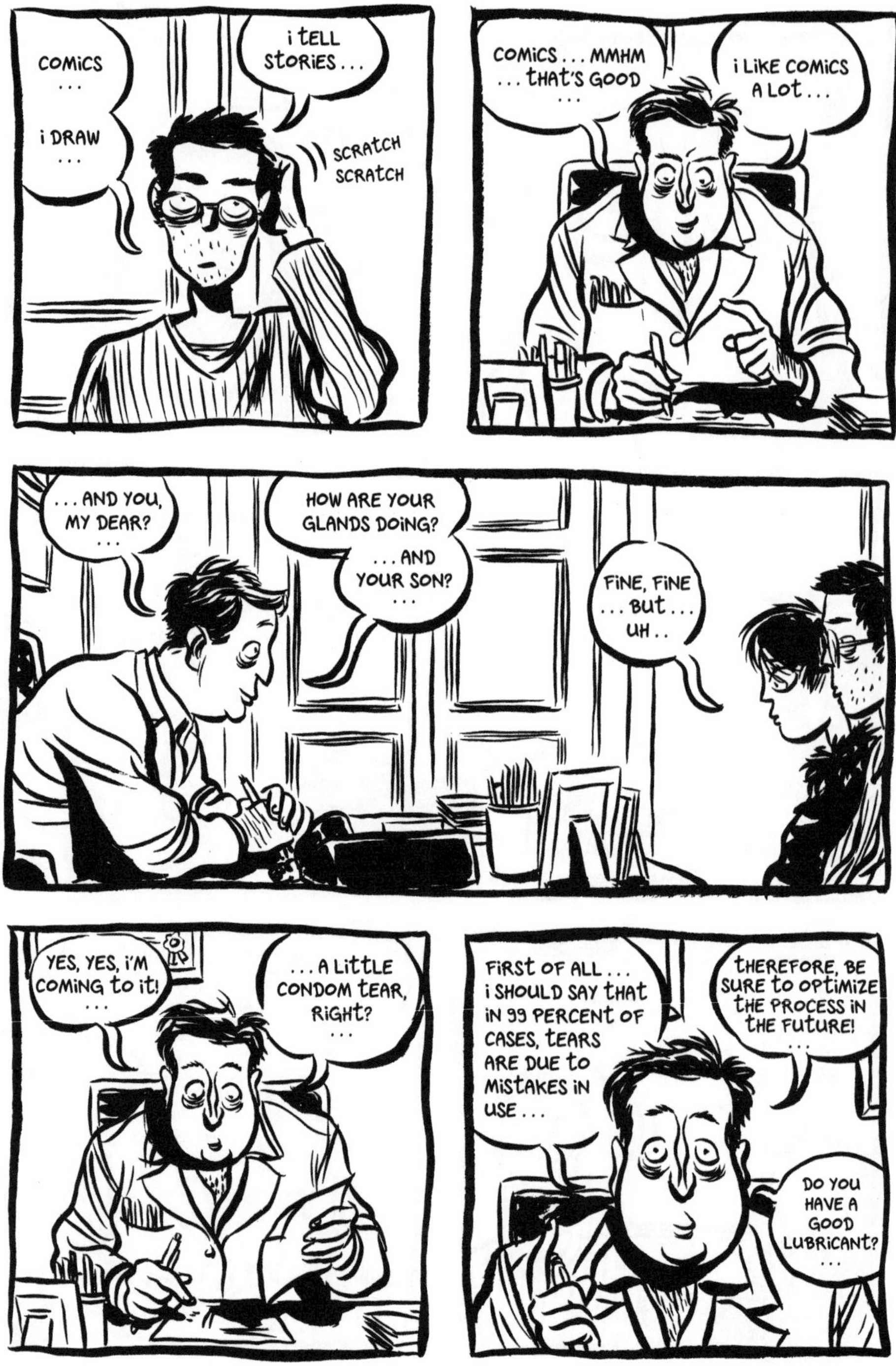

COMICS ... i DRAW ...
i TELL STORiES ...
SCRATCH SCRATCH
COMICS ... MMHM ... THAT'S GOOD ...
i LiKE COMICS A LOT ...
... AND YOU, MY DEAR? ...
HOW ARE YOUR GLANDS DOiNG?
... AND YOUR SON? ...
FiNE, FiNE ... BUT ... UH ..
YES, YES, i'M COMiNG TO iT! ...
... A LiTTLE CONDOM TEAR, RiGHT? ...
FiRST OF ALL ... i SHOULD SAY THAT iN 99 PERCENT OF CASES, TEARS ARE DUE TO MiSTAKES iN USE ...
THEREFORE, BE SURE TO OPTiMiZE THE PROCESS iN THE FUTURE! ...
DO YOU HAVE A GOOD LUBRiCANT? ...

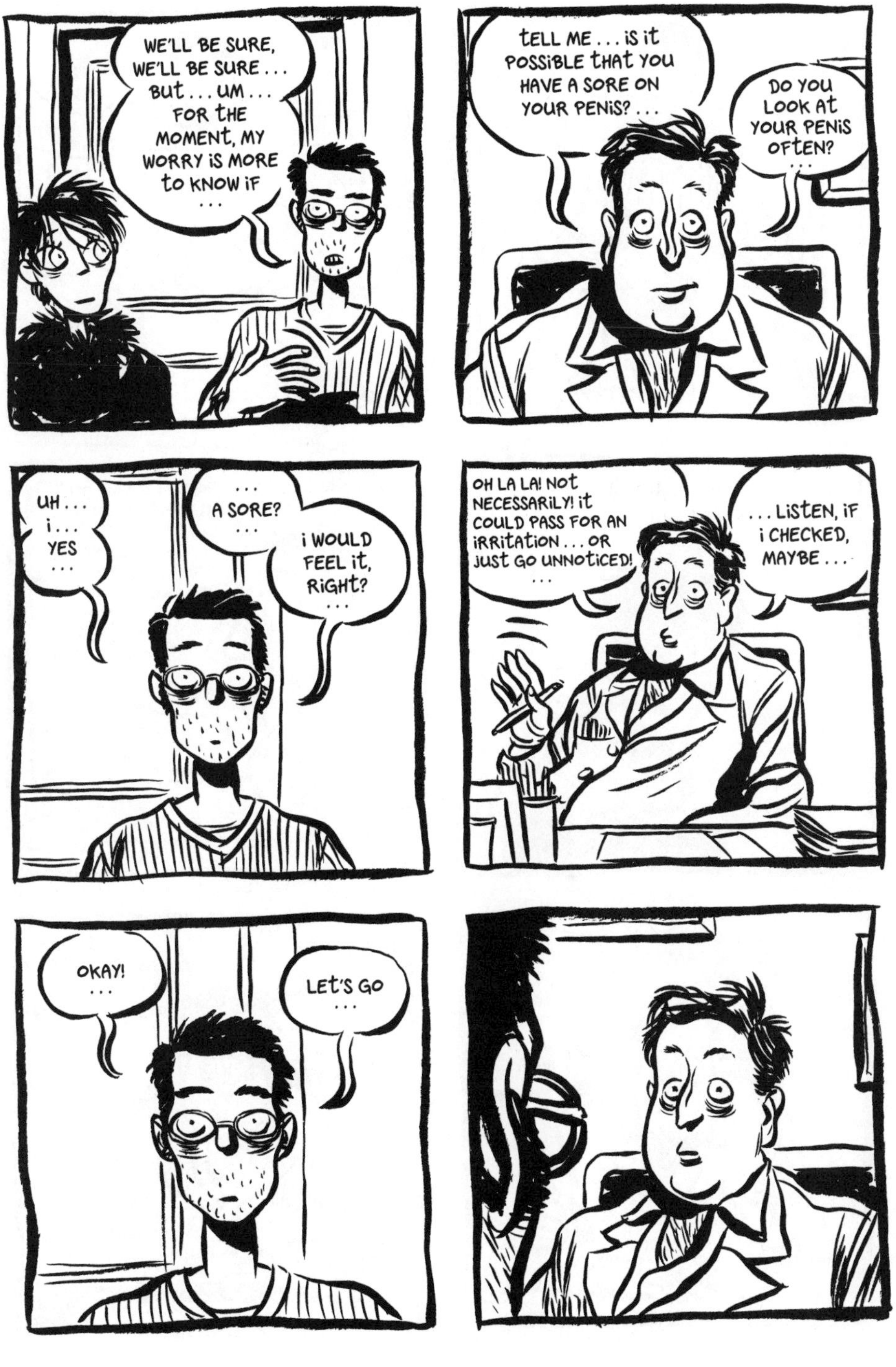
WE'LL BE SURE, WE'LL BE SURE . . . BUT . . . UM . . . FOR THE MOMENT, MY WORRY IS MORE TO KNOW IF . . .
TELL ME . . . IS IT POSSIBLE THAT YOU HAVE A SORE ON YOUR PENIS? . . .
DO YOU LOOK AT YOUR PENIS OFTEN? . . .
UH . . . I . . . YES . . .
. . . A SORE? . . .
I WOULD FEEL IT, RIGHT? . . .
OH LA LA! NOT NECESSARILY! IT COULD PASS FOR AN IRRITATION . . . OR JUST GO UNNOTICED! . . .
. . . LISTEN, IF I CHECKED, MAYBE . . .
OKAY! . . .
LET'S GO . . .

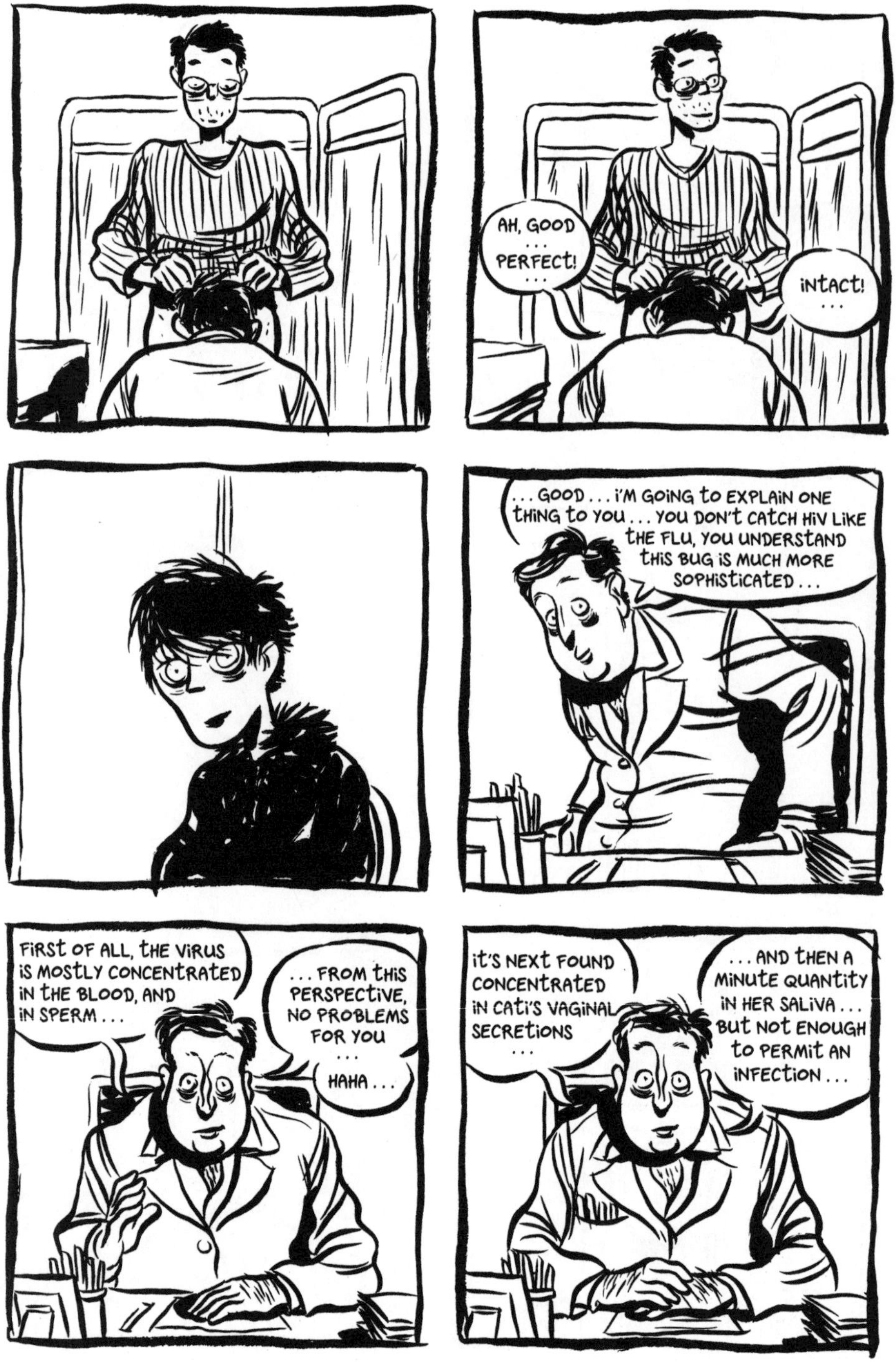
AH, GOOD . . . PERFECT! . . .
iNTACT! . . .
. . . GOOD . . . i'M GOiNG TO EXPLAiN ONE THiNG TO YOU . . . YOU DON'T CATCH HiV LiKE THE FLU, YOU UNDERSTAND THiS BUG iS MUCH MORE SOPHiSTiCATED . . .
FiRST OF ALL, THE ViRUS iS MOSTLY CONCENTRATED iN THE BLOOD, AND iN SPERM . . .
. . . FROM THiS PERSPECTiVE, NO PROBLEMS FOR YOU . . . HAHA . . .
iT'S NEXT FOUND CONCENTRATED iN CATi'S VAGiNAL SECRETiONS . . .
. . . AND THEN A MiNUTE QUANTiTY iN HER SALiVA . . . BUT NOT ENOUGH TO PERMiT AN iNFECTiON . . .

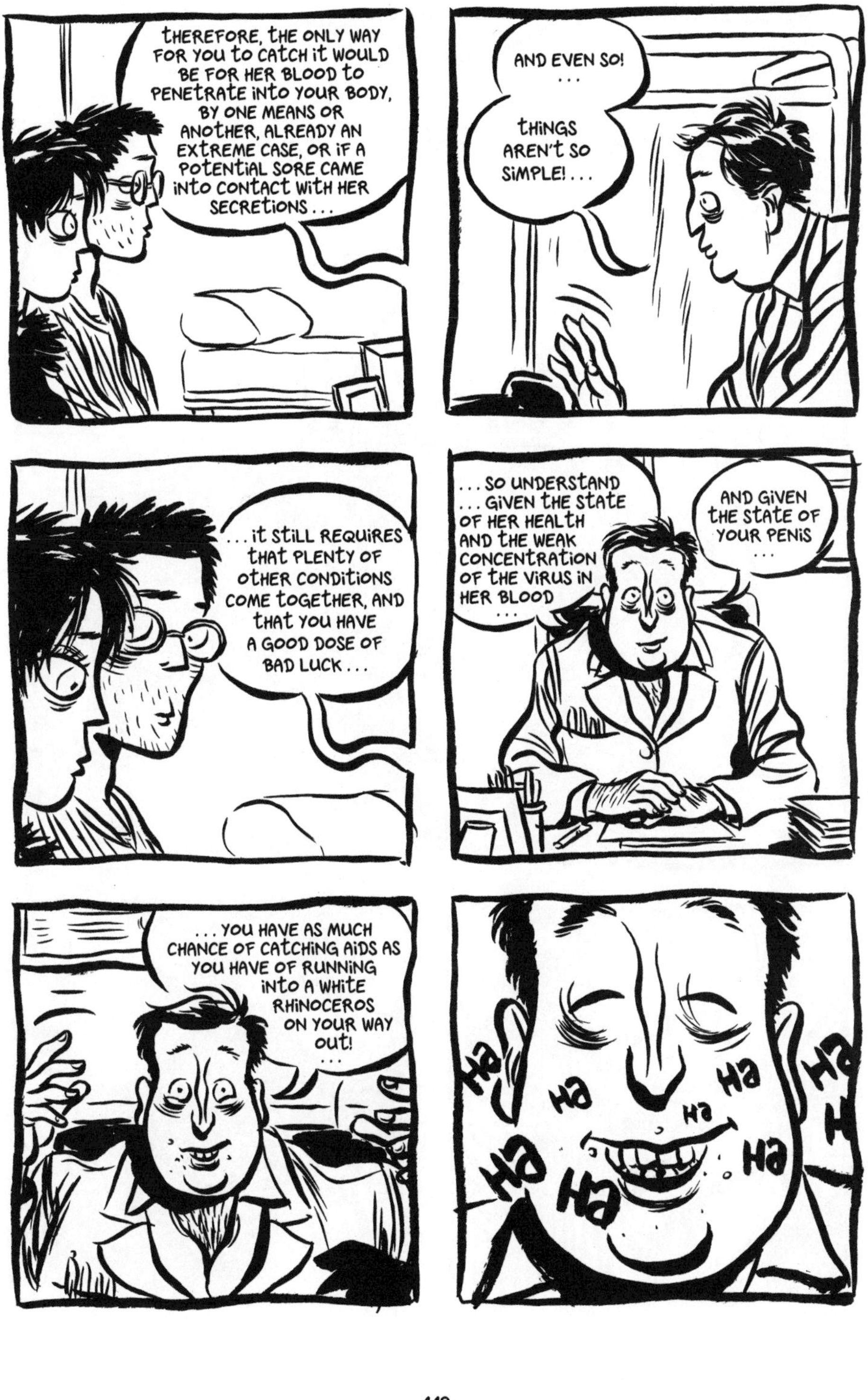

THEREFORE, THE ONLY WAY FOR YOU TO CATCH IT WOULD BE FOR HER BLOOD TO PENETRATE INTO YOUR BODY, BY ONE MEANS OR ANOTHER, ALREADY AN EXTREME CASE, OR IF A POTENTIAL SORE CAME INTO CONTACT WITH HER SECRETIONS . . .
AND EVEN SO! . . .
THINGS AREN'T SO SIMPLE! . . .
. . . IT STILL REQUIRES THAT PLENTY OF OTHER CONDITIONS COME TOGETHER, AND THAT YOU HAVE A GOOD DOSE OF BAD LUCK . . .
. . . SO UNDERSTAND . . . GIVEN THE STATE OF HER HEALTH AND THE WEAK CONCENTRATION OF THE VIRUS IN HER BLOOD . . .
AND GIVEN THE STATE OF YOUR PENIS . . .
. . . YOU HAVE AS MUCH CHANCE OF CATCHING AIDS AS YOU HAVE OF RUNNING INTO A WHITE RHINOCEROS ON YOUR WAY OUT! . . .
HA HA HA HA HA HA HA HA HA

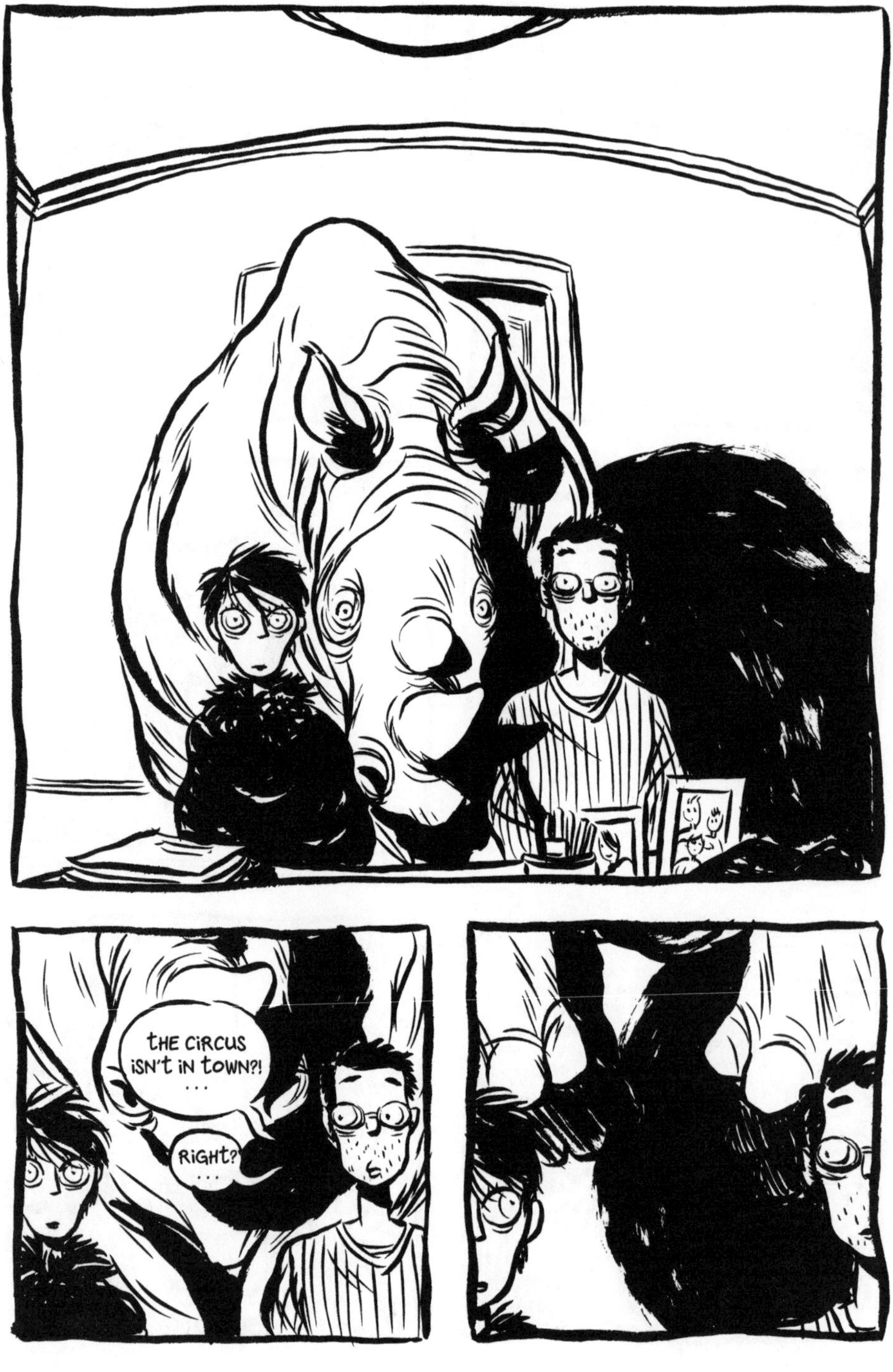
THE CiRCUS iSN'T iN TOWN?! ...
RiGHT? ...

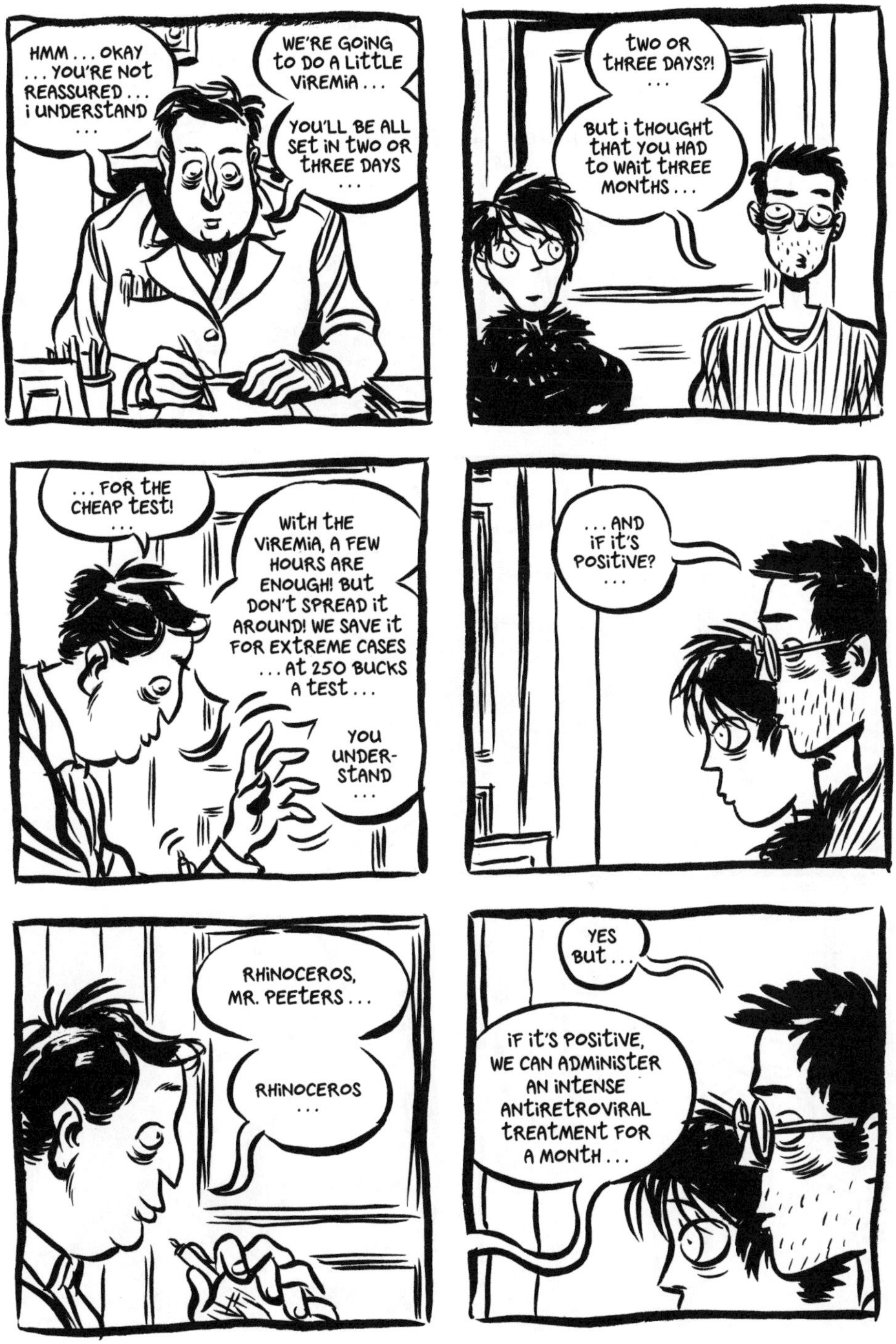
HMM . . . OKAY . . . YOU'RE NOT REASSURED . . . i UNDERSTAND . . .
WE'RE GOiNG tO DO A LittLE ViREMiA . . .
YOU'LL BE ALL SEt iN tWO OR tHREE DAYS . . .
tWO OR tHREE DAYS?! . . .
But i tHOUGHt tHAt YOU HAD tO WAit tHREE MONtHS . . .
. . . FOR tHE CHEAP tESt! . . .
WitH tHE ViREMiA, A FEW HOURS ARE ENOUGH! But DON'T SPREAD it AROUND! WE SAVE it FOR EXTREME CASES . . . At 250 BUCKS A tESt . . .
YOU UNDER-StAND . . .
. . . AND iF it's POSitiVE? . . .
RHiNOCEROS, MR. PEETERS . . .
RHiNOCEROS . . .
YES But . . .
iF it's POSitiVE, WE CAN ADMiNiStER AN iNtENSE ANtiREtROViRAL tREAtMENt FOR A MONtH . . .

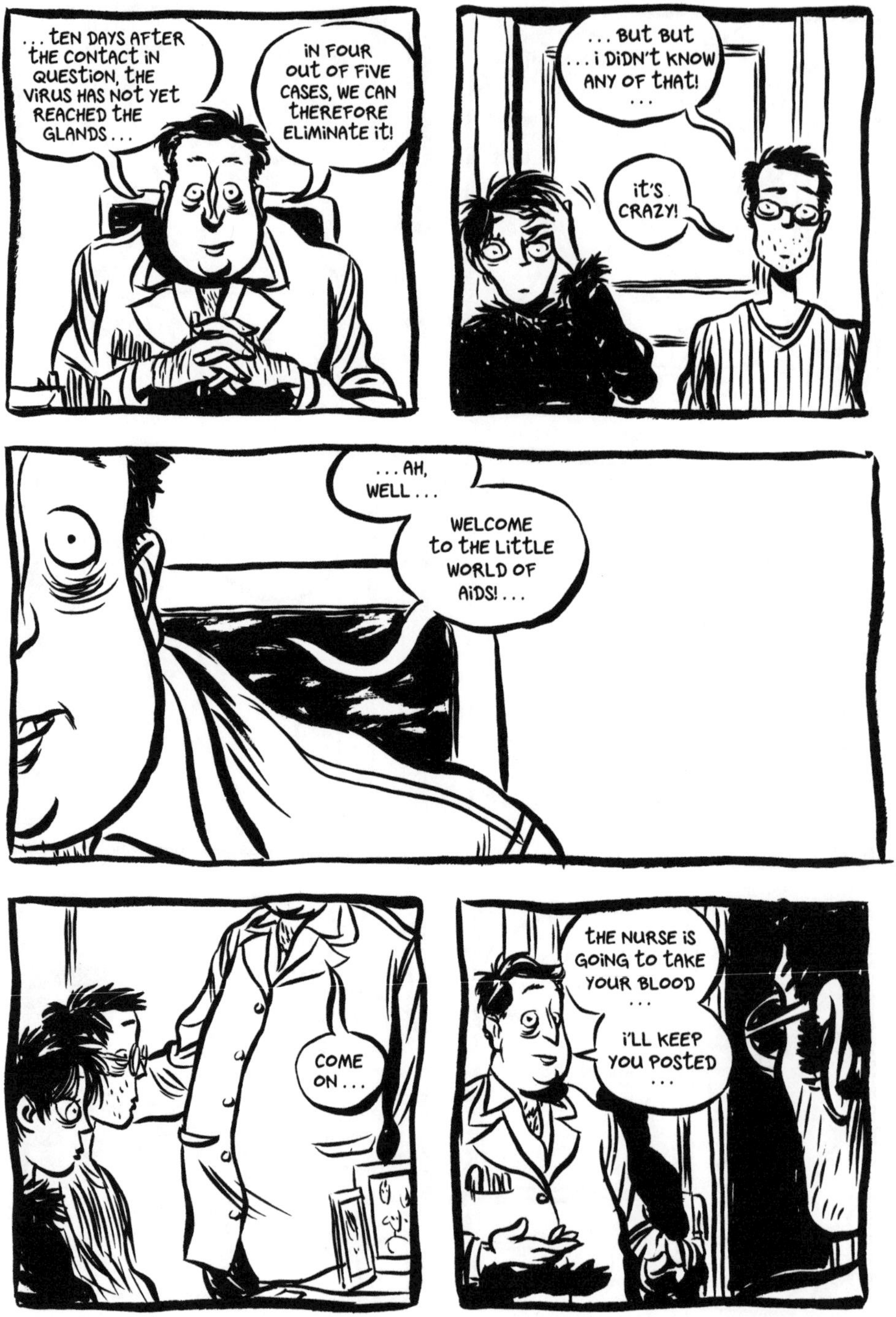
... TEN DAYS AFTER THE CONTACT IN QUESTION, THE VIRUS HAS NOT YET REACHED THE GLANDS ...
IN FOUR OUT OF FIVE CASES, WE CAN THEREFORE ELIMINATE IT!
... BUT BUT ... I DIDN'T KNOW ANY OF THAT! ...
IT'S CRAZY!
... AH, WELL ...
WELCOME TO THE LITTLE WORLD OF AIDS! ...
COME ON ...
THE NURSE IS GOING TO TAKE YOUR BLOOD ...
I'LL KEEP YOU POSTED ...

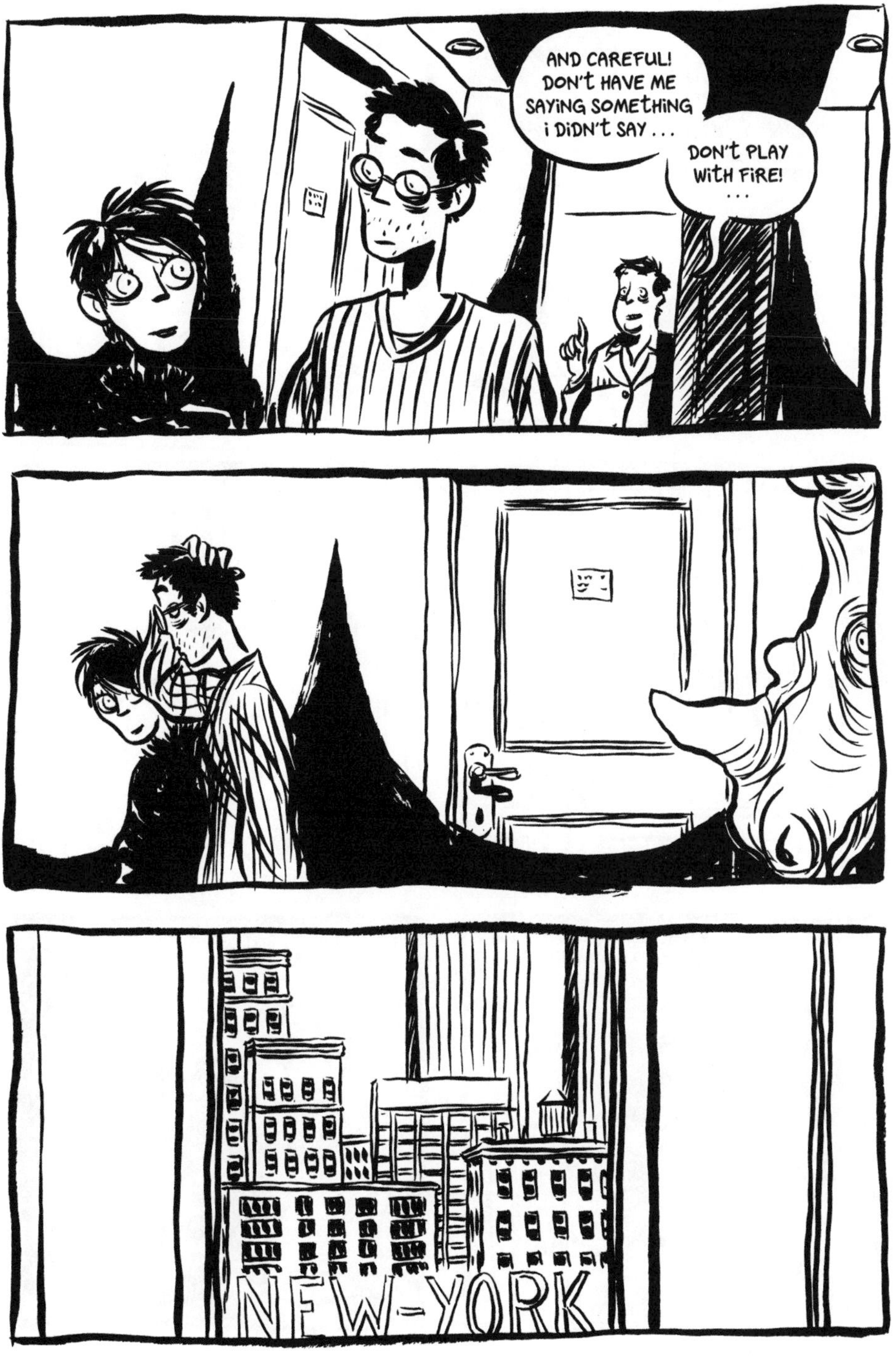
AND CAREFUL! DON'T HAVE ME SAYING SOMETHING I DIDN'T SAY . . .
DON'T PLAY WITH FIRE! . . .
NEW-YORK

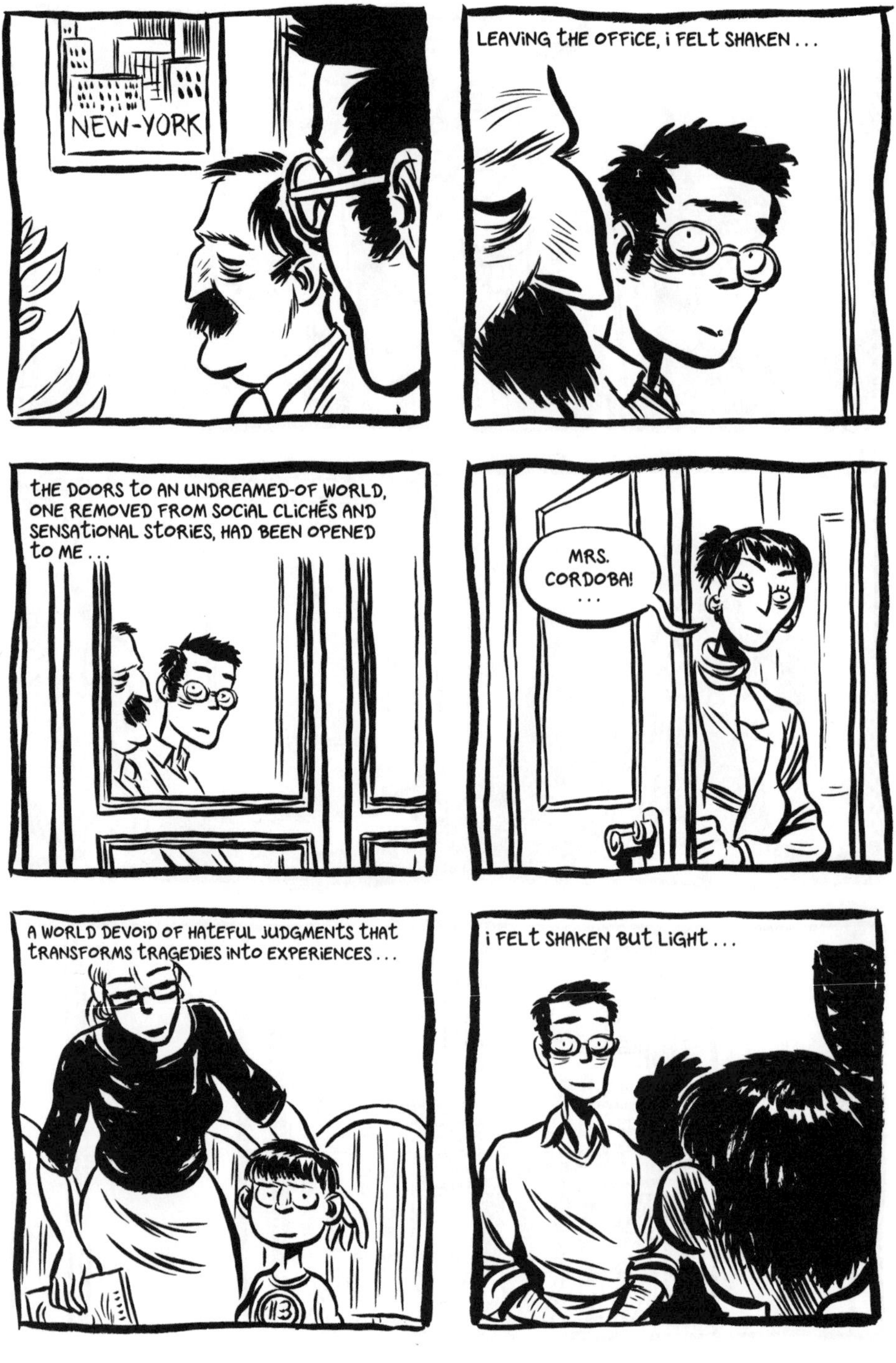
NEW-YORK
LEAVING THE OFFICE, I FELT SHAKEN . . .
THE DOORS TO AN UNDREAMED-OF WORLD, ONE REMOVED FROM SOCIAL CLICHÉS AND SENSATIONAL STORIES, HAD BEEN OPENED TO ME . . .
MRS. CORDOBA! . . .
A WORLD DEVOID OF HATEFUL JUDGMENTS THAT TRANSFORMS TRAGEDIES INTO EXPERIENCES . . .
I FELT SHAKEN BUT LIGHT . . .

AS FOR CATI, BURNED BY HER PAST EXPERIENCES, SHE PREFERRED TO WAIT FOR THE DEFINITIVE RESULTS...

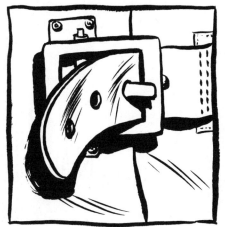

WHEN THE ANTICIPATED GOOD NEWS ARRIVED, IT MEANT LIBERATION...

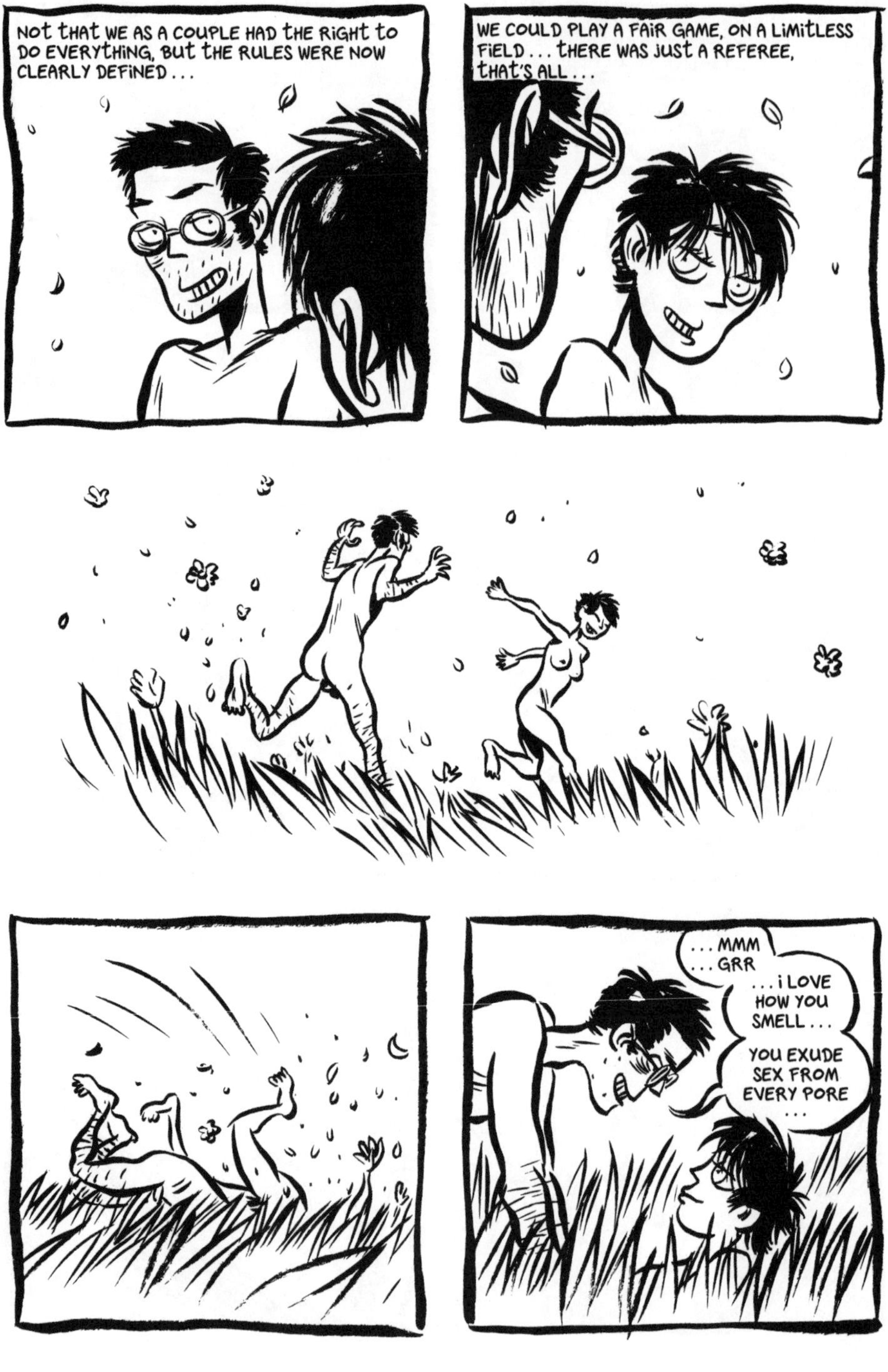
Not that we as a couple had the right to do everything, but the rules were now clearly defined . . .
We could play a fair game, on a limitless field . . . there was just a referee, that's all . . .
. . . MMM
. . . GRR
. . . I LOVE HOW YOU SMELL . . .
YOU EXUDE SEX FROM EVERY PORE . . .

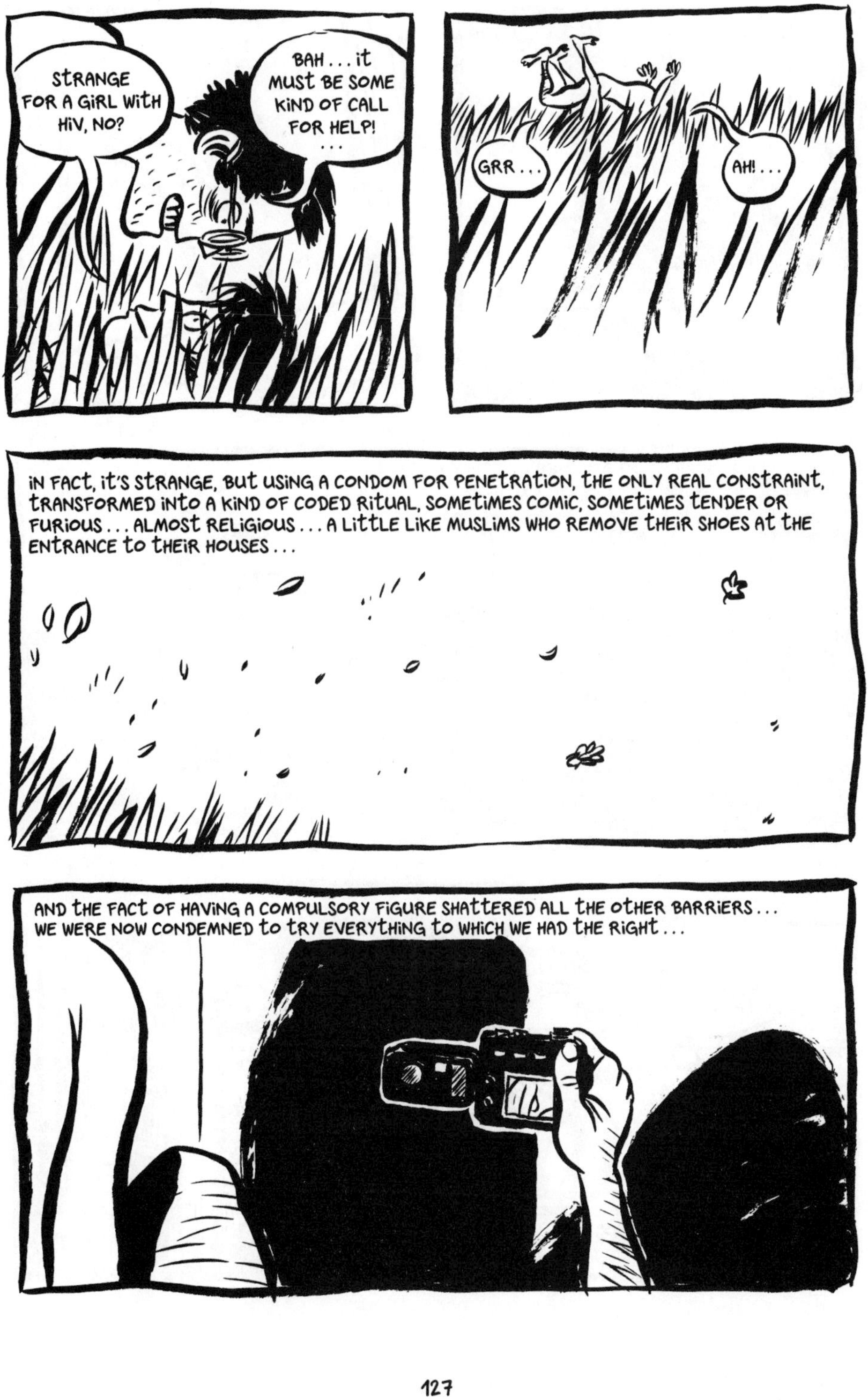
STRANGE FOR A GIRL WITH HIV, NO?
BAH . . . IT MUST BE SOME KIND OF CALL FOR HELP! . . .
GRR . . .
AH! . . .
IN FACT, IT'S STRANGE, BUT USING A CONDOM FOR PENETRATION, THE ONLY REAL CONSTRAINT, TRANSFORMED INTO A KIND OF CODED RITUAL, SOMETIMES COMIC, SOMETIMES TENDER OR FURIOUS . . . ALMOST RELIGIOUS . . . A LITTLE LIKE MUSLIMS WHO REMOVE THEIR SHOES AT THE ENTRANCE TO THEIR HOUSES . . .
AND THE FACT OF HAVING A COMPULSORY FIGURE SHATTERED ALL THE OTHER BARRIERS . . . WE WERE NOW CONDEMNED TO TRY EVERYTHING TO WHICH WE HAD THE RIGHT . . .

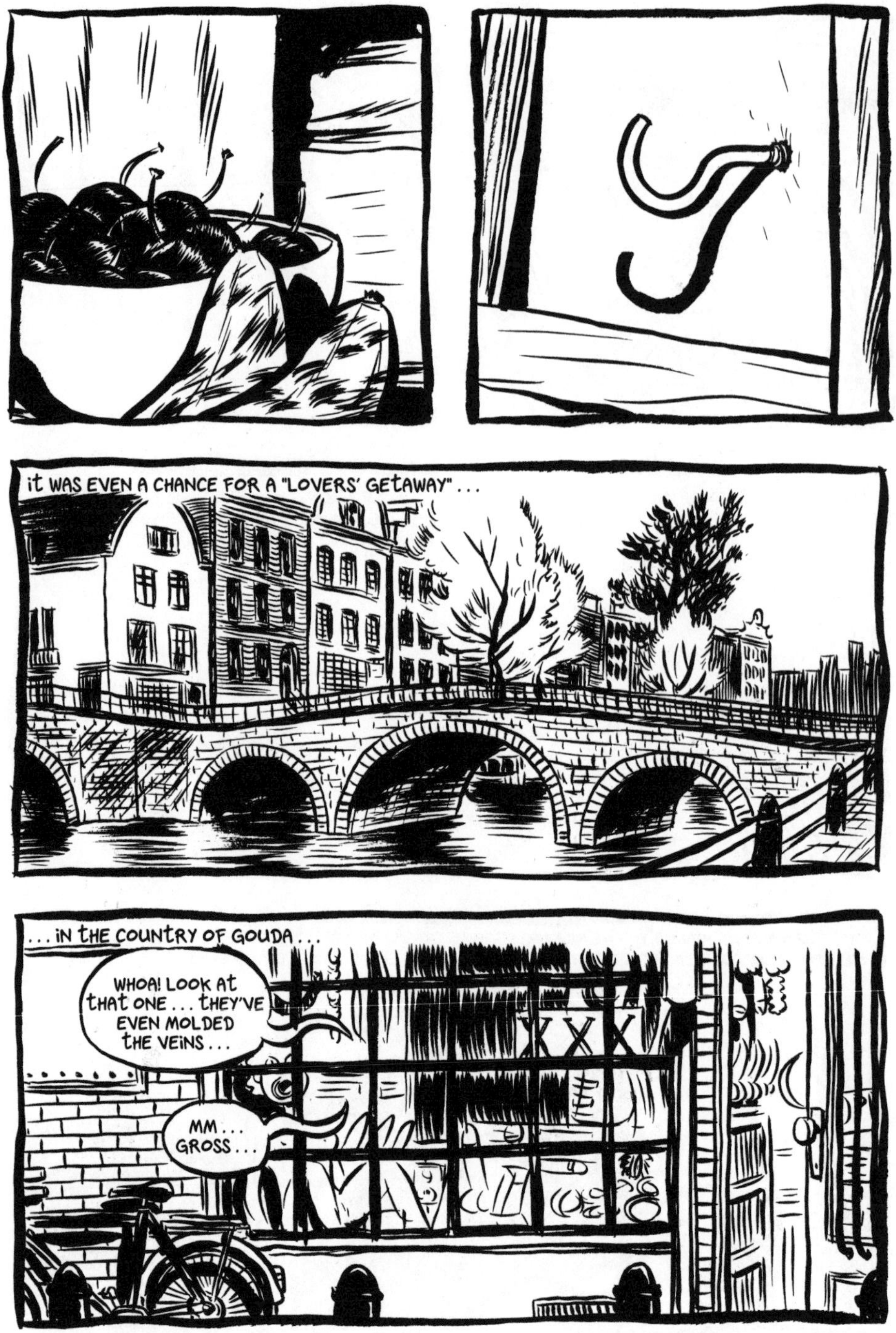
it WAS EVEN A CHANCE FOR A "LOVERS' GEtAWAY" . . .
. . . iN tHE COUNtRY OF GOUDA . . .
WHOA! LOOK At tHAt ONE . . . tHEY'VE EVEN MOLDED tHE VEiNS . . .
MM . . . GROSS . . .

APART FROM THAT, WE AUTOMATICALLY IMPOSED ON OURSELVES A LITTLE DISCIPLINE OF MAINTENANCE AND OBSERVATION OF OUR BODIES...

CRUNCH... SLURP...

BANDAGING CUTS... NO MORE CHEWING ON CUTICLES... KEEPING AN EYE ON MUCUS... IT ALL BECAME ROUTINE...

TSK TSK! ...

HMM ...

IN THIS EXERCISE, CATI DEMONSTRATED AS MUCH ZEAL AS, SOMETIMES, WEARINESS... INDEED, AT TIMES, ACCORDING TO THE LEVEL OF HER SPIRITS, HER TIREDNESS, OR THE DENSITY OF DIFFICULTIES IN HER LIFE, ROUTINE WEIGHED ON HER...

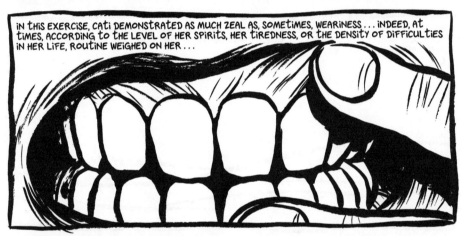

AND I UNDERSTAND THAT ONE CAN, EVERY SO OFTEN, FIND IT TRYING TO LOOK AT ONE'S ILLNESS IN THE MIRROR EVERY DAY...

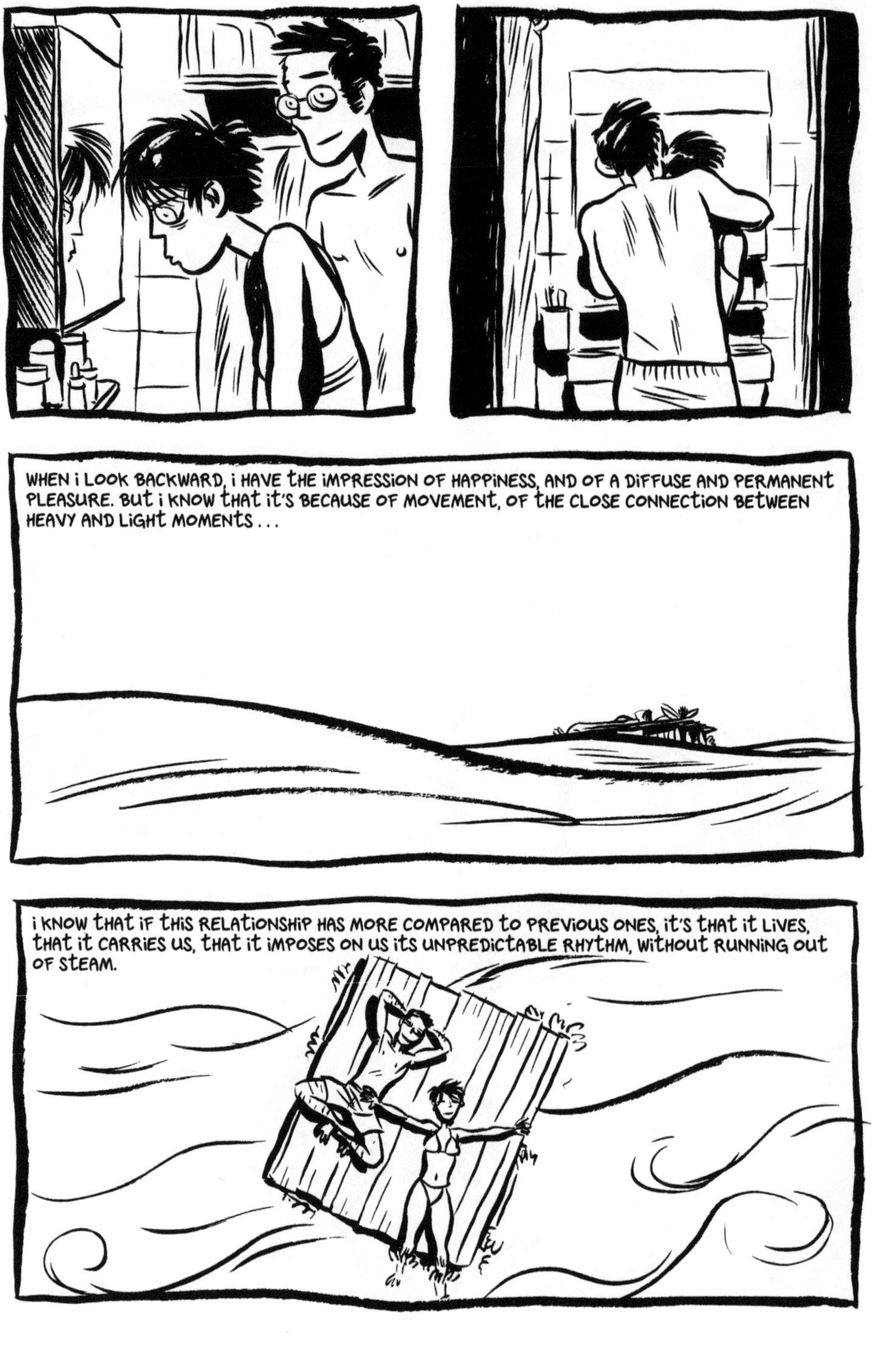
WHEN i LOOK BACKWARD, i HAVE THE iMPRESSiON OF HAPPiNESS, AND OF A DiFFUSE AND PERMANENT PLEASURE. BUT i KNOW THAT iT'S BECAUSE OF MOVEMENT, OF THE CLOSE CONNECTiON BETWEEN HEAVY AND LiGHT MOMENTS . . .
i KNOW THAT iF THiS RELATiONSHiP HAS MORE COMPARED TO PREViOUS ONES, iT'S THAT iT LiVES, THAT iT CARRiES US, THAT iT iMPOSES ON US iTS UNPREDiCTABLE RHYTHM, WiTHOUT RUNNiNG OUT OF STEAM.

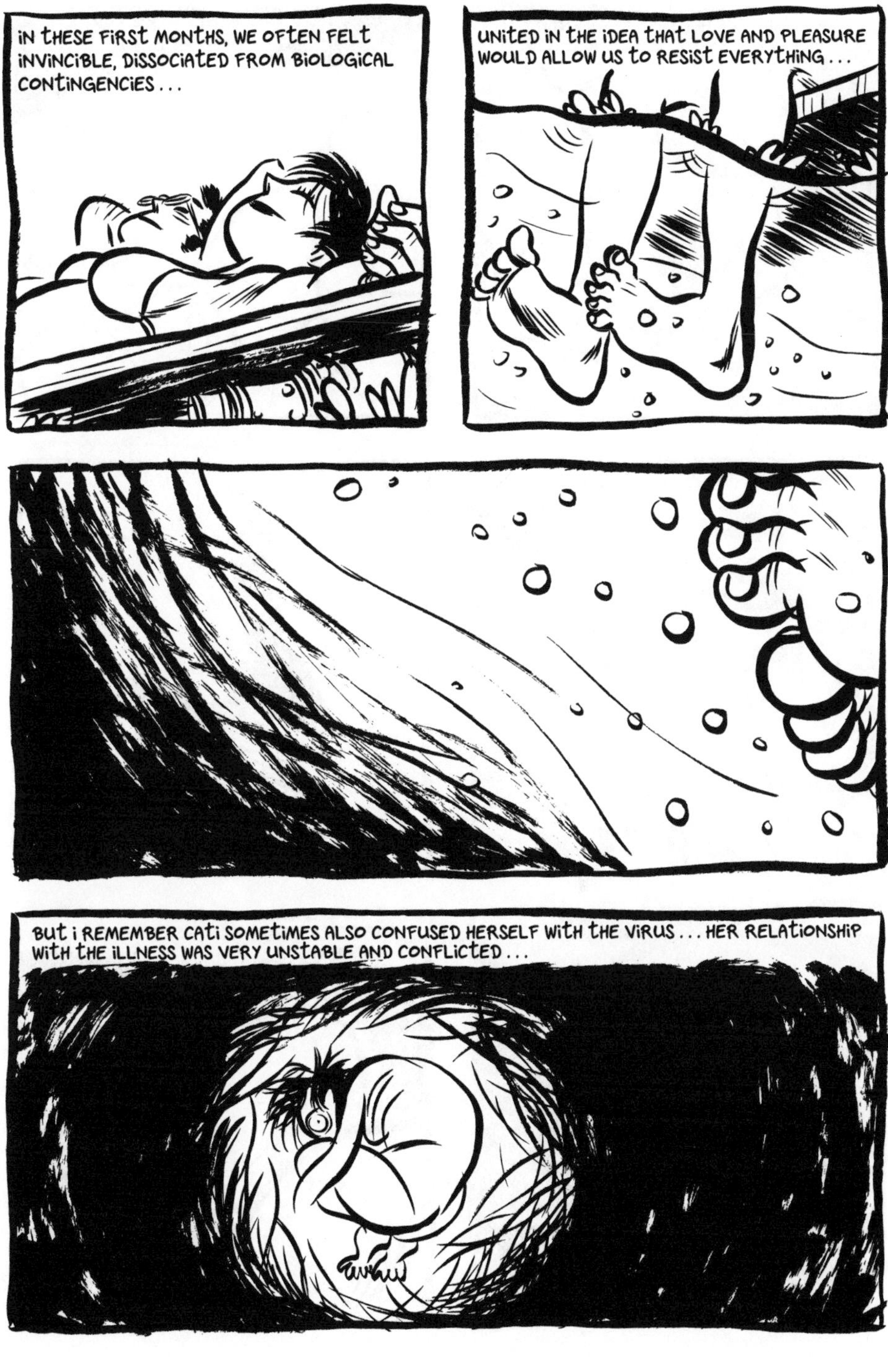
IN THESE FIRST MONTHS, WE OFTEN FELT INVINCIBLE, DISSOCIATED FROM BIOLOGICAL CONTINGENCIES . . .
UNITED IN THE IDEA THAT LOVE AND PLEASURE WOULD ALLOW US TO RESIST EVERYTHING . . .
BUT I REMEMBER CATI SOMETIMES ALSO CONFUSED HERSELF WITH THE VIRUS . . . HER RELATIONSHIP WITH THE ILLNESS WAS VERY UNSTABLE AND CONFLICTED . . .

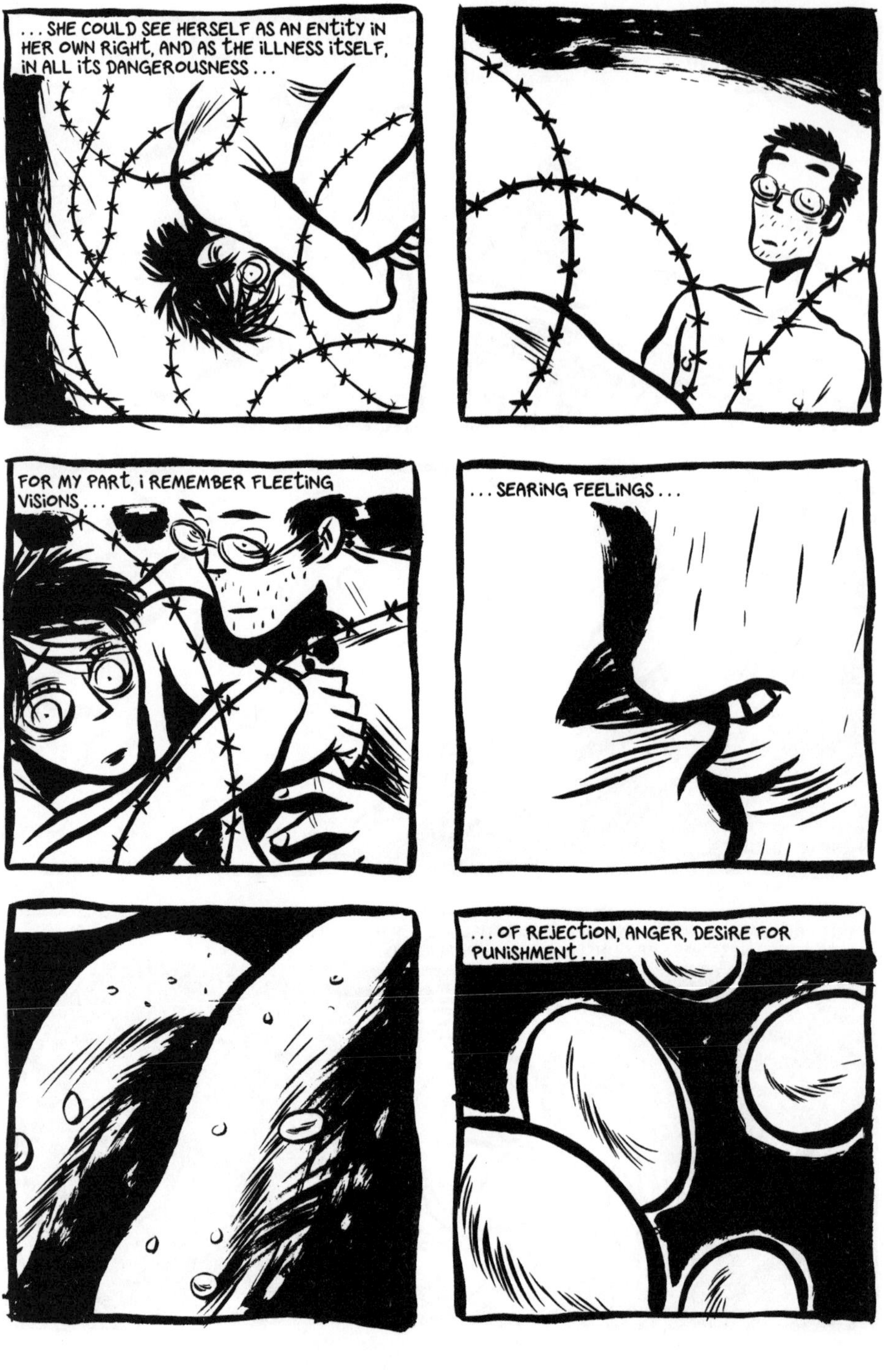
. . . SHE COULD SEE HERSELF AS AN ENTITY IN HER OWN RIGHT, AND AS THE ILLNESS ITSELF, IN ALL ITS DANGEROUSNESS . . .
FOR MY PART, I REMEMBER FLEETING VISIONS . . .
. . . SEARING FEELINGS . . .
. . . OF REJECTION, ANGER, DESIRE FOR PUNISHMENT . . .

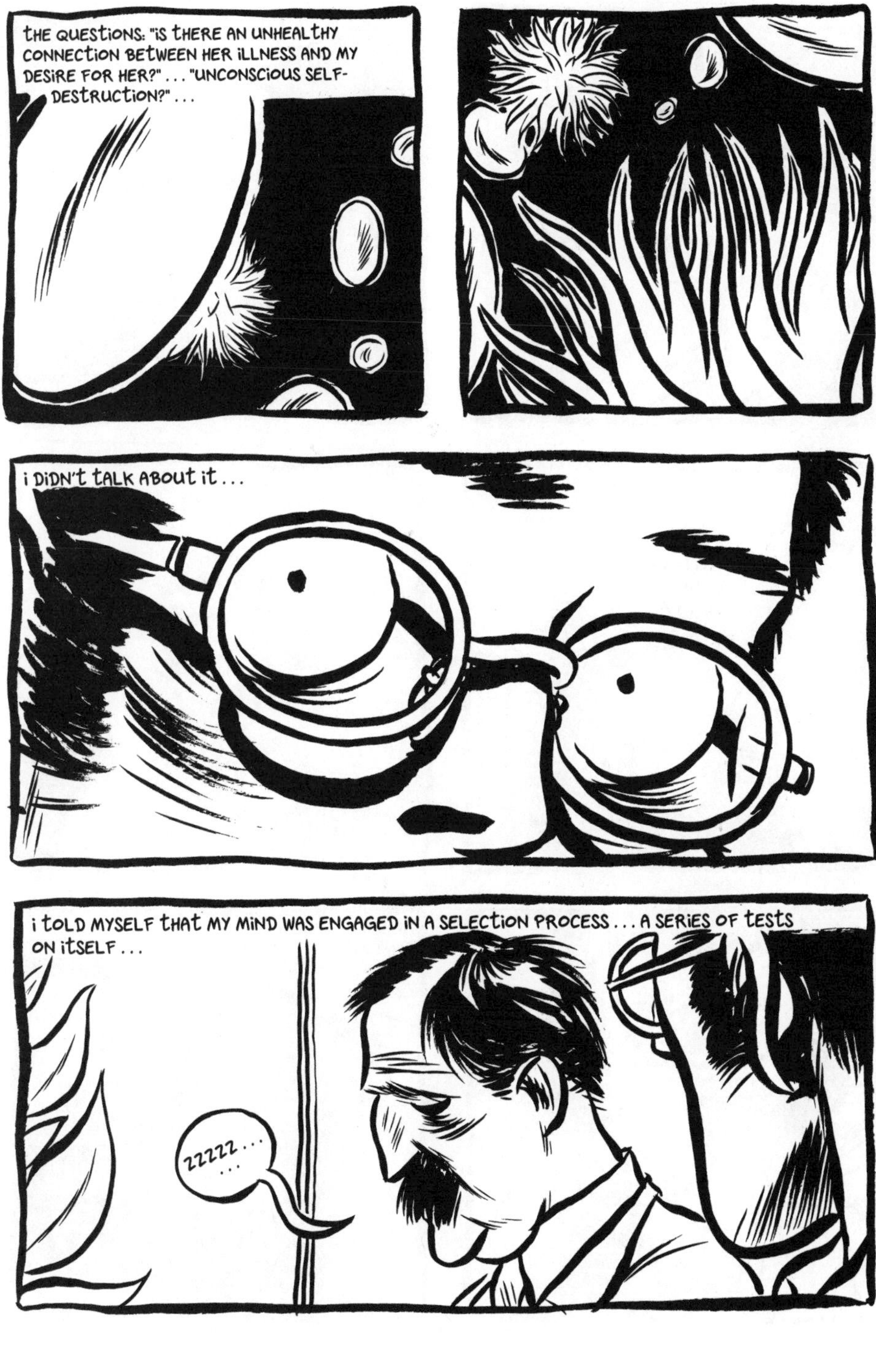
THE QUESTIONS: "IS THERE AN UNHEALTHY CONNECTION BETWEEN HER ILLNESS AND MY DESIRE FOR HER?" . . . "UNCONSCIOUS SELF-DESTRUCTION?" . . .
I DIDN'T TALK ABOUT IT . . .
I TOLD MYSELF THAT MY MIND WAS ENGAGED IN A SELECTION PROCESS . . . A SERIES OF TESTS ON ITSELF . . .
ZZZZZ . . . . . .

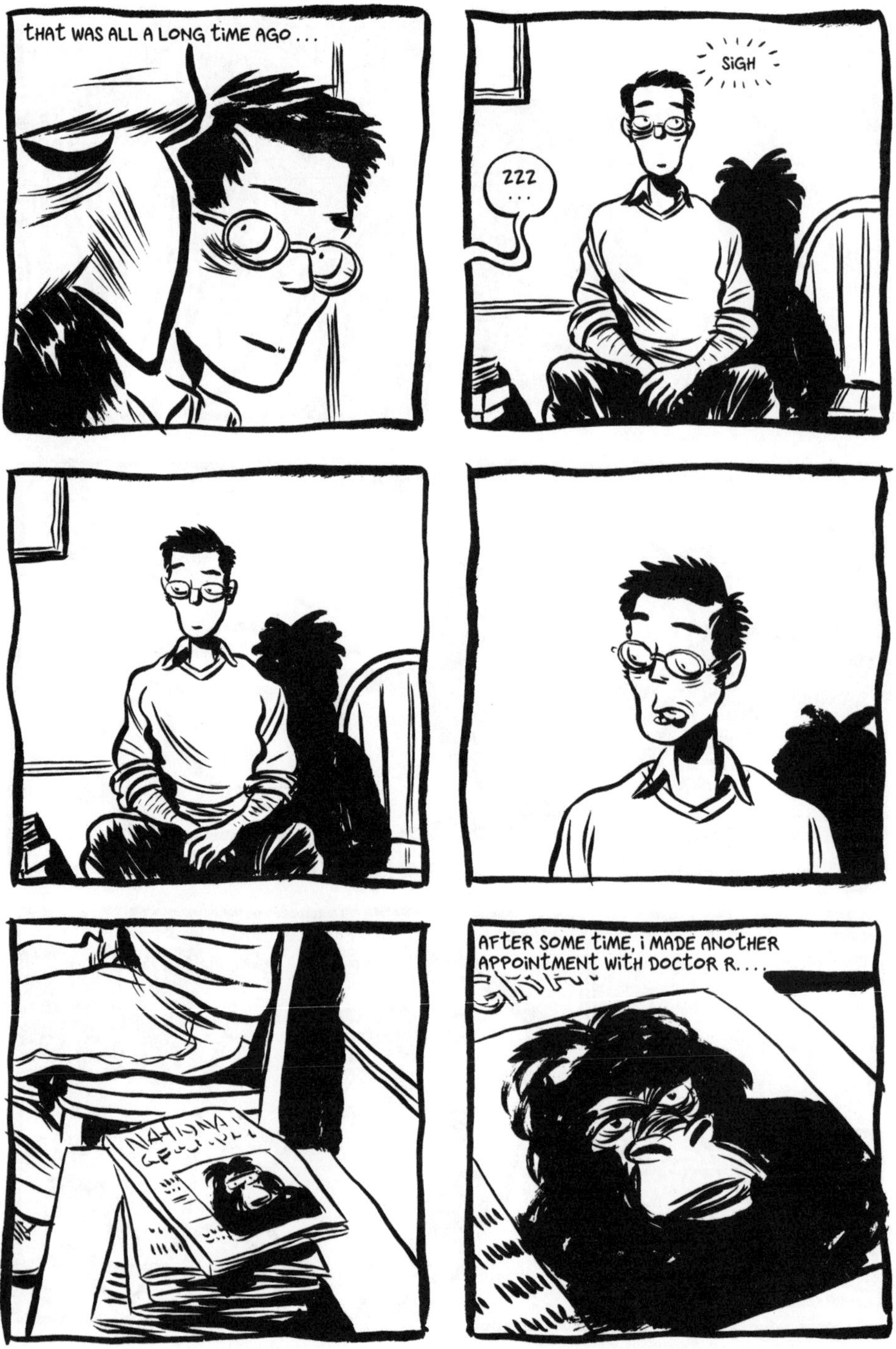
that WAS ALL A LONG timE AGO . . .
SiGH
ZZZ . . .
AFTER SOME timE, i MADE ANOTHER APPOINTMENT WITH DOCTOR R. . . .

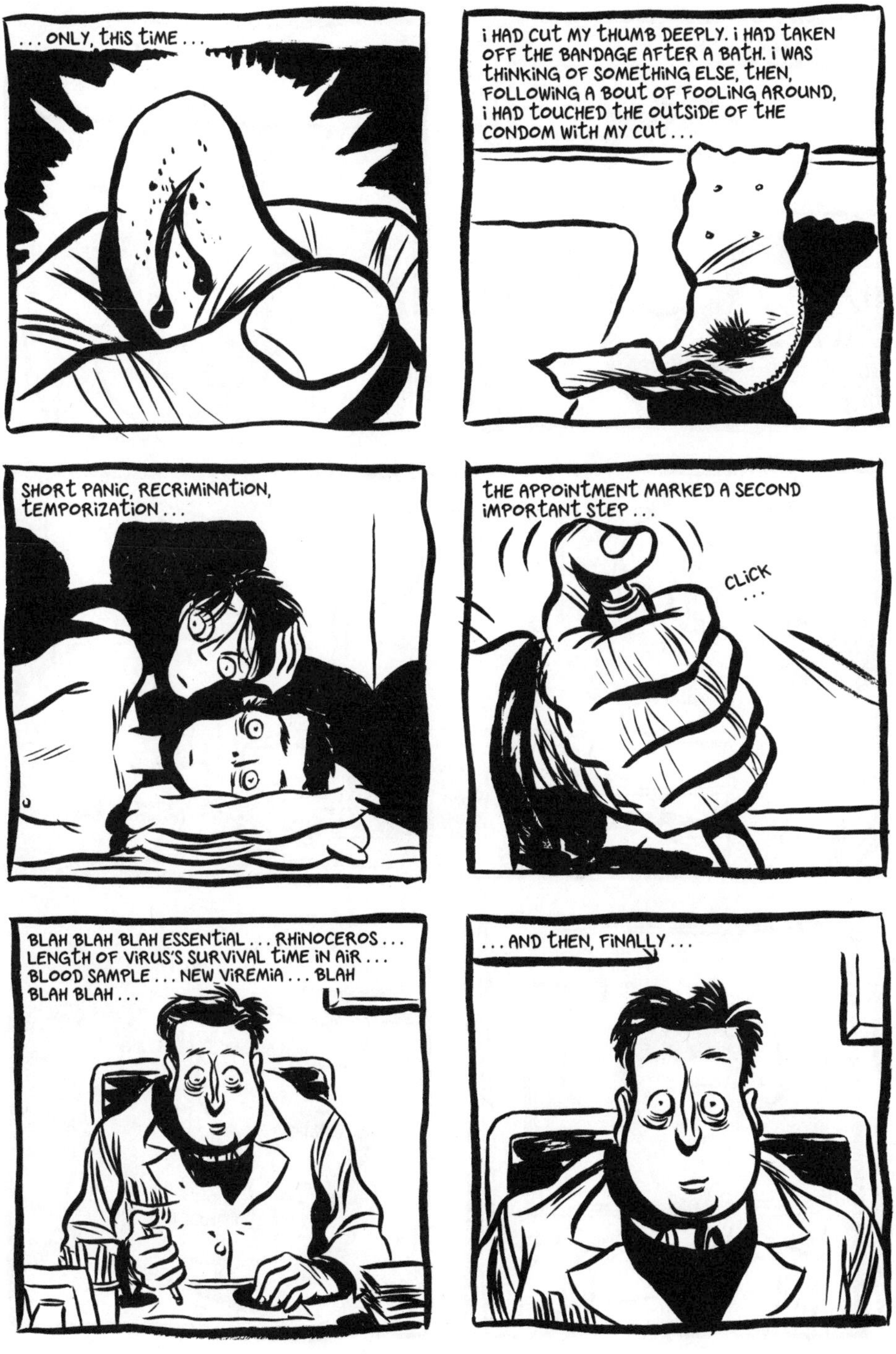
. . . ONLY, THIS TIME . . .
I HAD CUT MY THUMB DEEPLY. I HAD TAKEN OFF THE BANDAGE AFTER A BATH. I WAS THINKING OF SOMETHING ELSE, THEN, FOLLOWING A BOUT OF FOOLING AROUND, I HAD TOUCHED THE OUTSIDE OF THE CONDOM WITH MY CUT . . .
SHORT PANIC, RECRIMINATION, TEMPORIZATION . . .
THE APPOINTMENT MARKED A SECOND IMPORTANT STEP . . .
CLICK . . .
BLAH BLAH BLAH ESSENTIAL . . . RHINOCEROS . . . LENGTH OF VIRUS'S SURVIVAL TIME IN AIR . . . BLOOD SAMPLE . . . NEW VIREMIA . . . BLAH BLAH BLAH . . .
. . . AND THEN, FINALLY . . .

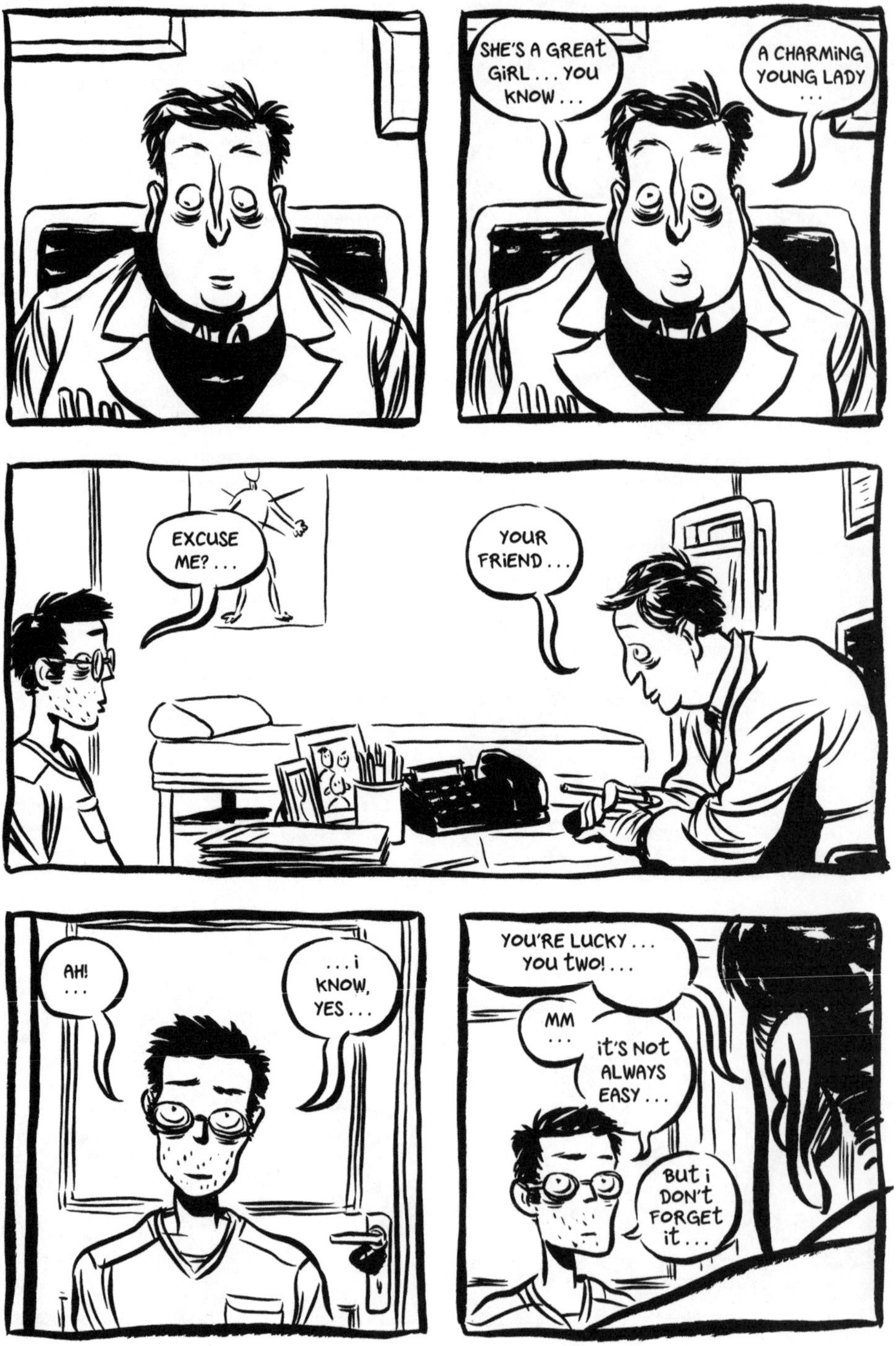
SHE'S A GREAT GIRL... YOU KNOW...
A CHARMING YOUNG LADY...
EXCUSE ME?...
YOUR FRIEND...
AH! ...
...I KNOW, YES...
YOU'RE LUCKY... YOU TWO!...
MM...
IT'S NOT ALWAYS EASY...
BUT I DON'T FORGET IT...

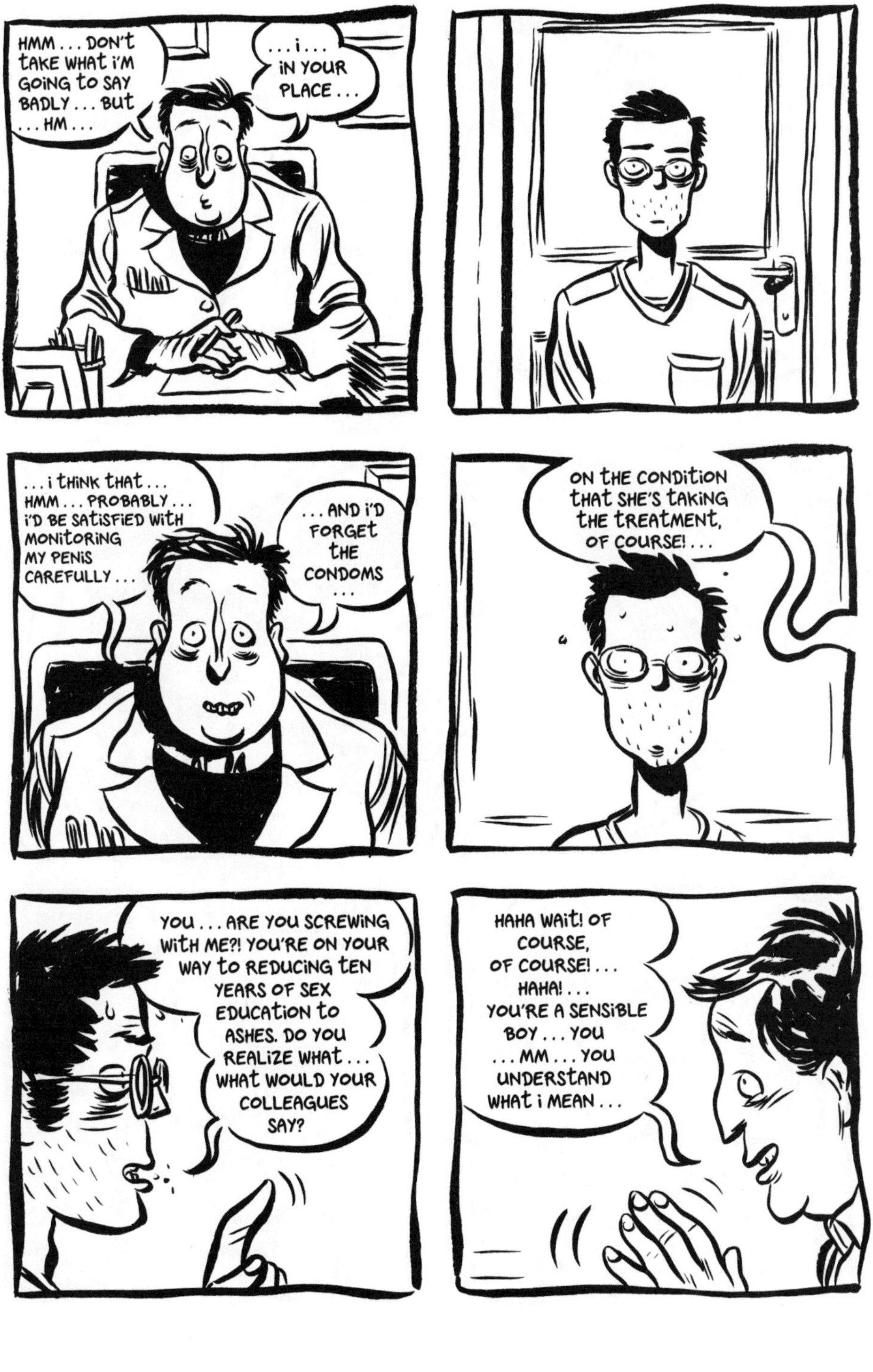
HMM . . . DON'T TAKE WHAT I'M GOING TO SAY BADLY . . . BUT . . . HM . . .
. . . I . . . IN YOUR PLACE . . .
. . . I THINK THAT . . . HMM . . . PROBABLY . . . I'D BE SATISFIED WITH MONITORING MY PENIS CAREFULLY . . .
. . . AND I'D FORGET THE CONDOMS . . .
ON THE CONDITION THAT SHE'S TAKING THE TREATMENT, OF COURSE! . . .
YOU . . . ARE YOU SCREWING WITH ME?! YOU'RE ON YOUR WAY TO REDUCING TEN YEARS OF SEX EDUCATION TO ASHES. DO YOU REALIZE WHAT . . . WHAT WOULD YOUR COLLEAGUES SAY?
HAHA WAIT! OF COURSE, OF COURSE! . . . HAHA! . . . YOU'RE A SENSIBLE BOY . . . YOU . . . MM . . . YOU UNDERSTAND WHAT I MEAN . . .

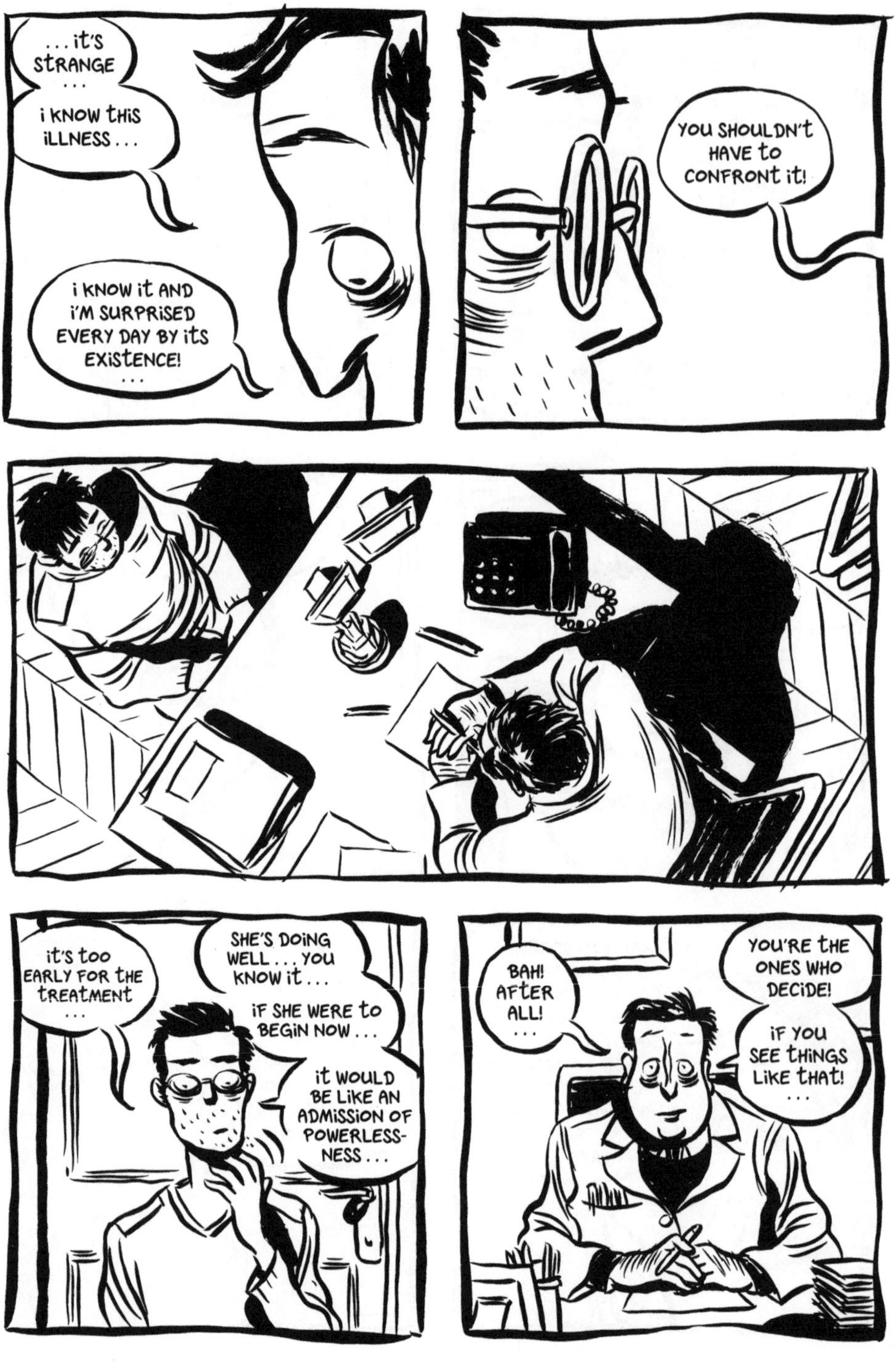
. . . it's STRANGE . . .
i KNOW tHiS iLLNESS . . .
i KNOW it AND i'M SURPRiSED EVERY DAY BY itS EXiStENCE! . . .
YOU SHOULDN'T HAVE to CONFRONt it!
it's too EARLY FOR tHE tREAtMENt . . .
SHE'S DOiNG WELL . . . YOU KNOW it . . .
iF SHE WERE to BEGiN NOW . . .
it WOULD BE LiKE AN ADMiSSiON OF POWERLESS-NESS . . .
BAH! AFtER ALL! . . .
YOU'RE tHE ONES WHO DECiDE!
iF YOU SEE tHiNGS LiKE tHAt! . . .

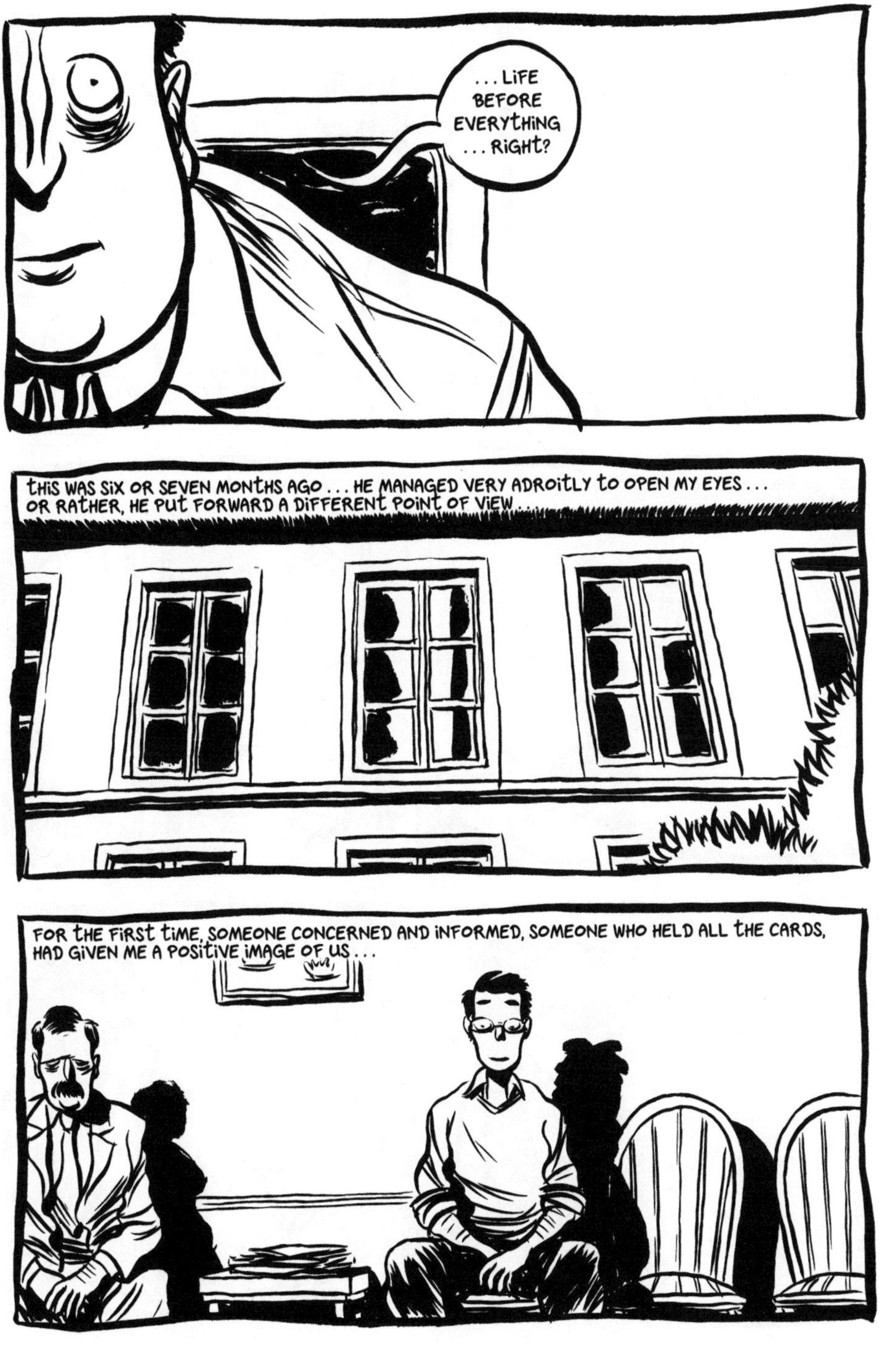

. . . LIFE BEFORE EVERYTHING . . . RIGHT?
THIS WAS SIX OR SEVEN MONTHS AGO . . . HE MANAGED VERY ADROITLY TO OPEN MY EYES . . . OR RATHER, HE PUT FORWARD A DIFFERENT POINT OF VIEW . . .
FOR THE FIRST TIME, SOMEONE CONCERNED AND INFORMED, SOMEONE WHO HELD ALL THE CARDS, HAD GIVEN ME A POSITIVE IMAGE OF US . . .

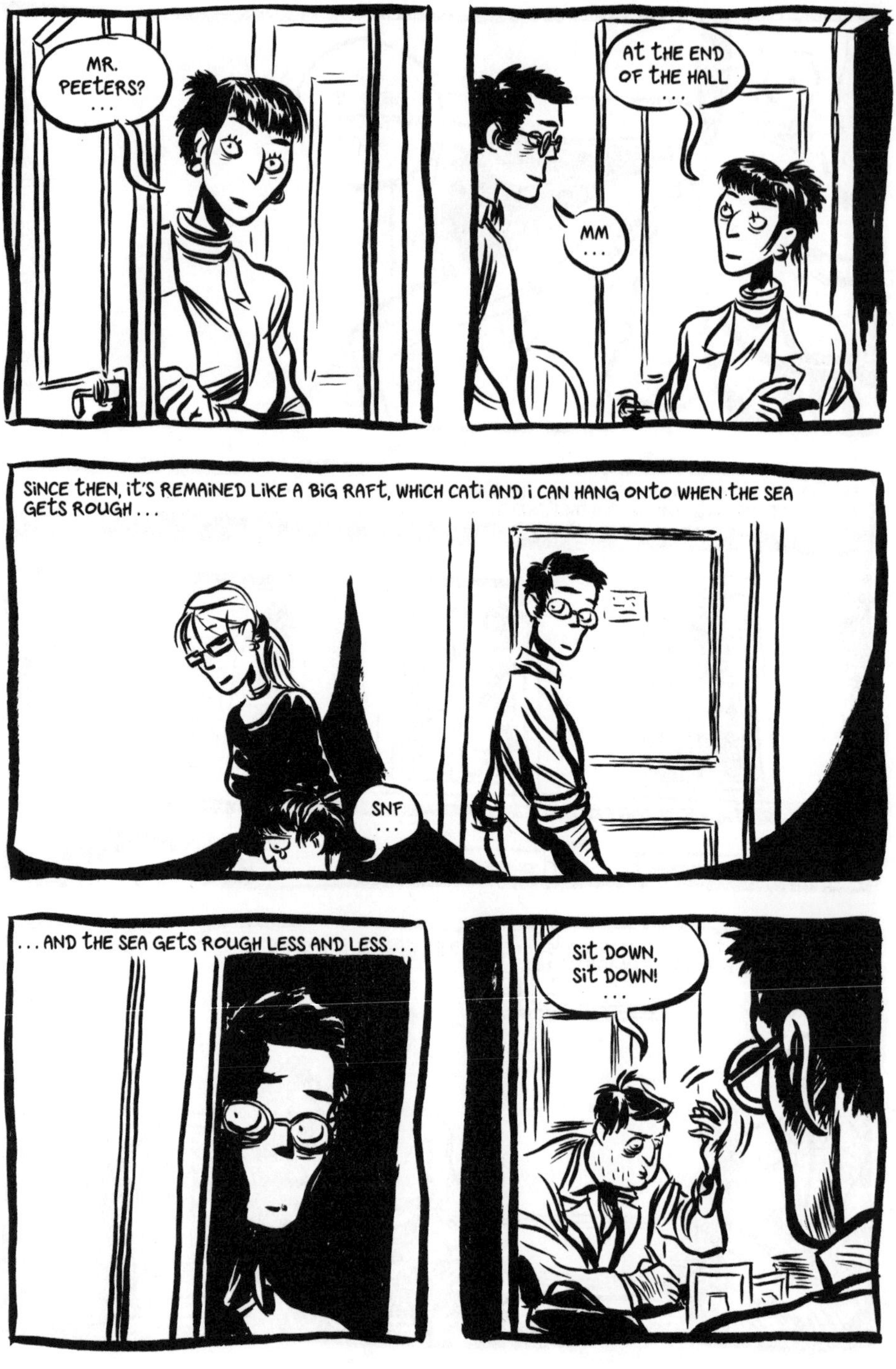
MR. PEETERS? ...
AT THE END OF THE HALL ...
MM ...
SINCE THEN, IT'S REMAINED LIKE A BIG RAFT, WHICH CATI AND I CAN HANG ONTO WHEN THE SEA GETS ROUGH...
SNF ...
...AND THE SEA GETS ROUGH LESS AND LESS...
SIT DOWN, SIT DOWN! ...

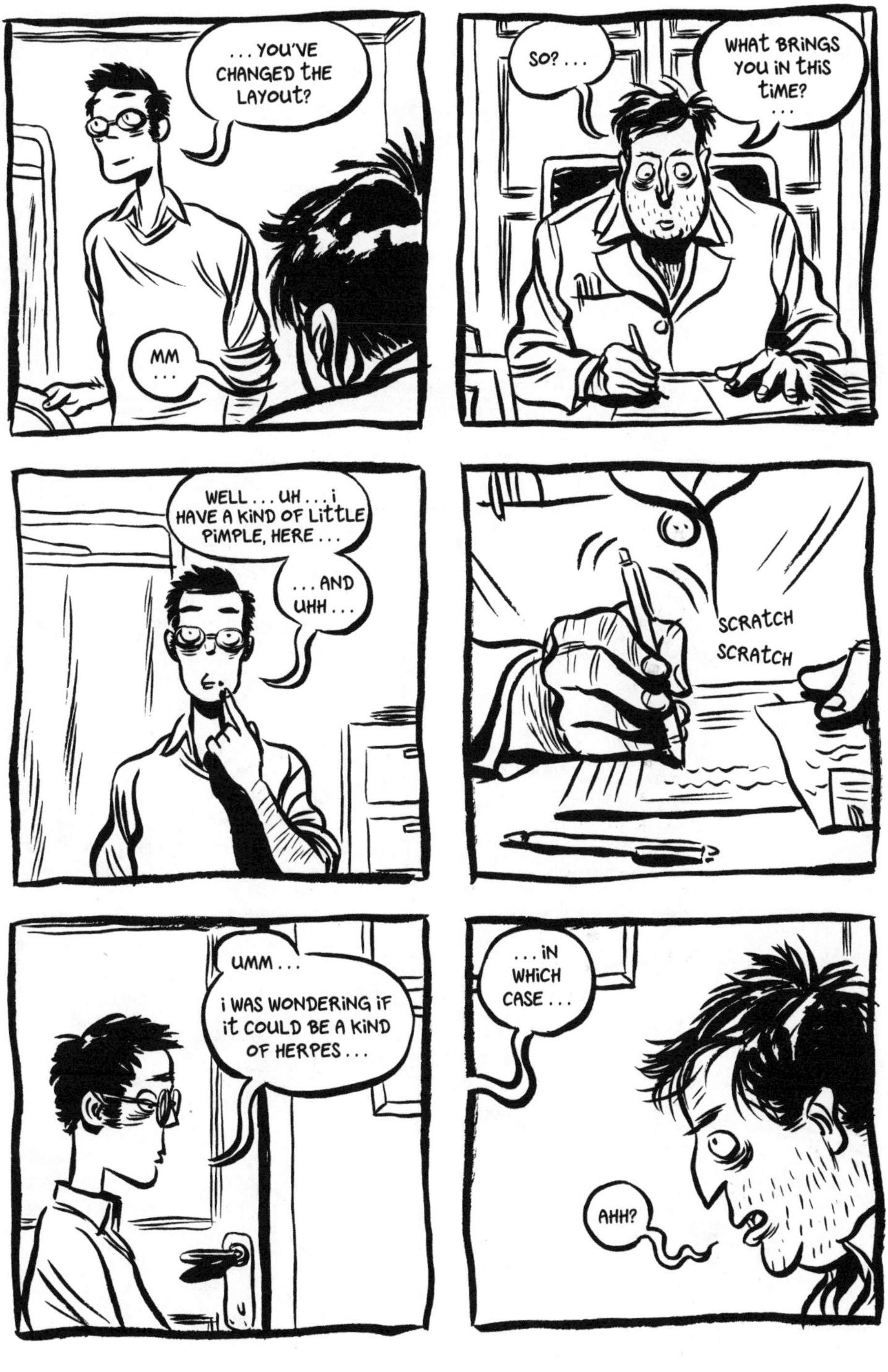
. . . YOU'VE CHANGED THE LAYOUT?
MM . . .
SO? . . .
WHAT BRINGS YOU IN THIS TIME? . . .
WELL . . . UH . . . I HAVE A KIND OF LITTLE PIMPLE, HERE . . .
. . . AND UHH . . .
SCRATCH
SCRATCH
UMM . . .
I WAS WONDERING IF IT COULD BE A KIND OF HERPES . . .
. . . IN WHICH CASE . . .
AHH?

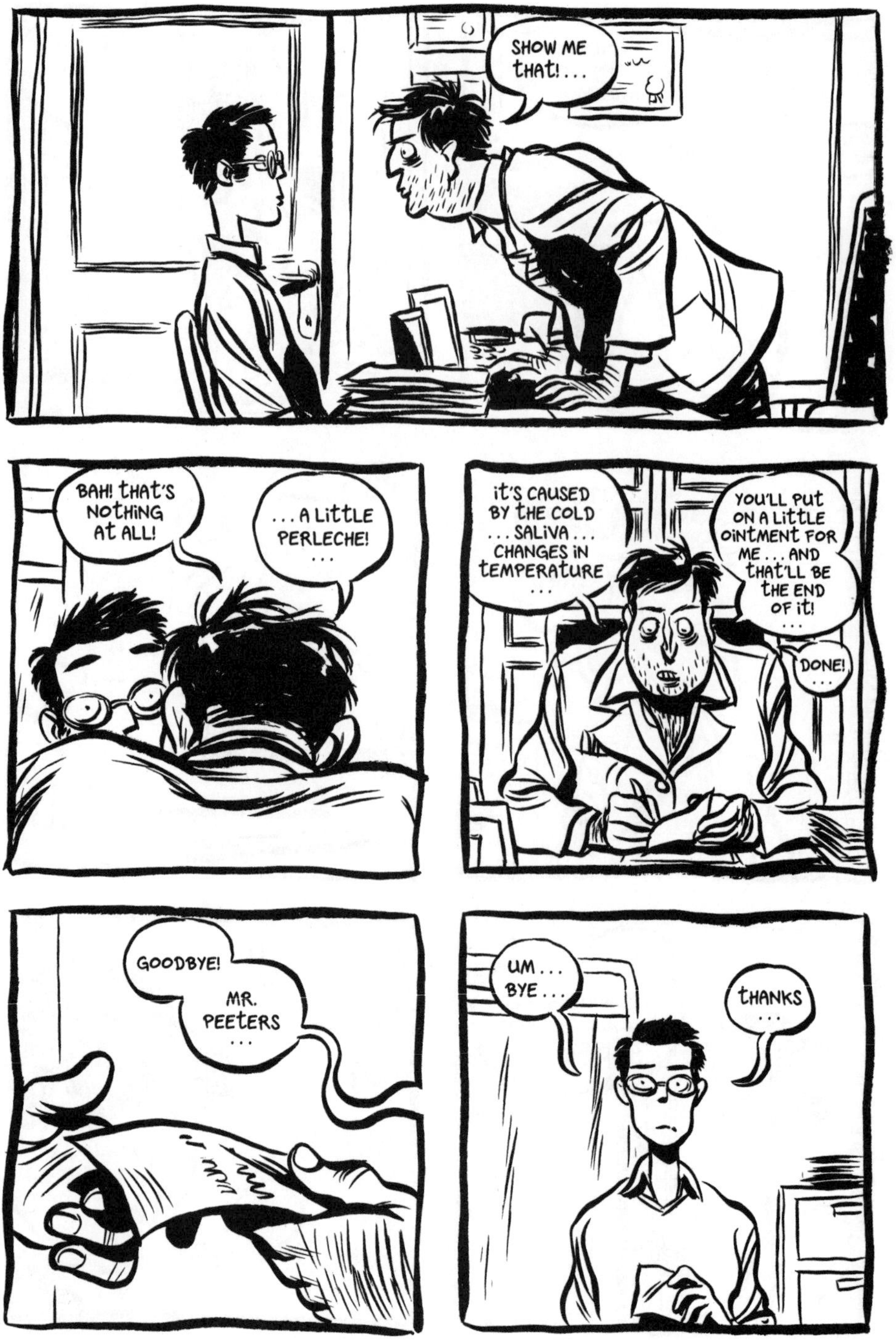
SHOW ME THAT!...
BAH! THAT'S NOTHING AT ALL!
...A LITTLE PERLECHE! ...
IT'S CAUSED BY THE COLD ... SALIVA ... CHANGES IN TEMPERATURE ...
YOU'LL PUT ON A LITTLE OINTMENT FOR ME ... AND THAT'LL BE THE END OF IT! ...
DONE! ...
GOODBYE!
MR. PEETERS ...
UM ... BYE ...
THANKS ...

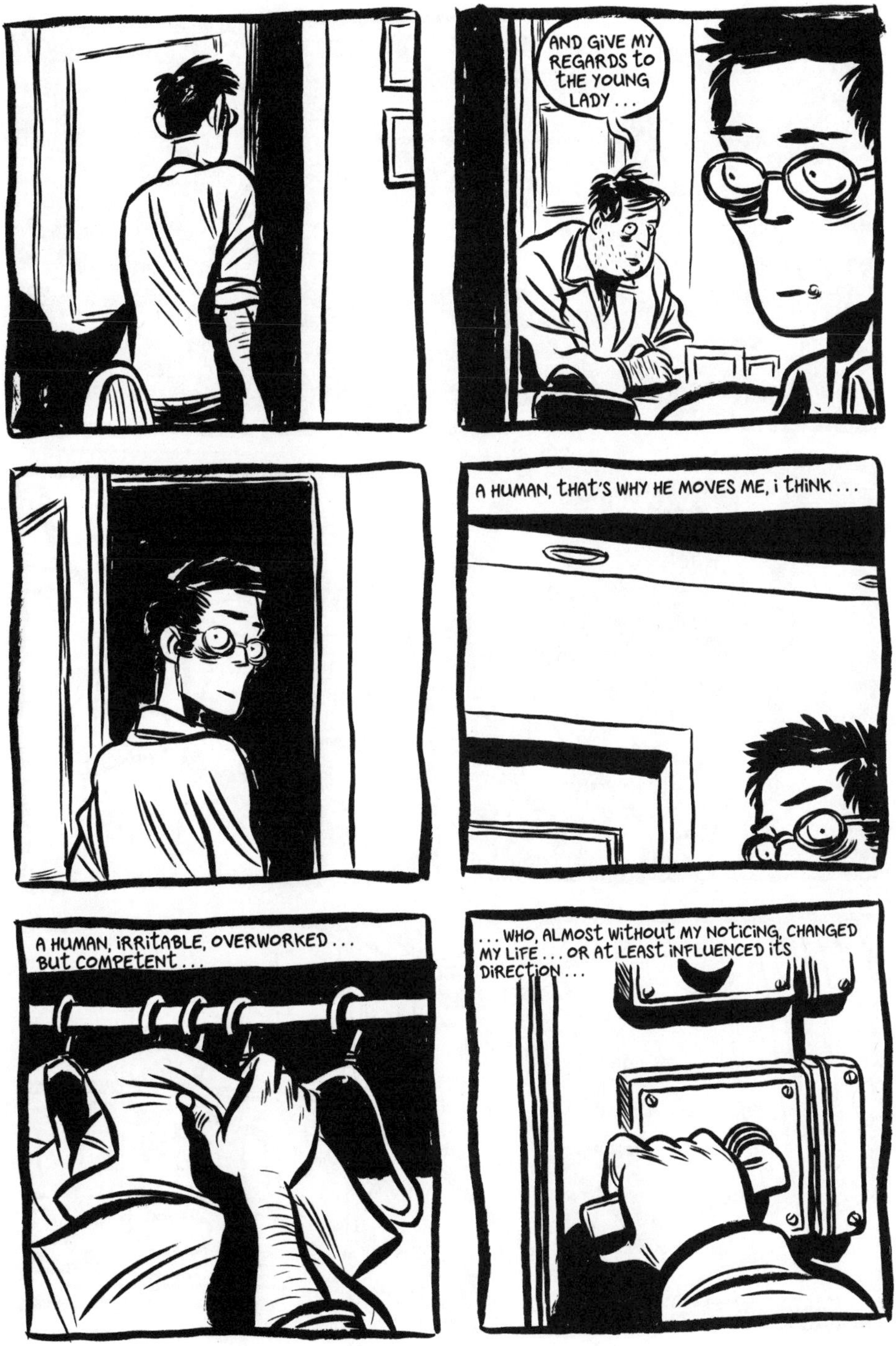
AND GIVE MY REGARDS TO THE YOUNG LADY . . .
A HUMAN, THAT'S WHY HE MOVES ME, I THINK . . .
A HUMAN, IRRITABLE, OVERWORKED . . . BUT COMPETENT . . .
. . . WHO, ALMOST WITHOUT MY NOTICING, CHANGED MY LIFE . . . OR AT LEAST INFLUENCED ITS DIRECTION . . .

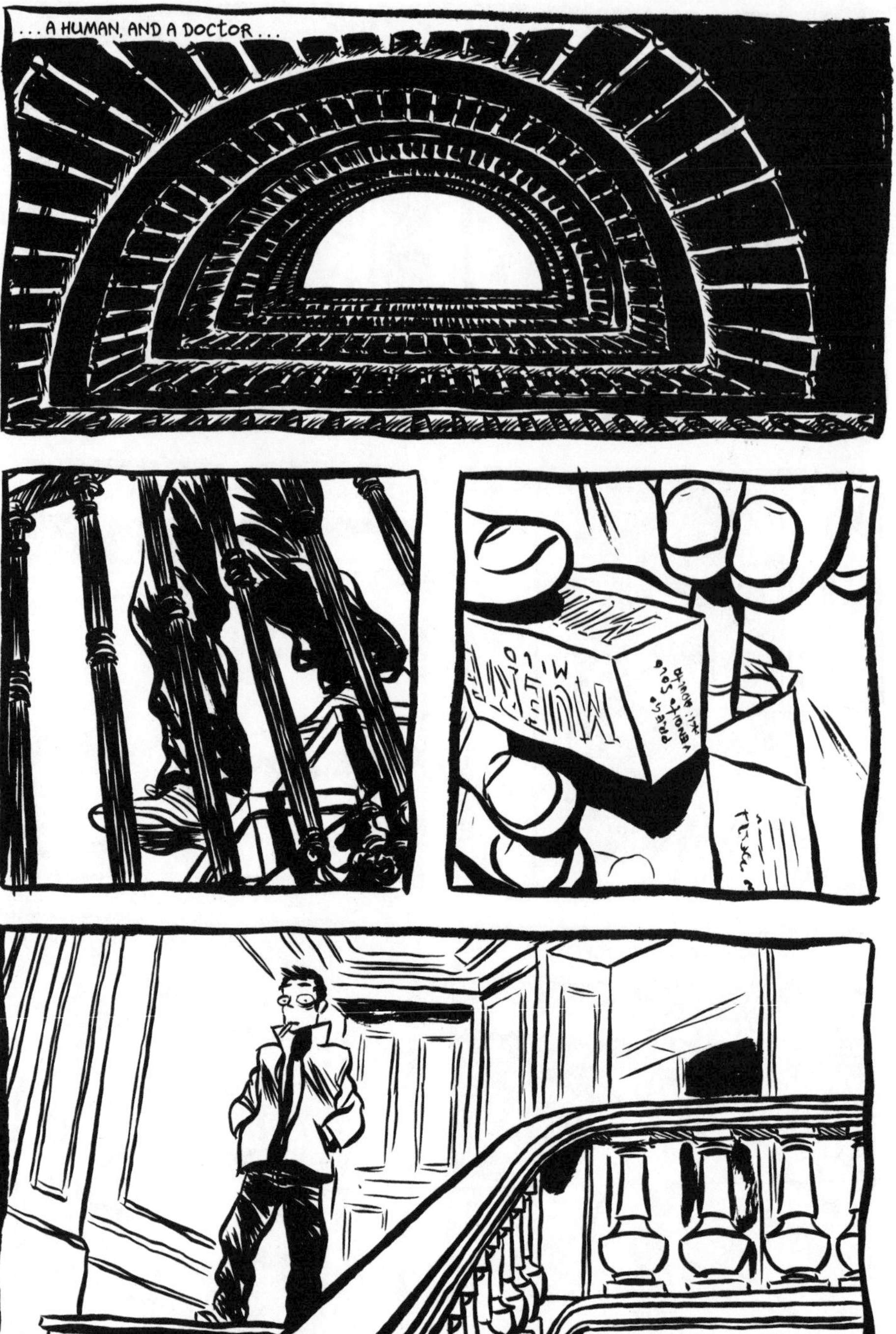
. . . A HUMAN, AND A DOCTOR . . .

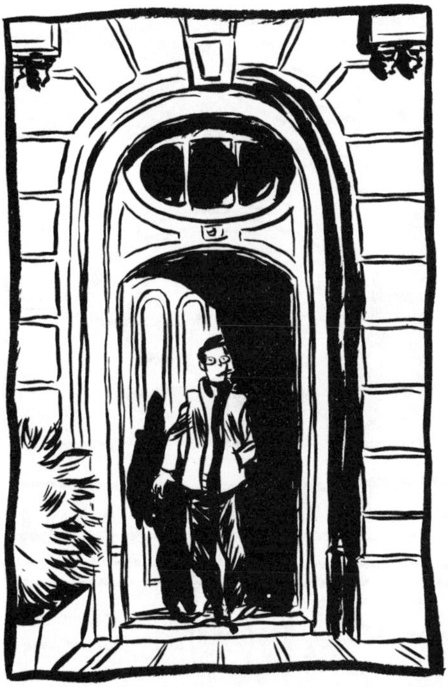

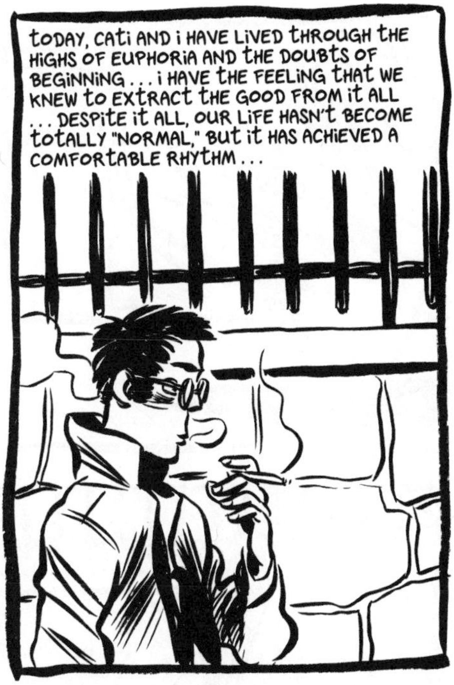
TODAY, CATI AND I HAVE LIVED THROUGH THE HIGHS OF EUPHORIA AND THE DOUBTS OF BEGINNING . . . I HAVE THE FEELING THAT WE KNEW TO EXTRACT THE GOOD FROM IT ALL . . . DESPITE IT ALL, OUR LIFE HASN'T BECOME TOTALLY "NORMAL," BUT IT HAS ACHIEVED A COMFORTABLE RHYTHM . . .

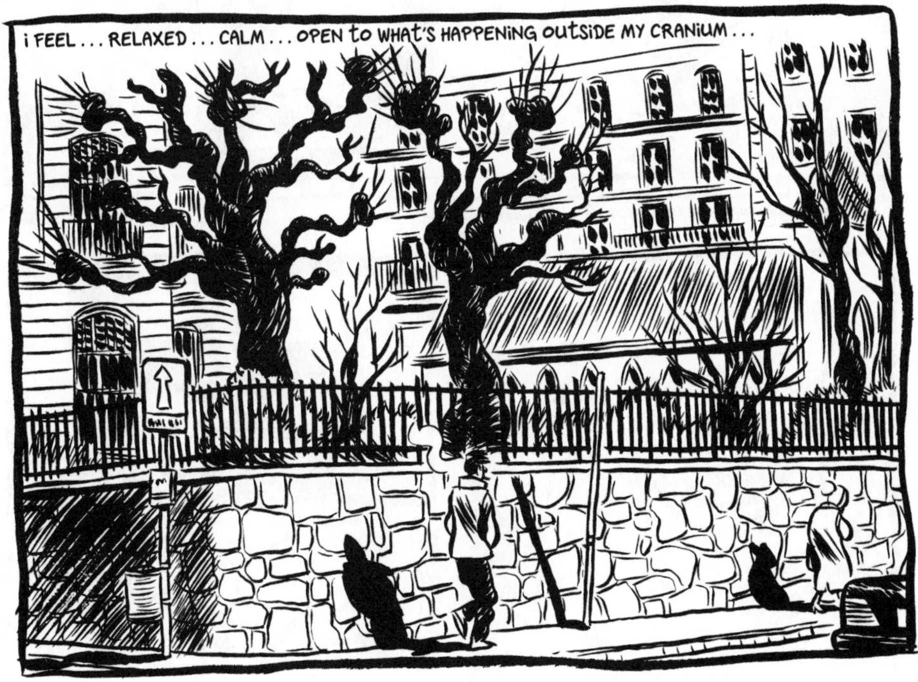
I FEEL . . . RELAXED . . . CALM . . . OPEN TO WHAT'S HAPPENING OUTSIDE MY CRANIUM . . .

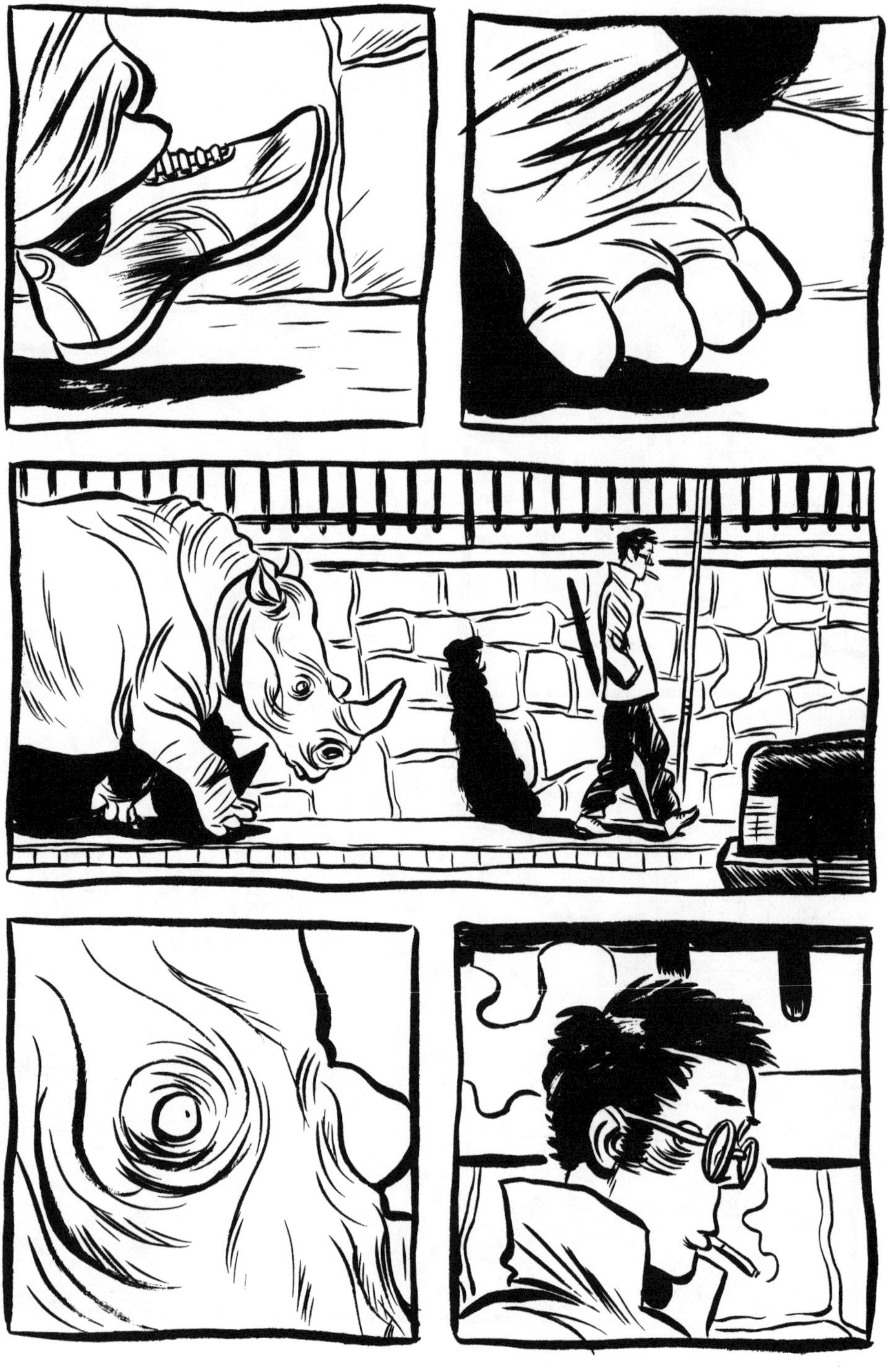

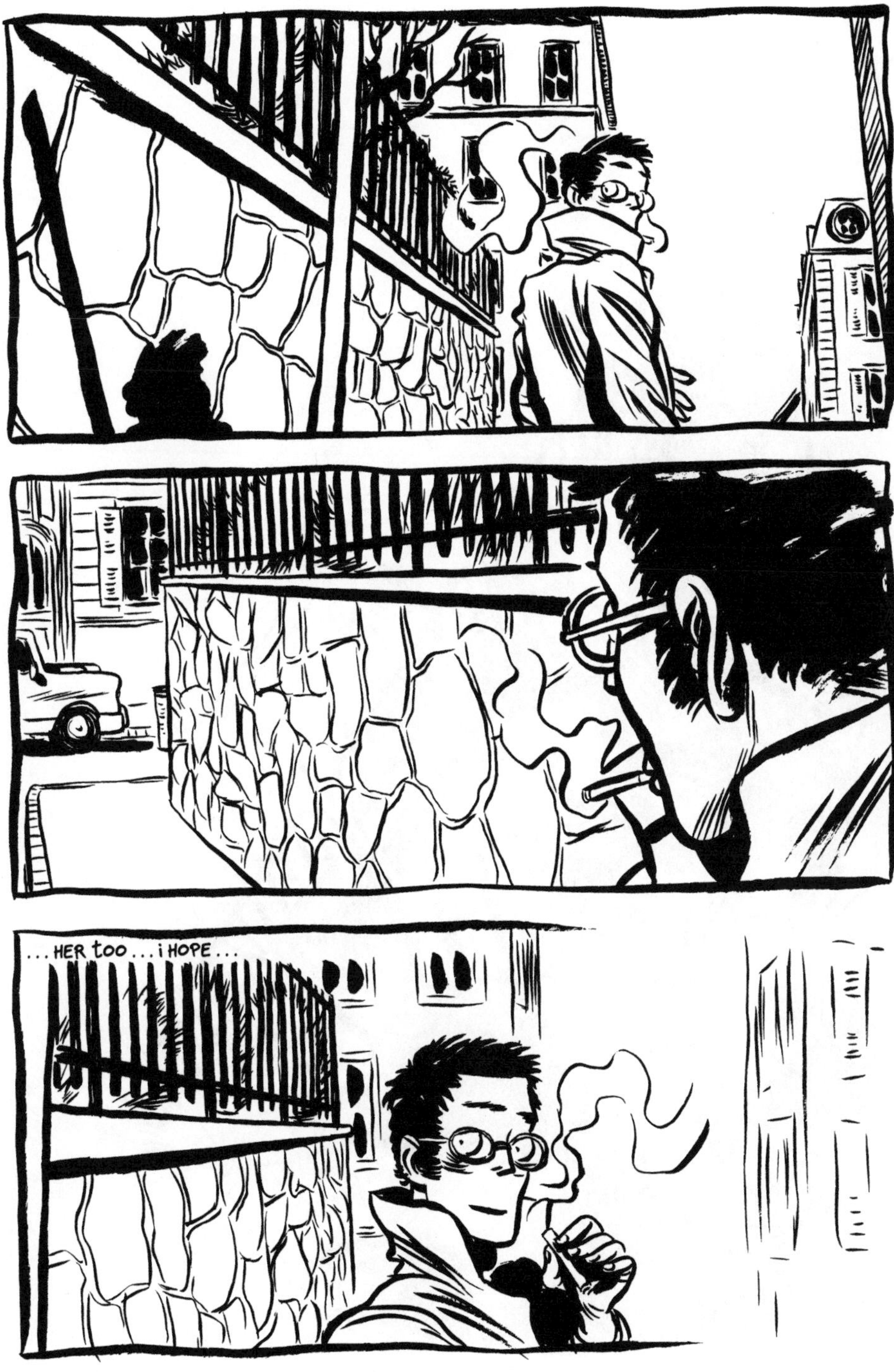

...HER too...i HOPE...

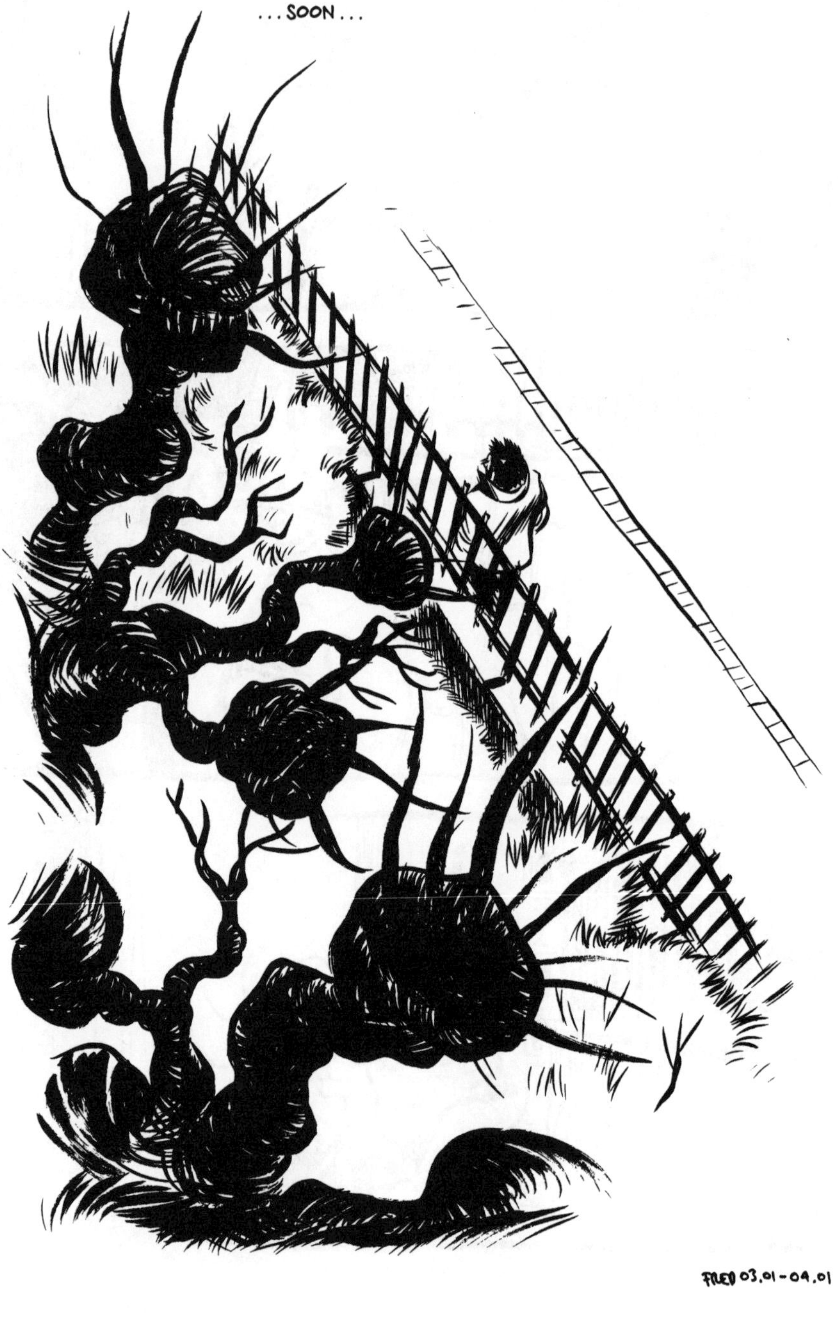
...SOON...
FRED 03.01-04.01

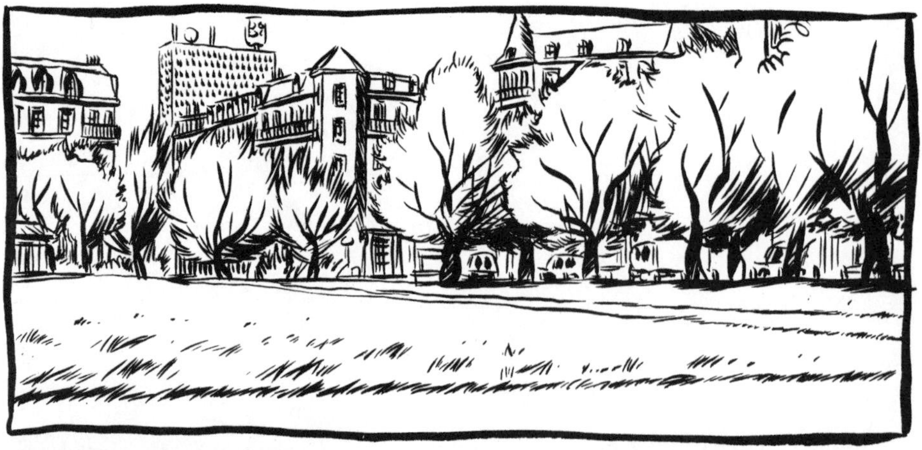

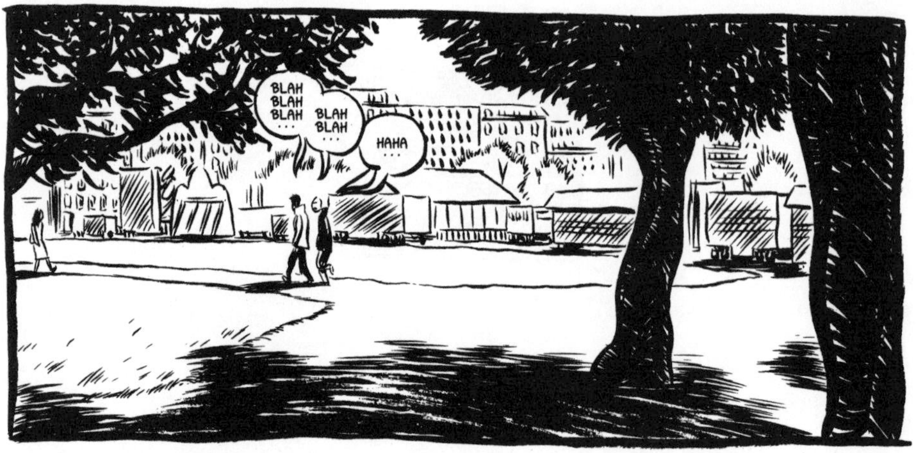
BLAH BLAH BLAH ...
BLAH BLAH ...
HAHA ...

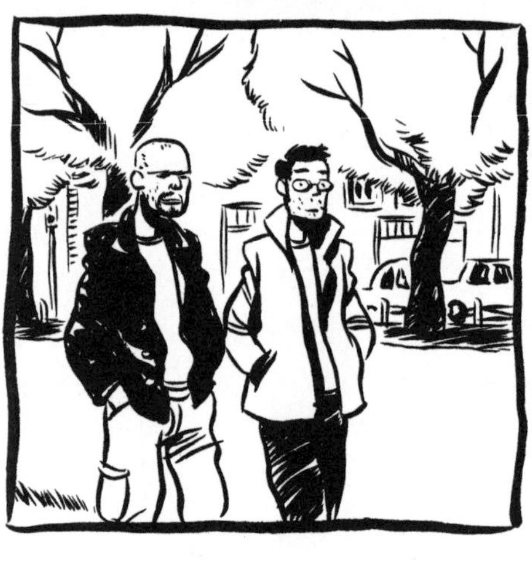

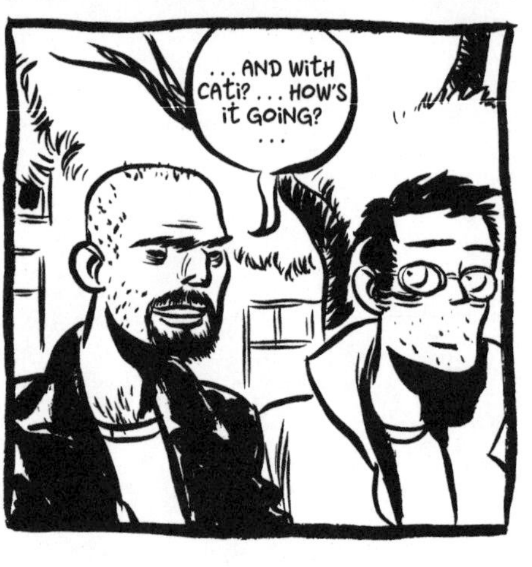
... AND WITH CATI? ... HOW'S IT GOING? ...

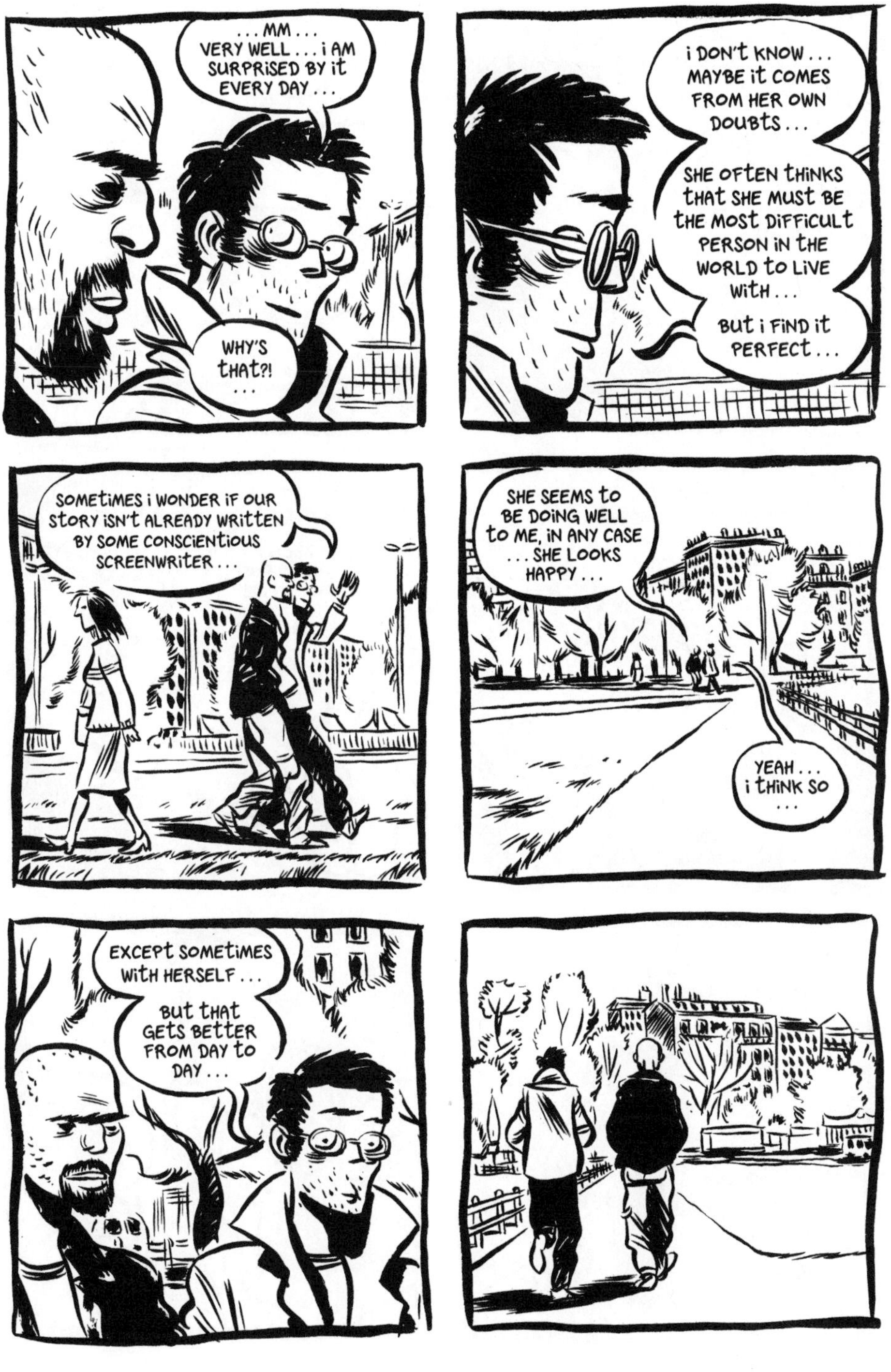

. . . MM . . . VERY WELL . . . i AM SURPRISED BY it EVERY DAY . . .
WHY'S THAT?! . . .
i DON'T KNOW . . . MAYBE it COMES FROM HER OWN DOUBTS . . .
SHE OFTEN THINKS THAT SHE MUST BE THE MOST DIFFICULT PERSON IN THE WORLD TO LIVE WITH . . .
BUT i FIND it PERFECT . . .
SOMETIMES i WONDER IF OUR STORY ISN'T ALREADY WRITTEN BY SOME CONSCIENTIOUS SCREENWRITER . . .
SHE SEEMS TO BE DOING WELL TO ME, IN ANY CASE . . . SHE LOOKS HAPPY . . .
YEAH . . . i THINK SO . . .
EXCEPT SOMETIMES WITH HERSELF . . .
BUT THAT GETS BETTER FROM DAY TO DAY . . .

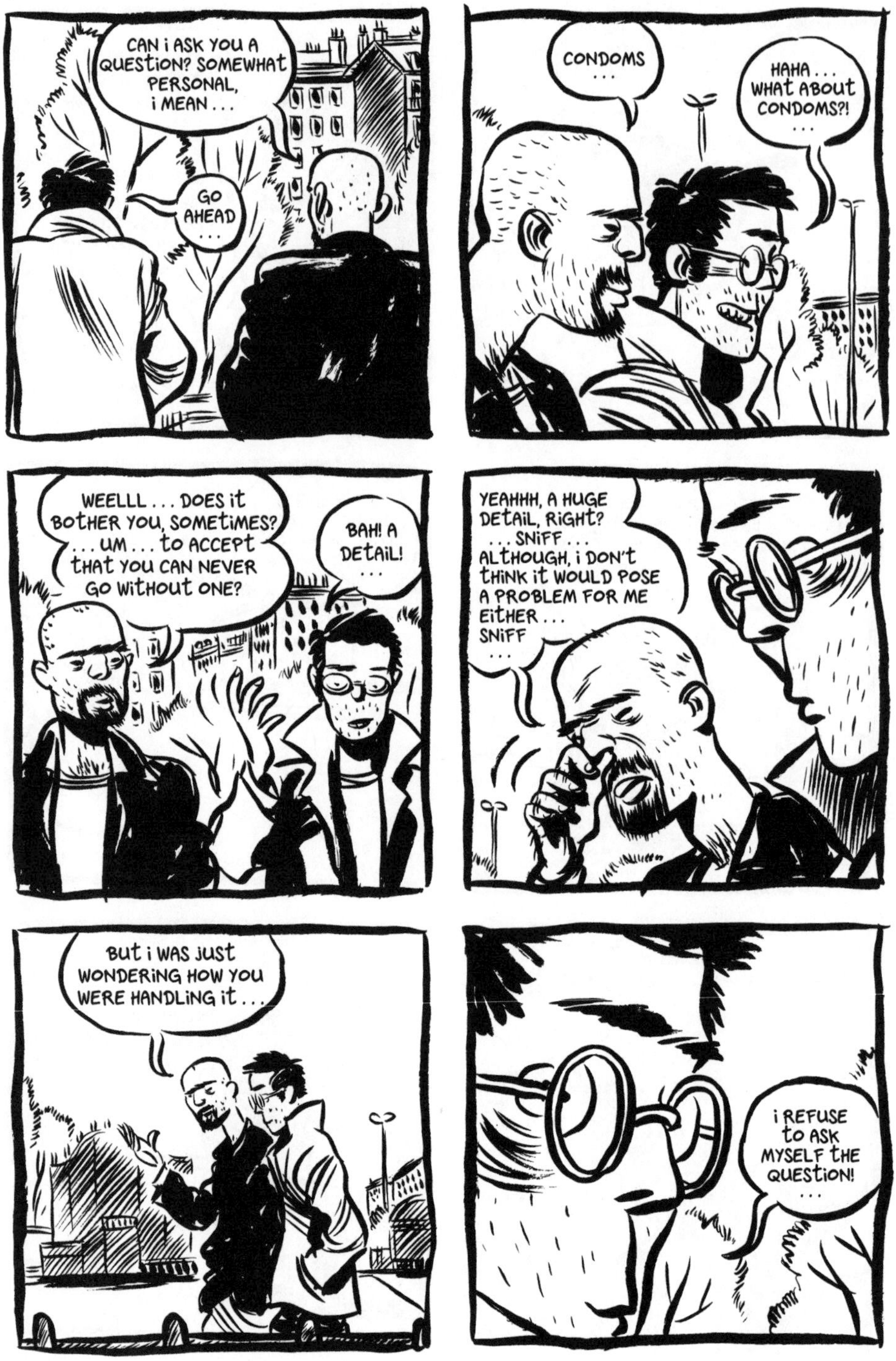
CAN i ASK YOU A QUESTION? SOMEWHAT PERSONAL, i MEAN . . .
GO AHEAD . . .
CONDOMS . . .
HAHA . . . WHAT ABOUT CONDOMS?! . . .
WEELLL . . . DOES it BOTHER YOU, SOMETIMES? . . . UM . . . to ACCEPT THAT YOU CAN NEVER GO WITHOUT ONE?
BAH! A DETAIL! . . .
YEAHHH, A HUGE DETAIL, RIGHT? . . . SNIFF . . . ALTHOUGH, i DON'T THINK it WOULD POSE A PROBLEM FOR ME EITHER . . . SNIFF . . .
But i WAS JUST WONDERING HOW YOU WERE HANDLING it . . .
i REFUSE to ASK MYSELF THE QUESTION! . . .

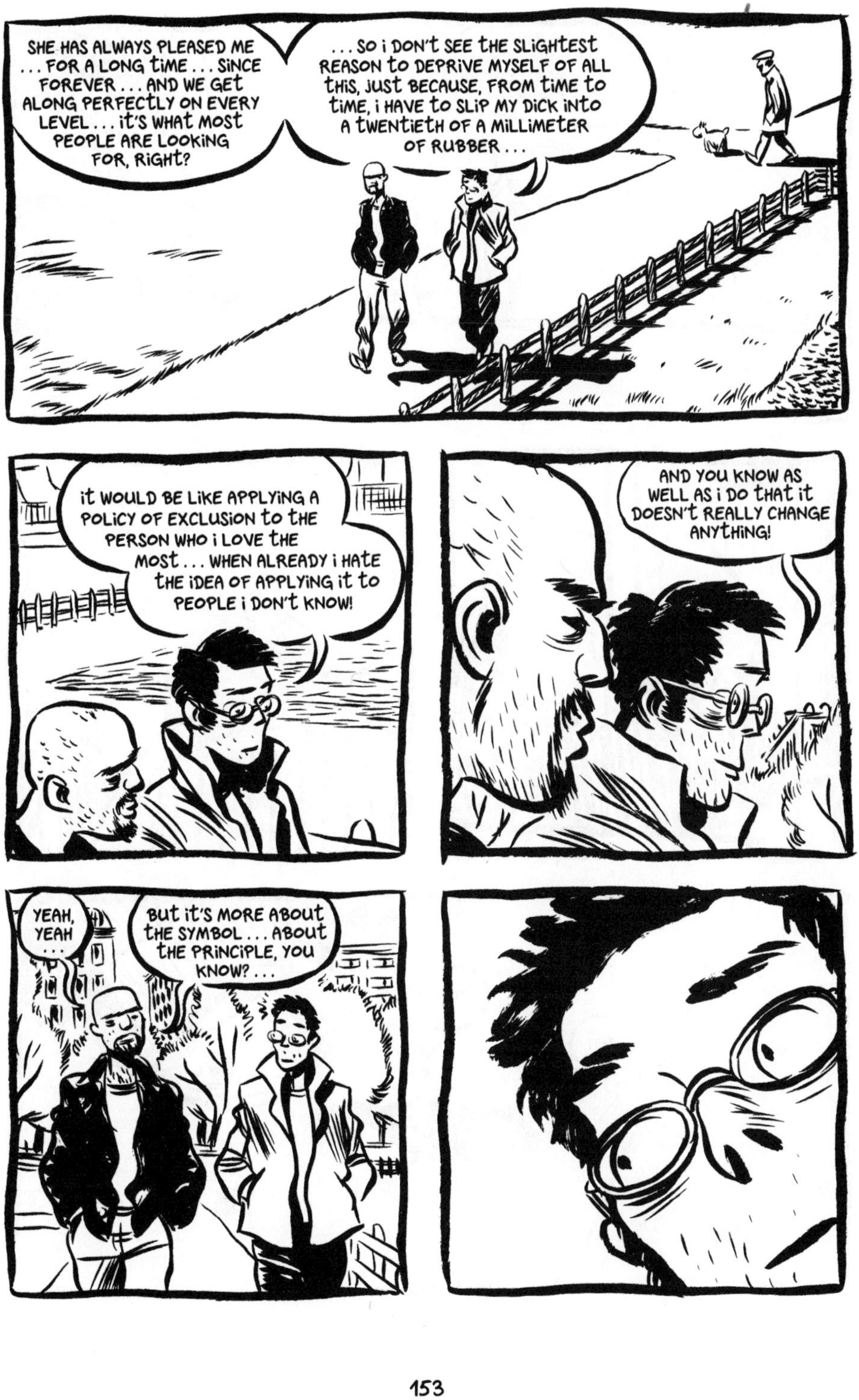
SHE HAS ALWAYS PLEASED ME . . . FOR A LONG TIME . . . SINCE FOREVER . . . AND WE GET ALONG PERFECTLY ON EVERY LEVEL . . . IT'S WHAT MOST PEOPLE ARE LOOKING FOR, RIGHT?
. . . SO I DON'T SEE THE SLIGHTEST REASON TO DEPRIVE MYSELF OF ALL THIS, JUST BECAUSE, FROM TIME TO TIME, I HAVE TO SLIP MY DICK INTO A TWENTIETH OF A MILLIMETER OF RUBBER . . .
IT WOULD BE LIKE APPLYING A POLICY OF EXCLUSION TO THE PERSON WHO I LOVE THE MOST . . . WHEN ALREADY I HATE THE IDEA OF APPLYING IT TO PEOPLE I DON'T KNOW!
AND YOU KNOW AS WELL AS I DO THAT IT DOESN'T REALLY CHANGE ANYTHING!
YEAH, YEAH . . .
BUT IT'S MORE ABOUT THE SYMBOL . . . ABOUT THE PRINCIPLE, YOU KNOW? . . .

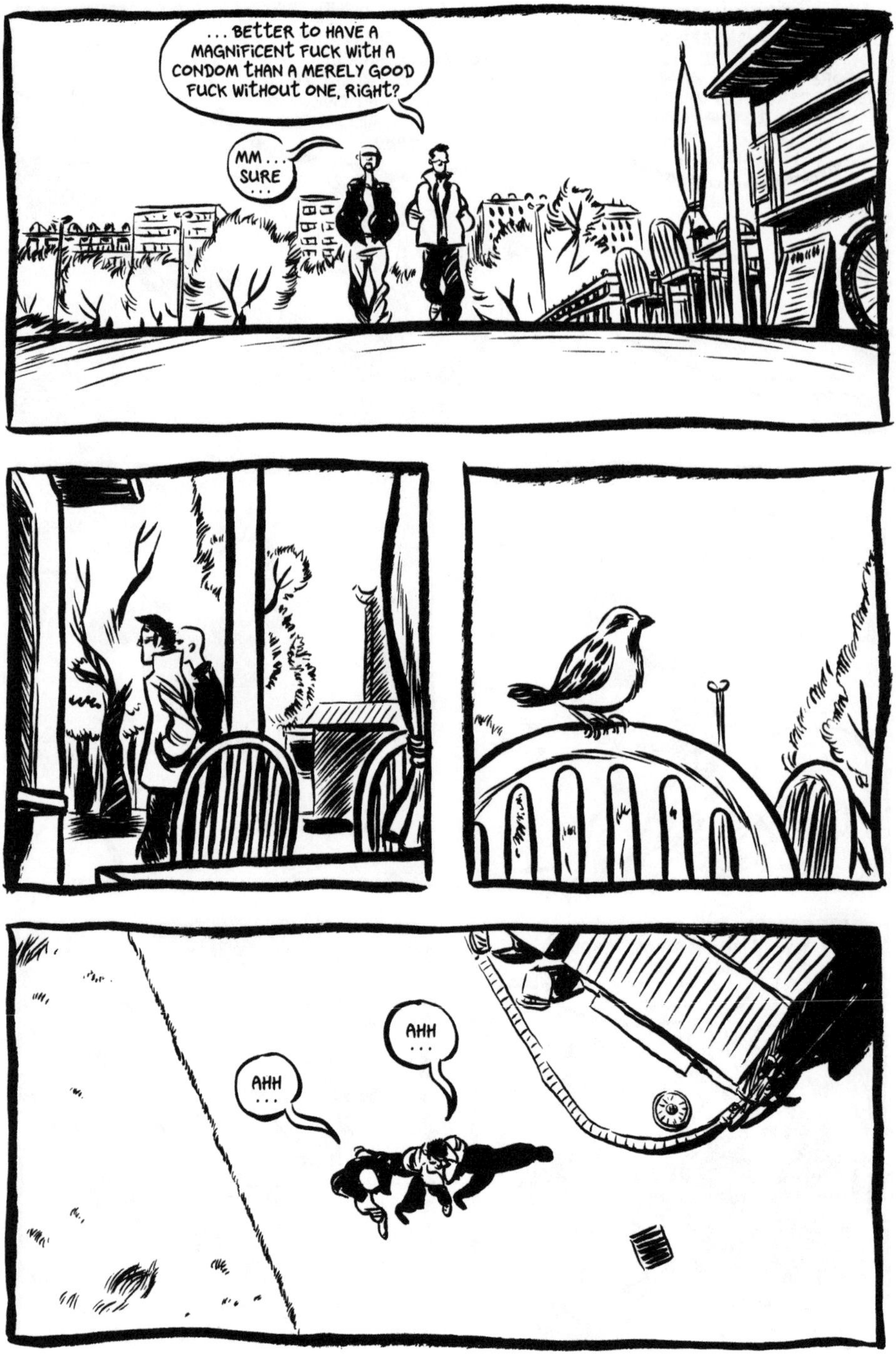
... BETTER TO HAVE A MAGNIFICENT FUCK WITH A CONDOM THAN A MERELY GOOD FUCK WITHOUT ONE, RIGHT?
MM... SURE ...
AHH ...
AHH ...

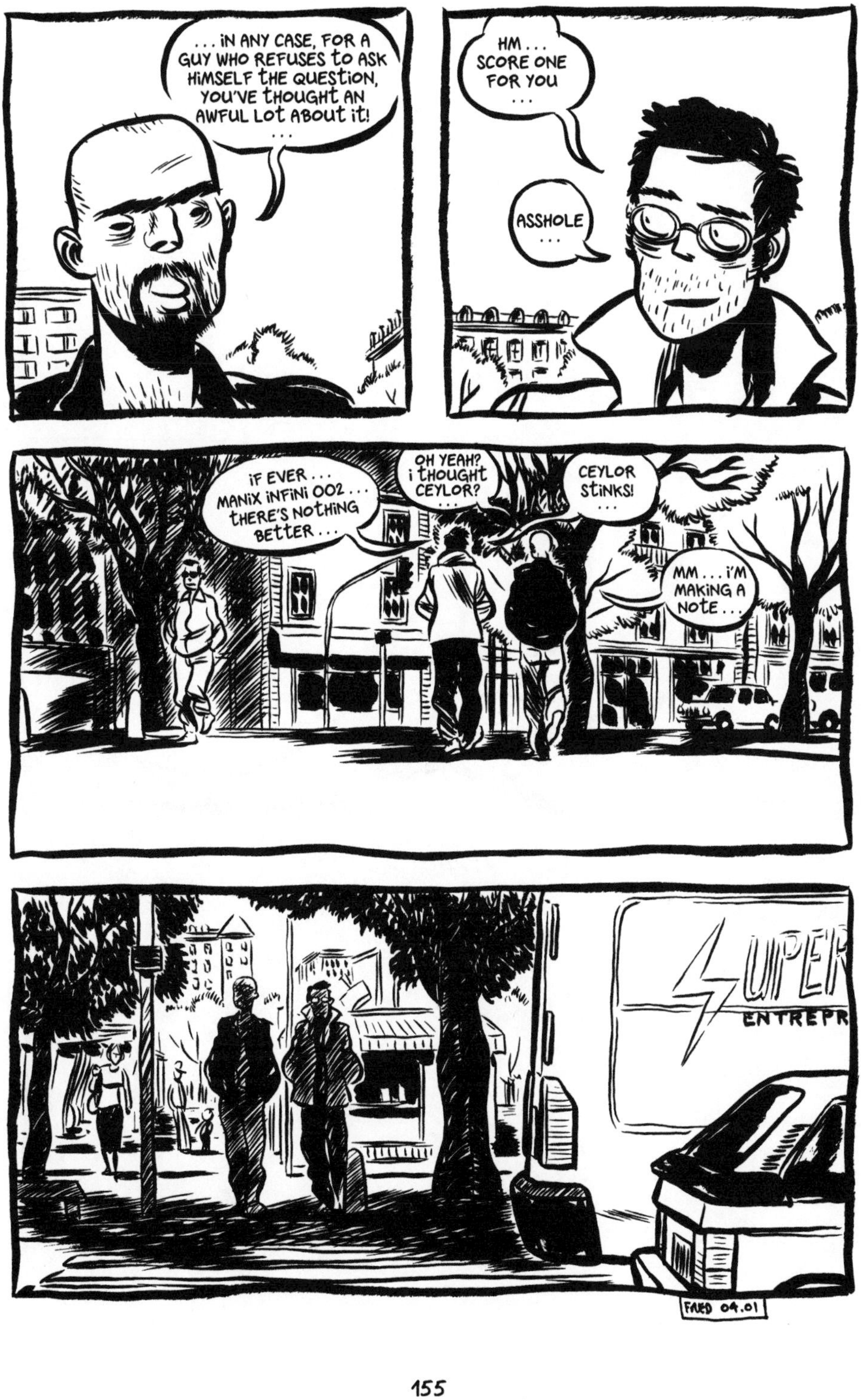

. . . iN ANY CASE, FOR A GUY WHO REFUSES tO ASK HiMSELF tHE QUEStiON, YOU'VE tHOUGHt AN AWFUL LOt ABOUt it! . . .
HM . . . SCORE ONE FOR YOU . . .
ASSHOLE . . .
iF EVER . . . MANiX iNFiNi 002 . . . tHERE'S NOtHiNG BEttER . . .
OH YEAH? i tHOUGHt CEYLOR? . . .
CEYLOR StiNKS! . . .
MM . . . i'M MAKiNG A NOtE . . .
SUPER
ENTREPR
FRED 04.01

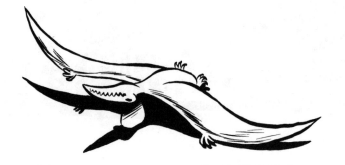

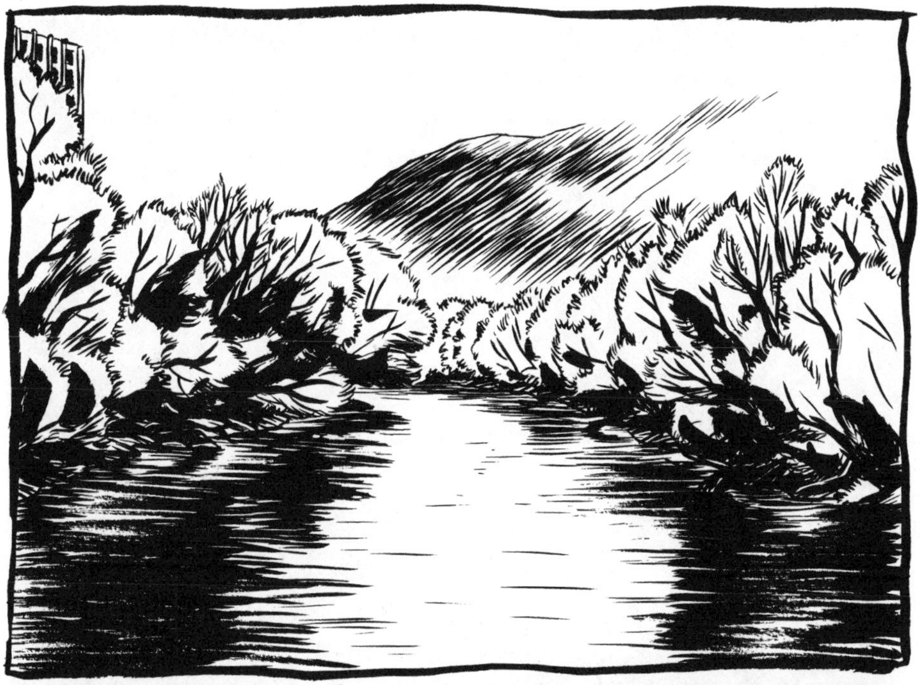

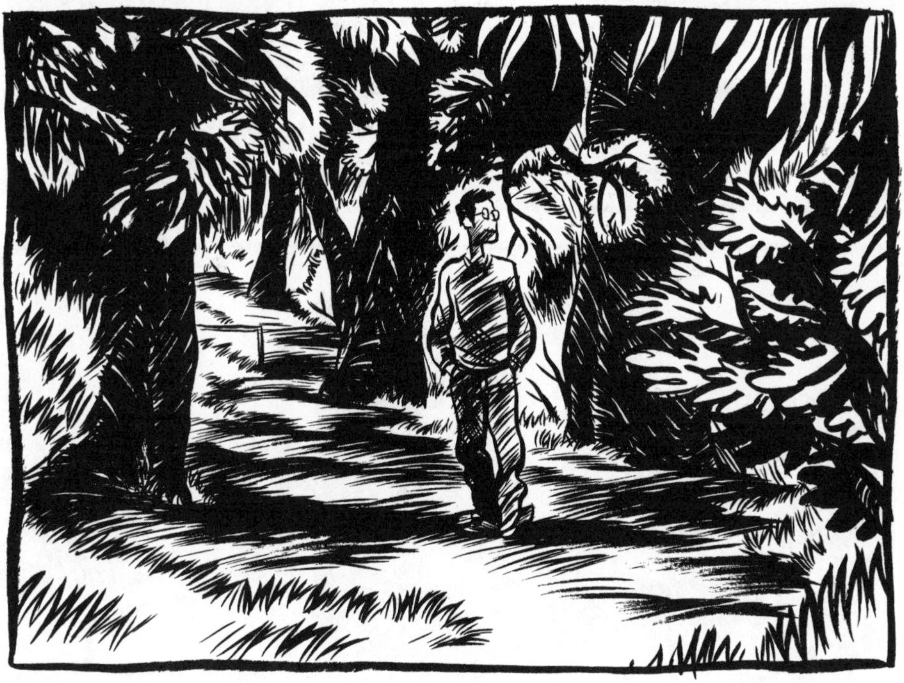

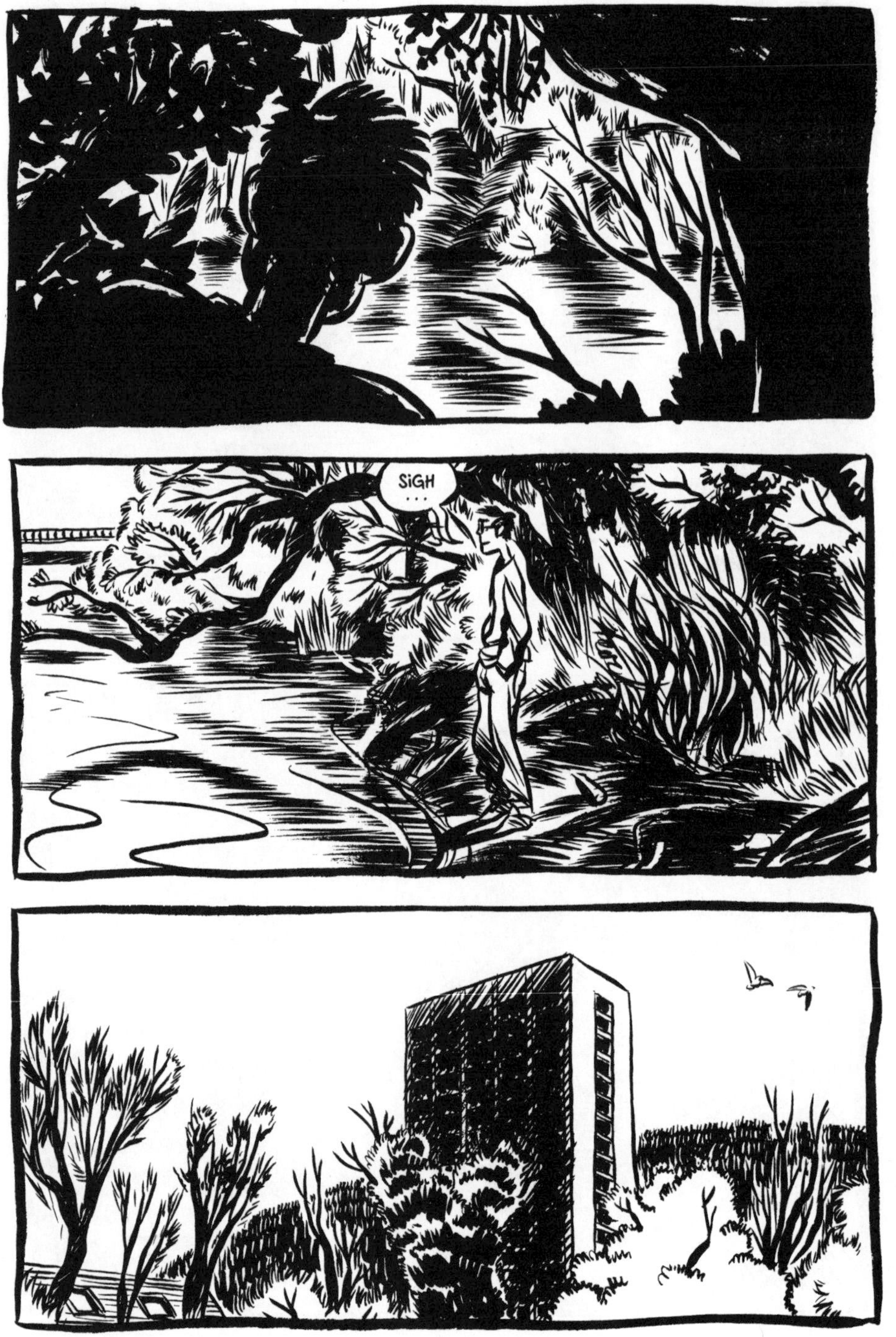
SiGH
...

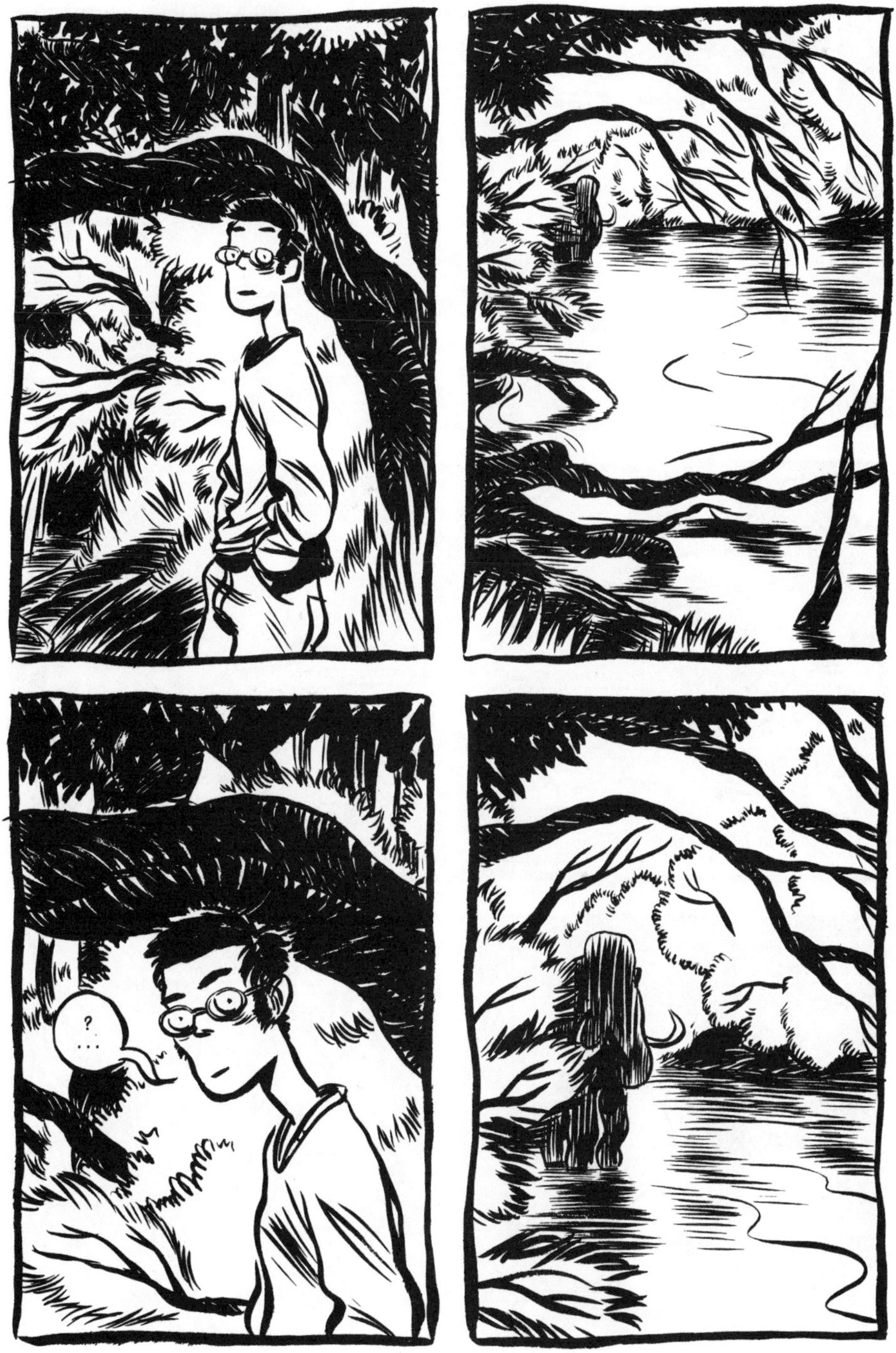
?
...

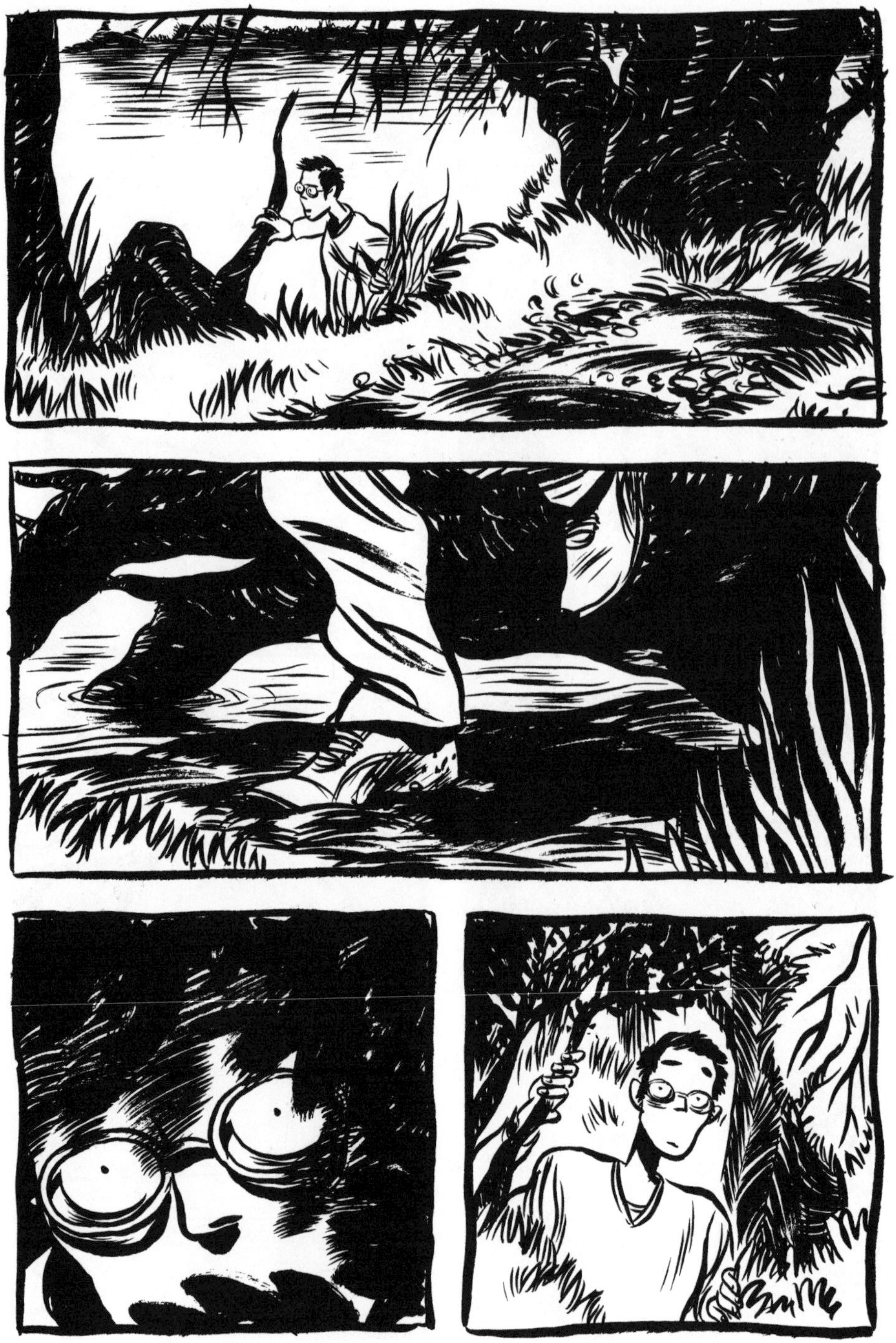

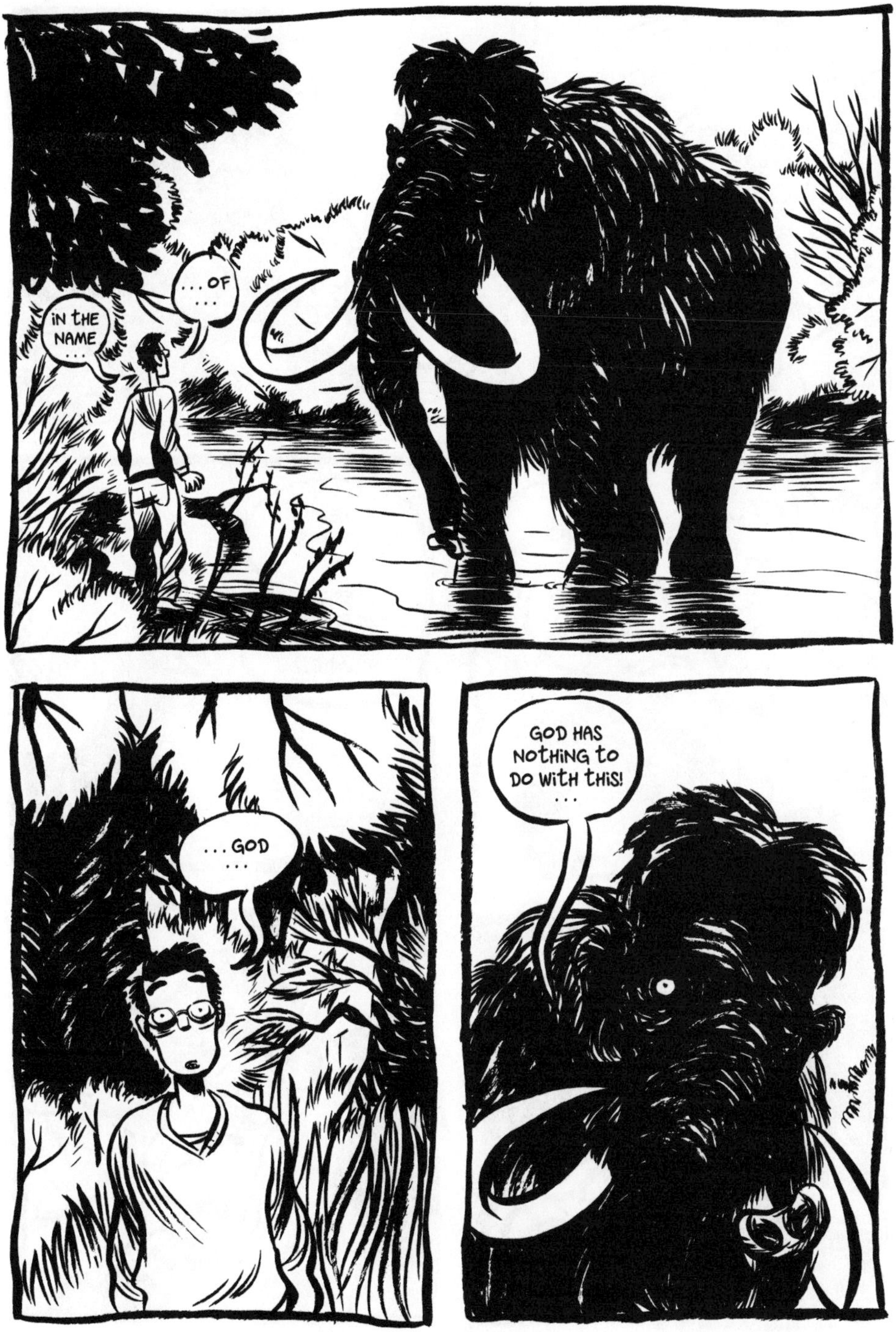
IN THE NAME . . .
. . . OF . . .
. . . GOD . . .
GOD HAS NOTHING TO DO WITH THIS! . . .

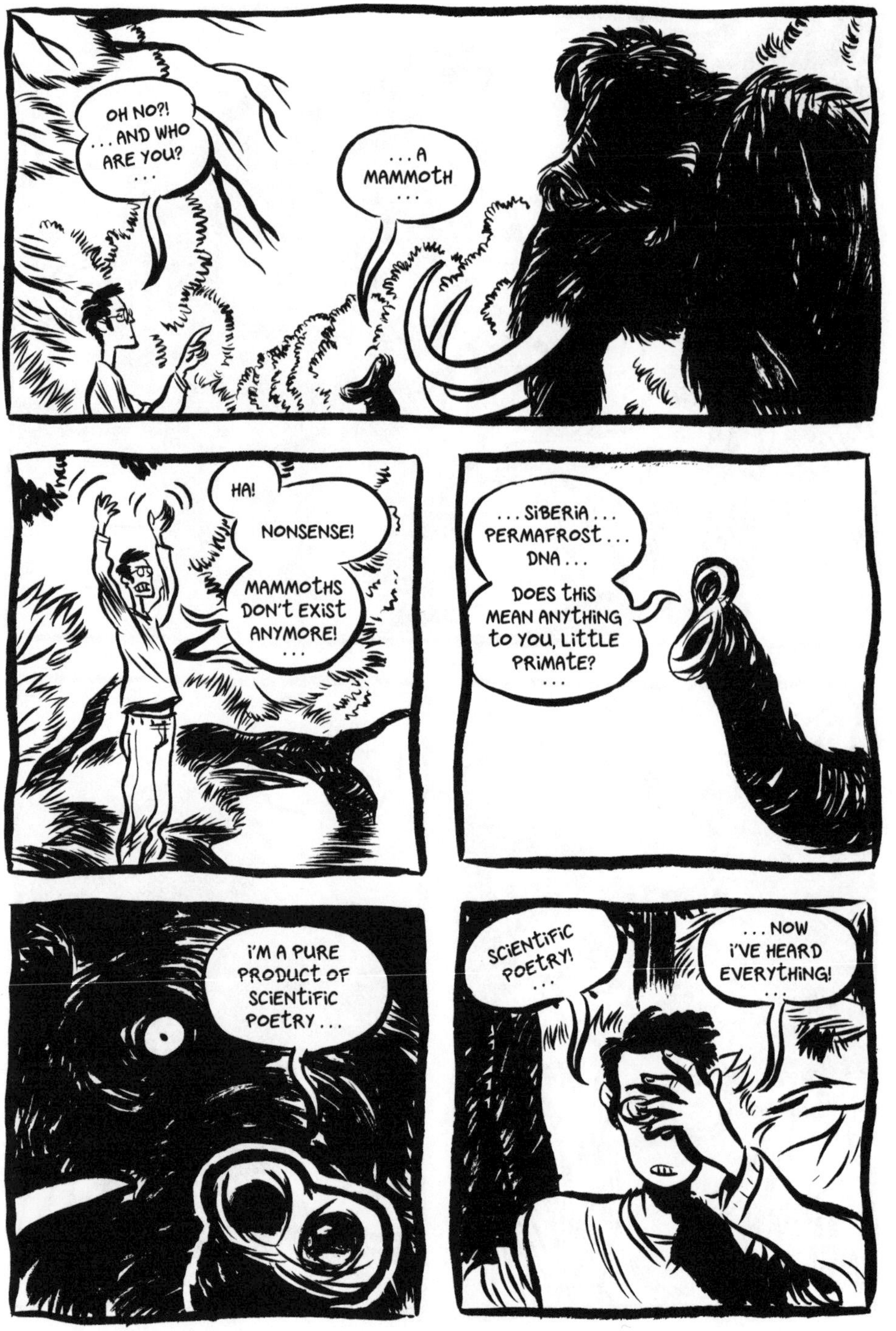
OH NO?! . . . AND WHO ARE YOU? . . .
. . . A MAMMOTH . . .
HA!
NONSENSE!
MAMMOTHS DON'T EXIST ANYMORE! . . .
. . . SIBERIA . . . PERMAFROST . . . DNA . . .
DOES THIS MEAN ANYTHING TO YOU, LITTLE PRIMATE? . . .
I'M A PURE PRODUCT OF SCIENTIFIC POETRY . . .
SCIENTIFIC POETRY! . . .
. . . NOW I'VE HEARD EVERYTHING! . . .

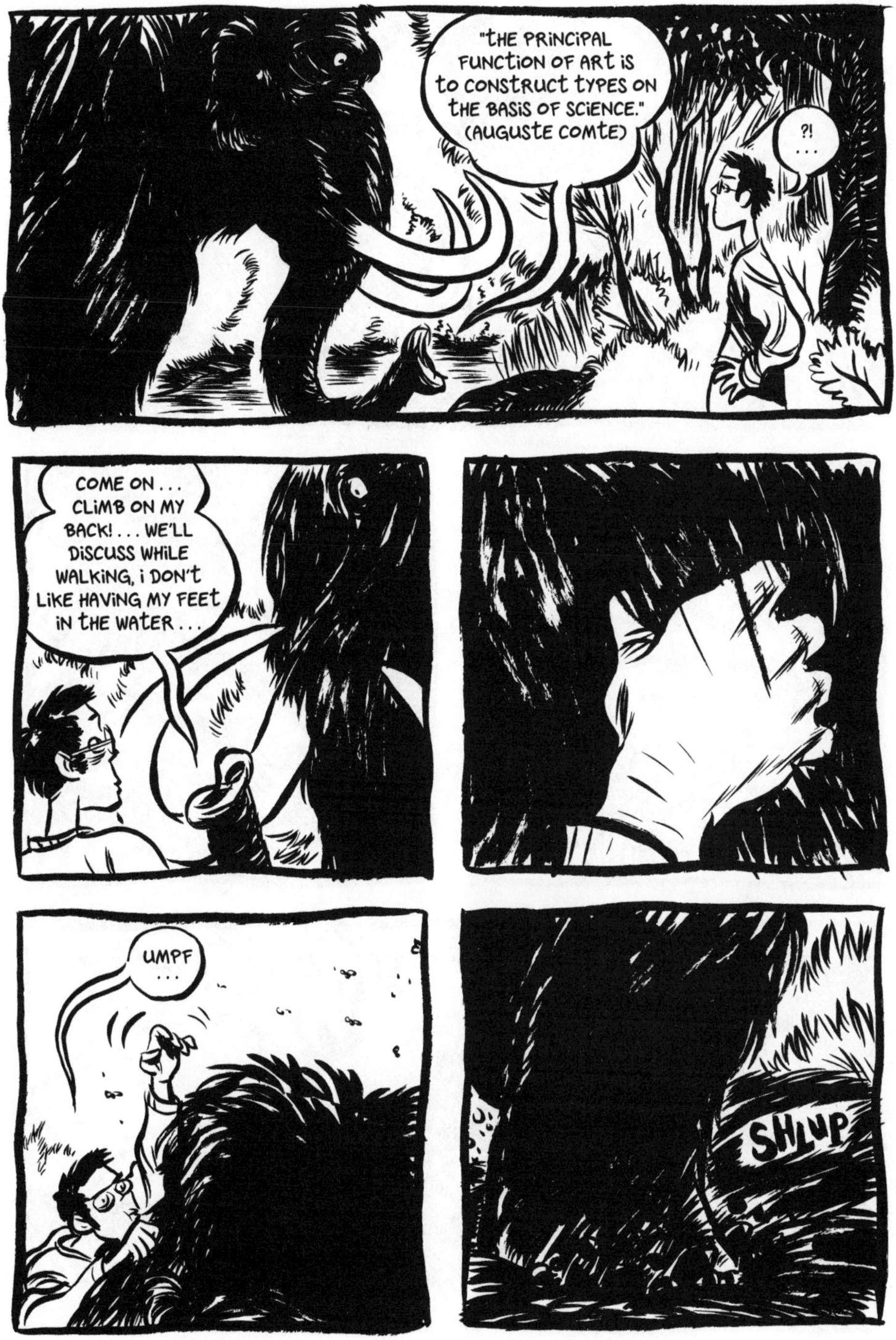
"THE PRINCIPAL FUNCTION OF ART IS TO CONSTRUCT TYPES ON THE BASIS OF SCIENCE." (AUGUSTE COMTE)
?! ...
COME ON... CLIMB ON MY BACK!... WE'LL DISCUSS WHILE WALKING, I DON'T LIKE HAVING MY FEET IN THE WATER...
UMPF ...
SHLUP

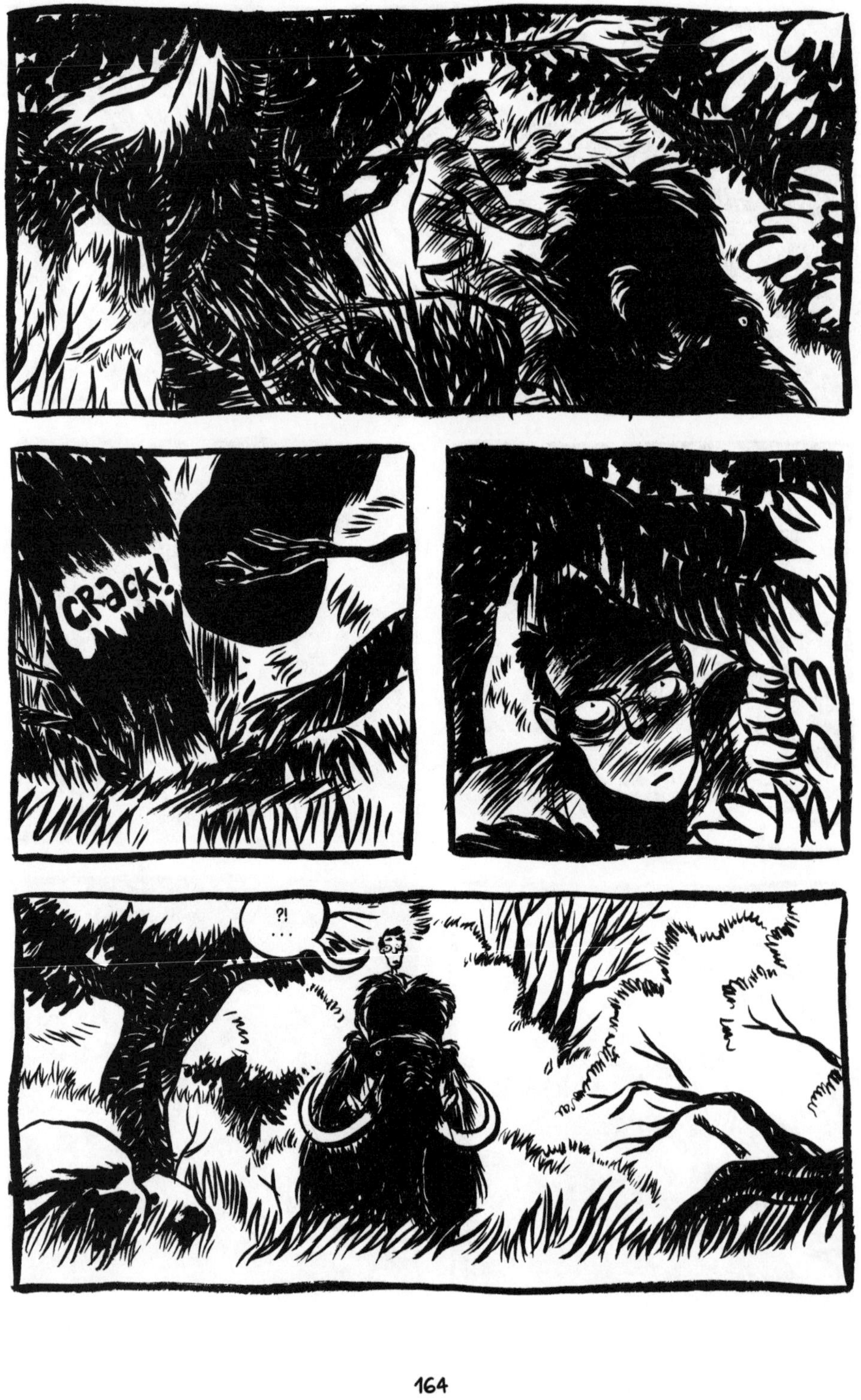
CRACK!
?!
...

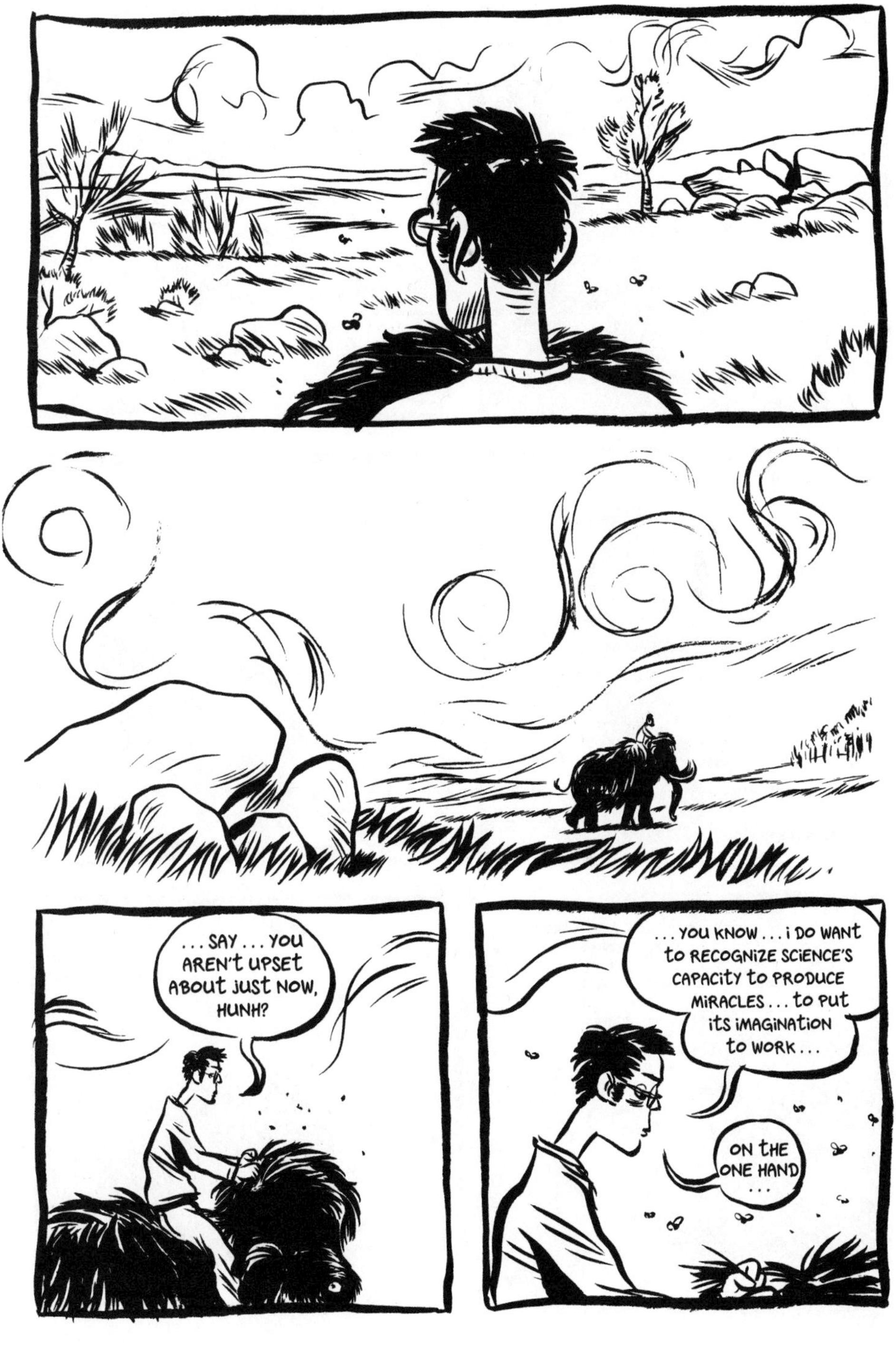
...SAY...YOU AREN'T UPSET ABOUT JUST NOW, HUNH?
...YOU KNOW...I DO WANT TO RECOGNIZE SCIENCE'S CAPACITY TO PRODUCE MIRACLES...TO PUT ITS IMAGINATION TO WORK...
ON THE ONE HAND ...

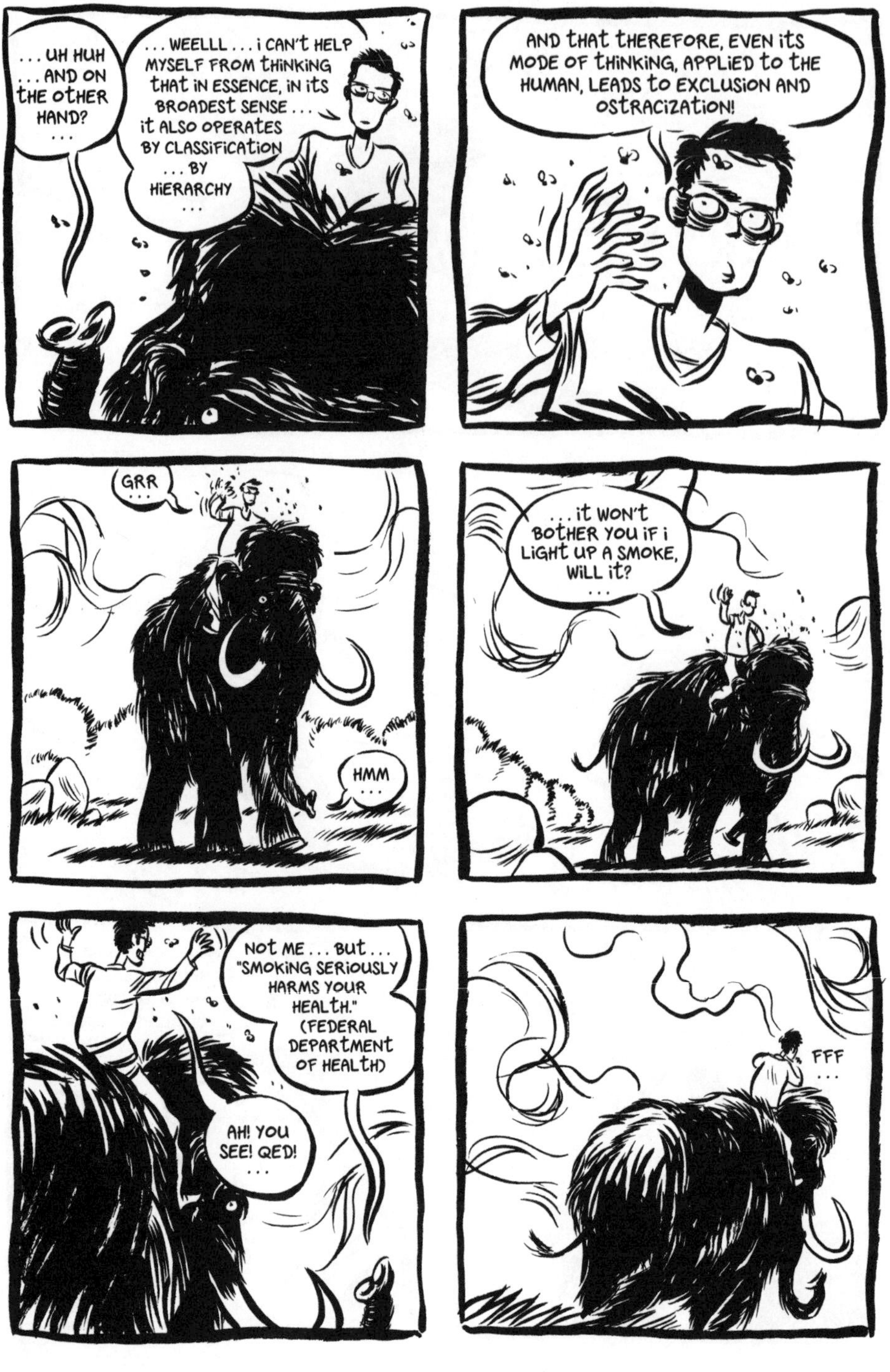
. . . UH HUH . . . AND ON THE OTHER HAND? . . .
. . . WEELLL . . . I CAN'T HELP MYSELF FROM THINKING THAT IN ESSENCE, IN ITS BROADEST SENSE . . . IT ALSO OPERATES BY CLASSIFICATION . . . BY HIERARCHY . . .
AND THAT THEREFORE, EVEN ITS MODE OF THINKING, APPLIED TO THE HUMAN, LEADS TO EXCLUSION AND OSTRACIZATION!
GRR . . .
HMM . . .
. . . IT WON'T BOTHER YOU IF I LIGHT UP A SMOKE, WILL IT? . . .
NOT ME . . . BUT . . . "SMOKING SERIOUSLY HARMS YOUR HEALTH." (FEDERAL DEPARTMENT OF HEALTH)
AH! YOU SEE! QED! . . .
FFF . . .

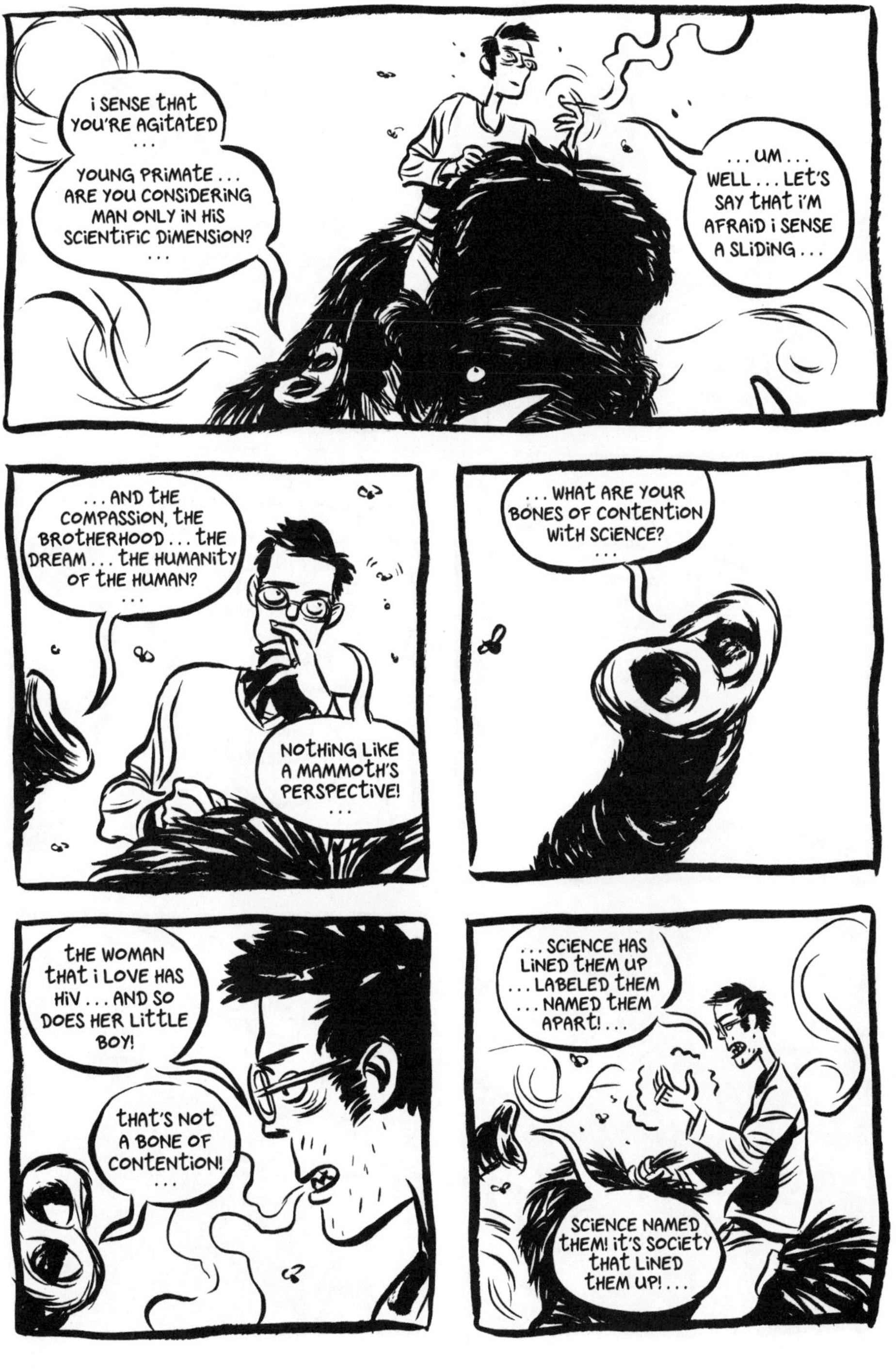
i SENSE tHAt YOU'RE AGitAtED . . . YOUNG PRiMAtE . . . ARE YOU CONSiDERiNG MAN ONLY iN HiS SCiENtiFiC DiMENSiON? . . .
. . . UM . . . WELL . . . LEt'S SAY tHAt i'M AFRAiD i SENSE A SLiDiNG . . .
. . . AND tHE COMPASSiON, tHE BROtHERHOOD . . . tHE DREAM . . . tHE HUMANitY OF tHE HUMAN? . . .
NOtHiNG LiKE A MAMMOtH'S PERSPECtiVE! . . .
. . . WHAt ARE YOUR BONES OF CONtENtiON WitH SCiENCE? . . .
tHE WOMAN tHAt i LOVE HAS HiV . . . AND SO DOES HER LittLE BOY!
tHAt'S NOt A BONE OF CONtENtiON! . . .
. . . SCiENCE HAS LiNED tHEM UP . . . LABELED tHEM . . . NAMED tHEM APARt! . . .
SCiENCE NAMED tHEM! it'S SOCiEtY tHAt LiNED tHEM UP! . . .

AND WHY DID SCIENCE NAME THEM?

TO BETTER TREAT THEM...

EXCUSE ME...

HAHAHA

HA HA HA

LOOK AT AFRICA! HAHAHA! IT'S FLAGRANT!...

NO NO NO... THOSE ARE STILL OTHER SPHERES... THE END OF THE HUMAN... THE END OF SCIENCE

...THERE IT'S BIG MONEY AND THAT'S ALL!...

THE RESULT OF ALL THIS CYNICISM, LAST YEAR IN IRAN A FATHER KILLED HIS SON WITH AN AX BECAUSE HE WAS HIV POSITIVE...

PFF... TO TREAT!...

YOU'RE MIXING UP EVERYTHING... YOUNG PRIMATE...

THE ROOTS OF YOUR ANGER GO DEEP...

HMM...

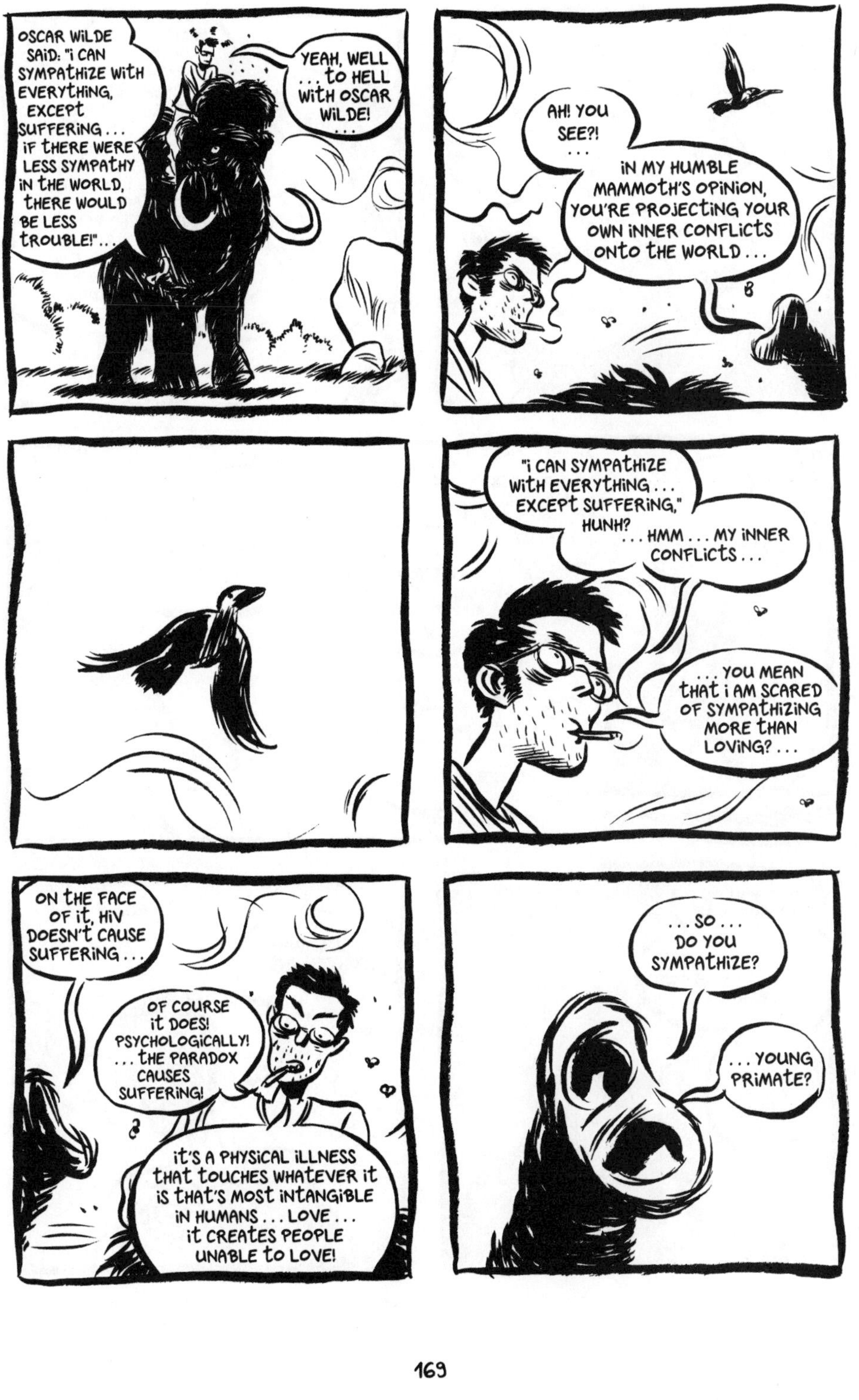
OSCAR WILDE SAID: "I CAN SYMPATHIZE WITH EVERYTHING, EXCEPT SUFFERING . . . IF THERE WERE LESS SYMPATHY IN THE WORLD, THERE WOULD BE LESS TROUBLE!" . . .
YEAH, WELL . . . TO HELL WITH OSCAR WILDE! . . .
AH! YOU SEE?! . . .
IN MY HUMBLE MAMMOTH'S OPINION, YOU'RE PROJECTING YOUR OWN INNER CONFLICTS ONTO THE WORLD . . .
"I CAN SYMPATHIZE WITH EVERYTHING . . . EXCEPT SUFFERING," HUNH?
. . . HMM . . . MY INNER CONFLICTS . . .
. . . YOU MEAN THAT I AM SCARED OF SYMPATHIZING MORE THAN LOVING? . . .
ON THE FACE OF IT, HIV DOESN'T CAUSE SUFFERING . . .
OF COURSE IT DOES! PSYCHOLOGICALLY! . . . THE PARADOX CAUSES SUFFERING!
IT'S A PHYSICAL ILLNESS THAT TOUCHES WHATEVER IT IS THAT'S MOST INTANGIBLE IN HUMANS . . . LOVE . . . IT CREATES PEOPLE UNABLE TO LOVE!
. . . SO . . . DO YOU SYMPATHIZE?
. . . YOUNG PRIMATE?

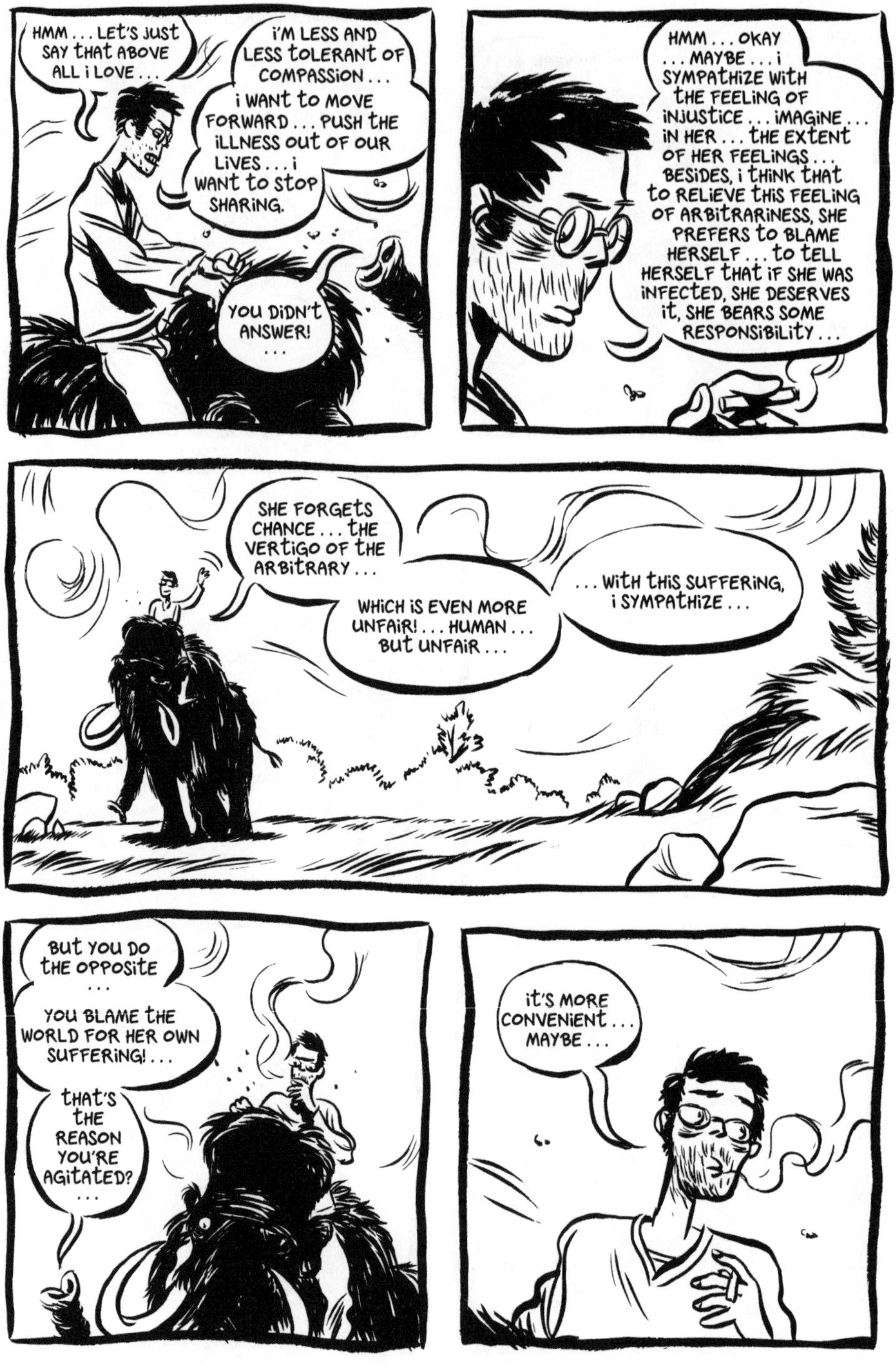
HMM . . . LET'S JUST SAY THAT ABOVE ALL I LOVE . . .
I'M LESS AND LESS TOLERANT OF COMPASSION . . . I WANT TO MOVE FORWARD . . . PUSH THE ILLNESS OUT OF OUR LIVES . . . I WANT TO STOP SHARING.
YOU DIDN'T ANSWER! . . .
HMM . . . OKAY . . . MAYBE . . . I SYMPATHIZE WITH THE FEELING OF INJUSTICE . . . IMAGINE . . . IN HER . . . THE EXTENT OF HER FEELINGS . . . BESIDES, I THINK THAT TO RELIEVE THIS FEELING OF ARBITRARINESS, SHE PREFERS TO BLAME HERSELF . . . TO TELL HERSELF THAT IF SHE WAS INFECTED, SHE DESERVES IT, SHE BEARS SOME RESPONSIBILITY . . .
SHE FORGETS CHANCE . . . THE VERTIGO OF THE ARBITRARY . . .
WHICH IS EVEN MORE UNFAIR! . . . HUMAN . . . BUT UNFAIR . . .
. . . WITH THIS SUFFERING, I SYMPATHIZE . . .
BUT YOU DO THE OPPOSITE . . .
YOU BLAME THE WORLD FOR HER OWN SUFFERING! . . .
THAT'S THE REASON YOU'RE AGITATED? . . .
IT'S MORE CONVENIENT . . . MAYBE . . .

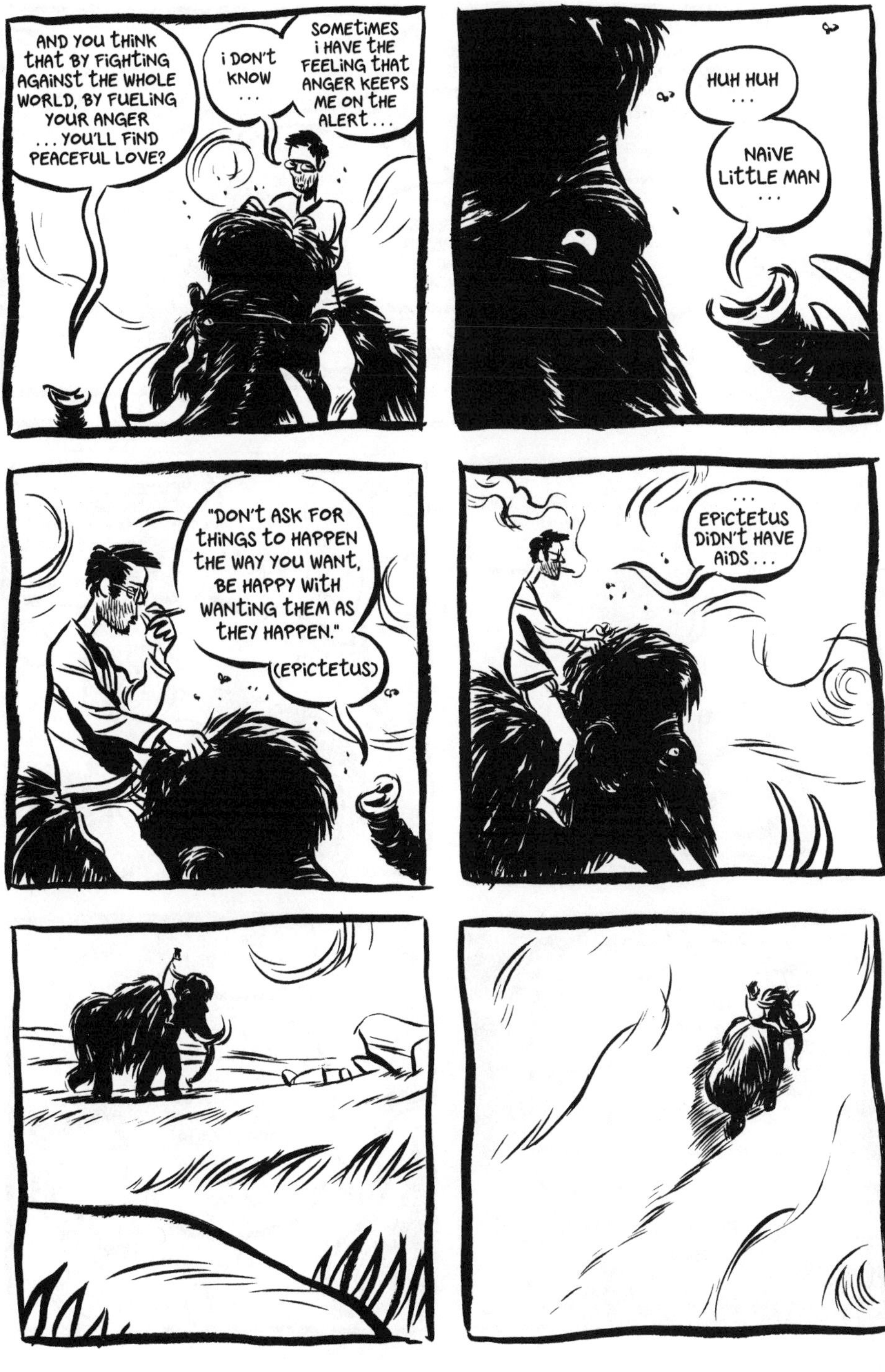
AND YOU THINK THAT BY FIGHTING AGAINST THE WHOLE WORLD, BY FUELING YOUR ANGER ... YOU'LL FIND PEACEFUL LOVE?
I DON'T KNOW ...
SOMETIMES I HAVE THE FEELING THAT ANGER KEEPS ME ON THE ALERT ...
HUH HUH ...
NAIVE LITTLE MAN ...
"DON'T ASK FOR THINGS TO HAPPEN THE WAY YOU WANT, BE HAPPY WITH WANTING THEM AS THEY HAPPEN."
(EPICTETUS)
... EPICTETUS DIDN'T HAVE AIDS ...

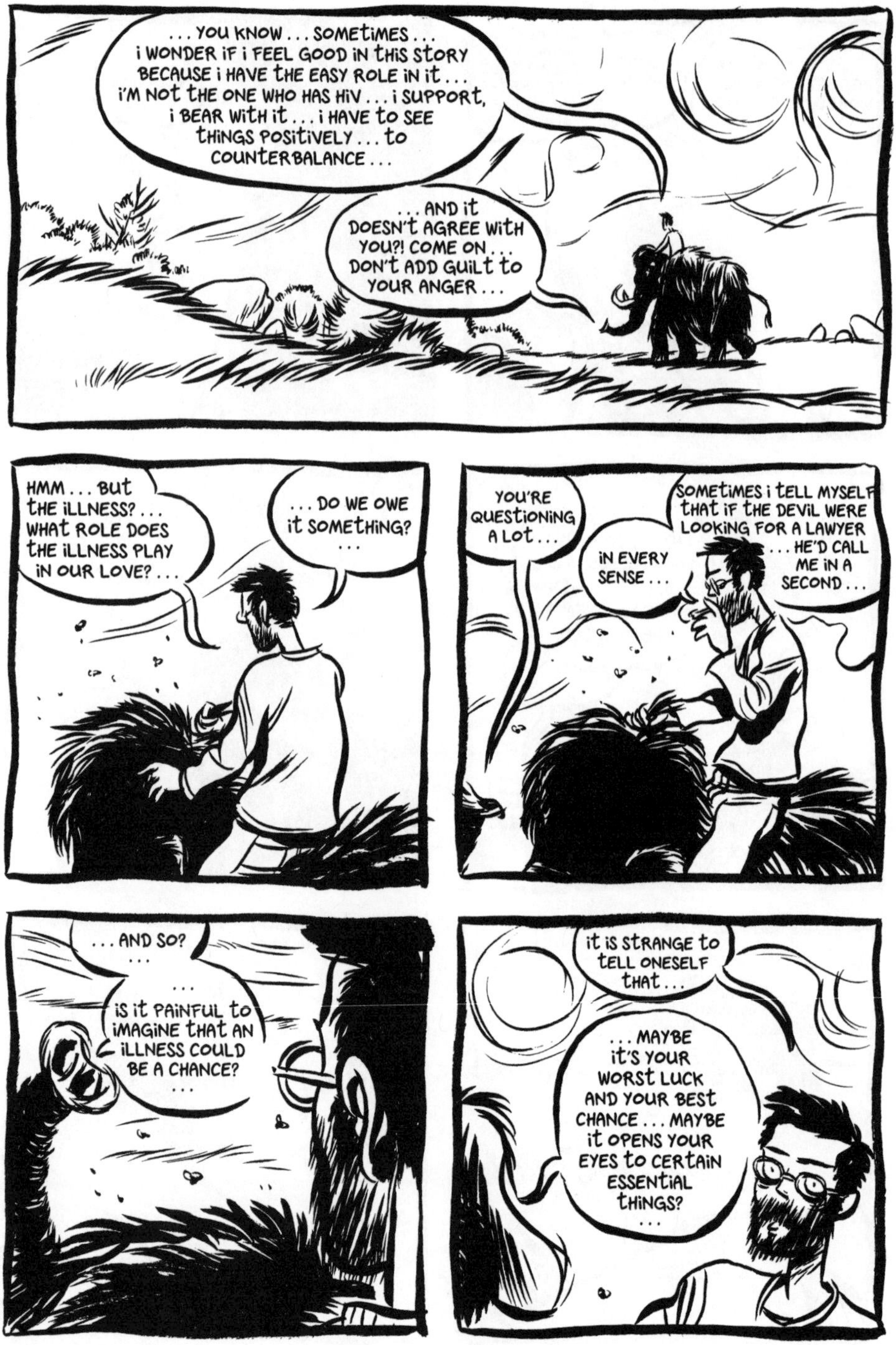
... YOU KNOW ... SOMETIMES ... I WONDER IF I FEEL GOOD IN THIS STORY BECAUSE I HAVE THE EASY ROLE IN IT ... I'M NOT THE ONE WHO HAS HIV ... I SUPPORT, I BEAR WITH IT ... I HAVE TO SEE THINGS POSITIVELY ... TO COUNTERBALANCE ...
... AND IT DOESN'T AGREE WITH YOU?! COME ON ... DON'T ADD GUILT TO YOUR ANGER ...
HMM ... BUT THE ILLNESS? ... WHAT ROLE DOES THE ILLNESS PLAY IN OUR LOVE? ...
... DO WE OWE IT SOMETHING? ...
YOU'RE QUESTIONING A LOT ...
SOMETIMES I TELL MYSELF THAT IF THE DEVIL WERE LOOKING FOR A LAWYER ... HE'D CALL ME IN A SECOND ...
IN EVERY SENSE ...
... AND SO? ...
... IS IT PAINFUL TO IMAGINE THAT AN ILLNESS COULD BE A CHANCE? ...
IT IS STRANGE TO TELL ONESELF THAT ...
... MAYBE IT'S YOUR WORST LUCK AND YOUR BEST CHANCE ... MAYBE IT OPENS YOUR EYES TO CERTAIN ESSENTIAL THINGS? ...

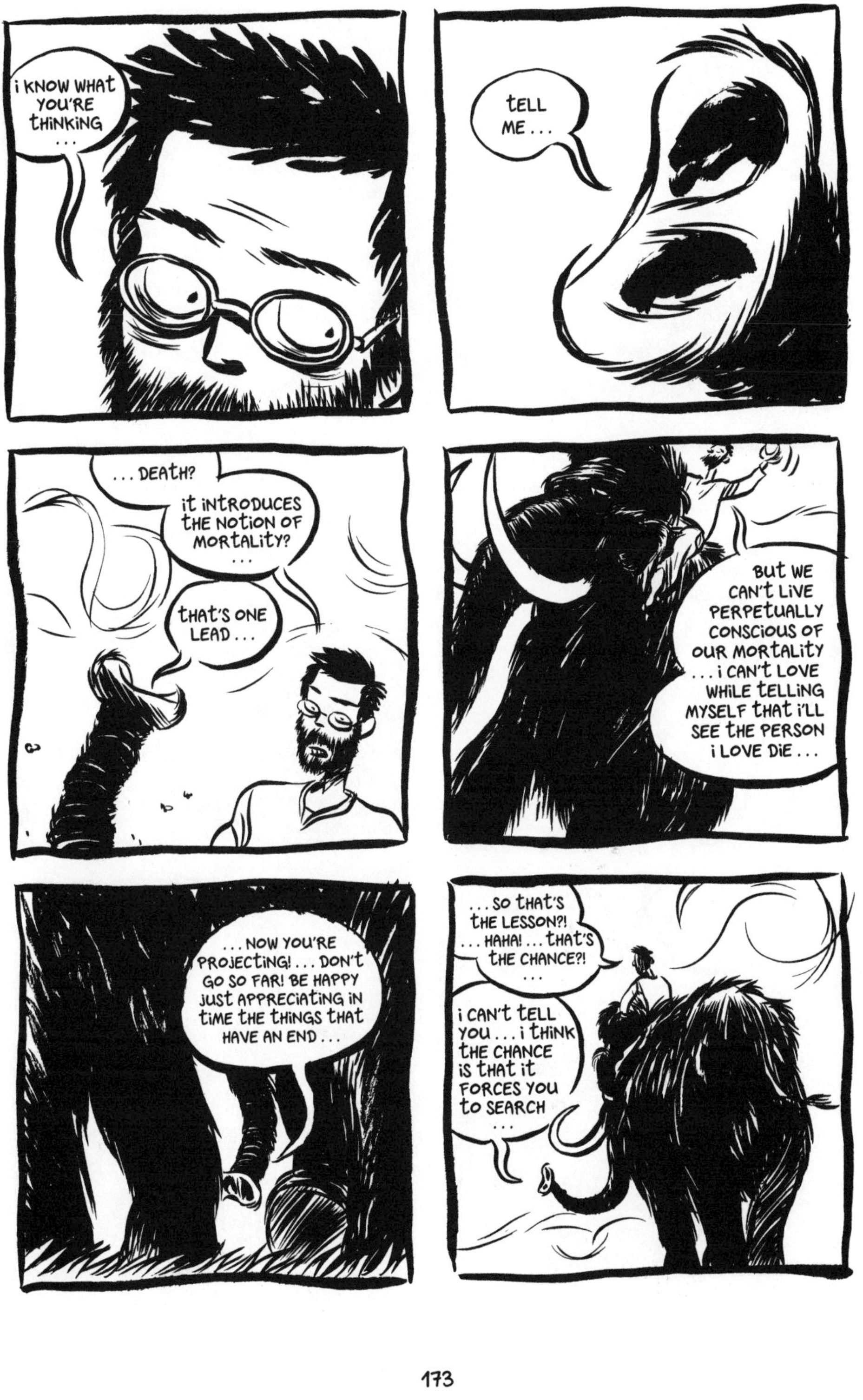
i KNOW WHAT YOU'RE THINKING . . .
TELL ME . . .
. . . DEATH?
it iNTRODUCES THE NOTION OF MORTALITY? . . .
THAT'S ONE LEAD . . .
BUT WE CAN'T LIVE PERPETUALLY CONSCIOUS OF OUR MORTALITY . . . i CAN'T LOVE WHILE TELLING MYSELF THAT i'LL SEE THE PERSON i LOVE DiE . . .
. . . NOW YOU'RE PROJECTING! . . . DON'T GO SO FAR! BE HAPPY JUST APPRECIATING IN TIME THE THINGS THAT HAVE AN END . . .
. . . SO THAT'S THE LESSON?! . . . HAHA! . . . THAT'S THE CHANCE?! . . .
i CAN'T TELL YOU . . . i THINK THE CHANCE iS THAT iT FORCES YOU TO SEARCH . . .

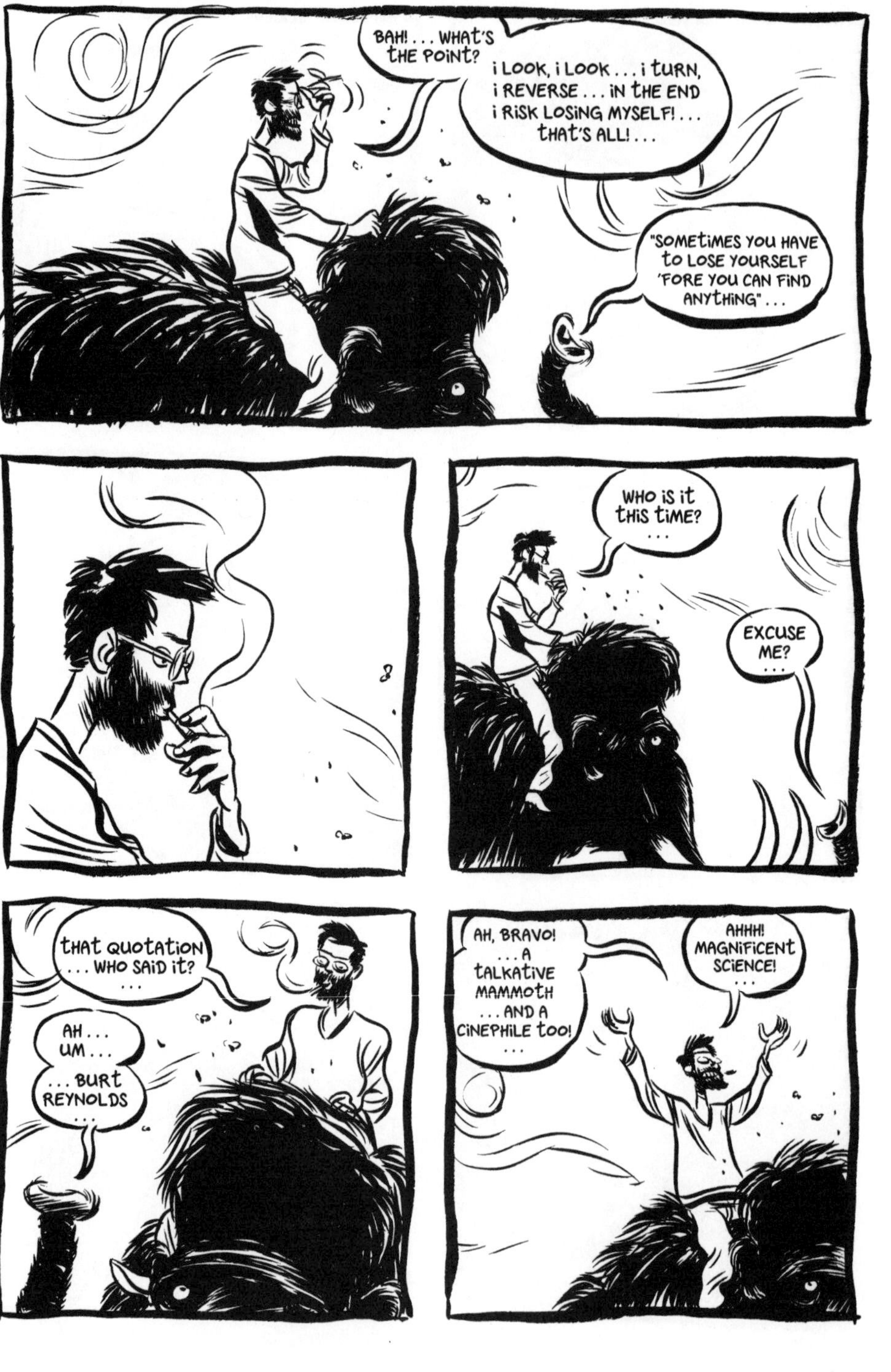
BAH! . . . WHAT'S THE POINT?
i LOOK, i LOOK . . . i TURN, i REVERSE . . . iN THE END i RiSK LOSiNG MYSELF! . . . THAT'S ALL! . . .
"SOMETiMES YOU HAVE TO LOSE YOURSELF 'FORE YOU CAN FiND ANYTHiNG" . . .
WHO iS iT THiS TiME? . . .
EXCUSE ME? . . .
THAT QUOTATiON . . . WHO SAiD iT? . . .
AH . . . UM . . . . . . BURT REYNOLDS . . .
AH, BRAVO! . . . A TALKATiVE MAMMOTH . . . AND A CiNEPHiLE TOO! . . .
AHHH! MAGNiFiCENT SCiENCE! . . .

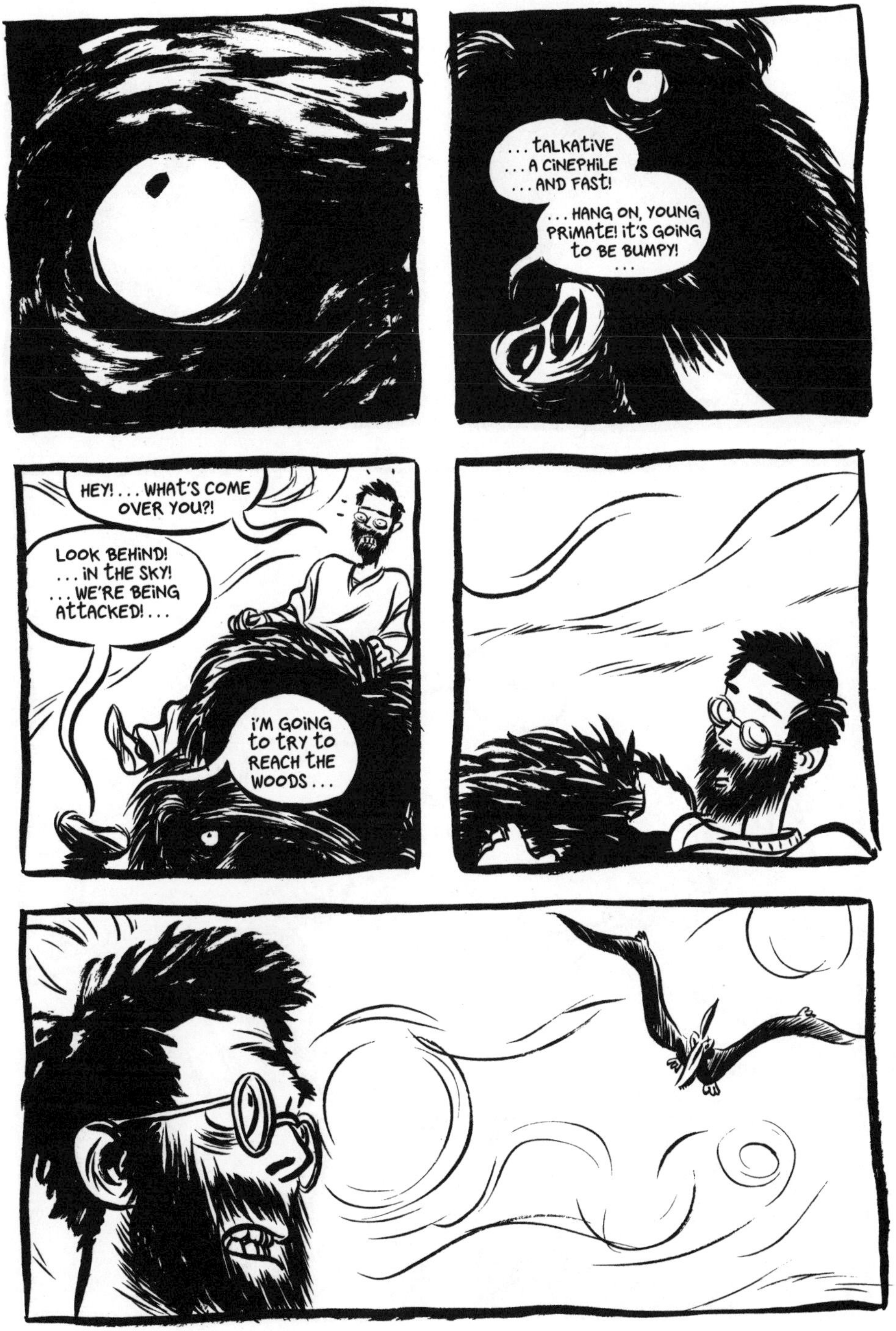

... talkative
... a cinephile
... and fast!
... hang on, young primate! it's going to be bumpy!
...
hey! ... what's come over you?!
look behind!
... in the sky!
... we're being attacked! ...
i'm going to try to reach the woods ...

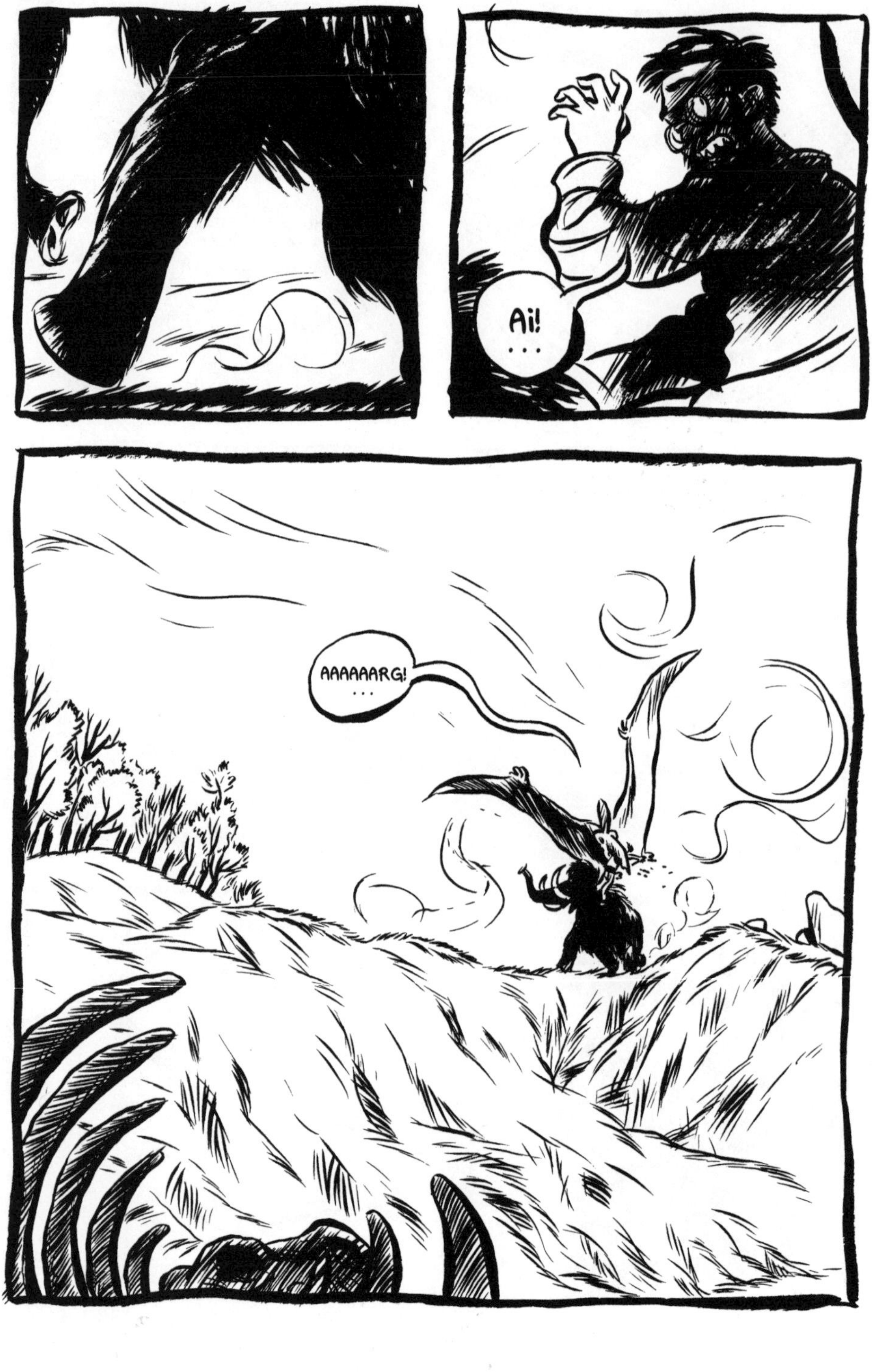
Ai!
...
AAAAAARG!
...

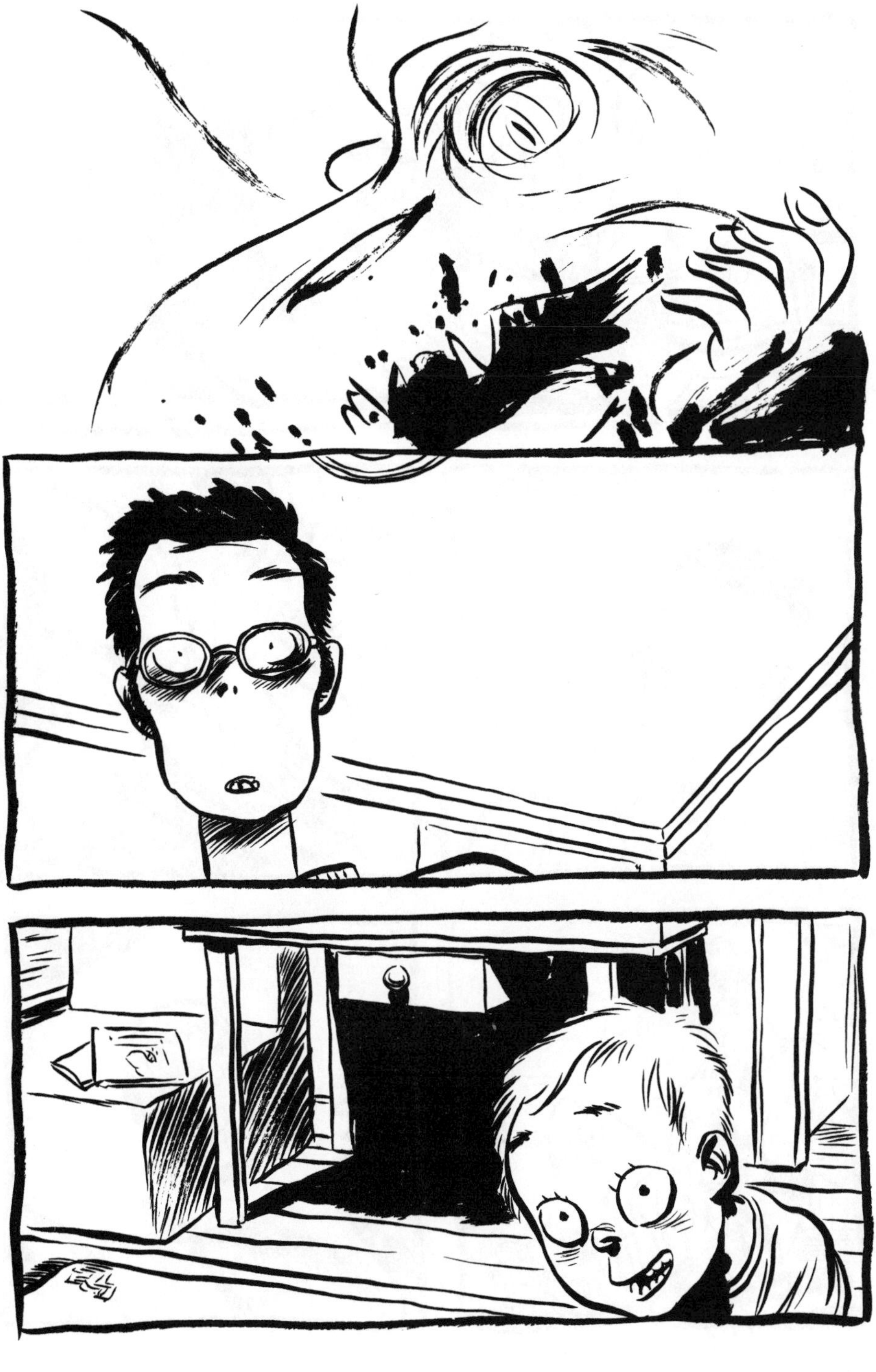

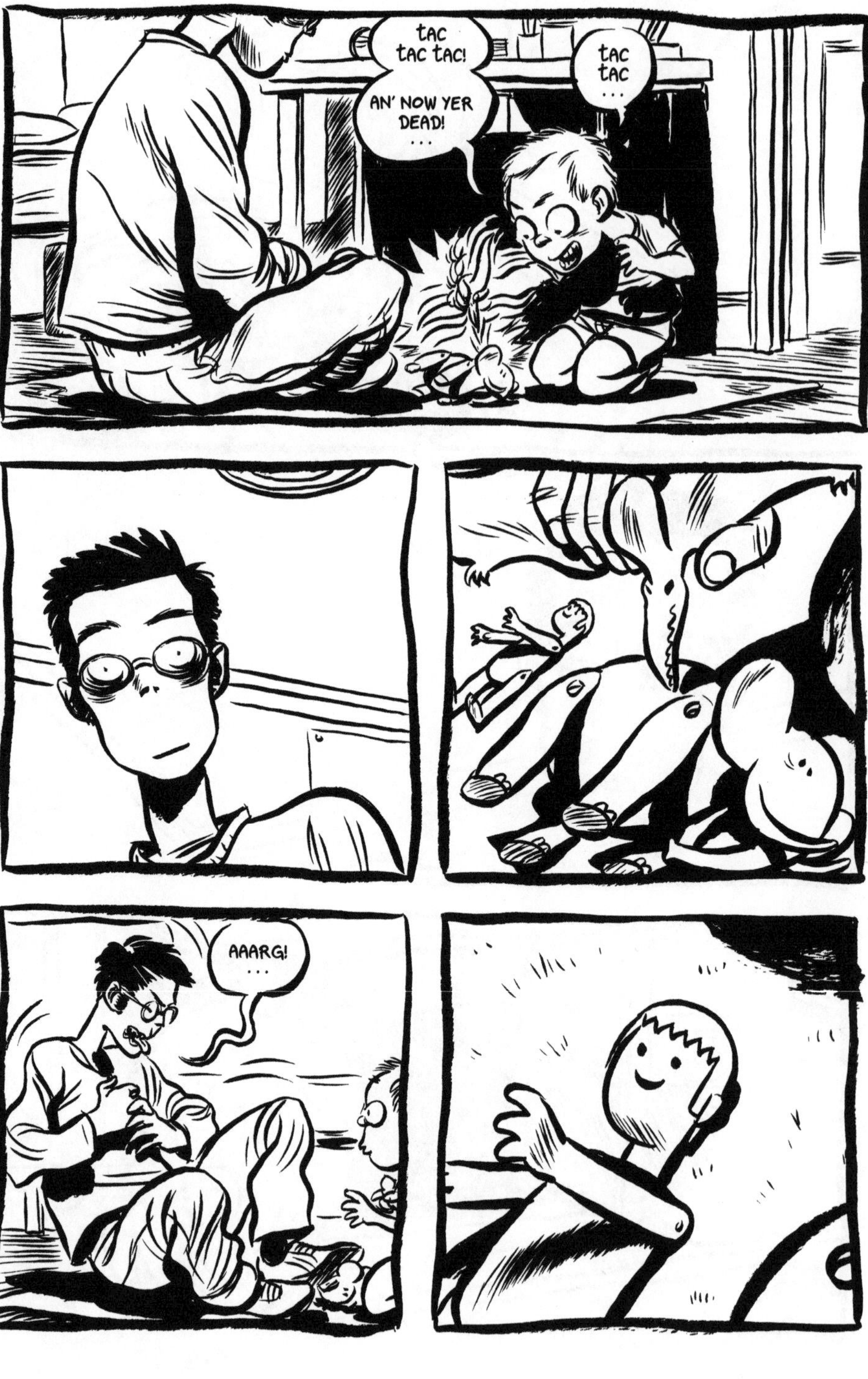
tac
tac tac!
AN' NOW YER
DEAD!
. . .
tac
tac
. . .
AAARG!
. . .

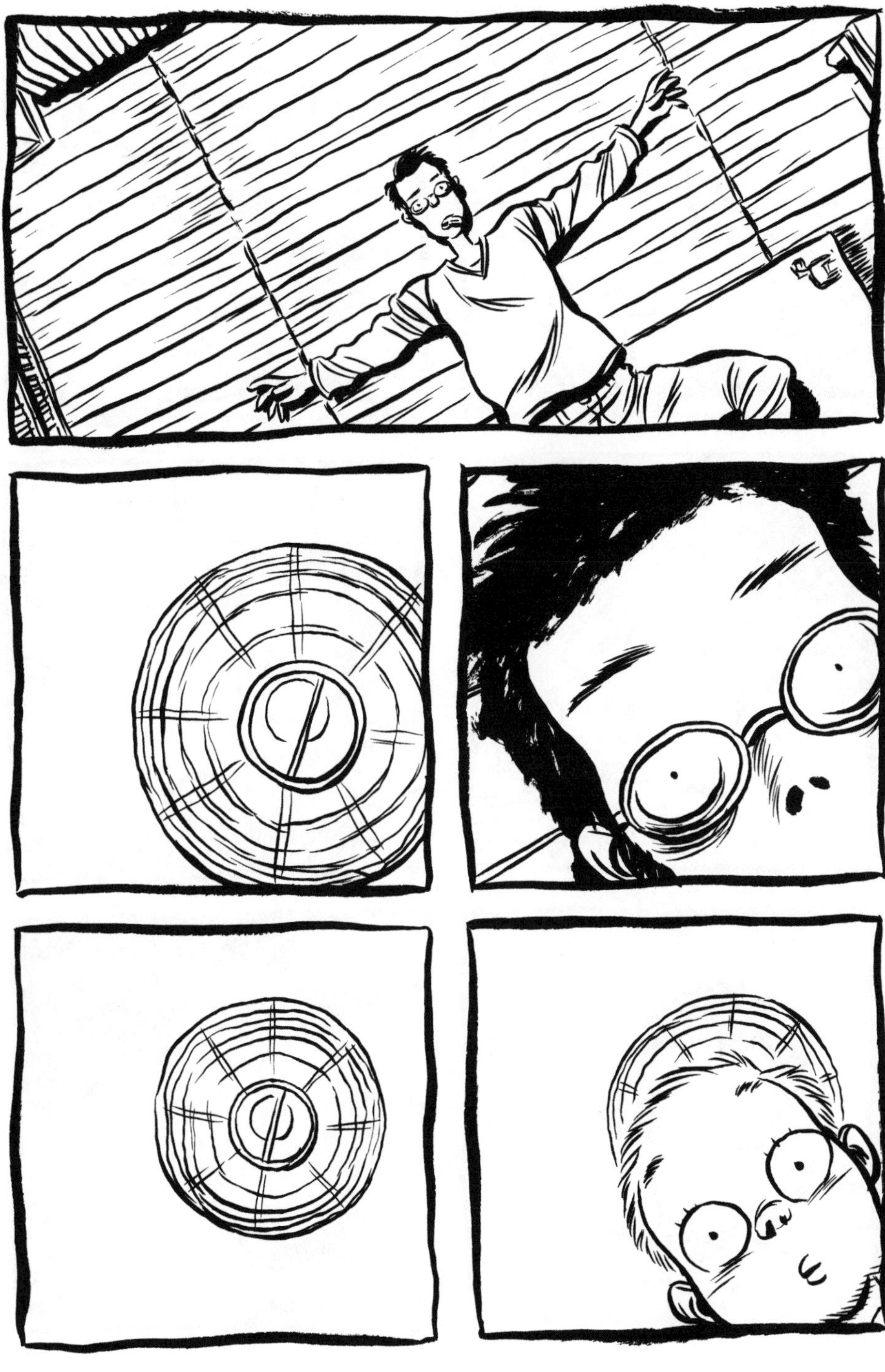

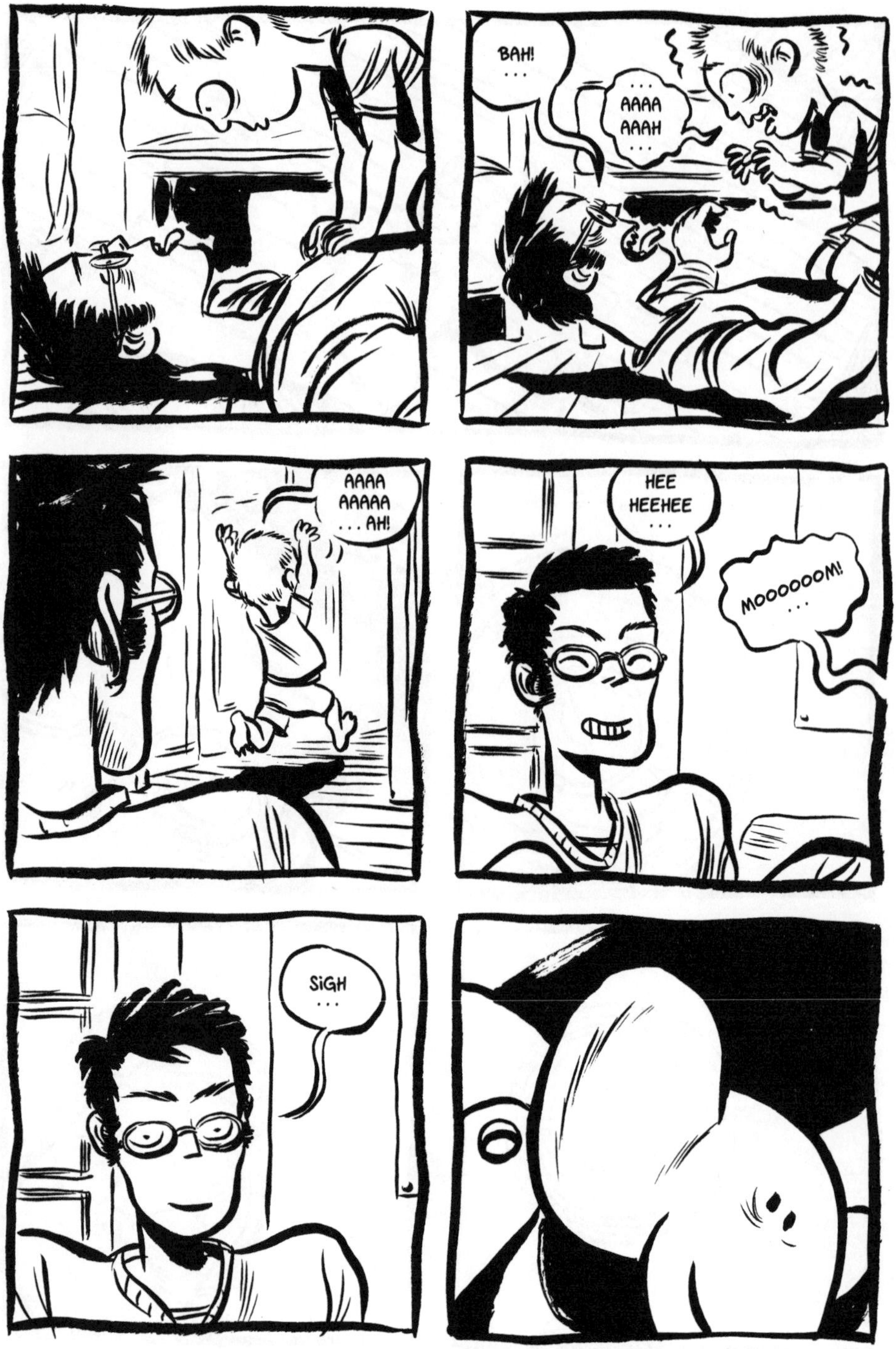
BAH! ...
... AAAA AAAH ...
AAAA AAAAA ... AH!
HEE HEEHEE ...
MOOOOOOM! ...
SiGH ...

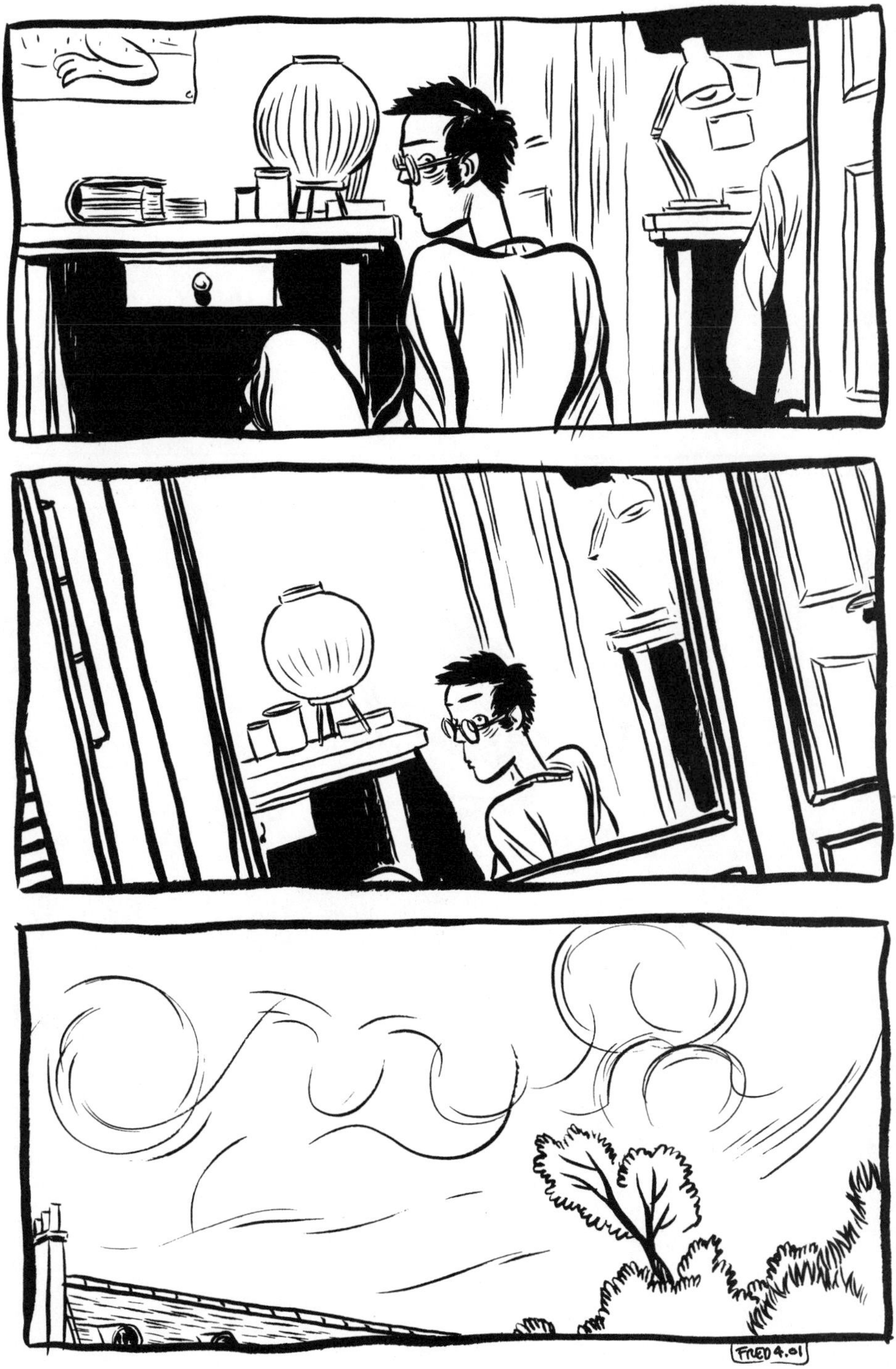
FRED 4.01

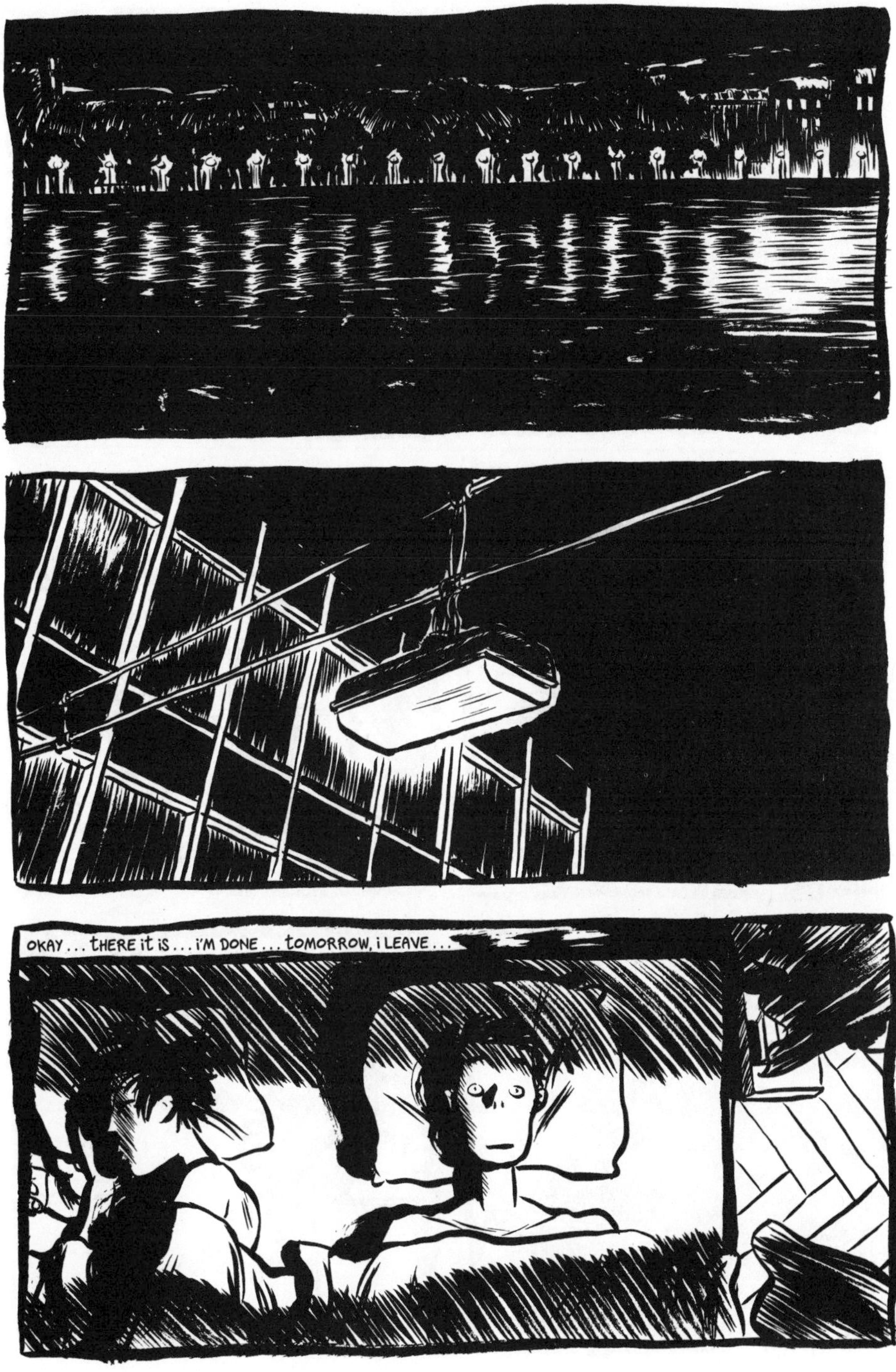
OKAY... THERE IT IS... I'M DONE... TOMORROW, I LEAVE...

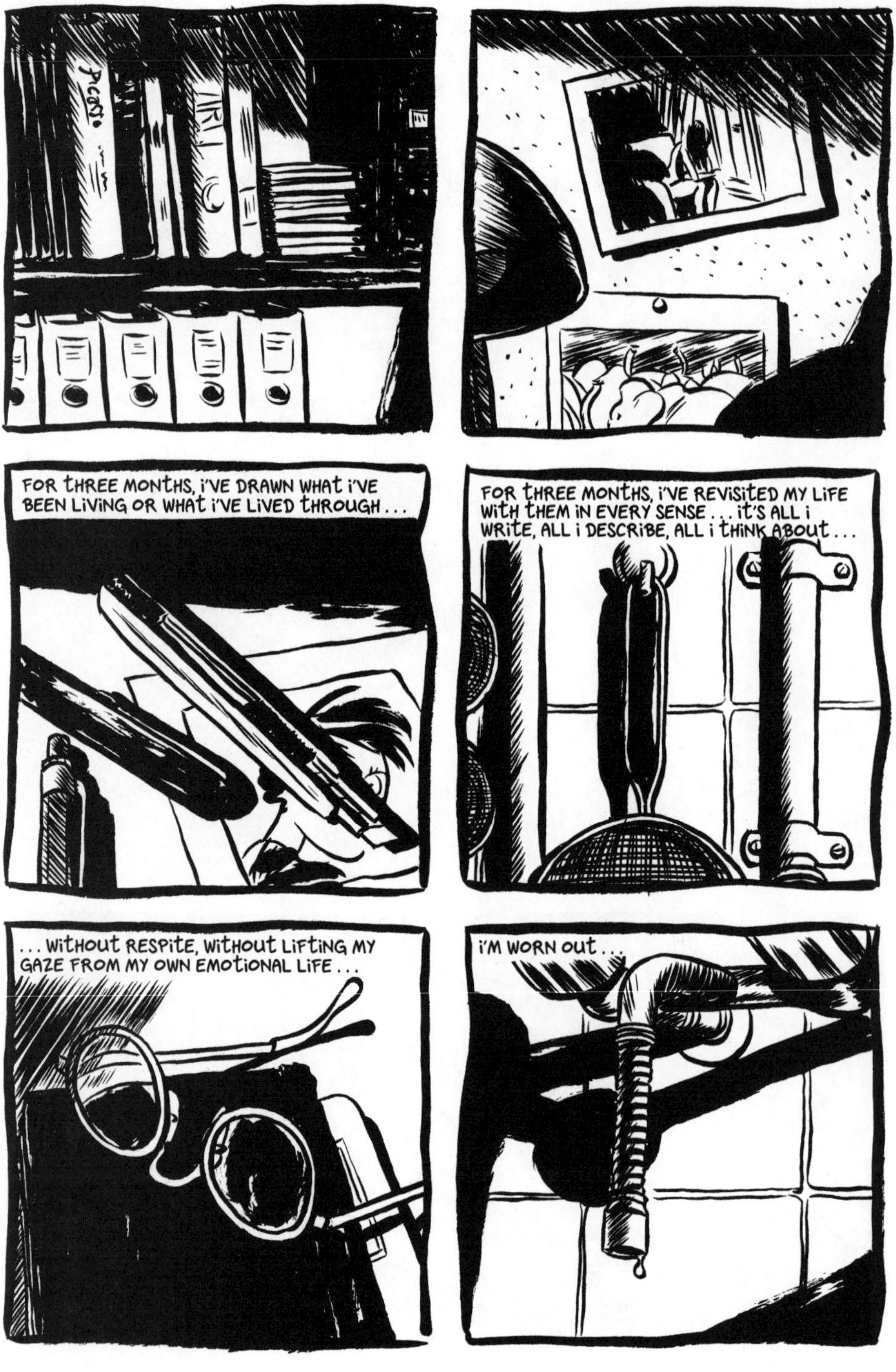
FOR THREE MONTHS, I'VE DRAWN WHAT I'VE BEEN LIVING OR WHAT I'VE LIVED THROUGH . . .
FOR THREE MONTHS, I'VE REVISITED MY LIFE WITH THEM IN EVERY SENSE . . . IT'S ALL I WRITE, ALL I DESCRIBE, ALL I THINK ABOUT . . .
. . . WITHOUT RESPITE, WITHOUT LIFTING MY GAZE FROM MY OWN EMOTIONAL LIFE . . .
I'M WORN OUT . . .

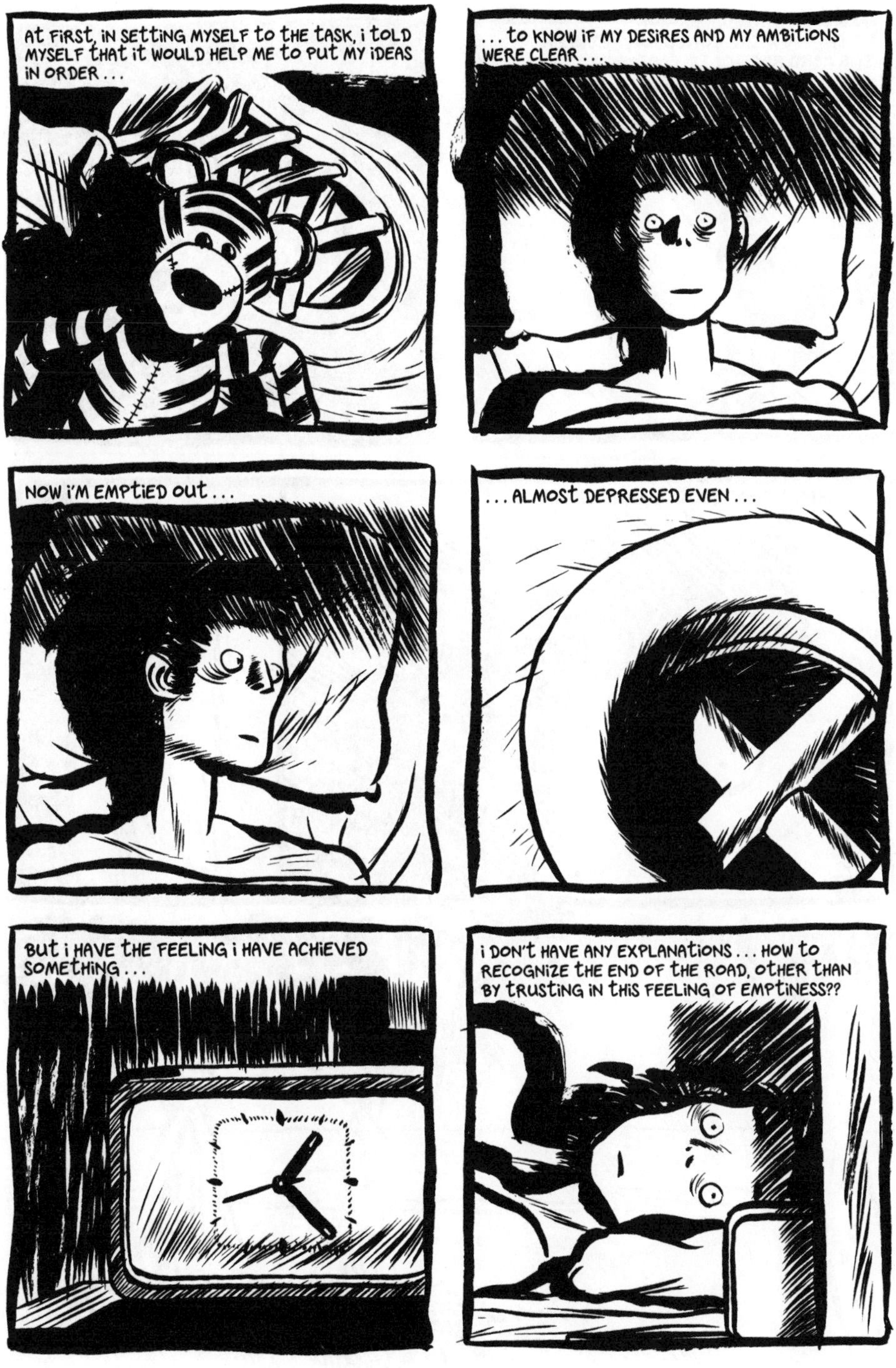
At first, in setting myself to the task, i told myself that it would help me to put my ideas in order . . .
. . . to know if my desires and my ambitions were clear . . .
Now i'm emptied out . . .
. . . almost depressed even . . .
But i have the feeling i have achieved something . . .
i don't have any explanations . . . how to recognize the end of the road, other than by trusting in this feeling of emptiness??

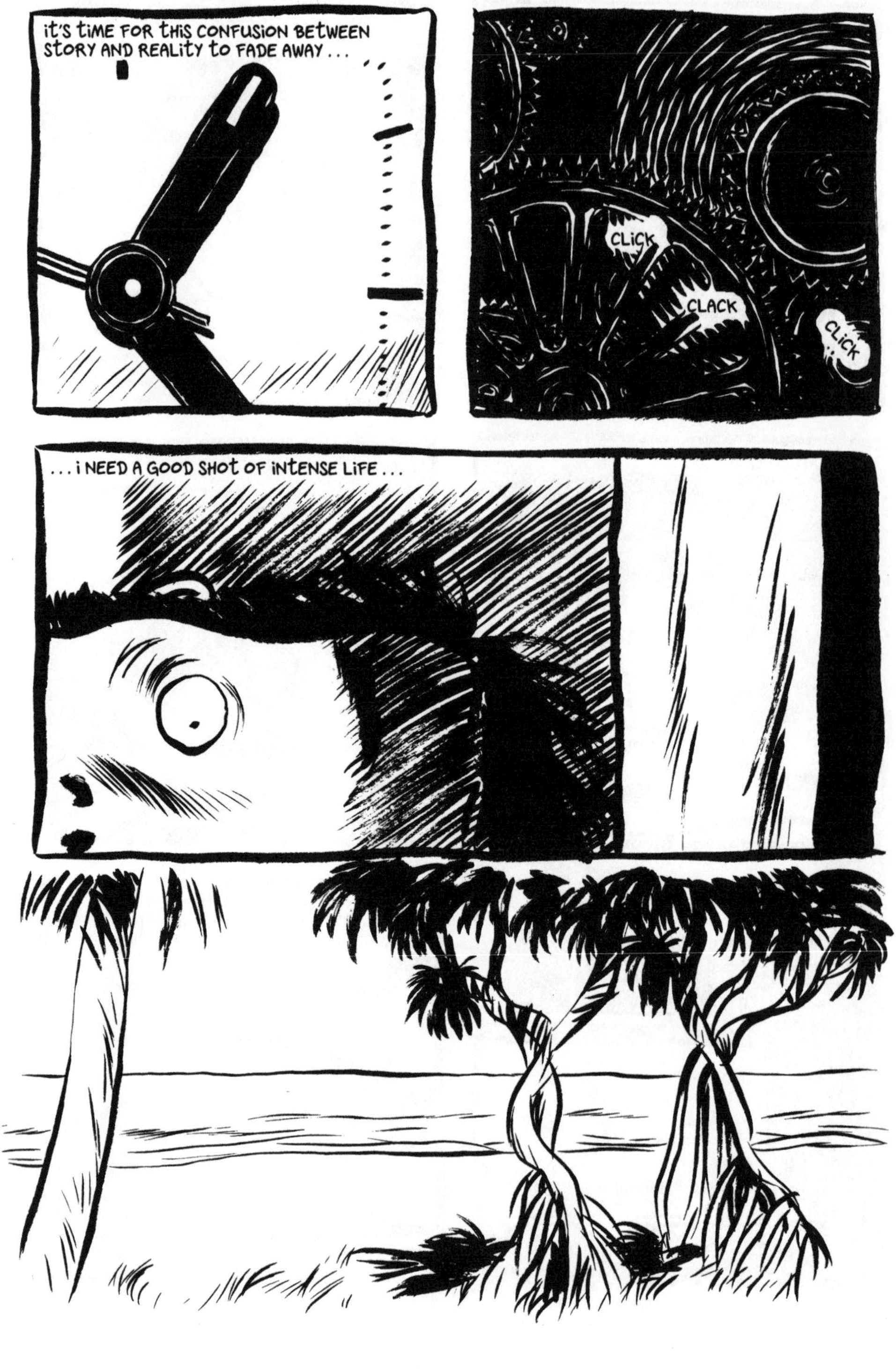
it's time for this confusion between story and reality to fade away . . .
CLICK
CLACK
CLICK
. . . i need a good shot of intense life . . .

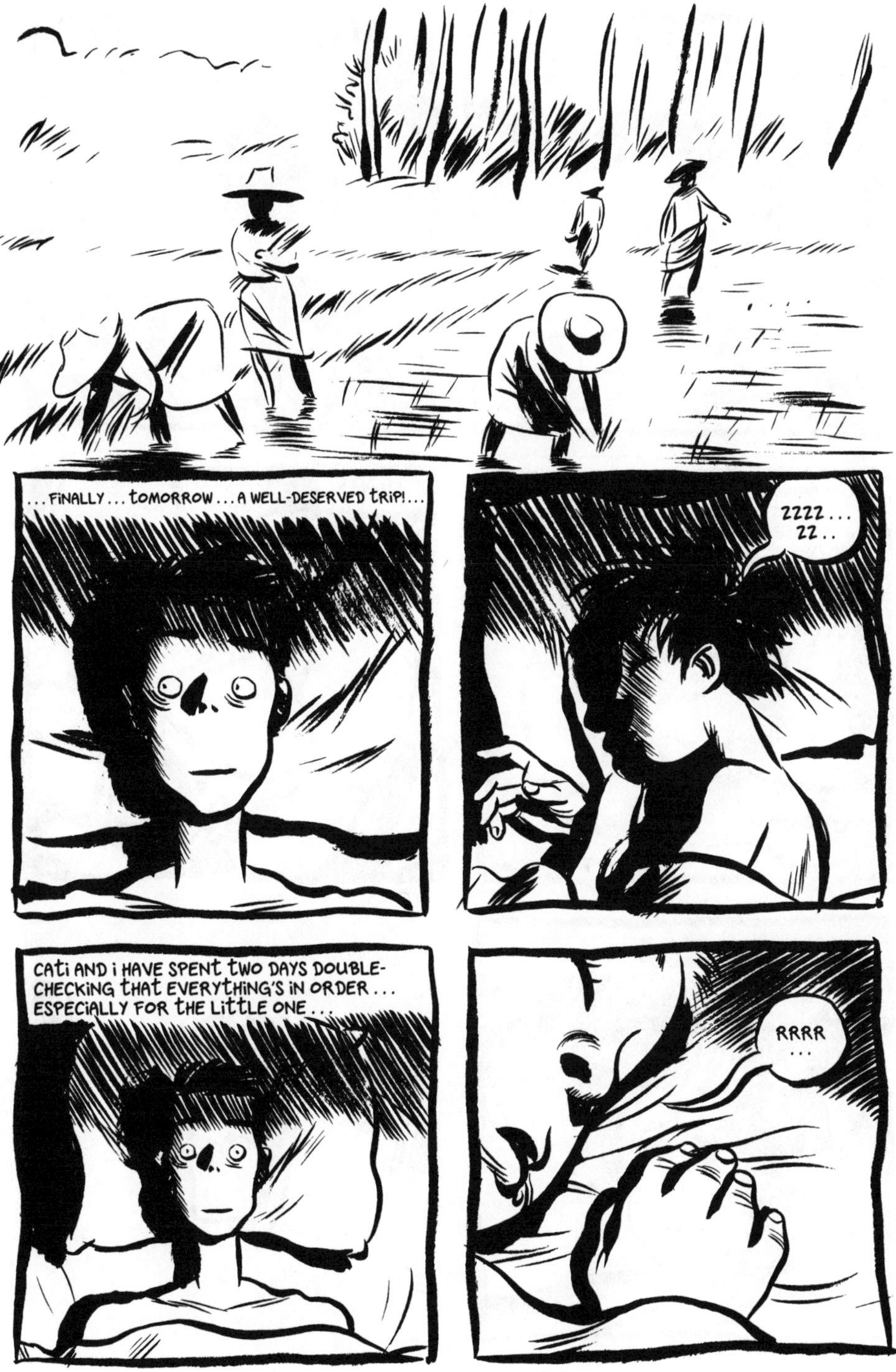
...FINALLY... TOMORROW... A WELL-DESERVED TRIP!...
ZZZZ... ZZ..
CATI AND I HAVE SPENT TWO DAYS DOUBLE-CHECKING THAT EVERYTHING'S IN ORDER... ESPECIALLY FOR THE LITTLE ONE...
RRRR...

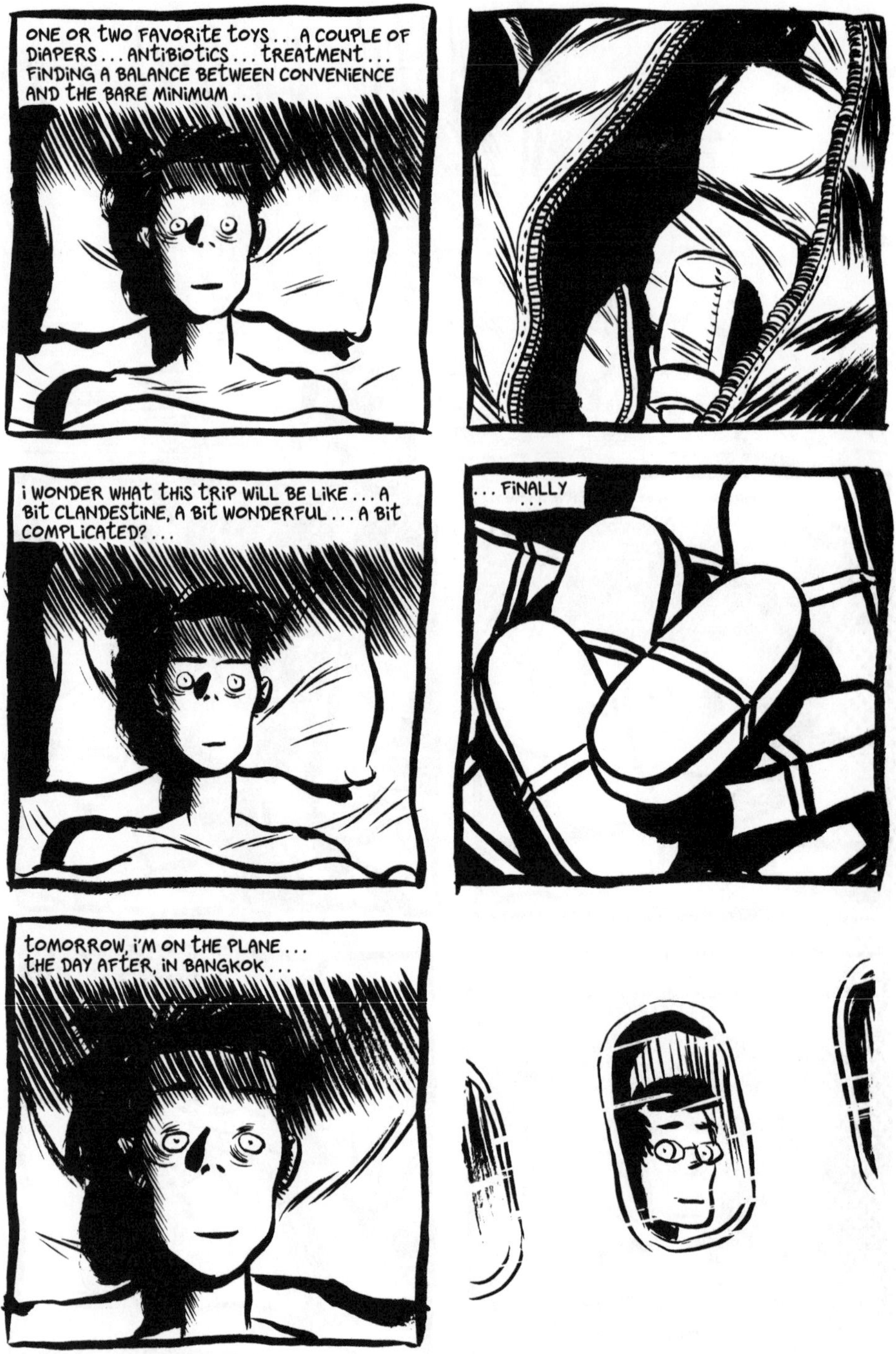
ONE OR TWO FAVORITE TOYS . . . A COUPLE OF DIAPERS . . . ANTIBIOTICS . . . TREATMENT . . . FINDING A BALANCE BETWEEN CONVENIENCE AND THE BARE MINIMUM . . .
I WONDER WHAT THIS TRIP WILL BE LIKE . . . A BIT CLANDESTINE, A BIT WONDERFUL . . . A BIT COMPLICATED? . . .
. . . FINALLY . . .
TOMORROW, I'M ON THE PLANE . . . THE DAY AFTER, IN BANGKOK . . .

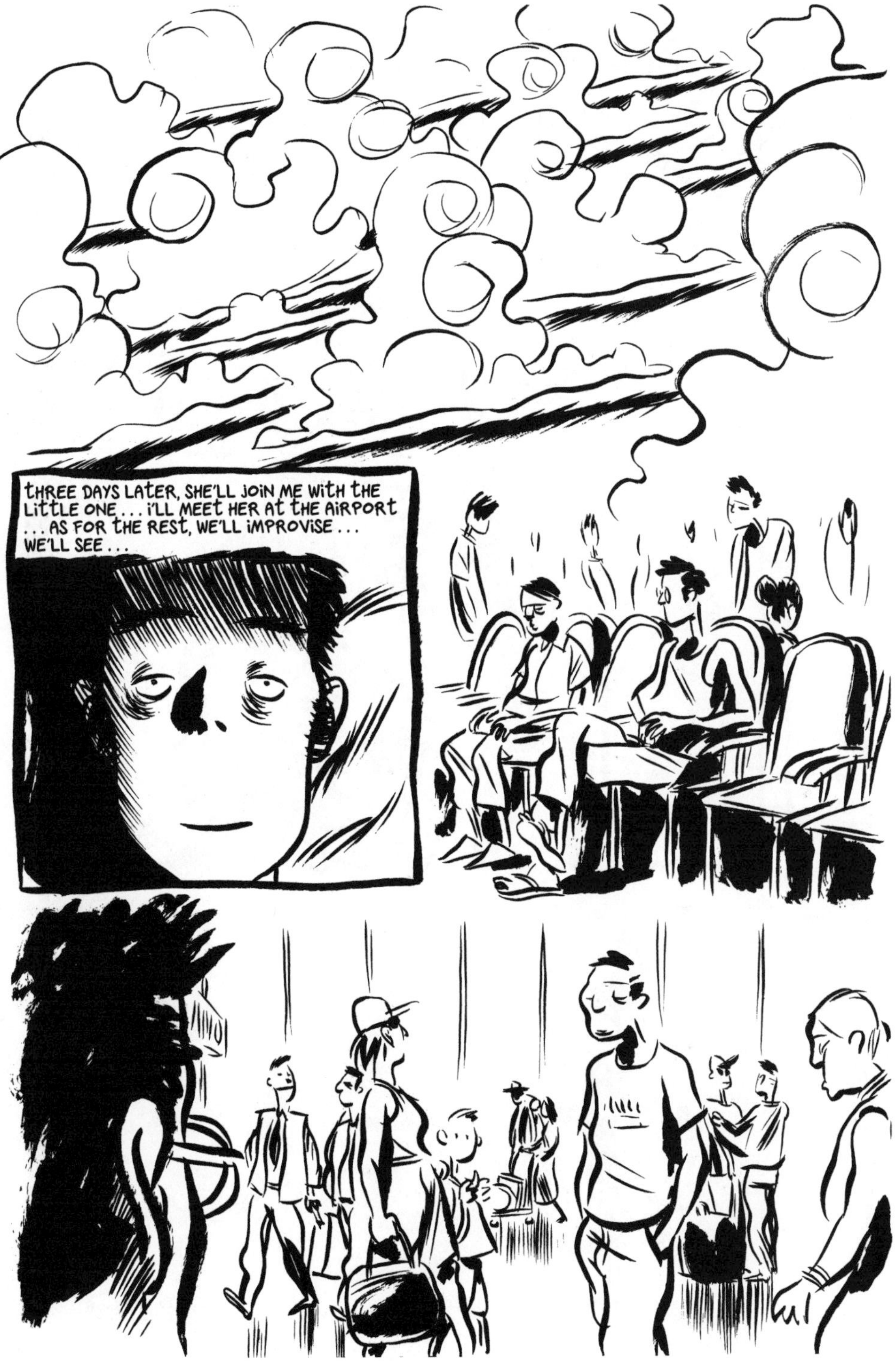
THREE DAYS LATER, SHE'LL JOIN ME WITH THE LITTLE ONE . . . I'LL MEET HER AT THE AIRPORT . . . AS FOR THE REST, WE'LL IMPROVISE . . . WE'LL SEE . . .

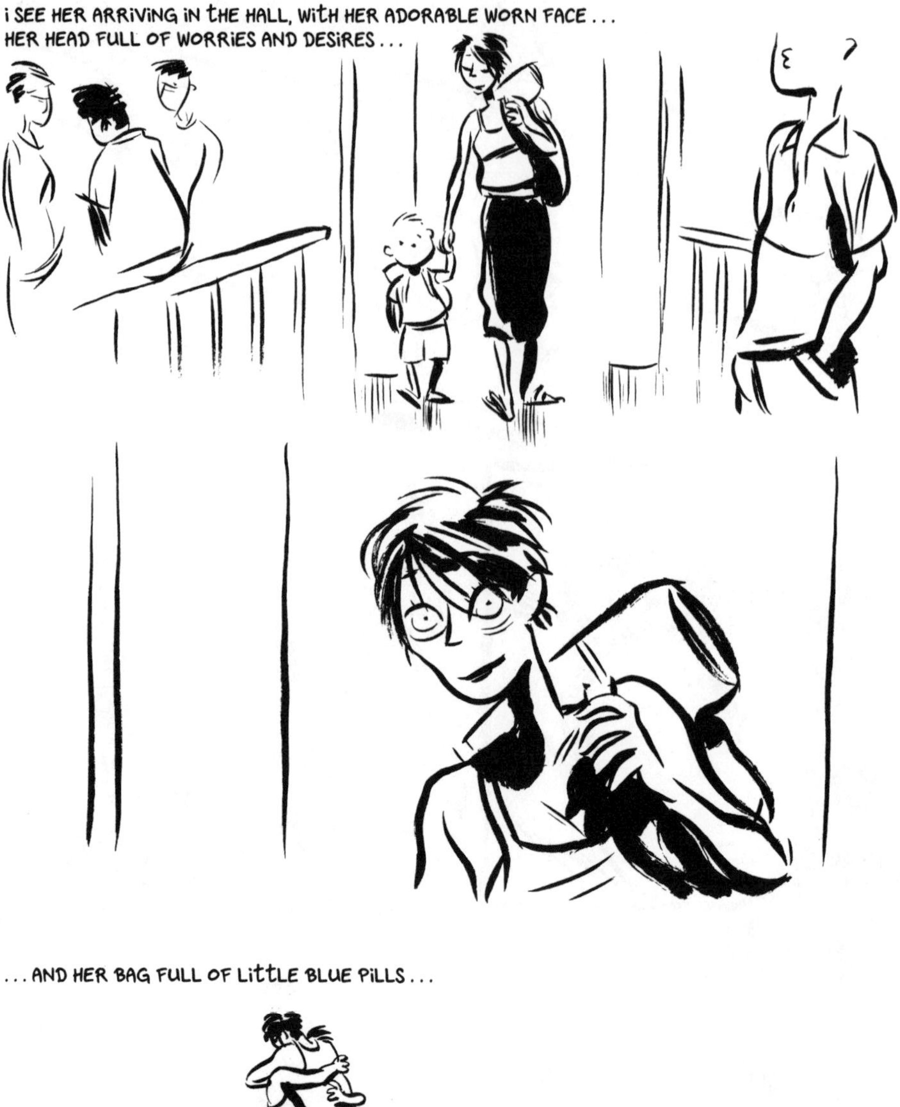
I SEE HER ARRIVING IN THE HALL, WITH HER ADORABLE WORN FACE . . .
HER HEAD FULL OF WORRIES AND DESIRES . . .
. . . AND HER BAG FULL OF LITTLE BLUE PILLS . . .
FINFREDAVR2001

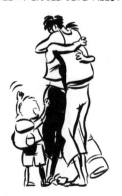